The Psychology of Astro*Carto*Graphy

Jim Lewis with Kenneth Irving

Copyright © Estate of Jim Lewis, and Kenneth Irving, 1997, 2012
Printed in the USA. All rights reserved, including the right of reproduction in whole or in part in any form.

Second Edition
Published by Words and Things
wordsandthings.com
P.O. Box 8034, FDR Station
New York, NY 10150-8034

ISBN: 978-0-9844280-0-7

First Edition (1997), Penguin Arkana

Cover and Book Design by Kenneth Irving
Cover image: Jim Lewis' Astro*Carto*Graphy map

All Astro*Carto*Graphy maps courtesy of
Astro Numeric Service (astronumerics.com)

Charts created with Solar Fire Gold, Version 7
Courtesy of Astrolabe, Inc. (alabe.com)

Astro*Carto*Graphy® is a registered trademark of the Astro*Carto*Graphy Living Trust, and its use in this book with alternate spellings or abbreviations for purposes of readability should not be construed to indicate otherwise.

Contents

List of Figures v
List of Tables v
Introduction to the Second Edition vii

PART ONE: Lines Around the World

1. Space and Time in the Horoscope: The Dimension of
   Astro*Carto*Graphy 3
2. Lines and Crossings 18
3. Shadowed Planets: Stages of Psychological Growth 26
4. Grace's Saturnian Journey 36
5. Winds of Neptune, Fires of Mars 46
6. War Lines Across the World 60
7. Prisoners of the Horoscope No More 70

PART TWO: Your Planets and Their Lines: Natal Astro*Carto*Graphy

Introduction: Zen and the Art of (Not) Cookbooking 81
8. The Sun: Can Anyone Really Be a Star? 82
9. The Moon: Why Is Everyone So Emotional? 97
10. Mercury: The Taming Power of the Small 112
11. Venus: Is There More to Life Than Happiness? 125
12. Mars: Mary Poppins, Watch Out! 139
13. Jupiter: Does More Really Mean Better? 152
14. Saturn: It's Tough to Know When You Need Discipline 163
15. Uranus: Can Anyone Change the World? 174
16. Neptune: Materialists Beware! 184
17. Pluto: The Intensity Addict 193

PART THREE: Transits and Progressions: Cyclo*Carto*Graphy

Introduction: Location is the Key 203
18. The Sun: Let Your Big Light Shine 205
19. The Moon: An Emotional Interlude 210
20. Mercury: Link to the Network 216
21. Venus: A Time for Love and Pleasure 222
22. Mars: Stress, Competition, and Energy 229
23. Jupiter: Full Speed Ahead 235
24. Saturn: Responsibility is the Keynote 242
25. Uranus: Excitement, Change, and Nonconformity 249
26. Neptune: Go with the Flow 256
27. Pluto: The Beginning of the Rest of Your Life 262

Afterword and Resources

About Jim Lewis: Teacher, Friend, Humanitarian 268
Historical and Technical Notes on Astro*Carto*Graphy 276
Notes and Resources 288
Definitions of Some Useful Terms 296
Index 298
Author Biographies 305

LIST OF FIGURES

1. An example of birth for New York, February 4, 1950 5
2. Example birth relocated to San Francisco 5
3. Sun for example chart, showing rising/setting lines across the world 7
4. Paramahansa Yogananda: Teacher Sun versus student Moon 12
5. John F. Kennedy: an appointment with Pluto in Dallas 14
6. Grace: a Saturnian journey 37
7. Grace's journey in space and time 38
8. Jim Jones: Burned by Sun and Mars in Guyana 48
9. Jim Jones, the terror of Jonestown, Guyana 49
10. Harvey Milk, at his birth place in Woodmere, New York 56
11. Harvey Milk, relocated to San Francisco 57
12. Dan White, at his birth place in Bellflower, California 58
13. Dan White, relocated to San Francisco 59
14. Harry S. Truman, whose Pluto line struck Hiroshima 64
15. Harry S. Truman, natal, progressions and transits for Hiroshima 68
16. An Alternative Map for the United States of America (Boyd) 72
17. USA (Boyd chart): the mise-en-scène for a Martian progression 76

LIST OF TABLES

1. Four Stages in the Emergence of a Shadowed Planet 29
2. Possible Indicators of a Shadowed Planet 31
3. Transiting Mars and the Gulf War 67
4. Truman's Natal, Progressions, and Transits for Hiroshima 69

The Psychology of Astro*Carto*Graphy
Introduction to the Second Edition

Astrology was created and nurtured in a relatively small part of the world, and the horoscope that astrologers used to map the birth heavens of people from ancient to modern times was itself a small world, as everything about a person from past, to present, to future, was said to be found within the bounds of the horoscope itself. Possibly sometime in the late 19th century and certainly by the early 20th century, with civilizations connecting across the world, astrologers began to think globally, and began to consider how to extend the reach of the birth chart beyond the birthplace in order to understand how a person's life might be changed by moving.

Some of those astrologers even tried to map a horoscope onto the globe itself, though before the 1970s the various ways of doing this were mostly the province of technical astrologers and they were used mostly for looking at world events, not people. Thus when full-page advertisements bannered "You Can Change Your Life by Changing Your Address" began appearing in astrology magazines in 1976, offering the reader something called an Astro*Carto*Graphy map and an interpretation booklet that would allow them to do this for themselves, it set in motion what became a sea change in the way both astrologers and the public thought about the birth chart. The ancient horoscope, with its limits of time and space, touched and was forever touched by the world around it.

Due to Jim's lecturing, writing, and teaching on the system of mapping and interpretation he had developed, by the time the first edition of this book appeared in print, chart services around the world were offering maps similar to Jim's, and mapping modules were beginning to appear in software for personal computers. What is generically referred to as locality mapping software is now a commonplace, and most students of astrology can produce a map that looks much like one of Jim's originals at the touch of a button. Unfortunately, many such maps, whether from software or charting services, are not the same as Jim's, either in the basic conception or the details, and some are even based on faulty mathematics or wrong assumptions.

This new edition of *The Psychology of Astro*Carto*Graphy* will bring the understanding of locality mapping back to the basics by introducing Jim Lewis' work to a new generation, and providing both students and working astrologers a resource that explains the basic ideas underlying these maps and makes clear the way in which their beautiful lines depend directly on the birth chart for meaning. A new section in this revised edition introduces Jim himself to those who never had the pleasure of meeting with him, working with him, learning from, or knowing him as a friend. More than that, it will outline Jim's philanthropic legacy, as though Jim passed away in 1995, all royalties from his products (including a portion of the profits of this book) are passed along to others in the form of grants-in-aid, scholarships, and other funding. Equally important, the updated historical and technical section should help astrologers both now and in the future understand the distinct mark Jim Lewis left on astrological history.

Anyone with an interest in astrology can use this book, but in order to understand how, let's take a brief look at how it is organized.

The first section is an overview of Astro*Carto*Graphy, beginning with the basic ideas and then illustrating how they work out in the lives of average individuals, people of achievement and power, and nations. The first three chapters explain the key concepts, and the fourth and fifth show how they can work out (both for good and for ill) in individual lives. The sixth chapter is also focused on individual lives, but since the subjects are all U.S. presidents, its narrative focuses on how their power to pick and choose the places around the world where they engage in open conflict is affected by the location of important lines in their maps. The final chapter in the first part of the book is about the use of these maps in mundane astrology (the astrology of world events), through the lens of a particular U.S. chart. All such charts are speculative to some degree, and each has its fans, but whatever the reader might think of the particular chart used, some of the ideas introduced here can be used in people's charts as well.

The second and third sections of the book lay out the specifics of the interpretation of natal planetary lines, and progressed and transiting lines, respectively. Jim's interpretations in these two sections can be used cookbook style, with map in hand, if you wish, but unless you've read the first six chapters and used the information there to get a better understanding of how each line relates to your whole chart, arriving at a relocation decision by cherry-picking benefic lines might give unexpected, and unwanted, results.

The final section of the book includes a profile of Jim Lewis as astrologer, teacher, friend, mentor, and humanitarian, an updated and revised historical and technical appendix, plus the end notes for the chapters, and a brief listing of sources for further study that is important for anyone who really wants to get a firm foothold in understanding Astro*Carto*Graphy. If you're a serious student, you should definitely consult the notes while reading the earlier chapters, and would probably benefit from reading the historical and technical appendix right after you read Chapter Seven. Doing that will give you a good grasp of the subject matter and help you make more out of the interpretive chapters.

***

A final note here, but a very important one, is to make sure that everyone who reads *The Psychology of Astro*Carto*Graphy* understands the place that astrologer, author, and editor Erin Sullivan played in making this book happen. As the Series Editor of Penguin's Arkana Contemporary Astrology list in the early 1990s, Erin managed to convince her somewhat reluctant friend Jim to write this book. Not long after he gave in to her friendly pressure, and

INTRODUCTION

a contract was signed, he was diagnosed in the terminal stages of metastatic lung cancer, so Erin got Penguin to agree that if Jim could contract with someone to make sure the book would be finished, everything could move forward. Erin not only acted as editor but provided helpful suggestions that vastly improved the original edition of the book in its final form.

Someone else due my personal thanks is my wife Ronnie Dreyer, who prompted Jim to ask me to do this at a time when he felt I would be too busy to take up the task. Too busy? Never for Jim. I had known him for 20 very good years at that point, had edited many of his articles during that time, and had many long discussions with him over the years about astrology, politics, the world, and everything in it. Our astrological roots included much time spent honing our craft through an early association with *American Astrology* magazine, something that had made us both highly aware of the importance of well-understood facts as the foundation for sound technique.

Finally, a very special thanks to Ron Makha, Trustee of the Astro*Carto*Graphy Living Trust, for making it possible for us to go ahead with this new edition. I would also like to thank Madalyn Hillis-Dineen, Angel Thompson, Ken Bowser, Robert Currey, Bert Fannin, Jodie Forrest, Grace, Gregg Howe, Colleen Mauro, Karen McCauley, and Maria Kay Simms for their support and for their help with various editorial and technical aspects of this book.

Kenneth Irving

PART ONE

Lines Around the World

1

Space and Time in the Horoscope: The Dimension of Astro*Carto*Graphy

THE FAMILIAR everyday astrology which uses the wheel-shaped horoscope is mainly concerned with measuring time, as it attempts to explain when inner and outer realities or potentials of self will manifest. There is, however, another kind of astrology, which concerns itself with both space and time, asking when and where the possibilities in the birth pattern might actualize themselves. Known as "locality astrology" in the recent past, this technique also used the traditional horoscopic wheel, though the astrologer would cast it for a place of residence (or intended residence) rather than the place of birth. However, late in the 20th century both the form and the interpretation of this type of chart were changed with the advent of Astro*Carto*Graphy, a new kind of geographic astrology, which is much broader in scope. In this type of astrology, the wheel is replaced by a map that shows the planets as they relate to the entire world through the continuous curves of rising, setting, and culmination for each planet that existed at the moment of birth. Though this map can be used for the usual exoteric and concrete interpretations, which deal with love, money, and health, its most interesting use lies in its ability to help us understand how particular places can come to symbolize the accepted, suppressed, or projected parts of the self.

Geography is very powerfully linked with the psyche, as just a little consideration will tell us. In Europe in the 1980s tremendous changes occurred as the walls of the Iron Curtain between East and West suddenly, and very surprisingly, began to fall. Is it a coincidence that this occurred during the time marked by a conjunction of Uranus, Neptune, and Saturn? It was almost as if there were an unconscious overflow from a hitherto repressed part of the Western psyche into its consciousness, symbolized by the breach in the Berlin Wall and the sudden interchange between the two halves of the world mind. Could it be that there is a longitudinal line, a real geographical line, that runs where the Iron Curtain stood, defining the frontier between Eastern and Western thought? South Africa, which witnessed the unraveling of a racial "iron curtain" around the same time, is not far east of the same longitude in the southern hemisphere.

Thus at the time of the conjunction of Uranus, Neptune, and Saturn, the wall separating two disparate halves of the Western psyche, the conscious and the unconscious, suddenly was broken. If this analogy is appropriate, an amazingly creative and positive period of time will result from such events, as the conscious mind is opened to the many exciting possibilities available to us in ways hitherto suppressed. In a similar way, the potential both for good and for ill inherent in the psyches of individuals and the collective psyche of nations can be unlocked by astrological patterns specific to certain areas of the world. Though we may not be certain of the precise link between firmament and terra firma that brought about the startling events in Eastern Europe and South Africa, if we have a known date and time of birth we can in fact plot lines of planetary influence on a map, showing which places on earth might relate to the energies of which planets in a given case. Before considering more specifically the individual, national, and cultural reactions to place, and the way the birth moment demonstrates them, we should first understand something about how these planetary lines are plotted.

A horoscope is simply a map of the sky at the moment and the place of birth, but if the individual whose birth is being charted had been born at a place halfway across the world, though at the same Greenwich or Universal Time, the planets would have fallen into different houses, i.e., sectors of the sky. Consequently, in the example shown in Figures 1 and 2, if an individual born on February 4, 1950 at 10:15 A.M. Eastern Standard Time (15:15 Universal Time) in New York City had instead been born on the same date in San Francisco at 7:15 A.M. Pacific Standard Time (also 15:15 Universal Time), a relatively weak 11th house Sun would instead be strong by virtue of being directly on the Ascendant. In other words, because the Ascendant is the more powerful position, this individual would be expected to act out more of a solar personality in San Francisco than in New York. It is important to reiterate that this kind of relocation chart is *movable in space but fixed in time*. Thus, the San Francisco relocation chart for the person born in New York still shows each planet in the same sign, degree, and minute, even though the house positions have changed completely. And houses, especially angles, show how the planet's agency is enacted or embodied.

In the course of the day at a given place, the Sun rises in the east, moves to its "noon" position in the south (called upper culmination), sets in the west, then moves to its "midnight" position to the north (called lower culmination).[1] Astrologically, these four points correspond to the Ascendant, Midheaven, Descendant, and Imum Coeli, or the cusps of the 1st, 10th, 7th and 4th houses, respectively. Similarly, each of the planets, as well as the Moon, has a "day" in which it rises, sets, and culminates at a particular place. A planet placed at any of these four important *angles* of the chart expresses itself most clearly and directly. An individual with Mars, for example, in such an angular zone is more apt to be eminent in athletics or to show other typically Martian traits than will a person with Mars elsewhere in his or her chart. A planet placed near a birth angle is expected by astrological tradition, as confirmed by the scientific work of the Gauquelins, to manifest more powerfully in the outward personality.[2] Although no scientific research has yet been done about relocated planets as such, the experience of many with Astro*Carto*Graphy indicates that they also express themselves with equal power.

SPACE AND TIME IN THE HOROSCOPE

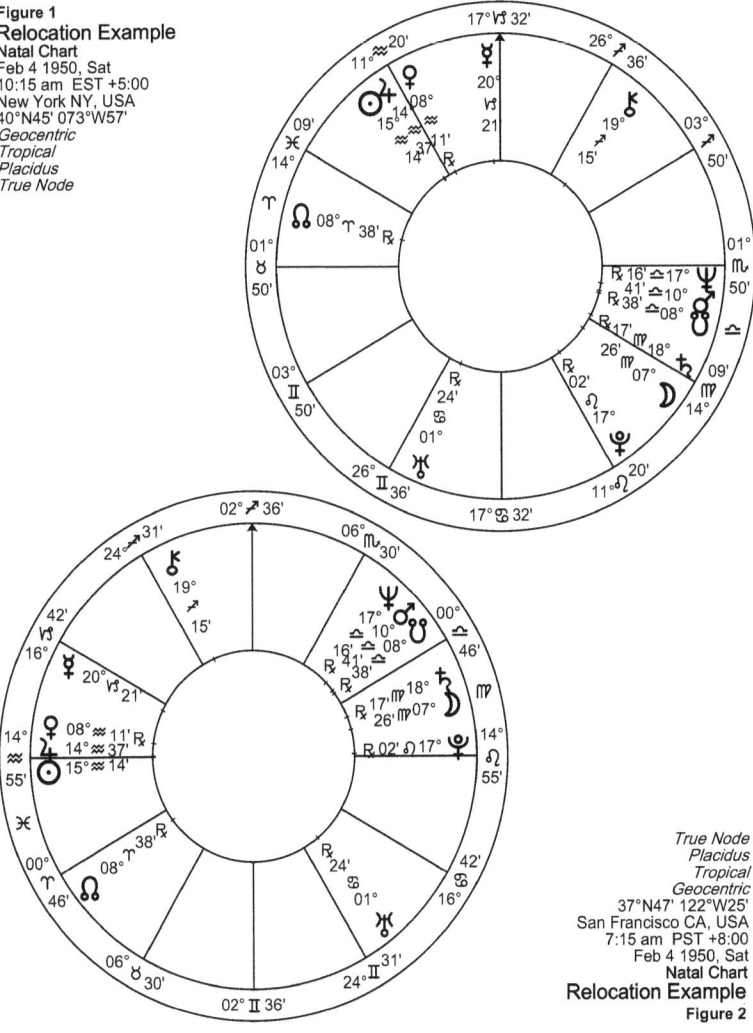

Figure 1
Relocation Example
Natal Chart
Feb 4 1950, Sat
10:15 am EST +5:00
New York NY, USA
40°N45' 073°W57'
Geocentric
Tropical
Placidus
True Node

True Node
Placidus
Tropical
Geocentric
37°N47' 122°W25'
San Francisco CA, USA
7:15 am PST +8:00
Feb 4 1950, Sat
Natal Chart
Relocation Example
Figure 2

In order to gain an understanding of the astronomical principle underlying Astro*Carto*Graphy, first consider the fact that there is no single place where the Sun rises or sets, and that we can always find many places on the Earth where it is either daylight or dark, sunrise or sunset. In fact, at any given moment the Sun will be either rising or setting along a curve that stretches from one side of the International Date Line to the other, peaking at those extreme northerly or southerly latitudes where at certain times of the year the "midnight sun" is visible 24 hours a day, and where at other times the Sun will not be seen at all for extended periods. (Figure 3 shows this solar "world line" at the time of our example birth.) At the same time, the Sun can be found at upper or lower culmination (i.e., noon or midnight) all along a straight line that stretches from pole to pole. The same is true of the other planets, and an ACG[3] map simply diagrams these rising, setting, and culmination lines for all planets as they appeared across the world at the time of birth for a person, a nation, or anything else for which an astrologer might draw up a horoscope.

Like planets in a regular horoscope, the lines on the ACG map are subject to alterations over time: transits can activate them; they progress eastward across the map when direct in motion, westward when retrograde; you also can derive subsidiary charts such as solar returns and then plot the planetary lines for these. The Earth somehow "remembers" such lines—the angular presence of planets at pivotal moments of individual or collective history—and when they are activated at a later date, the potential of the original lines is released.

How can we use this type of map? The most obvious way is to apply it to exoteric and concrete astrological interpretation. If you go to a place graced by a Venus line, you are apt to become more occupied than usual with relationships and their place in your life, perhaps getting married or making some other important long-term move of a similar nature. Less obviously, however, these lines each represent untapped and even suppressed psychological potentials; your degree of assimilation of what each line represents will lead you to a set of experiences that are in keeping with the desire of these archetypes to seek outer manifestation in your life.

If as a youth you go to a place where a planet whose archetypal principle you have suppressed is angular, you will be caught up in external realities relating to that planet's principle, including some which may be rather distasteful to you. For instance, young people have a generally difficult time dealing with Saturn or living on their Saturn lines, unless, for example, they have several planets in Capricorn. In maturity, however, those who feel a strong need to experience wholeness seem to be drawn toward places accenting planets that require outer manifestation. Thus, an individual may well be drawn to Saturn lines in later life in an attempt consciously to manifest that archetype more outwardly and openly. Several individuals of our acquaintance (one of whom is discussed in Chapter Four) gravitated to

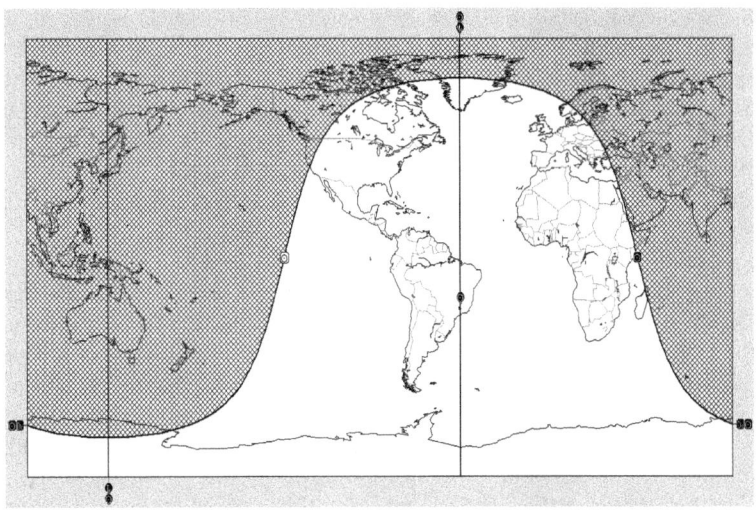

Figure 3 - Sun for example chart, showing rising and setting lines across the world

their Saturn lines at the time of their Saturn returns, a move which shows a definite geographical outreach toward Saturn and its archetype.

To understand how a planet is going to manifest, it is necessary to understand how you feel about that planet and what it represents, though in truth, honesty sufficient to understand such feelings in full is probably rather rare. Carl Jung once said, "every part of the psyche seeks outer manifestation,"[4] a concept which has considerable significance for astrology, since it suggests that each planet equally seeks external manifestation for its unique blend of energy in the individual's life. This is particularly true if we think of the planets as the key symbols of archetypal fundamentals in astrology. Some might identify signs or other astrological factors as of primary significance, but it seems more to the point to consider the planets as the sources of the archetypal energies from which all other elements of astrology derive their meaning and significance. After all, it was the planets that prehistoric humans first distinguished as different from stars on account of their varying motions on the celestial sphere. A translation of Jung's words into astrological language might thus read: "Every planet in the horoscope seeks outer manifestation." The process of assimilation and expression of these disparate energies is the fundamental dynamic underlying psychological growth. Jung also said that "when an inner situation is not made conscious, it happens outside as fate,"[5] a point of view equally significant for astrologers. Exploring and amplifying the implications of these two concepts can give us some insight into the depth interpretation of an ACG map.

Especially interesting is the way in which different age groups seem to react differently at a psychological level to the various planetary polarities, as suggested above. Another avenue of approach to this subject is the understanding of hostile planets, i.e., those planets which individuals for various reasons consider to be alien to themselves or inimical to their innermost feelings. Residing in a locality which falls under such a planet's angular influence is obviously likely to lead to a very particular type of experience.

Carl Jung also was among the few psychiatrists early in the 20th century to describe qualitative differences between the two halves of a human life. The Western world view, stemming as it does from logical positivism and the materialistic science of Newton and Descartes, would have us believe that you grow mentally and physically until you're about 21, reaching a level of maturity at which you remain until you reach 60 or so years of age and begin to fall apart, declining from the plateau of youth until you reach death in the bottom lands of physical and mental decay. This view is in keeping with the cause-and-effect philosophy of the 19th century in which an object was considered to remain static or inert if discrete forces were not acting on it. No allowance was made for qualities related to experience or time, since such subjective perceptions could not be quantified or outwardly analyzed.

Only in the 20th century, with Heisenberg and Einstein, did such qualitative realities begin to be allowed some existence. In his own field of psychology, Jung pioneered ideas of qualitatively different stages of life that emerged as differing types of consciousness at various times in our lives—and for this the entire Western world is in his debt. Frequently throughout his *Collected Works*, he describes life as "morning" and "afternoon," two qualitatively different periods of time that are perceived under different psychological rules by the individual.

In adolescence and the first half of life, the outer world is very real, resisting the ego and its desires in order to forge it in the fires of challenge; the ego is thus created and strengthened by its interaction with what is perceived mostly as a hostile environment. At this time of life, the polarities we all deal with seem to be most starkly contrasted. For example, the sexes are most opposite in their activities and interests at this time, and thus there is no doubt when pre-teenagers dress themselves just who the boys are and who the girls are. Youthful peer groups tend to be mutually exclusive, with two different groups often adopting an entirely different manner of dress and speech, something which can actually lead to physical confrontation if someone from one group happens to intrude on the territory or interests of another in some way. A strongly "tribal" and collective ethos prevails.

During youth, more than at other times, things are identified either as belonging to the self, or as alien to and opposite to the self—in other words, as "self" or "not-self." Planets and their archetypes are sensed in this way as well. Every child, for instance, is probably closely in touch with his or her Moon, but children are very out of touch with their Saturns, tending to see Saturnian modes of thought and action as somehow coming from an external authoritative force, via parents' restrictions, teachers' rules in schools, the curfew, and other laws enforced by the police, or limitations placed on them by the government. Adolescents in fact seem to form themselves into subgroups that can be exclusively associated with certain planets astrologically. We can see this in high schools in the United States, where we find two social groups that have been categorized in various times and climes with terms such as the "rockers" or "hippies" versus the "nerds" or "jocks." The main thing distinguishing the groups on one side of the divide from the groups on the other is that those who constitute the first group tend to be very rebellious, wear clothes that push the edge of the fashion envelope (and often violate dress codes), tend to experiment with drugs, have artistic interests, and generally do things that bring approval from their peers; the nerds and jocks, even though themselves somewhat antagonistic to each other, are both straitlaced compared to the rockers and the hippies, tend to do as they're told, and attempt to excel in ways likely to gain the approval of higher-ups, through activities in academics or sports. The two planets that might be associated with each end of this polarity are, of course, Uranus and Jupiter.

Jung suggested that beginning at midlife such polarizations tend to evaporate as the individual seeks to bring about a synthesis between them. As we grow older, it becomes less interesting to add even more experience to the particular archetype we specialized in developing when young, and the things we haven't been hold more allure and fascination for us. Consequently, after midlife, planets in the horoscope which we have projected outward onto other people or inward to ourselves as polarized modes of consciousness begin to emerge as parts of our outer consciousness. The collective or tribal affiliations of adolescence become subordinate to individuation—to becoming an individual.

Often the first emergence of these planets is marked by a certain amount of hostility. The poet Robert Bly said, "Every part of our personality that we don't love will become hostile to us."[6] An archetype and part of self that has been suppressed for many years releases an enormous amount of pent-up psychic energy when it suddenly bursts forth. Frequently, such emerging planetary archetypes are associated with distant places. Just as the psyche is seen as the home for the self, distant places, whether those that we visit or those which manifest in our lives in some involuntary way, become significant and symbolic of emerging potentials that are begging for manifestation. Bly describes this as the "Hotspur in Wales problem." Readers familiar with Shakespeare will remember that King Henry IV was plagued by a rebellious young nobleman named Hotspur, who was finally defeated at Shrewsbury. The image of an urgent and vigorous noble, plotting rebellion or otherwise fomenting problems from afar, has much in common with the way the planets work in our charts, especially when we try to ignore or even suppress them. This idea of emerging planets first manifesting in connection with some distant place is obviously one that will be developed in our exploration of Astro*Carto*Graphy.

When different planets are associated either with the self or the not-self, varying types of polarization will manifest. Obviously, the simplest of these to understand is the male/female opposition. The sexes seem to be most unlike in youth—boys and girls, while they enjoy each other's company in childhood, begin to polarize in the early teen years and thus find each other bothersome, troublesome, and almost impossible to coexist with. The sexual relationship is then undertaken as the only way to bridge the polarization. As time goes on, of course, the sexes become less disparate and by the eighth decade it may actually be rather hard to tell them apart in some cases.

Different sociological planetary polarities are also interesting to observe. As already noted, in high schools in the United States we often find two groups which might well be symbolized primarily by Uranus versus Jupiter. In a more general fashion, the conformers and enforcers of majority opinion are certainly associated with Jupiter and perhaps to some degree Saturn, as well as, of course, with the athletic Mars. On the other hand, the individualists who dare the group to make them conform are represented by Uranus, or perhaps Neptune or Pluto. These groups will polarize in relation to each other and will often seem to be irreconcilably opposite, especially in the early years of life. Class differences are also symbolized by such polarization. Mercury and Jupiter are the two planets that seem to symbolize the working class and the professional class, respectively. Individuals who find themselves attracted strongly to the things in life represented by one of these planets will probably be polarized to the other.

The planets and associated archetypes opposite to those with which an individual has identified in youth begin to emerge at various times throughout the life when activated by astrological factors. The Saturn return at the age of 29 is a very well-known and clear-cut period when a planet that has hitherto been projected outward onto authorities, the police, or academic leadership begins to be internalized in some way; the individual is forced to accept that Saturn lies within as well as without. The Saturn return will in fact be painful in proportion to how closely one has identified with either Jupiter or Uranus or Pluto or any of the planets that seem to be most opposite to Saturn in nature. Those who do well with the Saturn return are usually spared because they have a well-placed Saturn, or perhaps several planets in Capricorn. These people often wait until the Uranus opposition (or perhaps the Neptune square) at midlife to experience the kind of crisis others go through earlier with Saturn. The individual who has mastered a particular planet will find that its aspects come and go without causing much difficulty, while the individual who has ignored that planet and projected it outward will deal more intensely with external confining circumstances or with the emergence of a part of himself that he or she is not particularly happy to see.

A very complex series of reactions occurs when a new planetary archetype emerges from its hitherto unconscious situation. The first evidence of this reaction often is total denial, a contention that what this planet or its archetype represents simply is not there. Children often do this when the sexual archetypes of Mars and Venus begin to manifest in their lives, for example. As the planet continues to manifest, denial is soon followed with a pattern of projection and repression. Projection, despite its bad reputation, is not all wrong, as it can often be an important stage on the way to assimilating an archetype. After all, only denial—insisting there's no point in the individual even dealing with an urgent issue—absolutely ignores a planet's existence, something which can build the repressed energy to uncomfortable and even dangerous levels. With projection, at least the planet's existence is acknowledged, albeit in some outward form. Despite this, in projecting the symbolism and energies of a particular planetary archetype outward, one is giving away power that is properly one's own. The energy of projecting the planet outward onto some institution or person means that the power the individual could normally direct toward his or her own undertakings is now wasted in trying to create an external reality.

In addition, it is more likely that the energy of such a rejected or projected planet will manifest itself externally—remember what Jung said about the inner situation not made conscious happening "outside, as fate." Traveling to a location at which a projected planet is found angular can often be fateful indeed, as an essentially hostile planet is then brought into consciousness with little preparation, often in the form of an event or a person who seizes control of the native's life in some way. So the best relationship to have with any planetary archetype is that of assimilating it, assuming it to be part of self, and making an effort to learn it and apply it. In this way, the individual can best come to utilize its positive aspects. Such assimilation often occurs through an important personal relationship in which the attributes of the partner, at first irksome because they are opposite to self, are soon made part of the conscious personality.

In certain cases, especially for those who have reached the top in some social, political, or personal sense, there's a further stage beyond assimilation, which might be called exemplification, in which an individual acts out a particular planetary archetype so well that he or she is called upon to epitomize it for other people in his or her society. Everyone who projects a planet needs a willing (or unwitting) person upon whom to project it. An example of this is the Pope or the Dalai Lama, each of whom embodies the principle of Jupiter for hundreds of millions of Roman Catholics or Buddhists all over the world. Presidents and other national leaders act out Saturn, and perhaps Jupiter, for people both inside and outside their countries; and there are movie stars who excel at portraying particular archetypes such as the *puer aeternus* and the beautiful *anima*. Projection is, however, always a two-

LINES AROUND THE WORLD

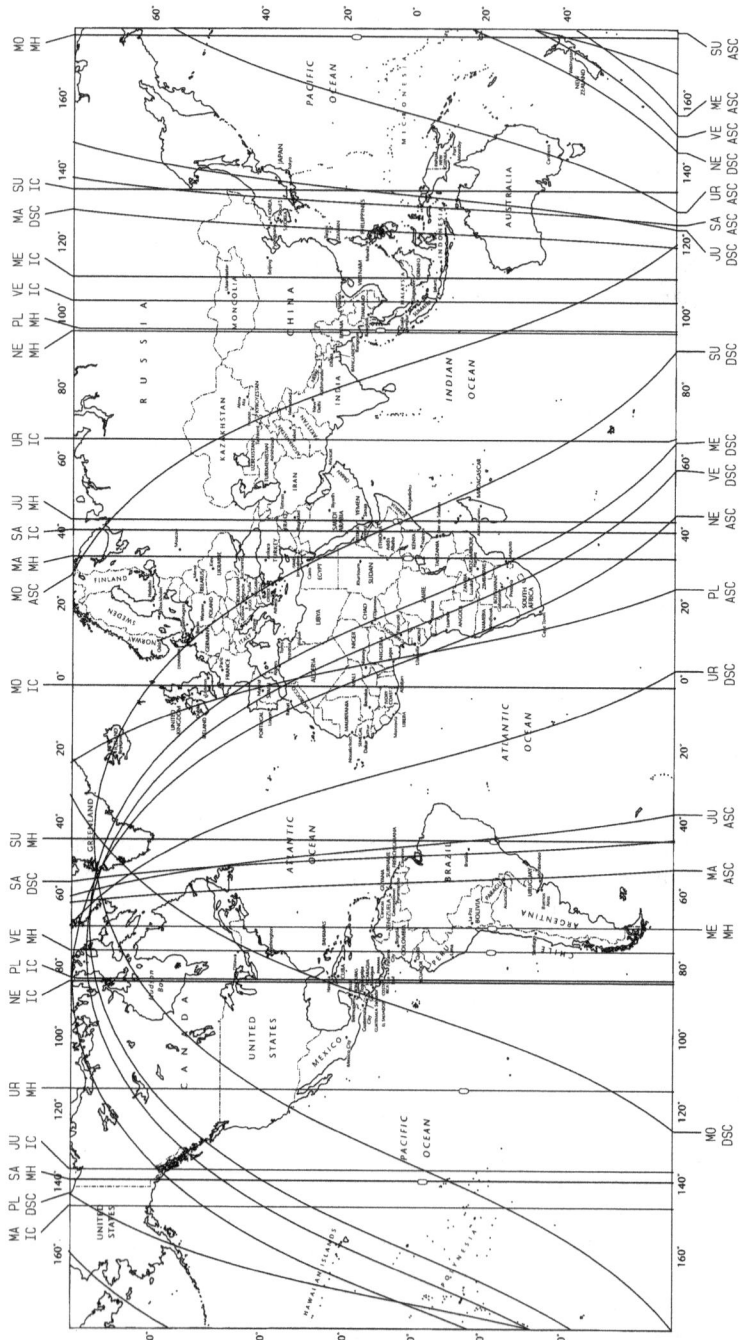

Figure 4 - Paramahansa Yogananda: Teacher Sun Versus Student Moon

way street, as it is only through the assimilation of each archetype that an individual can reach wholeness.

Our reactions to "self" and "not-self" archetypes change, though, and are modified by the stage of life we are in. In youth, the things that resemble one's own chosen archetypes are seen as good, while those archetypes that are polarized and opposite are seen as bad and as representing something that needs to be resisted, destroyed, or somehow suppressed. In maturity, by contrast, the archetypes associated with self come to be seen as rather boring, while those that are not-self often become fascinating and imbued with numinosity. In this neutralization of the "change" of archetypes lies an important reason for the high number of divorces in midlife—what was seen in the spouse as "good" later seems just "boring."

We have stated that some planetary archetypes will be seen as not-self and others will be seen as self. Those which are associated with not-self in the later stages of life usually become far more attractive and far less repulsive to us than they were in the earlier stages. In any case, all planets seek outward manifestation at all times, so the more we project a particular planet, the more it will act outside ourselves and beyond our control, as fate.

How might we feel about a place where a planet we had always rejected and projected outward was particularly strong? What could we expect to happen to us in such a "denial place?" To begin with, we probably wouldn't like people who come from that region, and yet at the same time we might tend to feel a peculiarly strong attraction to them, one that would cause people or ideas from this area to intrude frequently on our lives—a little like a bad dream that keeps repeating itself until we begin to understand the message it conveys. On the other hand, if a place is associated astrologically with a planet whose archetype we have thoroughly assimilated, things and people from those places will in some way make us feel and act most like ourselves, reinforcing our egos. These places will urge us to continue being ourselves as we are and as we always have been.

Because of this, it should become clear that the techniques associated with Astro*Carto*Graphy represent a great deal more than a travel itinerary, more than just a way of determining where to have a pleasant vacation. Its prime value lies in its ability to identify those places of the world that are correlated with the archetypes which are emerging in one's consciousness as one matures. Let us look at some examples and see how this has worked in different individuals' reactions to some of the same archetypes. Figure 4 is the ACG map for the spiritual leader Paramahansa Yogananda,[7] who began life in India, where he studied under his own guru. India is east of his Uranus IC line and on his Moon Ascendant line. This is fitting symbolism for a person who was going to give up his "4th house" identification as a Hindu, an Indian, a Brahman—everything he had been up until then—in order to seek spiritual enlightenment with his master. The role of a student is particularly shown by his Moon Ascendant line.

LINES AROUND THE WORLD

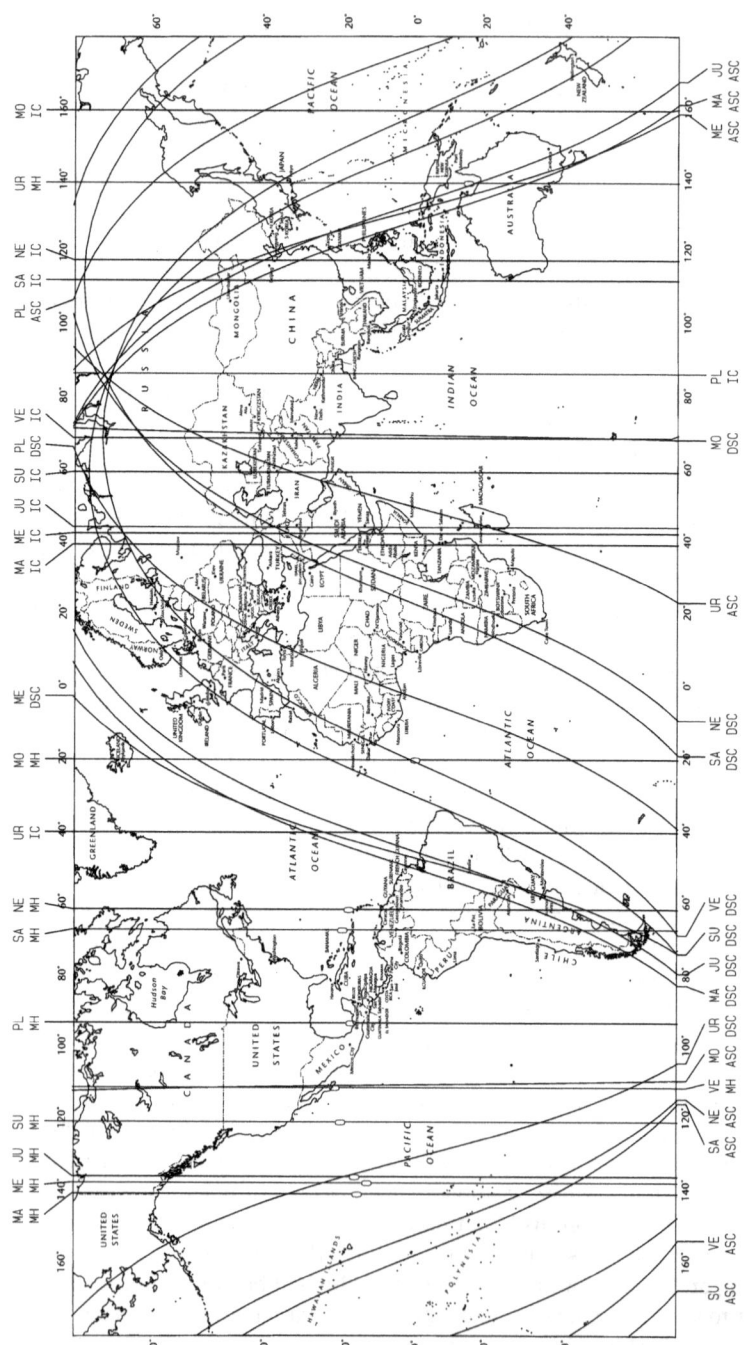

Figure 5 - John F. Kennedy: An Appointment with Pluto in Dallas

In his maturity, he came to Los Angeles, which is on his Uranus Midheaven line, reversing the polarity from the transformation of himself on an inner level to one in which he acted as the instrument for the external transformation of society on an outer level. Moreover, Los Angeles is exactly on his Sun Ascendant line, so that while the Moon rising at his birth equipped him for studenthood, as an adult he moved to a place where the Sun on the Ascendant made it possible for Yogananda himself to be a teacher and to transmit to others the very knowledge he had learned as a youth. Youth and age thus polarized themselves in the life of Yogananda: from self-transformation at Uranus IC, to a role as an active transformer of society under Uranus Midheaven; from a student under his Moon Ascendant line, to a teacher at his Sun Ascendant line.

Another interesting example is found in the map of John F. Kennedy (Figure 5),[8] in which the Pluto Midheaven line goes directly through Dallas, the place where the President was murdered. It would be foolish to assert that going to one's Pluto line means absolutely that one is going to die, and it is particularly important in assessing the potential of a planetary line to look at the chart of the individual in order to understand the context in which the planet is placed there. Kennedy had Pluto unaspected and cadent in the 9th house, and its closest aspects are semisquares to Mars and Mercury, suggesting perhaps problems in travel. It is clear from this that Pluto was not a planet with which John Kennedy was particularly comfortable, and that it was something he had not inwardly assimilated. Psychologically, this unassimilated Pluto was demonstrated by the charismatic power and sexual relentlessness he embodied. Also, his unintegrated Pluto led him to the underworld—as both champion and victim. Consequently, when Pluto manifested on his Pluto Midheaven line, it did so in an entirely external and devastating fashion. An interesting example of a Pluto Midheaven line operating from the inside out (rather than from the outside in, as with Kennedy) is seen in regard to a particular chart for the United States, as we shall see in Chapter 7.

C. G. Jung, in contrast to Kennedy, had Pluto angular throughout his life near Zurich, though in his case it was very close to his IC, with its exact distance depending on the precise time of birth out of several possibilities.[9] Jung's Pluto is widely square Uranus and square Saturn and widely conjunct the Moon, but above all it is angular in the natal location. Clearly, Jung was able to employ the energy of this planet in an entirely positive way since he spent his whole life going within himself in order to transform the base material of the psyche into the gold of conscious transformation. A planet on the IC usually refers to transformation on the deepest levels, with all the "givens" of self—family, home, religion, class identity—surrendered to some higher calling.

The Sun Descendant line also passes through Switzerland, so it was through his patients and his relationships to them that the inner transformation of Pluto on the IC manifested. He wrote in his autobiography that everything he knew had been taught to him by his patients. It should be mentioned here, incidentally, that perusal of Pluto lines in maps such as this will reveal differences between the standard horoscope and ACG mapping. The former considers only the longitudes of the planets, while the mapping process also makes use of a further dimension, the planet's latitude. Pluto's latitude is so great in Jung's case that its "true rise" moves its line several degrees closer to Zurich than one might suppose it would be when looking at Jung's standard horoscope.

Jim Jones[10] and Elizabeth Taylor[11] provide us with two other interesting examples and an interesting contrast as well. Jones was the cult leader whose 900+ followers committed mass suicide, or were simply murdered, under his direction in 1979. As we will see (Chapter 5), Jim Jones' Mars and Sun lines go right through Guyana. A little consideration of his birth chart will tell us that his Mars line is likely to produce problems since this planet squares his Sun in Fixed signs and forms other difficult aspects as well. Thus, Mars was for him in conflict with his inner self. Taylor, on the other hand, moved to a place where her Mars Midheaven falls near Sun, Mercury, and Neptune lines. In her early life in Hollywood she acted out some of the more negative and clearly projected manifestations of the Mars archetype with her countless marriages and the resulting string of scandals in the press. But in later years she took it upon herself to raise money for AIDS research and, in an era when President Ronald Reagan was afraid even to utter the name of the disease in public, she singlehandedly raised $60 million for medical research to combat it.

Speaking of American presidents, let us consider the ACG map of George Bush (41st president and father of George W. Bush, 43rd president) and see how well he assimilated some of his more problematical archetypes. The fact that Bush's Mars Descendant line goes right through the Panama Canal speaks for itself; it's quite clear he did not manage to assimilate his Aquarian Mars in a positive manner, despite the fact that it trines his Sun. Perhaps the opposition of Mars to Neptune was the source of the problem. Another Mars line, the Ascendant, crosses his Jupiter Midheaven line right in Beijing, obviously indicating his continued problems with China. As one example, the massacre in Tiananmen Square was a significant defeat for George Bush, and the fact that the Chinese gerontocracy absolutely refused to allow the reforms demanded by their people resulted in continued difficulties that extended into the administration of Bush's successor. Nearly every American president for whom a reliable birth time is available has had to engage in some military activity under one or another of his Mars lines. For Roosevelt, it was Pearl Harbor; for Truman, Japan and Korea; for Kennedy, Johnson, and Ford, Vietnam; for Carter, Iran; and for Reagan, one might say "everywhere."[12]

George Bush (senior, often known as "Bush 41") followed one of his Mars lines in Panama, though only after several false starts in which opportunities to let local leaders deal with the problem of General Noriega were missed. His most notable action, "Desert Storm," occurred under his natal Sun-Jupiter lines. Two things are interesting in this respect, the first of which is that much of Saddam Hussein's magnificent weaponry was accumulated with a generous shower of goodwill and cash from the Bush administration, as a result of the mistaken notion that Saddam would provide a stabilizing counterweight to the Iranians. The second interesting point is that, perhaps unfortunately for Saddam, his invasion of Kuwait was undertaken at a time when Mars was engaged in a long, slow transit of these two very planets in Bush's chart, Sun and Jupiter. Thus, acting as a "stand-in," transiting Mars ensured that Bush got the message and replaced his Sun-Jupiter blank check to the Iraqis with a Sun-Jupiter-Mars massive retaliation.

This movement of diplomats, soldiers, and military hardware to areas touched by Mars at the birth of a single individual is surely the most fascinating and often tragic example of the way in which our innermost thoughts, feelings, and fears can become events in the outside world. Though few reading this book can ever hope to have anything like the power of a national leader, the ways in which the astrological circumstances of our birth may affect how we relate to the world at large, and how the world in turn relates to us, are just as important in our lives. These lines across the world can tell us at least as much about ourselves as the planets, signs, and houses in a traditional horoscope do—and perhaps in showing how our innermost selves relate so precisely to space, time, and geography they can tell us more.

2

Lines and Crossings

AS WE HAVE SEEN, each planet in a standard horoscope for a given time and place can also be mapped as a set of lines that denote those places where it was rising, setting, or at upper or lower culmination around the world at the instant for which the chart was set. Though adding this new dimension to the standard horoscope can be very valuable in mapping and understanding the long-term psychological development of the native, in the shorter term the way in which the planets manifest in this global context is often more direct. The simplest application of an ACG map in fact uses the most rudimentary astrological principles to show where we might, for instance, be likely to find fame (Sun and Jupiter lines), or to find ourselves dealing with our emotional natures (Moon), to find romance (Venus), or perhaps to be more assertive (Mars). Along with these planetary principles there are, of course, basic modes of action which depend on which angles highlight the planets. Over the years, clients who have purchased these maps have provided a great wealth of anecdotes showing evidence of the way in which the planets work at this level.[1]

The stories of travelers passing through areas where individual lines are strong are particularly interesting for the way in which they illuminate the action of planetary lines. An extended stay along a particular line is likely to be psychologically important in much the same way as a slow transit or a progressed aspect, but the action of a planetary line encountered on a brief journey can at times be very striking. While these "travel transits" may shake us up or otherwise stand out as engaging memories years later, rarely do they bring us the kind of self-awareness or self-realization we can gain from longer experience in a particular location.

Consider, for example, the story of a young American woman traveling through Europe with a girlfriend, both in their early twenties. Having completed college and not being quite sure what to do with the rest of their lives, the young woman and her friend set off on a journey that took them from Greece to the Netherlands, working to pay their way along the road by picking up odd jobs available to students in those days. Along the journey, she resided for a few months on Crete, which is situated between her Sun Descendant and Moon IC lines. During her time there, she became very involved in writing, recording her daily activities and observations in journals, all of which is in keeping with the kind of creative urge often sparked by Sun lines. Leaving Crete, she then spent some time along the western edge of Greece, particularly on the island of Cefalonia. During her time there she continued her writing as she lived for a time in a rustic setting on the beach in a grass hut, but since in traveling from Crete to Cefalonia she had moved from between her Sun and Moon lines to a spot almost directly on her Pluto Midheaven line, her experiences began to take a new direction and a new tone.

The first signal that Pluto was involved came when she met a man a few years older than herself (she was in her early twenties at the time), who, as she would later put it, awakened her sexually. Though her generation was generally quite open in both talking about sex and experimenting with it, up to that point her own experiences had been, if interesting and educational, less than satisfactory. The man she spent time with on Cefalonia was, however, experienced and skilled enough for her to find herself really enjoying sex for the first time. Her experience with this man was one of several "epiphanies" (her word) she experienced on the road.

After leaving Cefalonia, she and her friend traveled north, hitchhiking through Yugoslavia (as it was called then), west of her Pluto Midheaven line, and it was here, just outside Skopje, that her youthful feelings of immortality were challenged as she came face to face with the prospect of her own death. As the two women traveled along the highway from Skopje, walking along in the warm afternoon, they were for a time mainly aware of the pleasantness of the day and the camaraderie, and not much concerned about the weight of the backpacks or the length of the journey ahead of them. Suddenly, as if startled awake from a dream, the two of them realized they were being watched by children who had suddenly emerged from the landscape around them. Though at first they were unconcerned, as the number of children grew and as older-looking ones filtered into the group, and as they began to move closer, the two began to worry. Then some of the group began to make animal noises, neighing like horses, while others moved closer and began striking their backpacks, all the while eyeing the two women to see their reaction. That reaction came like a blow to the stomach, as the two began to understand that they were in danger from these strange creatures, that they were being stalked and, as they were all alone in a strange country, they might in fact be in mortal danger.

All they could do was continue walking, trying not to seem afraid as the children came closer and the harassment increased. Just as they were beginning to wonder how they could possibly escape, a tourist bus came over a rise. Quickly they ran out onto the highway, directly in front of the bus, waving it to a stop. The bus driver picked them up, calming them by saying he would take them to the next town and safety, and as they looked back they saw that their tormenters, who the driver said were gypsies, had melted back into the scenery, disappearing as swiftly as they had appeared. The experience, which left an indelible mark on the young woman, was as unpleasant as her awakening on Cefalonia had been pleasant. From sex to death, she had experienced Pluto close up.

Other experiences in the ACG files offer similar meaningful personal triumphs and tragedies, such as the case of a woman with a 12th house Saturn debilitated by sign who traveled to her Saturn IC line a few months before her Saturn return was to take place. While there, she managed to experience political unrest, a romance which altered her life for quite some time to come, and, most interesting of all, hospitalization for treatment of a potentially life-threatening illness just a few weeks before her Saturn return. All of this, unfortunately, took place before Astro*Carto*Graphy had been fully developed and made available to the public, so it was only years later that she discovered the kind of peril in which her astrological situation had placed her. Because of the involvement of the Saturn return, this story parallels a similar "Saturnian journey" outlined in a later chapter, but also makes, with that parallel, two interesting points, the first of which is that not all lines related to a particular planet are the same; and the second of which, as anyone using standard astrology could tell us, is that planets in two different birth charts do not operate in exactly the same way.

In the case of the debilitated 12th-house Saturn, personal and social upheaval were followed by illness, while in the case of a Saturn in Scorpio in the 7th house tht we begin discussing in the next chapter, the focus of the Saturn return and the activities surrounding it ultimately involved partnership issues. The action of planetary lines is not always clear-cut in this sense, but cases such as these show that a planet's angularity at a particular locality takes place within the background of the natal chart itself.

These lines and their effects also involve the charts of others, especially in the case of close relationships (whether personal or business) that develop at locales where two people both have strong planetary emphasis.

A woman who was born near her Venus-setting (VE DSC) line has fond memories of her childhood when she was the center of attention and had an interest in the arts. When she was still fairly young, however, her family was forced to move a great distance to a place in which the planets emphasized were Mars, Saturn, and Neptune. Not only did she feel completely out of touch with the scene, but she also found that the people she met over the next few years had an entirely different set of values, and she was highly aware of their proclivity toward violence and the use of drugs (the latter of which she herself dabbled in for a time as well). Finally, she left that place for another which, while some distance away, was still close to those Mars, Saturn, and Neptune lines. Over the next decade or so she managed to learn skills that landed her a job in the film industry, though the work itself was difficult and demanding. When she finally realized that any effort to act independently would be squelched by those around her, she and the husband she had by now acquired left to move across the country. An additional factor in the move was the marital problems they had been experiencing, and both had strong 7th-house Venus lines in the place they decided to move to. Though it was a struggle, they managed to repair the problems in their relationship and both managed to make progress in their respective careers. Everything was not moonlight and roses, but the switch from Mars-Saturn-Neptune to Venus made a definite difference in easing their situation.

As the latter story with its relatively happy Venus-Descendant ending makes clear, the meanings for each type of line are roughly in keeping with the traditional meanings for each angle in a horoscope. If a planet is on the Midheaven, it means the planet's energy will manifest in terms of your position in society. If it's on the Ascendant, it shows itself in your outer personality, so that the people around you will see you as the outer expression—almost the personification—of that planet. If it's on the Descendant, this is most apt to represent a projection of the planet's energy, a place where other people will symbolize or act out that planet for you, as the Venus-Descendant couple acted out Venus for each other. The Imum Coeli, or IC, is probably the most interesting and most unexpectedly important of the angles. The IC represents the foundation with which you are equipped when you come into this world, or the particular individualized context into which you emerge when you are born—your family, your ethnicity, your race, your social class, your religion. A planet on that line indicates a change of that context into something else. For instance, if you go to a place where Uranus is on the IC, you very likely will transcend your family, your race, your background, or your class in order to become a more individualized, Uranian person.

Aside from the obvious differences between the angles, the operation of each planet is modified slightly, depending on which side of the line one is considering (few localities will in fact coincide precisely with a particular planetary line). For example, if you were considering a move to a place near a Jupiter-rising line, the usual promise of success might be less in your control if you were west of the line, and more in your control if you were east of it. Such differences result from the fact that the angles of the chart—the Ascendant, Midheaven, Descendant, and Imum Coeli, or IC, are still and all part of the house structure. Thus, if you were to live west of your Jupiter line, your Jupiter experience would be colored by the 1st house tendency to be directly aware of your personal identity as the focal point for much of what happens to you. On the other hand, east of the line, the more subtle 12th house influence would tend to make you feel that things which others see you as producing are actually coming to you from outside. Neither viewpoint is better or worse than the other, but the difference can at times be crucial. A general explanation of the differences to be seen in each zone follows.

THE ANGULAR LINES
Ascendant/1st House (West of line)

Among the possible manifestations you could see with a particular planet, those involving your direct perception of your own personality and identity should be the major focus of interest. You could come to identify strongly with the various functions, energies, personality attributes, and activities of this zone, and might consciously incorporate them into your repertoire of personality options. Real power can come from recognizing the nature and potency of this influence, a positive personal energy which you can come to symbolize in a very real way for others, whether through exaggerating it, or through consciously acting out the positive aspects of its role. This energy flows both ways, as you'll find that other people empower you, recognizing your instinctive ability to handle matters that either make them uncomfortable or escape their understanding perhaps because they strike too close to the core of their personality. In your personal relationships, you may tend to play the role assigned by this psychological influence, and your partner may well play whatever is opposite. Success comes from accepting this role and learning to manage and project it consciously.

Ascendant/12th House (East of line)

In this situation, your external personality is very strongly colored by the psychological principles of the planet. However, others may see this more clearly than you do, and in general you are inclined to see these principles and their role in your life as things that happen to you, rather than things you consciously do. Gaining control of these impulses can be difficult for this reason, and you stand the best chance to capitalize constructively on the power of this zone or to integrate the planetary potentials it highlights if you work toward understanding how events that frequently or repetitiously befall you here really are the product of a consistent, inner attitude toward yourself and your identity. This may sound abstract, but it is still important, because if you fail consciously to control your role in events that befall you here, you could unconsciously be working against yourself.

Midheaven/10th House (West of line)

Here a planet presents you with those possibilities which seem most outer-oriented, yet personally relevant. Since this influence will tend to act itself out in a social arena, you could find yourself thrust into situations in which imposed leadership or responsibility requires you to develop the capacities and skills of the planet in question. At first you are likely to be exposed to people and situations that command your attention or that force themselves on you, if these are concerns which you tend to deny having to deal with. In either case, they will pose examples of how you can assume the required authority and thus properly act it out, but quickly you'll find you've been left on your own, immersed in challenges and situations that clearly require you to develop the skills and awareness natural to this planet in a public and highly visible manner. If you feel the world is watching you, that's because it is, as your career or your vocational position in society demands acceptance of, and growth into, the potentials signaled by this planet.

Midheaven/9th House (East of line)

In a location such as this, those planetary potentials which seem most external, objective, and detached from your self and your personality are the ones most apt to manifest. The planet's influence will act itself out in a social arena, but more specifically and most often through people, situations, and social or cultural influences that represent external authority or the whole of society and its values. If you're in a position of authority at this locality, you will clearly exemplify the potentials of this planet, but more likely you will find yourself repeatedly exposed to others who act out this role for you and play the role of authority as well. You can assimilate your own leadership potentials from these experiences, as you are powerfully influenced by cultural, educational, legal, or religious institutions. Expect the people, gender, and social roles, and the professions connected with this planet to become dominant in your social and career life, and anticipate that they will offer important guidance and valuable insights about what your ultimate social power is and where it lies.

Descendant/7th House (West of line)

As manifestations of a strongly external nature are apt to predominate here, you will likely "project" the qualities you ought to be learning from the planet, and your mate, partners, and others closest to you will frequently seem to exhibit the patterns and potentials associated with it. It is very difficult for you to see how your own acceptance or rejection of parts of yourself can bring this all about, and thus you may blame others when you fall short in certain areas of your life. However, these other people are really teachers and pupils at the same time, as they first show you parts of yourself you are reluctant to accept, and then learn from your reactions. One thing you may find mystifying, in fact, is to hear people acknowledge your importance to them, since you yourself may be unable to see the very qualities in yourself that they are acknowledging. For that reason, here you will learn most by example, as the qualities of this planet often seem remote and opposed to who you are within.

Descendant/6th House (East of line)

Since a planet in this house for a given location is a little east of the actual planetary influence, it is likely to manifest in a more external and practical fashion. The planetary energies require your attention and understanding by repeatedly challenging you with problems, the solutions of which require you to accept and learn the potentials of that planet in ways that you might not have anticipated. Many of these problems will deal with other people, especially in day-to-day work and vocational situations. You will want to see this planet as operating externally to those things you identify as central to your concept of self and personhood, so if the concerns it represents happen to be repugnant to you, there is real danger of such elements intruding quite beyond your control, forcing you to come to terms with them, if only to "keep them in their place"—that is, out of your conscious mind. But such mental gymnastics can be very time-consuming, and a waste of energy as well, so it is far better to take the numerous hints offered by this planet and accept, develop, and mature the qualities and potentials of this zone.

Imum Coeli/4th House (West of line)

Planetary energies relating directly to the influence of your family, cultural, or ethnic background are most likely to manifest here. The planet tends to act outside of you, polarizing your self-image in opposition to its more negative potentials, requiring your development of its qualities by either positive example or direct coercion. Who you are—meaning in this case who your family, past, and "root" have been—becomes a potent force in this creation of who you are growing to be, a force whose nature will conform closely to the meaning of this planet. Living here will change your most inward concepts of self, often by bringing you into direct confrontation with your origins and your past.

Imum Coeli/3rd House (East of line)

Those planetary matters which relate most to your environment and to your growing awareness of it as an important influence in your personality will be most strongly emphasized here. You are sensitized to your immediate neighborhood and surroundings, challenged to react to external reality and day-to-day immediate concerns by altering your personal image, or your identity in order to better conform to what the planet in question represents.

In addition to the obvious ten basic lines, two other factors need to be considered. The first of these, which will not be a factor at latitudes greater than about 23° north or south, is the relative distance of a planet exactly at upper or lower culmination (MC or IC lines) from the nadir or zenith. These are the points directly overhead (zenith) for a culminating planet or directly opposite this (in essence, directly below your feet!) for a planet at lower culmination (nadir). The first point is indicated in a standard ACG map by a small oval at the latitude equal to that planet's declination, while the second would be found on the IC line at the same latitude, but in the opposite hemisphere. For example, if a planet has a north declination of 21°06', its zenith point would fall in the northern hemisphere on its Midheaven line at 21N06, and its "nadir point" (not shown on an ACG map) would fall in the southern hemisphere on the IC line at 21S06. In fact, this example fits John F. Kennedy (Figure 5), whose Midheaven line runs just east of Cuba, an island which covers latitudes from about 21° north to 23° north. Thus, the scene of Kennedy's greatest foreign-policy disaster is well within range of both the latitude and longitude where Saturn was at its greatest height above the horizon at the time when Kennedy was born.

More important than this, however, is the idea of "latitude crossings," also referred to as "line crossings," which are just what they sound like—the latitudes at which lines for two given planets cross on a map. As such crossings only involve the combination of a Midheaven or IC line on the one hand with a rising (Ascendant) or setting (Descendant) line on the other, they are somewhat like squares in their action, and have been found to be about one-third the strength of the lines themselves. Though most ACG interpretation emphasizes the lines more than the crossings, the latter are particularly important in those areas where one is not within "orb" of regular lines. An orb of about 4 to 7 degrees on either side (east or west) of an MC/IC or rise-set line, and about 1 to 2 degrees on either side (north or south) of a crossing are suggested based on experience, as well as feedback from Astro*Carto*Graphy users.[2]

Finally, just as we can "stack up" chart upon chart upon chart, so it is possible to consider questions of astrological geography from a variety of possible viewpoints, such as transits and progressions. Even within a horoscope, this can quickly become unwieldy, requiring a good knowledge of astrology and great care to interpret properly. When using a map, all the more care must be used. For this reason, the best method of going beyond the natal map to look at current indications is to combine progressions of the inner planets with transits of the outer planets, since the two sets of planets will move along at roughly the same speed.

These then are the basics of the mechanics of Astro*Carto*Graphy. Understanding them, we can now consider how they are used by an astrologer.

3

Shadowed Planets: Stages of Psychological Growth

AN ASTROLOGER'S clients generally have two types of problems: circumstantial and repetitive. A circumstantial problem is the product of a moment or a particular situation that is essentially of a transitory nature—for example, "I can't seem to get the contractors to fix the roof of my house." The circumstantial problem is usually easy to deal with because all the astrologer needs to do is to identify the transits or progressions in the chart that seem to have created it and then to explain exactly why it is happening. Following on with advice as to when the problem is likely to stop, and what transits would alleviate the problem with builders, the next step is therefore to identify the solution. For example, if Saturn is transiting Mars, and the client is having trouble in relationships with men, the astrologer could begin by noting that since that transit is the clear reason for these difficulties, a coming sextile of Jupiter to Mars might provide the solution by helping to expand consciousness of the latter planet, so to speak. This could be done through the client taking up athletics, or perhaps by doing something like taking a trip to a foreign country—in short, by engaging in some sort of Mars-Jupiter activity which would balance out or integrate the undermined or unfocused Mars.

The second basic type of dilemma, the repetitive problem, is much more difficult to deal with. For example, a common problem of this type is the complaint that "every time I get married, he turns out to be an alcoholic"; another typical example is the difficulty of holding a job. When the astrologer hears the phrase "every time" as the client is talking about himself or herself, and this leads to a history of two or three repeated events of the same kind, then it begins to become obvious that something at a deeper psychological level is at the source of it. The technique of dealing with such repetitive, deep-seated problems can be tied in to the geographic dimension of astrology, and thus directly concerns Astro*Carto*Graphy.

Before seeing how this works, we must understand something about the growth and maturation of the psyche. The psychological structure at the root of such things as our personalities, our interests, or our motivations does not emerge fully formed at birth, any more than our physical characteristics do. Obviously the growth of the psyche must be considered a process, just as the growth of the body is a process. For the human psyche, growth proceeds through the assimilation of unconscious contents into the conscious mind. In order to understand what is meant by this, just consider how most of the experience your brain has accumulated and categorized as you interacted with the world around you from childhood to your present age is not immediately available to you, but is rather suppressed into the unconscious mind. From time to time, elements of this unconscious emerge into consciousness in some form, but it is only when you directly acknowledge them and learn to deal with them—when you can integrate them and assimilate them—that they become part of your whole self as you reach a new stage in the growth of your psyche.

Specialization is a very important concept in human behavior. Why, for instance, do some people live in the Arctic, while others live in New York, or Paris, or Hong Kong? The answer to that question is that people do not enjoy competition that emphasizes their weaknesses, and choosing carefully where they live is one way of dealing with it. Those living things that inhabit the Arctic perhaps do so because they don't enjoy other things trying to kill them and eat their proteins. If you've ever had a lion, for example, try to kill you and eat your proteins, you know it is not a pleasant experience. Some will deal with this by living where the lions live and taking on the role of hunter. Others, neither willing nor able to be hunters, yet mindful that lions inhabit hot, tropical climates, say to themselves, "Well, I'm going to go live in the Arctic, so I won't get my proteins eaten."

In each person, the psyche also specializes in this way, so that not everyone equally expresses the mental structures associated with the planet Venus, or the planet Jupiter, or the planet Pluto, since some planets may be more suitable for that person's immediate environment than others. Partly as a method of adaptation, the psyche will choose one planet over the other, and while this may be good in the short term, the result of this kind of specialization is that certain parts of your psyche will become more developed, while others will lie dormant, at least until circumstances (either external or internal) challenge you to cultivate them.

If you're going to grow as an adult, then as you live your life and learn new things or are exposed to differing and changing situations, previously undeveloped parts of your psyche may begin to emerge and to demand first development and then assimilation into your conscious identity. This is in fact the reason underlying the astrological version of Carl Jung's very important observation that we mentioned in the first chapter: "every planet in the horoscope seeks outer manifestation." Every planetary principle in the chart needs to be expressed at some time in the life, and it will seek outer manifestation whether or not we wish this to be. A planet which is seeking outer expression, yet is being resisted by the conscious ego, is what is called a "shadowed planet," and these are usually at the root of repetitive problems.

Some planets, when their turns come to emerge upwards into the conscious personality, cause a great many problems, something which happens mainly in those cases when we force them back down each time they try to emerge. When we suppress them in this way, rather than accepting the situation we're trying to force, they go back down into the

Table 1 – Four Stages in the Emergence of a Shadowed Planet

1. Repression and denial
2. Projection
3. Assimilation
4. Exemplification

unconscious, do their planetary push-ups, and get a little stronger. Then, next time a transit or progression comes to trigger them, they emerge once again—only this time they're a little meaner, a little nastier, and a little more insistent on remaining out in the open. This cycle of a shadowed planet's emergence and repression lies at the root of nearly all repetitive problems.

Certain planets generally seem less welcome than others as participants in our emerging personalities, while others seem to emerge very easily. For instance, relatively few people have problems with the planet Mercury, though some indeed do. In our information age, Mercury is usually very well understood and appreciated, as there are educational institutions created by our society solely to encourage the perfection and expression of that planet. Thus, the planet of communication will rarely cause problems unless perhaps in the case of someone who suffers from a learning disability, deafness, or a speech problem, though when such problems have a psychological rather than physical origin, they may in fact indicate a suppression of Mercury for other reasons. In contrast to the situation with Mercury, the principles represented by Saturn or Pluto are less easy for most people to deal with, and thus they are more often likely to be shadowed.

A shadowed planet does not emerge into consciousness on the half-shell like Venus, fully formed from the Cytherian sea-foam, but instead goes through several typical stages mentioned previously (see Table 1 above). In the first of these, repression or denial, you refuse to accept the fact that this particular psychological process is going on, even though you are in some sense aware of it. An interesting example of the denial of a psychological pattern and the result of that denial is the story of Romeo and Juliet. Two happy teenagers in sixteenth-century Italy fall in love, as teenagers are wont to do, and yet in coping with the situation they deny and repress an emerging psychological potential which might control their passion and channel it to more socially useful ends. We can easily equate this potential with Saturn, as it represents the societal and familial structures that control them, whether they are aware of it or not. Freud called this function the "superego." In their incapacity and their inability to absorb this emerging Saturn, they suppress it, and the result is tragedy. When we suppress an emerging psychological potential, tragedy is not always the result, but we are usually highly aware of an intense level of discomfort nevertheless. Society, or the "superego," took precedence over Romeo and Juliet's own personal Saturn function of social consciousness.

The next stage in the acceptance of an emerging psychological potential is projection. At this stage, you are more aware of the planet, as you accept the fact that what it represents exists, but you see these things as existing in others more than yourself. Because of this, you are actually likely to find people who represent the very thing you are trying to suppress populating your life more and more, whether because you are unconsciously attracted to them in some sense, or simply because you are more aware of them. In part, then, this stage of projection allows you to study the way in which this potential has developed in others, familiarizing yourself with it while at the same time not overtly committing to solving its problems within yourself.

However, since you are still suppressing this potential within yourself, during those times when you are doing so more actively and aggressively, you are likely to find yourself in conflict with those on whom you are projecting the planet, and this can cause problems. A basic rule is that an emerging psychological potential will manifest as an external event to the degree that it is being repressed. The more it is repressed and not accepted, the more it is going to happen as an external event that seems to be fate, as Jung indicated.[1] Thus, seemingly fated occurrences that happen to people are not just things that happen randomly or foolishly or stupidly because of an unlucky throw of the dice, but rather they represent an emerging psychological potential that has been repressed and therefore is manifesting as fate.

In the next stage in the awareness of an emerging psychological potential, "assimilation," you actually begin to deal with the planet, making a conscious attempt to incorporate its particular energy into your personality. Just how one should do this is not necessarily self-evident, so assimilation may actually be a process of trial and error, and an astrologer or other counselor is often helpful in taking this step successfully.

The final stage beyond this, "exemplification," does not occur in every case. Reaching this level is the main way in which one becomes a celebrity. The Pope and other well-known religious leaders, for example, take care of our Jupiter for us. We ourselves can talk to God whenever we want to if we happen to be in touch with our own personal Jupiters—you just, so to speak, call the Deity up on the cosmo-phone and ask him or her whatever you want. But certain people who have set up institutions for handling communication with God will tell us, "Oh no, you have to go through us. We do the connection with the divine so much better than you that you really should give us your money and we'll take care of that Jupiter stuff for you!"

Those who act out a planet well can do it by proxy for those who are in denial about that planet and its potential within themselves. Even though this might sound like a desirable stage at which to be, being an object of other people's projections can be quite difficult, mostly because the people whom you are serving in this way will not let you be your own self. Thus, when it comes time to grow beyond that role you have taken on, those whom you have been relieving of the burden of dealing with their Jupiters or Saturns will now have to face them squarely. An example of this might be seen in the televangelist Jimmy Swaggart, who apparently developed a high-pressure, very secret, and somewhat bizarre sex life that seemed to deny everything he preached. Perhaps when Swaggart was a young man, he thought to himself, "I'm just so holy and great, and God's talking to me." As he grew older, he began to find out that there was more to his psyche than that, but he had placed himself in a position which made it difficult for him to change. As with so many others in this situation, he tried to repress and deny and project and then deal with these furious energies within himself through the back door, so to speak. But the end result of exemplifying one planet while denying others is often the same as it was in Swaggart's case—someday somebody catches you, and then everyone involved in the situation must change, quickly and traumatically.

Thus we see that through a series of steps, every planet, every potential, in the horoscope seeks outer manifestation, eventually emerging into conscious acceptance. Some planets encounter more resistance than others—resistance by the ego—and these are the ones we call "shadowed planets." Remembering that when an inner situation is not made conscious it happens outside as fate, we can see that an encounter with a shadowed planet is more apt to manifest as an event. This is particularly true in relation to Astro*Carto*Graphy, as when you travel to a place where a shadowed planet is angular, you are most likely to experience it as external events that relate to that planet. When you are brought face to face with the very thing you have been avoiding, it must show itself in some way.

The longer a shadowed planet is ignored and the more it is forcibly repressed, the greater the "change" it will have when it tries to emerge the next time. Thus, it will become more fateful and eventful, and probably negative, in its manifestation. Traveling to a place where that planet is angular is almost a guarantee that something like this will happen, as it brings the urgency of the issues it represents in your life front and center.

How can we identify a shadowed planet in a horoscope? Where would we expect it to fall in a chart? If it's on the angles, it's probably not shadowed, but if it's cadent, it could be. Stressful aspects, especially by outer planets, are also a good indicator. A square or opposition to the Sun or the Moon can be problematic as well, as these are the two planets more closely identified with yourself. Thus, for example, if your Sun (your consciousness) is opposite Saturn, you would tend to see that planet as an external factor that would be difficult for you to assimilate, to merge with your consciousness. Any planet on the western side of the chart (which itself represents the external side of reality) is likely to be a little more shadowed than the same planet

Table 2 – Possible Indicators of a Shadowed Planet

- in a cadent house (3rd, 6th, 9th, but particularly 12th)
- stressful aspects, especially from outer planets
- square or opposite the Sun or Moon
- generally on the western ("other") side of the chart, though particularly in the 6th through 8th houses
- debilitated through sign placement
- unaspected
- a singleton (a planet alone in one hemisphere of the chart)
- "combust" by being within a degree of the Sun

A planet conditioned by any of the above aspects or placements should be examined carefully to consider whether it might present the native with some difficulty in expression of its energy. The more items in the list that apply to a particular planet, the more likely it is to be shadowed.[2]

would be if found in the east. Other things that might show a shadowed planet include placement in an adverse sign or house, being unaspected, or being a singleton.[3]

In general, we can say that any planet which is associated with a not-self idea is also more likely to be shadowed than are others in a chart. The planets of the self are, of course, the Sun and the Moon, plus Venus for a woman, or Mars for a man. Other planets, such as Saturn, Uranus, Neptune, or Pluto, are essentially not-self and thus will usually be more difficult to assimilate. Saturn, in fact, is almost always shadowed for everybody to some degree. Venus may be difficult for a man to understand, given the way our culture distinguishes between men and women. Conversely, it is usually more difficult for a woman to understand Mars. So one of these last two planets is often shadowed by virtue of it being the opposite gender from the person in question.

As an exercise in finding shadowed planets, consider an example chart, which is that of a woman named Grace (Figure 6 in Chapter 4). Saturn in the 7th is the Sun's ruler, but this planet, which, as noted, tends to be shadowed more often than not, is in the west, reinforcing this. Mars is placed in the 12th house in Pisces, a mutable water sign, and if not technically a classic singleton is very close to being so—all of which contributes to making it shadowed. Since this is the chart of a woman, Mars would most likely be a problem for her anyway, but this is almost certain, given its placement. So we can see for this woman that Saturn and Mars are definitely shadowed, and even though this is not unusual for her sex (since Saturn archetypally represents the father and Mars is the opposite sex), they are shadowed for her even more than usual. Also, Saturn is exactly square the Moon, and as a woman identifies with her Moon, this is one more reason to consider Saturn as highly shadowed. Despite this, neither planet is badly aspected overall. Mars is part of a loose Grand Trine with the 7th-house Venus and the 4th house Jupiter-Uranus, and it widely sextiles the Sun. Saturn itself is sextile the Sun. Because of this, despite the fact that we can see both planets as shadowed, they do not represent any sense of urgency or crisis.

How are shadowed planets such as these activated astrologically? When are they likely to start pounding on the ceiling of the basement we keep them locked in for the first 20 or 30 years of our lives? Most of their time in that basement will be spent pulling strings and doing things like attracting us to bosses who resemble our fathers or getting us into relationships with people who resemble our mothers or our sisters. In other words, for much of its existence the average shadowed planet is just a quiet yet insistent source of psychological tension. It is much like the Wizard of Oz as it pulls your levers and jerks your strings, and all the while your psyche whispers soothingly, "Pay no attention to that planet behind the curtain!"

When does a shadowed planet finally come into conscious awareness? When does it demand attention, saying, "No more basement for me! I'm going to come upstairs in the living room and march around in front of all your friends!" Three circumstances familiar to astrologers might activate this emerging psychological potential. The first of these is time, as exemplified by progressions and transits. Obviously if a planet is strongly aspected by an important progression or transit, this will activate it and bring it out of the closet. For example, in 1984 the progressed Sun in Grace's chart moved to 19°11' Aquarius, at which time it had just passed its opposition to the Moon and was exactly square Saturn. To an astrologer this should have indicated that during this time the whole Moon-Saturn problem in this chart would demand some sort of conscious acceptance.

Similarly, in 1984 there was a Saturn return, and therefore transiting Saturn was square Grace's progressed Sun. During that period, the progressed Sun was activating Moon square Saturn, while transiting Saturn at its own natal place was adding its own insistent pressure at the same points in the chart. This kind of pattern involving transits and progressions is the thing that most often brings repressed planets up out of our psychological basements to start marching around in the living room, so to speak. Thus, no matter who you are or where you are, time will eventually bring about either the emergence of psychological potentials or events that signal they are trying to emerge.

A second astrological factor that can bring shadowed planets out into the open is a relationship. When you become involved in a relationship, you are putting yourself into a specific astrological climate, as shown in the chart of the other person and its aspects with your chart, and this can put pressure on shadowed planets. If you marry someone whose Saturn conjoins your Sun, it is much like having a transit of Saturn to your Sun every single time you interact with that person. This will inevitably bring a psychological stress to bear on your Sun, forcing you to confront the energies and potentials of both Sun and Saturn. If either happens to be shadowed, the relationship will more than likely bring them out in the open.

The third means of identifying an emerging psychological potential, and one that is not often considered by astrologers in this light, is locality. Just as with a relationship, moving brings you into a new astrological environment, though in this case it is your own planets' relationship to the angles of that chart which can bring one or another of these planets into consciousness. Whether you are ready or not, the potential of a shadowed planet on a local angle will cause it to intrude on your consciousness in a very direct way. Even when you do not move to a place where a particular planet is prominent, events or people related to that area can have the same effect, stimulating any shadowed planets angular there.

So we can see three different ways in which an astrological potential can emerge: transits and progressions (time), relationship (personal connections), and either travel or long-distance communication (space). More often than not, some combination of these three will act to trigger the emergence of a planet. If the psychological potential is really demanding its time in the sun, then you can find all three of those operating at the same time, which is what we will see as we look further at Grace's story in this chapter and the next.

Repetitive problems are thus an indication of emerging archetypal or planetary potentials that are being repressed. Encounters at earlier ages and stages of consciousness occur when it is not possible to assimilate what that planet represents. In these cases, traumatic experiences often result as a psychological potential tries to push its way into consciousness, only to be repressed. Such repression begets the cycle that itself becomes the repetitive problem, as despite the repression, a planet not yet assimilated stays just beneath the surface of awareness, wreaking mischief in our daily lives.

In order to help a client solve this type of problem, the astrologer must do several things, beginning with an examination of the chart for aspects that might serve to link the psychological potential with other more productive life activities. Another approach is to look at the astrological picture in place when this problem occurred in the past, and to note when similar progressions or transits will occur in the future. Finally, the astrologer must explain these things to the client, show what mitigating factors the client can call on to deal with the difficulty, and, first and foremost, explain in just what sense this recurring problem represents an important stage in psychological growth that must be reached in order to get rid of the repetitive problem more or less permanently.

Where Astro*Carto*Graphy is concerned, the line closest to a particular place will identify the planetary energy most likely to emerge there. If you consciously want to bring that planet to the surface, you can go directly to a place under one of the lines on your ACG map, meaning that you don't have to wait for transits or progressions. On the other hand, if your job or other circumstances require you to move to a particular line, this could clue you in to the fact that this psychological potential is seeking to emerge in your life in some way.

As already pointed out, you don't have to go to a place under a planetary line in order for that planet to manifest. For instance, Jimmy Carter had his Mars and his Jupiter lines strong in Iran, and he obviously did not have to go there, since in essence it came to him. Mars and Jupiter happen to be very shadowed planets in Jimmy Carter's chart, so when he became president, and thus had a worldwide span of influence, Iran came to him in the person of the Ayatollah Khomeini. His Mars and Jupiter lines thus manifested outside as fate, and we all know the result of that.

Different planets will react differently for different people. Not everyone going to a Jupiter line will have the same experience. For example, if you happen to be a Sagittarian and thus enjoy telling off-color jokes at church socials in order to see the reaction, then you will get along much better on a Jupiter line than will a Virgo, who finds the buffoonery unpleasant and more than a little vulgar. Also, if you're a woman, your experiences under a Mars line will be different than they will be if you're a man. If a man moves to his Mars line, he is likely to be more aggressive, unless his Mars happens to be a shadowed planet, as it was in Jimmy Carter's case. Carter is meek and mild, not at all "Marsy," so when his Jupiter and Mars (inflated aggression) manifested together, it could hardly manifest in any way but outside, as fate.[4]

The typical man, however, will go to his Mars line and become more aggressive unless he is a person with a shadowed Mars. A woman, on the other hand, will have to begin the process of assimilating her Mars when she goes to a Mars line. This will probably happen in the form of an external event—and often through an association with a man. After spending a certain amount of time with him, she will learn enough about Mars to assimilate it herself.

Let's look again at Grace's horoscope now and consider this woman's two most outstanding shadowed planets—Mars because of the 12th house and Pisces, and Saturn because of the 7th house and Scorpio. Both of them, by the way, are actually tied up with her 7th house, because one is the co-ruler of the 7th and the other is an occupant. So we know that when these planets are activated we're going to have some 7th-house type of activities, mainly relationships.

When is this particular problem going to be most manifest in her entire life? Most astrologers would probably single out the time around her Saturn return, that point in the 29th year when transiting Saturn returns to its natal place. As we have already noted, her Saturn return happened to coincide with the opposition of her progressed Sun to her natal Moon. Note in her chart that one of the closest aspects she has is Saturn square the Moon, meaning that anything concerning Saturn will also involve her Moon. Capricorn and Cancer are on her Midheaven and IC, meaning this entire theme must play itself out in relation to home and family. And, as we shall see, this is exactly what happened.

4

Grace's Saturnian Journey

HAVING SEEN how shadowed planets can be found in the chart, and having discussed the various mechanisms by which they can emerge, let's take a closer look at the geographical dimension of this emergence and the role it plays along with the other better-known factors. Of the three main triggers of astrological potential, perhaps time is the best-known, and in this case the time factor is most obviously involved through the return of Saturn to its natal position, which happens to everyone around the age of 29. The second trigger, relationship, is less obvious in its import, though it might become more so if we had data on some of the main players in Grace's life during the time period we'll be discussing. Most striking in this case, however, is the geography of Grace's journey through her Saturn return, as the series of events we will describe took place mainly along Saturn lines and at the latitudes of important crossings of Saturn with other planets.[1]

First, let's consider an essential part of the background to the events that transpired around the time of her Saturn return, beginning with the disintegration of her family with the divorce of her parents during her teen years. Though in many ways what happened to her is not too different from other stories we might hear in this day and age, the most tragic part of it for Grace was the effect it had on what had been a wonderful relationship with her father. Before puberty arrived and her sexuality began to burgeon, she was in fact her father's favorite, and she was even invited into his life by being allowed to attend various social functions related to his profession, a role that might normally be taken on by a wife. However, as her mother had little interest in such things, Grace for a time played the role of a kind of social surrogate for her mother, just one bit of evidence of the affection her father had for her, as well, as the interests they held in common.

At puberty, around 1968, Grace began to distance herself from her father. She was growing up and moving on in a normal way, establishing her own network of friends as well as pursuing activities usual to someone her age. Her father, however, was losing his surrogate marriage companion and he was angry and, as we shall see, vengeful. A month after she was allowed to begin dating at the age of 16, her father stormily announced that he wanted a divorce from Grace's mother and, in almost the same breath, told Grace he didn't love her anymore. Though he never repeated this statement, for years Grace felt devastated and perplexed by his outburst, which she felt should have been aimed at her mother. Only years later did she begin to understand that he was merely lashing out at her for leaving him in an

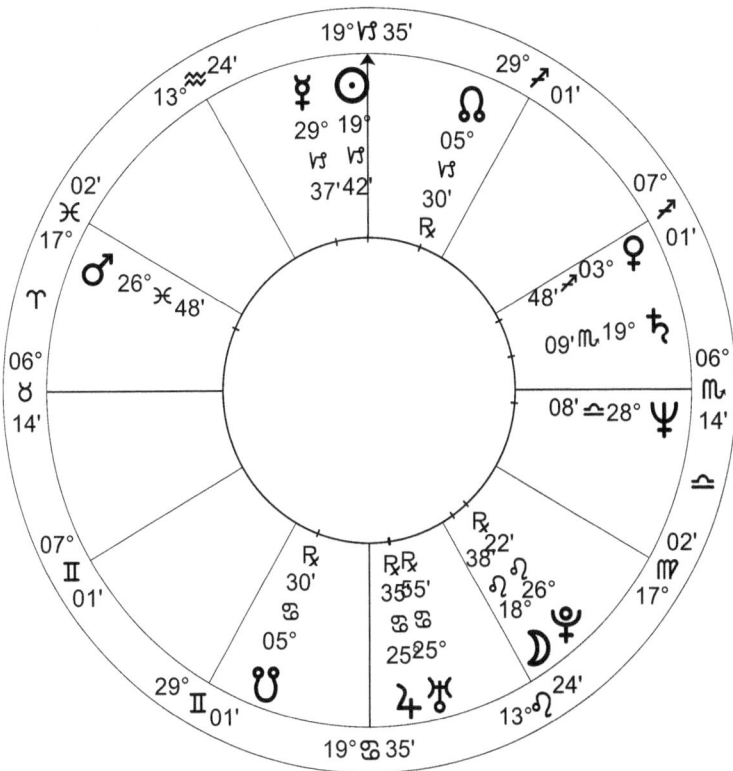

Figure 6- Grace's Saturnian Journey

empty marriage as she began to date. Almost overnight, he became critical of her in a way he had not been in the past, in particular, attacking her for any attempt she made to make herself more attractive and appealing. Perhaps far worse than that, for legal reasons he stayed in the house as the divorce proceeded, creating a strained situation which was only aggravated when both her parents, who weren't speaking to one another, made Grace their "confidante and courier," as she described it. She often refers to this grim situation as her first counseling job. Interestingly, her father announced that he wanted a divorce to end this marriage of 19 years almost coincident with a lunar eclipse that occurred within two degrees of Grace's natal Moon, and squaring her Saturn, of course.

During the divorce process, and while her parents were living separated in the same house, her mother, in an attempt at revenge, took a lover. This was a grave mistake from a legal point of view, because, as the law stood in that time and place, it gave her husband leverage that allowed him to keep the bulk of their common wealth. Between the relatively small amount allotted

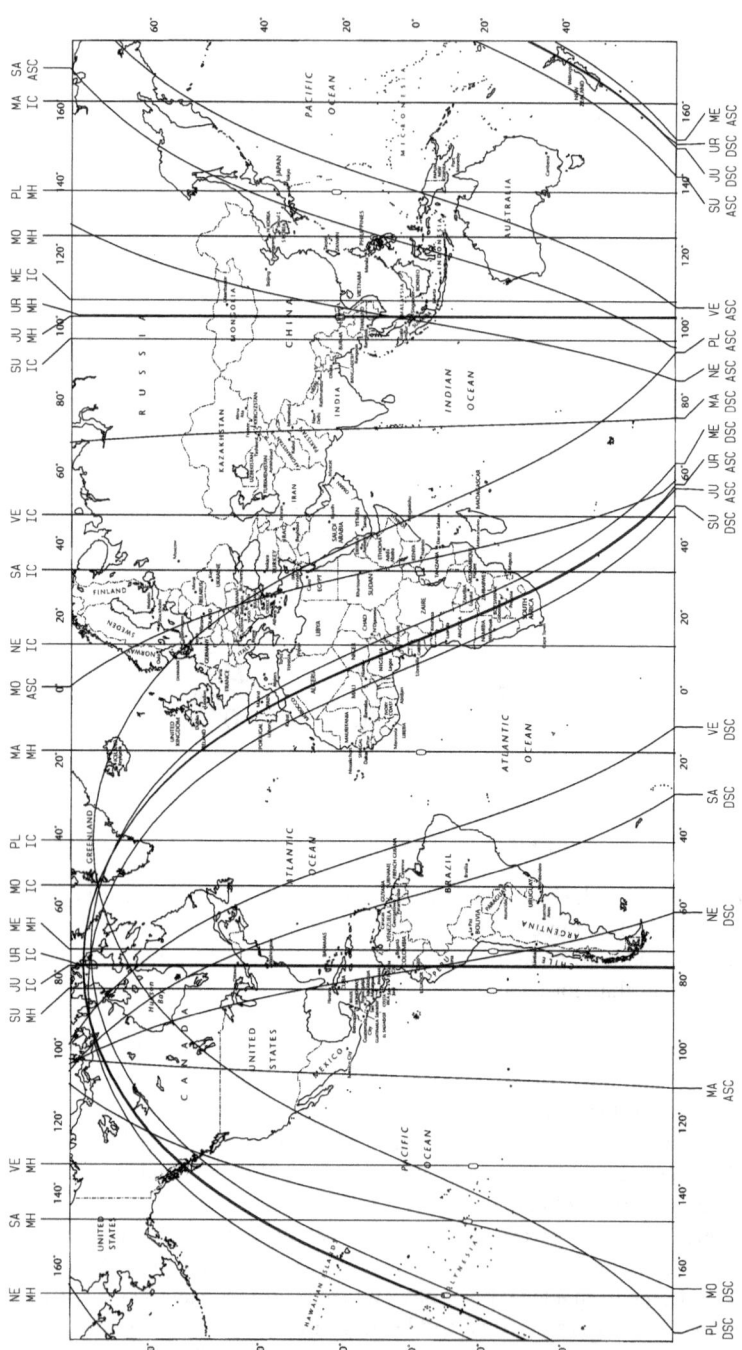

Figure 7 - Grace's Journey in Space and Time

to her and her naive mismanagement of it, in her later years it was a struggle for Grace's mother to make ends meet. Thus, the situation that began in 1971 played itself out agonizingly over many years. Grace and her siblings watched from afar as their father, distancing himself from them and rejecting their mother, built a new life for himself while their mother's prospects withered on the vine. Grace herself left home, moving as far away as she could possibly go and still be in the same country, as soon as she finished high school in early 1974. Following after Grace's "great escape," as she called it, came a period of her life that coincides well with the repression and denial phase of a shadowed planet—or in this case two of them, Mars and Saturn.

For someone observing from the outside, her life from that point on would have showed the same kinds of ups and downs experienced by many of her generation. She attended a university for a year, then moved to the west coast of Canada at the invitation of a friend, ditching both her university career and the last geographical ties with her family, though she would return occasionally for visits. During the first six or seven years on the west coast, she fell in and out of love a few times, hung out in a high-powered community of performance artists with political connections, and developed an interest in becoming a psychologist, which she in fact eventually became. At this time, Grace slowly began to separate herself from the life of the artistic community. After attending a large conference in Los Angeles in November 1982, she made a firm commitment to her career.

It was during this period in which she began exploring the best way to begin her studies that Grace made the contact which was to provide the theme (both geographical and psychological) that ran through her Saturn return, signaling the painful process of Saturn's emergence. In the summer of 1983, while in Toronto, she had occasion to meet an in-law, a native of Trinidad who casually invited her to visit him during Carnival in the spring of the following year. Grace accepted, though at the time she was quite sure her finances wouldn't allow her to make the trip. When the time came, however, she somehow managed to scrape together the money to take what turned out to be a fascinating journey to her Saturn line (see her map, Figure 7).

In February 1984, when he sent her a postcard saying that he was expecting her to come down to Trinidad for Carnival, she decided at the last minute to make some quick travel plans to visit this place where she had never been before. When she arrived at the Port of Spain airport in early March 1984, with Carnival in full swing and the country crowded with visitors from all over the world, she immediately found herself, in her own words, "immersed in a sea of black men." As a fair-haired white beauty, she rather stood out in the airport crowd, and during her wait for her host to pick her up, an endless stream of cab drivers approached her, offering to take her wherever she wanted to go, and generally to show her a good time. That, along with her feeling of being quite alone, made her feel highly uncomfortable, but also made her more than ready for the vacation which was to follow. On many occasions she would find herself the only white person in crowds of black men and women, a new experience as in many ways her contact with this culture was like being on another planet. Funeral pyres burning along the rivers and by the oceans were evidence of the practice of Hinduism in this largely Catholic country. The local flora and fauna seemed exotic as well, and she sampled some by eating (iguana) and some by more direct contact (one day, while she swam in the sea, she was stung multiple times by jellyfish). The events surrounding a machete murder also made an impression on her that stays with her to this day. All of this, added to the partying and the sexual stimulation, served to deepen her Scorpio/Saturnian experience.

At the end of nearly a month of fun with a core group of new friends, something special occurred. An enormous black man her age, who was married with children and was a high-level harbor official, invited her to walk with him on the last evening of her visit. As they strolled out behind the house and into a big sugarcane field under a canopy of stars, Grace was shocked when he suddenly lifted her up high over his head and declared his love for her—and then began weeping. He confessed that until he met her he had hated all white people, and he shared some painful memories from his youth of the British and their influence over Trinidad. Getting to know her had now changed how he felt. Grace recalls this as her most cherished memory of the entire trip. She herself had, of course, met a similar (though certainly lesser) demon, recalling the difference between how she had felt in the airport, much of which came from her awareness of being the only white face in a sea of black ones, aggravated by menacing cab drivers, and how perfectly natural it seemed to be in this situation now. For the first few days there, she had in fact been quite uncomfortable, but had dealt with this in a consciously positive way by telling herself that here was a new experience and she had to embrace it in order to learn from it.

After leaving the scene in Trinidad, on the way home she took advantage of a brief stopover in Barbados to call up a friend of hers from a pay phone, a Capricorn man who lived in Ottawa, right along her Saturn Descendant line. She ended up spending a few days with him before she flew home to the coast, and though they got along well, there was no sexual involvement, although Grace was deeply attracted to him. Starting in July of that same year, just as Mars was finishing its long transit of Scorpio and as Saturn was beginning the forward motion that would bring it into contact with her natal Saturn, he sent her a ticket and she spent six weeks with him, though again it turned out to be a disappointing effort to take a nice friendship to a romantic level.

Around this time, and still in the depths of her Saturn return, she began to come face to face with a decision she had made back when her parents were divorced, especially considering how her mother ended up financially. This decision was simply that she never wanted to be put in the position of being financially dependent on a partner, either through marriage or a common-law relationship. However, she began to notice more and more that the men who wanted to be in her life tended to be wealthy and powerful, and in fact a millionaire even proposed to her at one point. The result of all this attention was simply to reinforce her decision not to be put in the position of becoming accustomed to a lifestyle she could not maintain financially on her own should the relationship dissolve. On one level that might have been a wise decision, but at the same time the interest she attracted from men of wealth (her father was, after all, himself a highly paid professional) signaled at least some movement from denial to projection in the emergence of her shadowed Saturn.

After the brief but unfulfilling fling with her friend in Ottawa, she journeyed to Montreal, where she made contact with someone who specialized in the style of therapy she wanted to study. In a few brief exchanges with him in August 1984 on the subject of setting up a study group, he encouraged her to pursue the idea. This led to a second meeting, in Vancouver, at which Grace proposed that he lead the group for a year, which he agreed to. At their third meeting in two years, though no previous sexual interest had been shown by either of them, the instructor surprised her over a late dinner one night by proposing an affair in Montreal, at a later date when his wife would be out of town. Though unprepared for this, especially since she hadn't sensed any initial attraction, she was nonetheless drawn into a long and often painful drama that took her to the next step in bringing her Saturn into consciousness—it was now at least tapping at the door, asking to be let out.

After a brief involvement with the instructor, in August 1981, she told him firmly that she wasn't going to rearrange her whole life by moving across the country from Vancouver to Montreal to study with him and take on the role of mistress in order to accommodate him. This, of course, meant he would have to tell his wife and, most likely, end the marriage if he seriously wanted to become involved with Grace. Not wanting to lose Grace, when his wife came back from her summer trip he in fact confessed to her about the affair, thus beginning the process of ending his marriage. Grace was on the edge of this, involved with him both as lover and student since she had, as she initially suggested, organized the study group. The ending of the marriage took nearly two years, during which time she finished her university education.

As the instructor's marriage came to an end, it became apparent that Grace's relationship with him had descended into routine, and she finally reached the conclusion that perhaps her major role in his life was to help him get out of a marriage he could no longer endure. Despite the almost two-year relationship, both partners had resisted moving in with each other, and she now decided that their time together was coming to an end. However, a few months after the final break in the spring of 1987, and after spending some months considering what kind of partner she really ought to be spending her time with, she met her future husband. After their meeting in late 1987, she began living with him immediately and ended up as an adviser to highly placed people in Canada's capital city, Ottawa (which was, as we have seen, on her SA DSC line). It was with him that she reached the final phase in coping with her Saturn.

Before continuing the account of her life, however, note that in Grace's story we have seen all three modes of triggering the emergence of a shadowed planet. First of all, the time dimension was attributable to the coincidence of her Saturn return with the opposition of progressed Sun to natal Moon—spiced, we might say, by transiting Mars. The personal dimension shows itself in two ways, the first of which involves the kinds of social relationships thrust upon her in Trinidad. There she had to learn to face some of her deepest fears, both racial and sexual, and her forthright effort to face both might have clued her in, at least unconsciously, to the fact that she could confront the dark side of Saturn in which were embedded her feelings and fears relating to both her mother and her father.

These two astrological dimensions, time and personal relationship, would probably be singled out by most astrologers as central to Grace's development. More interesting, however, are the distinct spatial and thus geographical triggers to the emergence of Grace's Saturn. In order to see this, look closely at Grace's ACG map and note that the Saturn Descendant line goes right through Trinidad, and also through Ottawa, through Montreal, and everywhere that was important in this whole chain of events. In other words, some of the most crucial events from her Saturn return actually took place right on her Saturn line, and transiting Saturn itself would have been present all along that line, or very close to it, in the context of Grace's natal map.

The events of that year and later events that flowed from them were replete with Saturn symbolism. To begin with, consider the Roman name for "carnival"—the Saturnalia. While the Romans were probably not drinking sugar cane moonshine, smoking marijuana, and "groin dancing" to Latin rhythms, the purpose of their Saturnalia was much like the Trinidad Carnival, as it was a time in which to shed one's inhibitions and for all to be equalized. However, in the Roman case, the orgiastic revelry was to symbolize the emergence from a Saturnian period, the depths of the winter solstice, while Carnival in Trinidad is related to the coming of a Saturnian period, Lent. In Grace's case, the time of Carnival signaled both, as her emergence from the shadow of Saturn perhaps began here, though only after she sank further into its grasp.

In addition to the presence of her Saturn line near Trinidad, that island's capital, Port of Spain, at 8°48' north latitude lies at the same latitude as a crossing of Saturn on the Ascendant and Moon on the Midheaven, and quite close to another at which Moon is on the Ascendant and Saturn on the IC. The involvement of two key planets in this whole complex of transits, progressions, and natal planets that were central to the time dimension of Grace's experience simply reinforces everything we have already noted. This is called a "paran," wherein two planet lines, one in Ascendant or Descendant and one in IC or Midheaven, cross each other, forming a "mundane square."

What is perhaps more interesting over the long term is that Grace's actual residence at the beginning of all this (and at the end as well) was on the west coast of Canada, yet somehow she seemed to gravitate to the Saturn line that dominated the other coast. Perhaps something inside was telling her that she could face her Saturn-bound fears just as surely as she faced certain personal and irrational fear by plunging into the Carnival scene. More time and effort were required, however, as a last effort at suppression kept the lid on Saturn for several years to come. In the meantime, her journey from the west coast of Canada to attend Carnival in Trinidad had led to Ottawa and thence to Montreal, and would finally lead her back to Ottawa once more–all along her Saturn line.

As Grace drew away from the affair with the instructor in Montreal, Saturn had by this time moved to trine her natal Moon, perhaps making her efforts to cope with the cosmic taskmaster less hectic and more stable. After a period of several months on her own, during which she had much time to think about what she wanted in a partner, she met the man we have mentioned whom she eventually married, and the chemistry between them was very good right from the start. So began several high-powered years in Ottawa, as her husband's work as a political consultant soon thrust her into the midst of the inner political and governmental circle surrounding the prime minister.

Though the upward surge in Grace's life and career may have fulfilled the positive side of Saturn, it served to aid her to remain unaware for a time of what negative complexes she had come to her Saturn Descendant line to face. However, she was reminded with full force at a time when transiting Pluto was approaching a conjunction to her natal Saturn, in February 1990. The Metonic cycle, which marks the repetition of the phases of the Moon in the same degree and sign every 19 years, began to bring Grace full circle on February 9th, when, at the time of the "same" lunar eclipse that had triggered her parents' divorce, Grace experienced something new in her life–a panic attack. Long ago and far away, as her mother had carried on her affair, her anxious daughter would sit reading while trying to stay awake in the living room, worrying and waiting for her mother to return. Every time a car would drive by her home in the early morning hours, it would startle Grace awake. It was 19 years later that the sound of a car driving by her home in the night would once again set her heart racing, and a torrent of seemingly irrational fears would cloud her mind. After the first attack, others followed, and over a year of various kinds of treatment, nothing could end the attacks. For locked in the critical degree of the lunar eclipse was the memory of her mother and father–Sun and Moon–the primal eclipse in her young life.

Finally, in January 1991 when both a solar eclipse and transiting Saturn touched her natal Jupiter-Uranus conjunction in the 4th house (Saturn was conjunct her Sun and opposing her natal Jupiter-Uranus), Grace suddenly realized the connection between her attacks and the painful feelings of many years ago. Awakening Saturn from its long slumber, Grace began to deal with the unresolved feelings from her parents' divorce. First and foremost she decided that her long stay (extended by circumstances to six years) on her Saturn Descendant line should now be over and that it was time to move back to where she would really like to be, on the west coast. That summer, as an eclipse exactly contacted her natal IC, she and her husband moved to Vancouver. This done, she still faced a struggle with those long-suppressed emotions, and as she moved deeper into her old feelings over the next few months, she became more and more depressed and exhausted. Then, in the spring of 1992 as transiting Pluto squared her Moon-Pluto midpoint, and the transiting Uranus-Neptune conjunction began to conjoin her Midheaven, she wrote a long letter addressed to her parents, which she also sent to her siblings, confronting them with her feelings and trying to open up a dialog, even though her parents had not spoken to each other since the divorce many years before. Her plea that they try to establish some open communication with each other, at least for the sake of their children, simply resulted in her father distancing himself further from her than he had done already.

Through the next two years, she continued to work on her own problems related to this widening of the gap between herself and her father and to the realization that he and her mother might never again speak to each other. After a series of eclipses from late 1993 through early 1994 leaned heavily on her 7th-house planets, Venus and Saturn, she accepted the fact that there was no way to heal the past with her family's cooperation, and thus it was time to move on by processing it in full by herself. Perhaps the last item on the agenda for Saturn's emergence was her understanding that her partnerships had been guided in part by the fear of becoming dependent in the way her mother had, something which had led her either to forgo relationships she might have had, to get involved only with men who were of lesser status and earning power or, as in her marriage, to keep a strict sense of financial separation and independence that made her feel comfortable. Grace began to realize that, in pursuing this course, her efforts to keep financial entanglements at a minimum meant she was free to exit the partnership at any time without fetters–a somewhat noncommittal, even fearful, approach to her most important relationship.

Oddly enough, though, in a sense she had ended up just where she did not want to be. Despite the many good things about her marriage, her partner in fact (and in part with her unwitting collusion) was financially controlling in the way her father had been. Thus began a series of discussions about how to bring about more equal sharing in the marriage, a sign that Grace was fully aware, if not yet in control, of the dark side of Saturn that had struggled for so long to see the light.

Grace's story is uniquely her own, but in many respects it reflects a broader range of the principles of Astro*Carto*Graphy better than many other personal examples the reader is likely to come across. On the other hand, illustrations that have at least some of the breadth and depth of Grace's individual Saturnian journey (both in time and space) are more easily found when we give our examination of this kind of astrology a more universal scope by looking at the charts of newsmakers, national leaders, and nations themselves. In the case of Grace and some of the less comprehensive examples we have discussed so far, the relationship between the individual's chart and factors such as the charts of other people are often not known to us, if only because we do not usually have access to the full range of charts that might apply to a given case. Moreover, changes in the lives of most individuals usually happen slowly over a period of time, as we saw with Grace, and thus may not be obvious without an in-depth interview or some other kind of vetting process.

When we look at the lives of people who have made an impact outside their immediate environment, bringing themselves to the attention of the world in some way, we often see a different type of pattern from the one we saw in Grace's case. Her chart showed an intensive and repetitive set of patterns over time. Most of the people (and nations) we will look at over the next few chapters may show similar patterns, but the events involved are more sharply focused in time—and in their effects on the people themselves and on those around them.

5

Winds of Neptune, Fires of Mars

THE GRIM STORY of the mass death of 913 followers of a cult known as the People's Temple in the South American country of Guyana on Saturday the 18th of November in 1978 was perhaps the most shocking news item of that year. Though the press mainly exploited the sensational aspects of the occurrence, while choosing to ignore some of the more complex political undercurrents, the fact remains that an extraordinary event took place—a whole community of people, willingly or unwillingly, gave up their lives, seemingly under the almost hypnotic influence of a mentally unstable and charismatic leader, Jim Jones. Perhaps as interesting as the event itself was the way in which it tied into another tragedy back in the city of origin of the People's Temple, San Francisco, a tragedy that would eventually take the lives of Mayor George Moscone and supervisors Harvey Milk and Dan White, affecting the political climate of California for years to come. But perhaps most fascinating of all is the central role in these events played by the astro-geography of Mars and Neptune and Pluto.

One must wonder what kind of power Jim Jones had to influence so many people to follow him into death. While his birth chart presents the picture of a magnetic leader who could easily project the power of his rising retrograde Capricorn Saturn onto people socially dispossessed, nowhere does it seem to suggest that he would become the very personification of the "Grim Reaper" for hundreds of trusting souls. As we have seen, location plays almost as important a role in astrology as does time itself, and the horoscope is in fact a product of both time and place. Furthermore, though we can choose consciously to take advantage of this spatial aspect of the horoscope, by moving to a locality where we wish some underdeveloped aspect of our psyche to emerge, we can also unwittingly release the power of parts of ourselves that we have repressed, and the consequences in these cases can be difficult to handle at best. In the case of Jim Jones, several factors might lead us to say that his Mars, one of the central points of identity for a man, was shadowed to the degree that it would be integrated into the personality only with some difficulty.[1]

One point in its favor is its placement in Leo, a fixed fire sign, but this is quickly mitigated by its placement in the western (other) half of the chart and its wide square to the Sun, which itself is in a sign favorable to Venus by rulership (and the Moon by exaltation), not the Sun. Under some circumstances, the trine to Mars from the Moon in the 3rd house might be a helpful factor, but here Moon is in Aries, a captive of Mars. All of this might lead us to believe that Jones would have trouble expressing the masculine energy of Mars, finding it suppressed by a need to do this only in ways dictated by others. The suppression of Mars is problematic because the red planet is almost by itself the primary significator of energy and aggression. Bottling these things up, or guiding them into unnatural outlets, can make for tremendous fury when it is released in its rawest form.

That there was a potential for this can be seen from a quick glance at Jones' map for Guyana, which shows that this troublesome Mars was exactly setting in that locality at the moment of Jim Jones' birth in Indiana. Under normal circumstances, one would expect that Jones' Martian potentials of violence, passion, sexuality, and paranoia might be encountered in that locality. However, aside from the shadowed nature of Mars in Jones' horoscope, other factors combined to unleash these potentials in a particularly lethal way.

Near the Mars line is another, labeled SU IC, showing that at the moment of his birth the Sun occupied the lower meridian (IC) in Jonestown—the midnight position known to horary astrologers as "the end of the affair," one associated with establishment of a home and a leading role in the community. The combination of Sun and Mars has long been associated by astrologers with excessive passion, sexuality, and recklessness. The late Cyril Fagan wrote: "Should you scan through the horoscopes of those of both sexes who have uncontrollable sexual passions, the vast majority have the Sun configured with Mars. Should Mars be configured at the same time with Neptune, their passions become a surging torrent, impossible to restrain." A glance at Jim Jones' natal horoscope will show Mars sharing the 8th house with Neptune, not conjunct, but certainly related.

A little deeper analysis of these two planets, which totally dominate Jim Jones' relocated horoscope in Jonestown, will furnish insight into the power he held over the masses he led to destruction. The Sun is associated astrologically with fame and leadership. In many ACG charts for the famous, it is often in prominent positions in those locations at which they made their most powerful public impression. Jiddu Krishnamurti had the Sun angular in Los Angeles, Timothy Leary had the Sun rising in San Francisco. Leontyne Price and Willie Mays both had the Sun prominent in New York, as did Enrico Caruso before them. Numerous movie stars have the Sun angular in Hollywood; in fact, it seems almost a requirement for stardom. For Astro*Carto*Graphy clients, the Sun areas have been those in which fatherhood, leadership, religious interests, and the outward expression of a paternalistic ego have been most prominent.

Mars, the god of war, of course, is associated with violence and assertion. Presidents become involved in wars under their Mars lines. Among those who have given feedback about their experiences under various ACG lines, the Mars Descendant line has been particularly unpopular, and the complaints include reports of car wrecks, fist fights, wife-beating, violence,

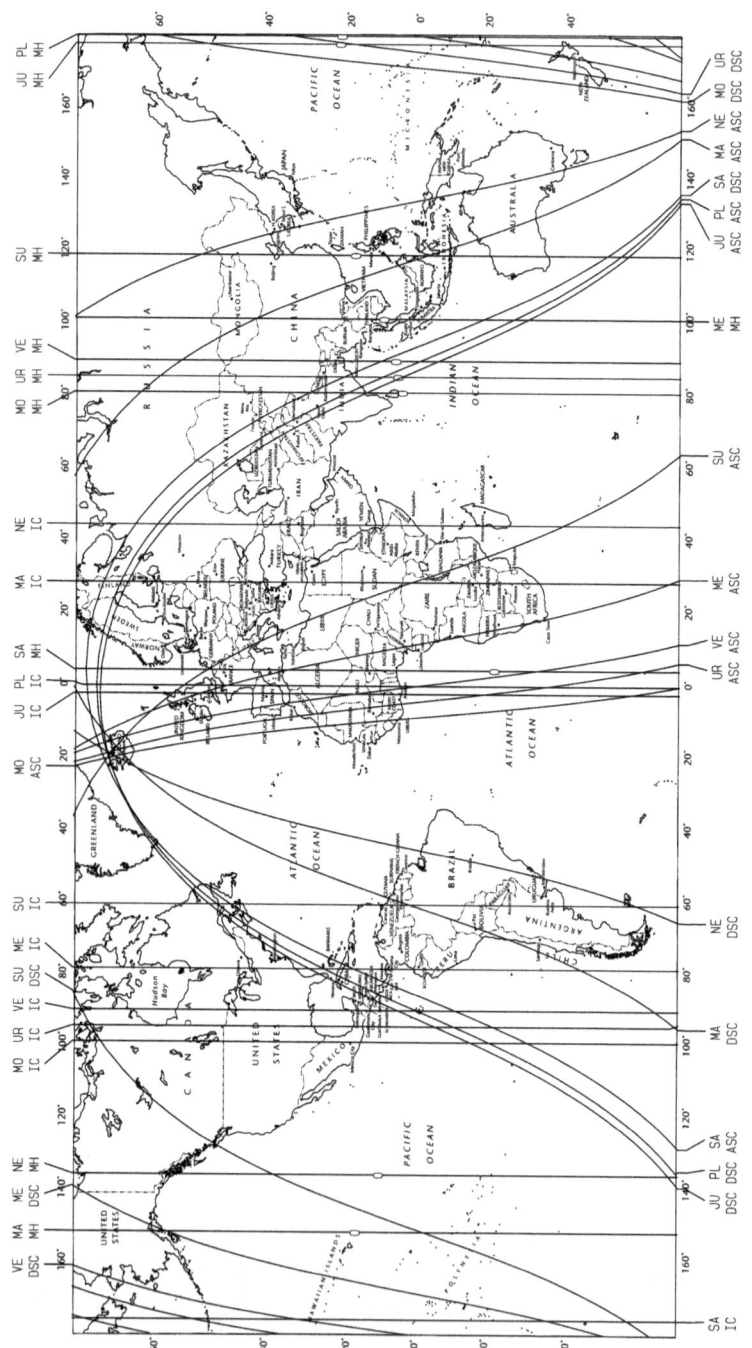

Figure 8 - Jim Jones: Burned by Sun and Mars in Guyana

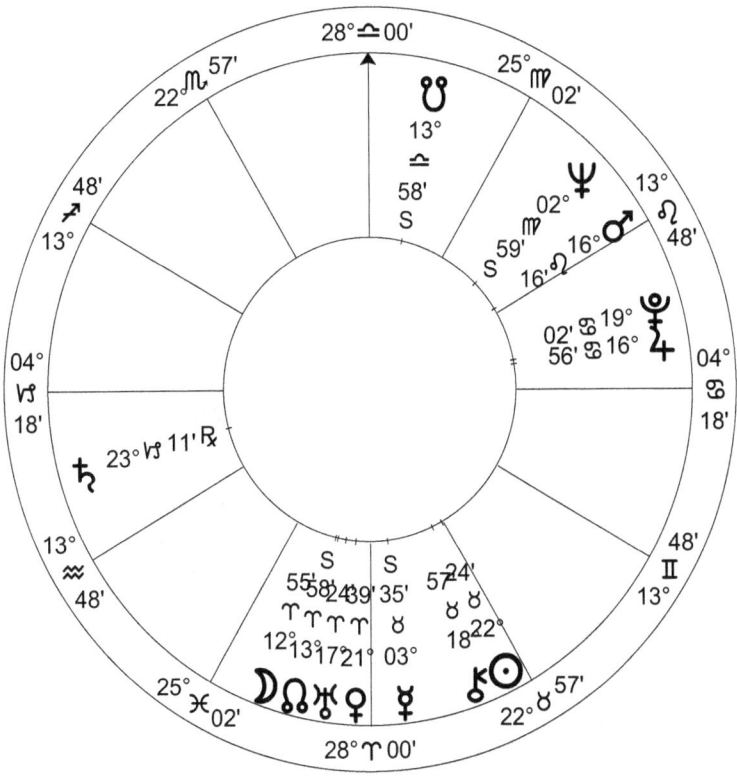

Figure 9 - Jim Jones, the terror of Jonestown, Guyana

injury, sexual coercion, and hostility in these locations. Why is this so? More often than not this placement makes for projection of Martian energy onto others, so that we are liable to see them as focusing their aggression on us, even when the opposite may be true. A grim feature of Jones' behavior in the Jonestown incident was the fear expressed to his followers that the Temple was under attack, and the visit of Congressman Leo Ryan (with news cameras in tow) to check out rumors of people being forced to stay against their will and take part in bizarre sexual rituals was simply taken as evidence by Jones of the truth of his paranoid fantasies. He dispatched gunmen to kill Ryan and his party, but when word reached him that some had escaped, Jones ordered his followers to commit suicide, killing their children in the process. Even so, to establish a pattern, more than just Jim Jones' example is needed. Does the relocated Mars Descendant line seem particularly favored by others whose violence involves many? It seems so.[2] John Wayne Gacy (March 17, 1942,

12:29 A.M. CWT, Chicago, Illinois) had his Mars Descendant line within 5° of Chicago, where he committed a chilling number of sexually motivated murders. Uranus was also nearby. Charles Manson's natal chart (November 12, 1934, 4:40 P.M. EST, Cincinnati, Ohio) has an exact conjunction of Mars and Neptune in the 5th house; but relocation to the southern California desert in which he organized his "family" puts those planets exactly on the Descendant, within a degree of arc.[3]

Thus, we see two patterns, both of which apply equally well to Jim Jones. Those places in which the Sun is angular at the time of one's birth are those at which one might expect to achieve fame or notoriety. Those places at which Mars is angular seem to be the ones at which one will encounter violence, coercion, and aggression, directed toward either oneself or others. Jonestown, Guyana, just happened to be one of the two places on the entire earth (the other is near Borneo) at which both of these conditions prevailed at the moment of Jim Jones' birth. It is not surprising that a short residence in that locality brought about the tragedy which so shocked the world in 1978.

Of particular importance is the exactitude of the contact—assuming the birth time to be accurate, the Mars line passes within one half a degree of Jonestown. Such precision often puts the person in touch with the planetary energy exaggerated to almost superhuman proportions; it is as if, under the direct, exact, angular rays of the planet, one becomes entirely dominated by its energy. This will, of course, be harmful in direct proportion to the degree to which the person in question has suppressed that planet's potentials, making him or her both unwilling and unable to cope with it.

In every person's ACG map, there are four intersections of the Sun and Mars lines somewhere on the planet; this does not mean that each of us has the potential to become a cult mass murderer at these locations.[4] What it does show is that each of us has a potential for intense assertion of our will in certain areas of the world. Conscious of this power, and having integrated it into the psyche, one should be able to channel it positively into constructive activities. Unaware of it, however, one could easily set the stage for a personal tragedy involving oneself and perhaps others. Knowledge is the key to transmuting the potentially disruptive energies of planets such as Mars, Uranus, and Pluto into productive channels.

One may also conjecture what might have happened had Jones tried to found his commune under a more favorable line. Central America shows Jupiter angular, and it was at such a location as this that Jacqueline Kennedy found her successful former residence in Greece. Under such lines, many ordinary individuals have met and befriended the powerful and wealthy, won competitions of various types at the international level, and generally prospered. One wonders what might have happened if only Jim Jones had paid more attention to his horoscope.

* * *

Not long before Dan White shot him down in cold blood, the openly gay San Francisco supervisor Harvey Milk said of him to a colleague, "Dan White is a closet case ... and he's dangerous."[5] Prior to that, Milk had made a similar assessment of the People's Temple, which had become a political force in the city over the last few years, calling it "weird and dangerous" and warning his own staffers and campaign workers to be on their guard and to be extra polite when dealing with Jim Jones' group. Tragic events in Jonestown had proved him right on November 18th, but little did he know that on the morning of the 27th, just nine days later, he would also be proved right about Dan White, at least insofar as his being dangerous was concerned.

White, who had served on the Board of Supervisors with Milk, was known to his constituents and the press as a clean-cut all-American boy, a high-school sports star who had gone on to prove himself in military service as well as in the San Francisco fire and police departments. In 1977, he emerged from a Catholic blue-collar district in San Francisco to run as a "traditional values" candidate, saying in one piece of campaign literature, "I am not going to be forced out of San Francisco by splinter groups of radicals, social deviates, and incorrigibles." White and Milk, the liberal, gay-activist politician, were natural political antagonists, and so they became when both were elected to the Board of Supervisors, their votes often falling on opposite sides of the political fence.

Despite this, there were times at the beginning when they seemed able to get along, with White toning down his conservative rhetoric and Milk opining from time to time that White was "educable." Milk himself was in many ways like White, at least superficially. He, too, was a high-school (and college) athlete, a college graduate, and a navy veteran (not dishonorably discharged, as he would later tell political gatherings, but rather just another swabbie who did his three-year stint and got out a month early for good behavior). His politics in the early years were quite conservative, and he was an avid enough supporter of right-wing Republican Presidential candidate Barry Goldwater in 1964 to get up early in the mornings with a friend to ride the subways in New York and hand out campaign literature before work. As an occupation, Milk settled on the business world, working as a researcher for a prestigious Wall Street firm for many years. A good friend from those days felt that he was just biding time and that, well as he did his job, he just didn't want to fit in.

One reason for this perhaps is that from high school on, straight-arrow, "man's man" Harvey Milk was living the kind of off-hours secret life gay men had to lead in the 1940s and 1950s. In fact, by the early 1960s he had established a middle-class existence that would have been the envy of most Americans, with a steady, high-paying job, a nice place to live, and a happy domestic life. The only difference, of course, was that his domestic companion was a nice-looking young man, something which few of his colleagues at work or in other areas of his social life knew about.

In the restless 1960s, Milk himself became restless about the same old surroundings, first transferring in his job to Dallas, Texas, where he was not at all happy, and then to San Francisco. Here, as one friend put it, he "fit in too well," and soon Mr. Wall Street's hair was sprouting a little too long, he was openly dissatisfied with the treatment of gays by the police, and was talking about running for mayor. Finally, after making a few waves in the press by burning his Bank Americard at an anti-war rally one lunch hour, Milk was given an ultimatum to cut his hair or be fired. He exited from the middle-class life with hair intact, fired for the first time in his life as he was nearing forty.

Within a few years, Harvey Milk was running a little camera shop on Castro Street and right in the thick of local politics. His penchant for fighting City Hall on behalf of both himself and others soon earned him the nickname "The Mayor of Castro Street," and he made his first run for the Board of Supervisors in 1973. Among other things he learned from losing was that if supervisors had been elected by district rather than city-wide, he would have won, so he duly supported a change to election by districts that passed before the next election, 1977, in which he was elected to office, along with Dan White. White may himself have benefited from Milk's efforts in changing the election process.

Over the next year, although Milk and White would occasionally find common ground, more often than not they were on the opposite sides of issues. White in fact at times seemed to be skirting the edge of political decorum in his statements about San Francisco's gay citizens. The main feature of his brief stint as a supervisor, however, was that Dan White did not like to lose; and lose he did on an important issue which had been part of his campaign—with Harvey Milk casting the deciding vote against him, after having first said he would vote with him. The issue itself was whether or not to use an abandoned convent in White's district for a psychiatric treatment center. The more Milk learned about it, the more he was for it, and after the vote, any cordiality between him and White seemed to be gone.

Even worse, while White felt himself mired in frustration and getting nowhere through the system, Harvey Milk played it like a finely tuned instrument, often netting press attention for his causes. Those causes themselves did not, as one might suspect, all center on the politics of gay versus straight, and in fact one of his best-known efforts centered around the simple idea of getting dog owners in the city to clean up after their pets. Surveys at the time showed that dog droppings in public areas was the number-one complaint about life in San Francisco, and Milk grabbed the headlines with his successful effort to bring that problem to heel. As he pointed out to friends, stories about this did not center on his gayness as such, but on the fact that he was a supervisor doing his job; and that, he told them, was a good education for the public.

Aside from his political frustrations, Dan White was a family man with a wife and a child who quickly learned that it was difficult to make ends meet on the lowly salary paid to supervisors in those days. Though his wife ran a small family-owned food stand in a local tourist area, between his meager salary and her troubles running the business, he decided that he would have to resign as supervisor. Little did this political amateur realize the repercussions, however, as his immediate relief was soon followed by trepidation when those who had supported him complained that he had left them with the prospect of a Board of Supervisors tilted against their political and economic interests. Moreover, some might have suggested that they liked him as a spokesman and that a great political future awaited him if he would simply stay the course. Within a few days, he tried to take back his resignation.

Mayor George Moscone[6], a liberal whose politics Dan White despised, was the key, as it was he who would have to appoint White's successor. At first Moscone said he had no problem with reappointing White, but then Harvey Milk lobbied hard against it, pointing out to Moscone that the right appointment would make it easier for both of them to get their pet projects through the board. More than this, however, was the strong threat of the large gay vote that now listened to Harvey Milk turning elsewhere when Moscone was up for reelection. Moscone relented and let word get out that he would not reappoint the frustrated conservative, a move which sealed the fates of himself, Harvey Milk, and Dan White.

On the morning of November 27, 1978, White, fueled by days of frustration and a sleepless night in which he had stoked himself with sugared soft drinks and cupcakes, methodically selected ten cartridges for his .38 police special (five had hollow points, which cause massive destruction, especially at close range), loaded five of them, strapped on his gun and then rode down to City Hall to confront both Moscone and Milk. After sneaking through a basement window to avoid the security checks at the door, White went upstairs and wrangled a quick appointment with the mayor. Though several people in the vicinity heard the muffled shots, no one paid much attention as White hurried out, already having pocketed four spent cartridges and one live shell, and reloaded his gun with the five hollow points. Almost casually, he asked Milk to leave his own office and go to White's old office for a private conversation. There he murdered Harvey Milk by firing five shots into him. The last shots for both Moscone and Milk were execution style to the head, causing instant death.

The end of White's story dragged out over the next few years, but the pertinent facts are these. First, in what amounted to a show trial, White was convicted only of manslaughter, the key being what the press called "The Twinkie Defense," in reference to a popular sugary snack cake—poor Dan White, according to his attorney, was so stoked up on junk food that he wasn't in his right mind.[7] Secondly, though he removed Harvey Milk from the scene, the outrage from the large gay community in San Francisco over the verdict completed what the gay rights movement had started and Harvey Milk had taken into electoral politics, as the gay community in San Francisco began to exercise its political power with a vengeance. As Harry Britt, appointed to fill out Milk's term, said to shocked reporters after the riots that followed the verdict: "Now the society is going to have to deal with us not as nice little fairies with hairdressing salons, but as people capable of violence. We're not going to put up with Dan Whites any more." Dan White himself served his time in jail for having killed two men while under the influence of cupcakes, and within a relatively short time after his release committed suicide.

There is an interesting contrast between the lives of Harvey Milk and Dan White that has a definite geographical feature to it, one which plays around a Mars-Neptune theme. For many years, as he stayed around his place of birth on the east coast, Harvey Milk lived a relatively normal middle-class life, despite the part of it that was secret to all but a few. Moreover, the life he led was not necessarily just for camouflage, as for a long while he really seemed to like its stability as much as anything else. Even politically in those years, he might have been closer, and sincerely so, to the Dan White of San Francisco days than to Supervisor Harvey Milk. The times, however, began to change him, and after his move to San Francisco, he "came out" in more ways than one, tapping into a potential he had only been dimly aware of before. His rise in politics was the result of a genuine talent that certainly would have carried him to higher office had he lived.

Dan White, on the other hand, seemed to be one of those people who reach their pinnacle of success in high school, and for whom life after graduation becomes a floundering for a way back to the glory days. White did well in the military, did well as a fireman, and did well as a policeman, yet in what should have been a natural role as a blue-collar populist expressing the frustration of stolid, conservative home-and-family types over the political and social turn their city was taking, White failed miserably. It was not simply that he could not make ends meet on a supervisor's salary, but that he seemed to feel powerless before the opposition he faced. After all, Harvey Milk probably lost more political battles than White by far, yet he would often turn a loss today into tomorrow's victory by keeping his shoulder to the wheel and his eye on the prize. Why the difference?

Consider first these two sets of positive and negative descriptive terms of Mars and Neptune, respectively, drawn from more comprehensive lists in Jeff Mayo's *Astrology: A Key to Personality*:[8]

Positive: Self-assertive, initiatory, enterprising, impulsive, competitive, persuasive
Negative: Combative, reckless, irascible, overexcitable, quarrelsome, brusque.

Positive: Sensitive, impressionable, tender, gentle, humane, idealistic, informal.
Negative: Impractical, unstable, touchy, hypersensitive, worrier, drug-addictive.

Perhaps the reader will agree that the first set, particularly the positive list, seems more in tune with Harvey Milk's situation in San Francisco, while the negative terms in both sets seem more in tune with Dan White during his rise and fall in local politics. Furthermore, it would not be too difficult to argue that the reverse (leaving the same emphasis on positive and negative, however, with regard to the sign and aspect conditions of the planets in question) might have held at earlier stages in their lives, when each lived close to his place of birth. The first set of terms identifies a "stimulus reaction" to Mars, while the second identifies the same in regard to Neptune. At his place of birth, Harvey Milk had Neptune setting almost exactly, while in San Francisco the planet closest to an angle was Mars (Venus and Jupiter are near angles as well). On the other hand, Dan White had Mars closer to an angle at his birth place, while Neptune was closer in San Francisco. Depending on the orb allowed, some would say that White had a conjunction of the two planets, though in any case both were certainly bound together by their placement near the same angle. While the difference between birth place and locality is not as stark as in Milk's case, it is there.

One difference that is stark, and which relates directly to the question of whether either might have had a problem in expressing Mars, is that while for Milk that planet is in Aries, its own sign, with a hard-edged square to Pluto (and to Saturn as well, if one allows wide orbs), White's Mars is in fact debilitated in the opposite Venus-ruled sign of Libra and flanked (if not closely aspected) by benefics Venus and Jupiter on the one side and fuzzy Neptune on the other. Thus, even though White's Mars is strong in being close to an angle, it is not in a particularly Martian environment, while Milk's back-channel Mars, so to speak, is much more healthy in a Martian sense.

Whether Milk was right or wrong about his "closet case" diagnosis of White in regard to sexual orientation, he may have been correct in sensing that White was someone whose Martian-sounding background came in part from overcompensation for some kind of inadequacy, for the feeling that somehow he did not measure up as a man unless he could perform brave deeds, handle a weapon and so on. Mars as a horoscopic factor alone indicates the need or ability to perform actions in a directed way, and to match one's performance against others. Neptune, on the other hand, is anything but directed or competitive, but by itself indicates a kind of "go along to get along" mentality that can be charming on the one hand, or frustrating (and frustrated) on the other. The heavily Neptunian individual is forever getting lost in the details of everyday life and while perhaps observant or even visionary in matters that don't concern him personally, he may be quite lacking in insight where his own place in the grand scheme of things is concerned. Looking at Milk in New York and White in San Francisco, one might say that a key term for Neptune could be "the invisible man."

In that light, consider Harvey Milk's first forty years, spent for the

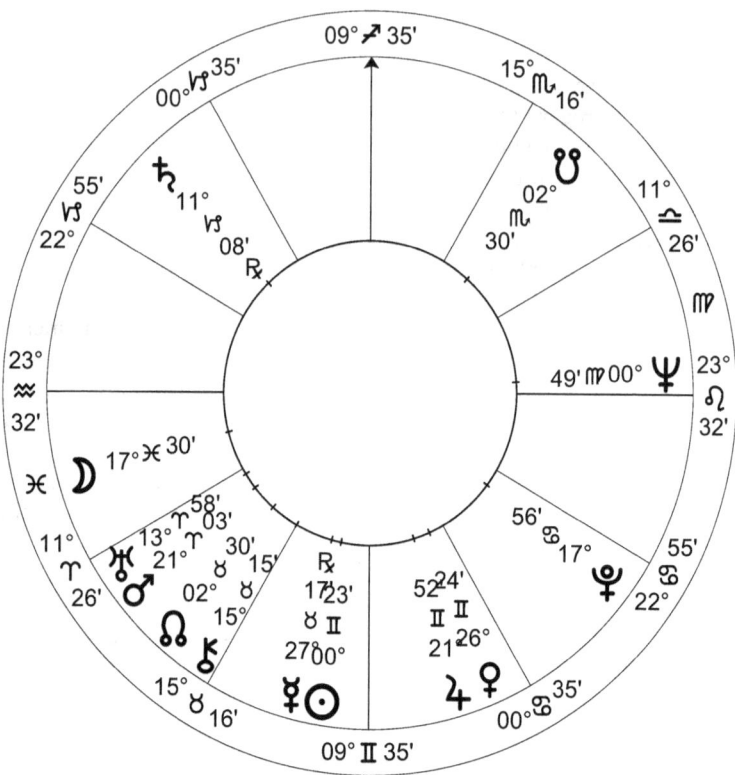

Figure 10 - Harvey Milk, at his birth place in Woodmere, New York

most part where Neptune was strong. Even though good at his job, since he was quite insightful where financial and economic matters were concerned, Milk was never exactly a team player and always, according to the observation of a good friend who was aware of his sexual orientation, seemed to be somewhere else, even if it was not exactly clear where that was. During this time, even though Milk played out his relatively strong Mars in certain areas of life, such as athletics, it never became integrated into his passionate (even pushy) interest in politics—until he hit San Francisco, where his gayness and his political feelings were shaped in the forge of Mars. Thus began the resolution of his own Martian dilemma, which for anyone is the problem of giving drive and direction to one's life based on one's own essential strength.

While Milk was in San Francisco, at last listening closely to his own inner drummer, Dan White had his ear to the ground, listening to everyone else's

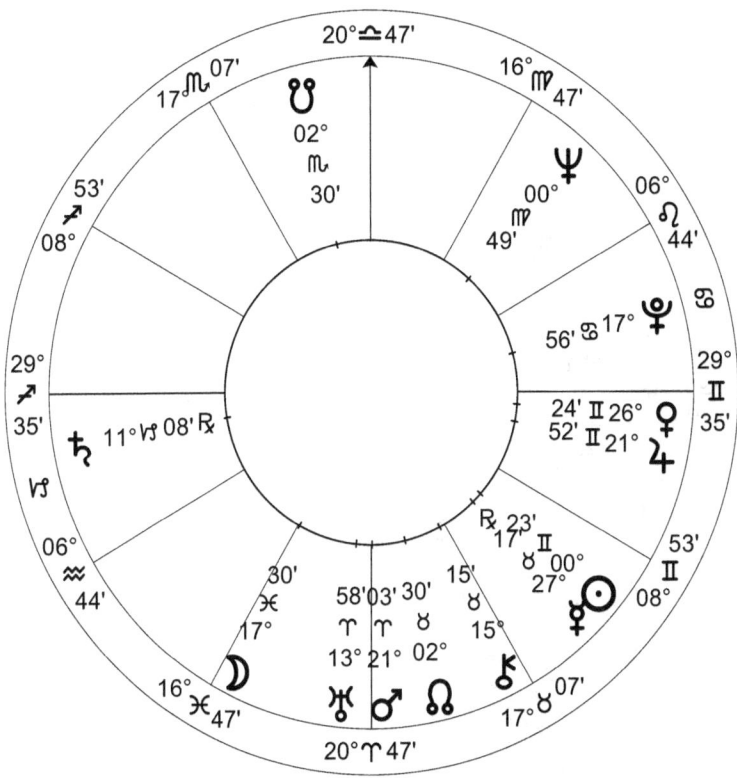

Figure 11 - Harvey Milk, relocated to San Francisco

rhythms, and many of his personal choices were most likely dictated by a need to do the right thing in the eyes of others. In part at least this can be explained by the tentative, not-self nature of his Libra Mars placement combined with the heavy influence of Neptune. Thus, as Mars waned and Neptune waxed in San Francisco, White's moral and psychological footing became uncertain, as indicated, for example, by his reputation for being a sore loser. In a sense, proving himself through winning was probably the only way he could be sure that he was in fact doing the right thing. His final assault on the problem may have been driven less by Twinkies than by the need to perform, by the *desire* to perform, an act that would make him a hero to those whose admiration he sought in everything. The denouement for him was the same as it is for many a surviving martyr who wakes up the morning after with the realization that those he sought to please must now treat him like a pariah in order to keep their veneer of respectability intact.

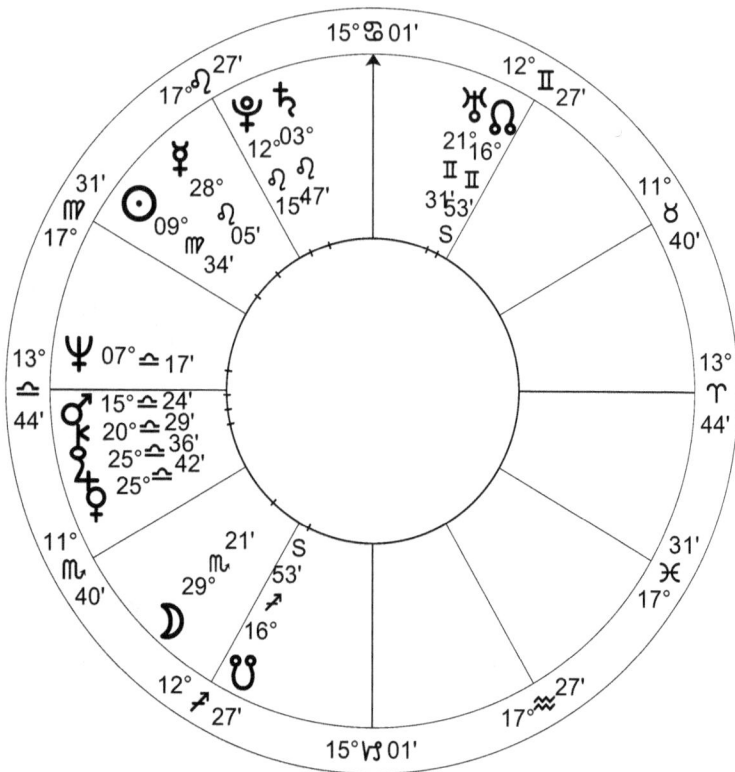

Figure 12 - Dan White, at his birth place in Bellflower, California

Moreover, the strong Martian hero had staked his life on convincing people that the cornerstone act of his time on the planet—the thing the world would know him for—had been laid not on the firm support of traditional values, but on a foundation made of Twinkies. The name for White's infamous defense is an apt expression for the marshmallow Neptune surprise inside his thin and brittle Mars.[9]

On the day of the murders in San Francisco, as for the Jonestown massacre a little over a week earlier, Mars and Neptune were conjoined in Sagittarius, emphasizing patterns suggested in the charts of Jim Jones and Dan White.[10] Other than the fact that a strong transiting or progressed aspect between two planets tends to resonate with and activate the same kind of aspect in a natal chart, the conjunction occurred within a degree or two of a conjunction to Dan White's South Node, and square to the natal Moon of Harvey Milk and to the progressed Midheaven of George Moscone's chart. Furthermore,

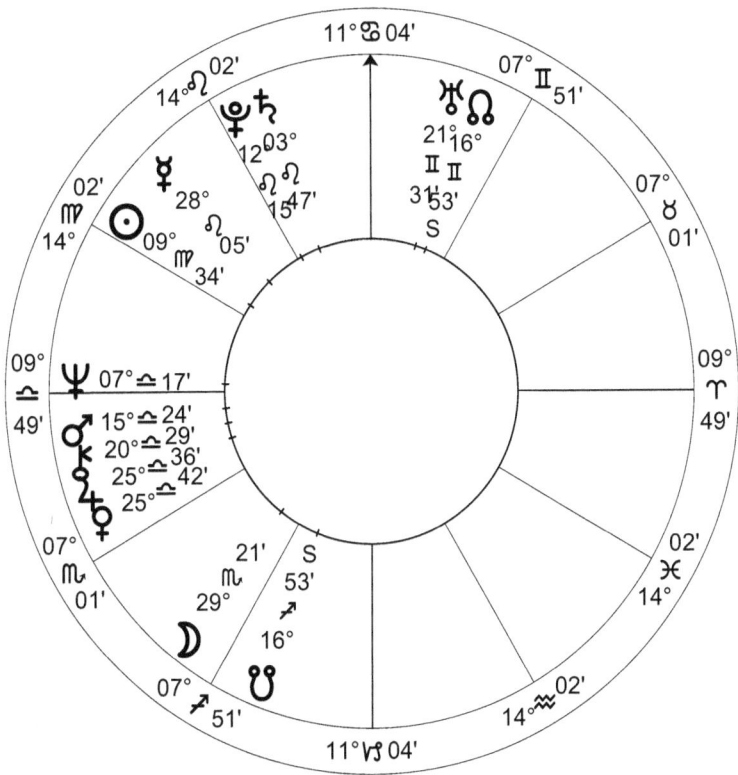

Figure 13 - Dan White, relocated to San Francisco

for Moscone, who natally had Pluto near the Midheaven in San Francisco, several Pluto themes were reiterated, the most striking of which was the fact that an opposition of progressed Sun and Venus to progressed Pluto was found across the horizon of the New Moon preceding his murder. Such Plutonian emphasis in the chart of a politician often presents the kind of danger that brought Moscone's life to so tragic an end.

No planet, even those usually classified as malefic, is wholly negative in its action, but when light and heat are turned up too high and too quickly on a shadowed planet hiding in the cool recesses of our minds, whether that comes from transits, progressions, or geographical emphasis, or all three, the results can be devastating. More than 900 lost souls at Jonestown in November 1978 attest to that fact, as do three more consumed in the Martian flames fanned by the winds of Neptune nine days later in San Francisco.

6

War Lines Across the World

WAR IS PERHAPS the most puzzling of human options. Love, ambition, and other motivations seem understandable for their rewards, but the perennial practice of pitting one society's strongest and best against another's in a fight to the death, in which more is destroyed than could ever be plundered, remains an unexplained enigma of human behavior. Societies never seem to learn; generation after generation, having just recovered from the previous conflagration, busies itself preparing for the next.

What has Astro*Carto*Graphy to say about this periodic human appetite for collective destruction? Can it shed light on the reason for and, perhaps, the future manifestations of this societal violence? From client feedback, as well as from the observation of cases such as those discussed in the previous chapter, certain correlations between these maps and personal behavior have become clear. Among the most consistent is that the Mars lines on an individual's map show places where he or she is apt to become either the victim or instigator of violence, assertion, belligerency, or aggression—as well as identifying those places where one can expect one's courage to be tested.

Many men have confessed to having become more combative and irritable in places where their natal Mars was angular—often responding to challenges to their masculinity and finding it more of an issue in a Mars zone than in other places. One basically non-aggressive personality wrote to tell of several fist fights and four auto wrecks while he resided under a personal Mars zone in Connecticut. Another, a Vietnam veteran, noted that he had been very lucky in Vietnam, surviving intense combat and prolonged exposure to danger under his Jupiter line there; however, as soon as he was ordered for an overnight stay in Cambodia, under his Mars line, his helicopter was hit by gunfire. Accidents, fights, enhanced sexuality, and generally assertive behavior seem consistent responses in people traveling through zones marked by Mars.

This should come as no surprise to the astrologer, as Mars has been known since antiquity as the god of war, and even modern research confirms this. To take one example, work by Michel and Françoise Gauquelin has demonstrated that Martian types (particularly those with Mars near the angles of a chart) seem able to succeed in professions such as surgery and the military. Even the planet itself—extolled by poets for its ruddy color—seems confirmed by space explorations to be a place of harsh extremes and climactic violence that fit well with the kind of temperament astrologers ascribe to Mars. And as we have seen in the cases of Jim Jones and Dan

White, at times the energy unleashed by a Mars line can be furious and far-reaching in its effect.

If Mars on an individual's map denotes where he or she is most apt to express assertion, initiative, or belligerency, is there some way to find a similar set of zones for the kind of war and conflict that engulfs entire nations or alliances of nations? Yes. The maps for many U.S. presidents show an inescapable pattern that usually has Mars as its central locus. A president is, of course, more than just an individual doing his job. He is a symbol for the whole nation during his time in office. Elections are a tremendously intricate process and seemingly select one member of society to act for the whole (or at least most of it), so it stands to reason that the person selected reflects to some extent the needs, desires, and specific intentions of the society that chose him or her. Thus, a president's Mars lines should show where the society he led or presently leads is most apt to wage war. At the same time, a purely personal element is involved as each president has his own personal demons to deal with, meaning that the growth processes of his own psyche are often reflected outwardly in the life and events of the nation he leads.

At least as interesting, if not more so in certain cases, is the relationship of Pluto lines to a president's war-making proclivities. Astrologers tend to speak of Pluto as a "higher octave" of Mars, and this seems amply confirmed by the history of military involvement directed by U.S. presidents, since this planet often serves as a stand-in when a close Mars contact is absent. Just as often, both planets will on occasion interact in some way to mark the location where the power of U.S. military might is to be felt.

To begin with Pluto, three presidents who led a military effort to control the tiny Central American country of Nicaragua had Pluto on the Midheaven (Calvin Coolidge[1] and Franklin D. Roosevelt[2]), or rising (Herbert Hoover[3]). A fourth president, who suffered the consequences of their actions some forty years later, Jimmy Carter,[4] showed Pluto on the Midheaven as a near miss to Central America, though it actually went through Mexico, a country with which Carter had somewhat strained relations. However, just off the coast of Nicaragua and running directly through Panama, Carter had Saturn rising, and it would not be too much to say that his foreign-policy dealings with these two countries alone would have caused major problems in his reelection effort, had they not been overshadowed by his disaster with American hostages in Iran.

Where Roosevelt's most notable military involvement is concerned, though it is difficult to localize a war whose battlefields were littered around the planet, it is interesting to note that since Mars and Pluto were within thirty degrees of longitude of each other, throughout the world the two flank many of the hot spots of the Second World War, with Pluto on the western edge of the war zones and Mars on the east. Pluto and Mars set on either side of Europe and North Africa, Burma, and areas of the Pacific.

Interestingly, though Mars rising passes near the scene of Roosevelt's major military failure at Pearl Harbor, his planetary set-up for the protagonist counter, in that case Japan, features Saturn, Neptune, and Jupiter. Though some conspiracy theorists have held that Roosevelt actually allowed Pearl Harbor to happen (something which makes no sense militarily, as the loss of men and equipment was too great, even if Roosevelt had been so callous as to permit their destruction), the major verdict seems to be that, despite ample warnings, the whole chain of command, including Roosevelt, was simply looking the other way, distracted by a Japanese show of diplomatic activity.

Given those three planetary lines in Japan, one wonders, in fact, what might have happened regarding Japan if President Roosevelt had lived to finish the war with that country. This task, however, was left to his successor, Harry S. Truman,[5] who of course made the decision to drop the atomic bomb on Hiroshima and Nagasaki—a decision whose military necessity is still argued at length by historians many decades later. Five years afterwards, Truman committed U.S. troops to yet another war, this time in Korea. His map (Figure 14) illustrates these events with much clarity and precision: Mars is on the IC exactly through the Korean peninsula, and Saturn was also on the Ascendant in the north, as well as near Japan. While Mars is near enough to Japan to affect it, Pluto rising is the planet that reigns over the cities in Japan on which Truman ordered the first A-bomb to be dropped, ushering in the atomic age.

It seems almost incredible that a planet which would not be discovered for 46 years rose at Truman's birth moment just west of the spot that would be obliterated by a device not to be invented for five decades. Truman's other major involvement of a military nature (though U.S. troops were not directly engaged) began with his maneuvering to end the Soviet occupation of Iran and to dampen Iranian nationalist fervor after the Second World War, one result of which was the long reign of the Shah and a steady supply of Iranian oil, so it is interesting that Truman's Mars sets exactly over Tehran.

Dwight D. Eisenhower did not wage war while in office, and as his birth time is somewhat disputed, his chart cannot be considered, unfortunately. John F. Kennedy[6] had the unenviable distinction of being the first president to commit troops to Vietnam, early in 1962; his map shows, not surprisingly, Mars, Saturn, and Neptune angular in the China Sea, a theme which we will find repeated in a particular U.S. chart as we explore it in the next chapter. Significantly, the Mars Ascendant line dominates in Southeast Asia, suggesting an initiative on his part. Of more than passing interest as well is the fact that his natal Pluto culminated in Dallas, where he was assassinated. While Pluto can on the one hand indicate force majeure turned against an enemy, it can just as often show the same turned against the native.

Lyndon Johnson's chart[7] shows less personal initiative where Vietnam is concerned, but rather hints at the great personal sacrifice the war cost him. Mars, Jupiter, and the Sun are on the Descendant near Vietnam; however, they rise in Washington, showing that his "Great Society" was to be clouded by the social cost of the escalating war and that his expensive and ambitious "War on Poverty" would seem insignificant next to the impossible war in the Far East. The conjunction of Mars and Jupiter, prominent in Kennedy's, Johnson's, and Nixon's charts, has been traditionally associated with extravagance, which is reinforced by the fact that the bills from Vietnam came due for most of the rest of the century in the form of inflation and cheapened dollars.

The horoscope of Richard M. Nixon[8] alone seems to vary from the established pattern; though Mars conjoins Jupiter again, it does not do so near Vietnam. Instead, Neptune, planet of deception and disillusion, lies at the IC in Cambodia, and (significantly) culminates over Washington. This suggests that Nixon's major personal contribution to the South-East Asia war was his covert invasion of Laos and Cambodia by CIA troops.

With Gerald Ford,[9] the old pattern returns, as his Mars dominates Saigon, and the MA DSC line again shows his less-than-willing role in the continuation of the conflict there. Mars is also near Cambodia, where the Mayaguez incident displayed Ford in his most assertive posture. His map is remarkable for other aspects, among which is Pluto exactly angular over San Francisco, where twice he was subject to assassination attempts (echoing our point about Kennedy and Dallas), and the Moon and Uranus lines crossing near Washington, indicating his unexpected elevation to the presidency.

Jimmy Carter has Mars rising with Jupiter at the Midheaven in Iran, a pattern which calls to mind the chart of Harry S. Truman, whose lines parallel Carter's almost exactly in this part of the world, though they are reversed in polarity—that is, the planet found on Truman's Ascendant there lies on Carter's Descendant, and so on. This might seem to suggest that Carter had to deal with some of the outcome of Truman's involvement in Iran, which some historians assert was the first act in a long drama driven by the Western world's need for petroleum. In fact, many of the twists and turns of the Iran hostage crisis were made understandable by a knowledge of both Truman's and Carter's Mars lines in this area.[10] Carter's natal Mars is opposed by longitude to his conjunction of Neptune and Venus—the two of which are also angular near the aforementioned areas, though more to the west, near Israel—so the scenario for Carter turned out to be quite different from Truman's. Venus with Neptune identifies the idealist. The opposition to Mars suggest that while Carter dislikes violence as a rule, as president he became involved in others' problems in part through pursuit of his ideals. The opposition seems aptly defined by his necessary involvement with repressive regimes such as that of the Shah of Iran or the South Korean government. As a private citizen he might not have supported these leaders, but as president he was bound to.

President Carter had long since moved on to build housing for the poor (among many things he never had time to do while in office) when President

LINES AROUND THE WORLD

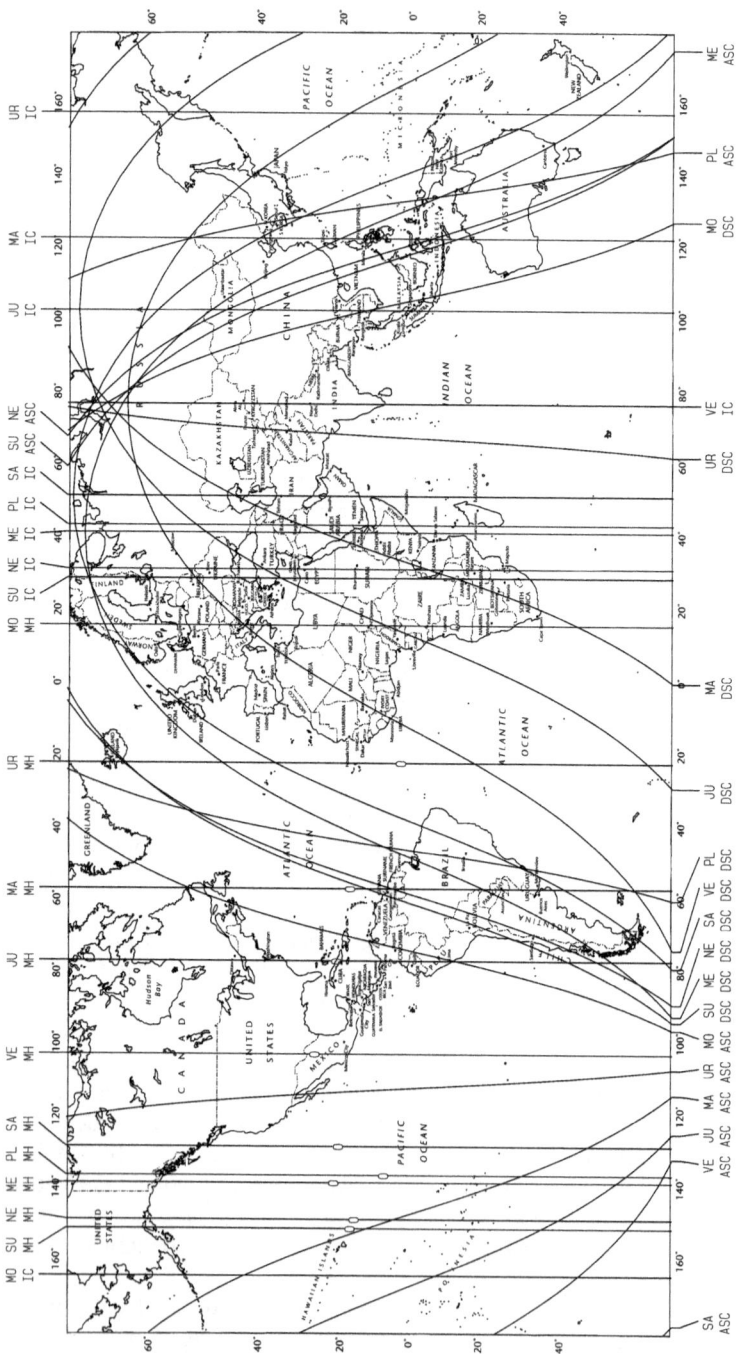

Figure 14 - Harry S. Truman, Whose Pluto Line Struck At Hiroshima

George H. W. Bush had to meet his own Mars crisis. Interestingly, several startling factors link Bush to Carter. For example, both presidents have Mars and Jupiter in exactly the same degrees: 27° Aquarius and 14° Sagittarius, respectively. In the four months that separated their births, Mars and Jupiter each turned retrograde, then direct, and by one of those coincidences that suggest some cosmic conspiracy to make astrologers pay attention, occupied exactly the same degrees on the two birthdays. For this reason alone, Bush's problems with Saddam Hussein can be seen as an extension of Carter's problems in Iran.

Bush's Mars lines fall in places that are of more than passing interest to the mundane astrologer. His Mars Descendant line falls right across Panama, while his Mars Ascendant crosses his Jupiter Midheaven line (Carter's fateful combo in Tehran) at Beijing. Readers may remember that among Bush's first crises in office was one touched off by the democracy demonstrations in Tiananmen Square, the suppression of which Bush didn't try very hard to prevent; nor did he hold the Chinese gerontocracy accountable for it on an important diplomatic occasion not long afterwards. His Mars IC and MH lines also emphasized Eastern Europe, Libya, Central and South-West Africa as areas which may also be under stress.

But what about Iraq and Kuwait, the scene of the massive military action known as the Gulf War? Surely his map must show something in this sandy oil patch which half the US Army was devoted to defending in 1990 and 1991? Given an 11:30 A.M. (June 12, 1924, Milton, Massachusetts) birth time,[11] Bush has expansive (the word takes on new meanings in this context) Jupiter squarely on the Ascendant in Baghdad. Does this mean victory? Surely, if anyone won a lottery in connection with Baghdad, it wasn't the US President, despite the political points he won for his handling of the Gulf War. After all, those points did not prevent him from losing the presidency less than two years later to Bill Clinton, whose political antagonists considered him a "draft dodger" at best. Is Mars also there somewhere in Iraq, as it was with Carter in Iran?

Near the end of the day on October 20, 1990, Mars paused in its orbit around the Sun as seen from Earth, and began apparent retrograde motion. This itself isn't news, since Mars does this routinely every two years or so. But this time it chose for its station 14°34' of Gemini. From that point it closely opposed the Carter/Bush Jupiter at 14°11' of Sagittarius. In short, October and November represented a critical and perilous time in which events occurred or decisions were made that affected the course of the conflict. (Bush announced the build-up on November 8, 1990.) Mars' station was the same transiting factor that provoked Jimmy Carter to try to rescue his hostages.

That station of Mars, which seemed to signal what might be called the failsafe point for military involvement, fell in exact opposition to Bush's Jupiter, which itself is angular at Baghdad. This would seem to have offered little hope for any other outcome of the confrontation between the United States and Iraq, especially since the aspect so closely reiterated what happened to Carter in 1980. Mars made its station conjunct Bush's Midheaven, and Jupiter rules Bush's 7th house, so it was not surprising that subsequent events led to an announcement of a military build-up of sufficient size to drive the Iraqi army from Kuwait.

Even less surprising, perhaps, in the light of what we have shown about the ways in which the geographical emphasis of Mars seems to drive and direct the aggressive energies of American presidents, is the set of aspects involving transiting Mars and President Bush's natal and progressed charts from the invasion through to the end of the Gulf War. Shown in Table 3, these make two interesting points. First of all, there is no doubt that transiting Mars was driving President Bush astrologically in both his natal and progressed charts relocated to Baghdad. In the history of his dealings with Iraq (possibly even going back to advice he proffered during the Reagan administration which became the basis for U.S. policy toward that country), Bush appears if anything to have acted like the proverbial sugar daddy. In fact, it does not stretch credibility to say that many of the more exotic weapons American and Allied soldiers faced had either been paid for with U.S. funds or their development allowed through a naive and over-generous U.S. policy that looked the other way in order not to see violations of international law—and winked at those it did see. Since Saddam Hussein was deemed to be a necessary foil to the destabilizing plans of the ayatollahs in Iran, he was given a blank check to go shopping in a weapons toy store and allowed to buy whatever his whimsies dictated. If this sounds like Jupiter, then so it should, since, as we have pointed out, Bush's own natal Jupiter was rising at Baghdad at his birth.

In fact, it was that kind of Jupiterian Santa Claus policy which, right up until the last minute before the invasion, seemed to make Saddam Hussein feel he could swallow Kuwait whole, like an oily delicacy on a sandy plate. Even the U.S. ambassador to Iraq seemed to signal that such an action would go unpunished, and one can only presume that at least her lack of a sense of urgency about the prospect of Kuwait being invaded came from instructions to handle Iraq as an important ally that could do no wrong. If George Bush later changed his mind, it might have been the result in part of a reported lecture about "backbone" from the British Prime Minister, Margaret Thatcher (compare her progressed Mercury on October 20, 1990, at 12°27' Sagittarius with Table 3). This in fact directs us back to the idea of shadowed planets and the way in which they are sometimes forced out in the open by either transits or progressions or locality considerations. All three seem to have played a part in Bush's case, with Thatcher as an additional relationship trigger letting him know the problem he faced on a personal level in dealing with this crisis.

As we can see from the table, during the entire crisis Bush's natal

WAR LINES ACROSS THE WORLD

Mars was rising in his progressed chart set for Baghdad, at times squared by transiting Mars after its station on October 20, 1990. Transiting Mars was also, of course, opposite both his natal Midheaven for Baghdad and his progressed Ascendant for the same place–with his natal Jupiter at 14° Sagittarius and his progressed Jupiter at 10° Sagittarius. This begins to sound like a cosmic message bellowing to Bush, "No more Mr Nice Guy!" These transits to Bush's natal and progressed angles and Jupiter are all the more interesting since, even after an earlier military adventure in Panama, he still had a "wimp" image with the public that was hard to shake. The Gulf War may have ended that, even given the later dissatisfaction among the public over his gentlemanly end to the war.

Fully as interesting as the transits to Bush's chart for the Gulf War are the transits and progressions relating to Truman's chart at the time when he ordered the dropping of the atomic bomb on Hiroshima. In

Table 3 - Transiting Mars and the Gulf War

	Nat. 25 ♒	A 13 ♉	B 11 ♊	C 4 ♊	D. 28 ♉	E 28 ♉	F 29 ♉	G 11 ♊	H 11 ♊
Natal									
MC 1 ♎	•	•	•	△	△	△	△	•	•
Asc 16 ♐	•	•	☍	•	•	•	•	☍	☍
Prog.									
MC 9 ♐	•	•	☍	☍	•	•	•	☍	☍
Asc 26 ♒	☌	•	•	•	□	□	□	•	•

Transiting and natal Mars to President Bush's natal (top) and progressed (bottom) Midheaven and Ascendant relocated to Baghdad during the Gulf War. Columns are identified below, with dates and times posted by Jamie Lankford in the library of the Astrology Roundtable on GEnie. Lankford noted that many times were derived from viewing live coverage of events.

Nat. - Natal Mars
Prog. - Progressed Mars
A - Iraqi Invasion, August 2, 1990, 3:13 a.m. Baghdad (BAT).
B - Bush announces troop build-up, November 8, 1990, 4:05 p.m. EST.
C - UN resolution, November 29, 1990, 5:28 p.m. EST.
D - Congress approves use of force, January 11, 1991, 3:00/3:50 p.m. EST.
E - UN deadline reached, January 15, 1991, 0:00 a.m. EST.
F - Bombing of Iraq begins, January 17, 1991, 2:30 a.m. BAT.
G - Allied ground offensive, February 24, 1991 4:00 a.m. BAT.
H - Bush announces cease-fire, February 27, 1991, 9:05 p.m. EST.

LINES AROUND THE WORLD

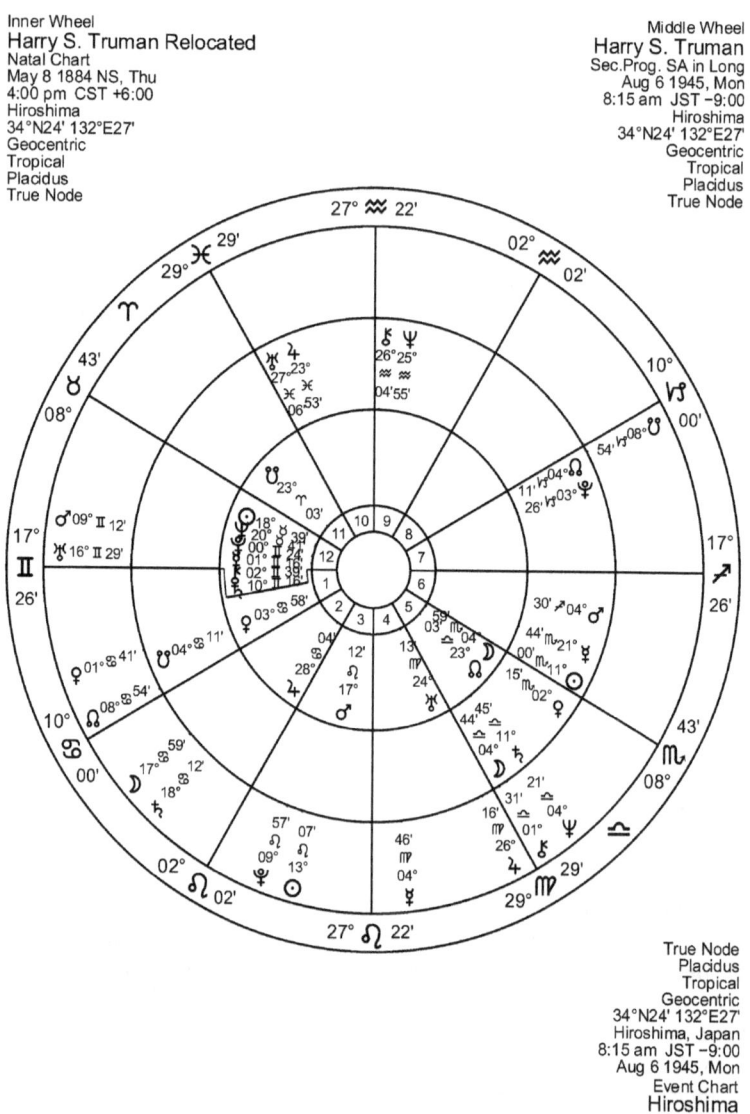

Figure 15 - Harry S. Truman's natal, progressions, and transits for Hiroshima

Astro*Carto*Graphy, the favored method for considering progressions is to look at the progressed planets within the framework of the natal chart (i.e., paying less attention to the angles of the progressed chart). Truman's natal and progressed chart along with the transits for that day (Figure 15 and Table 4) give a clear picture of the destruction his order to drop the bomb would engender. Truman's chart obviously repeats a theme shown later in

Table 4 - Truman's Natal, Progressions, and Transits for Hiroshima

	Rise	Set	Upper	Lower
Natal	•	•	•	•
♂	•	•	•	320°15'
♄	324°00'	•	•	•
♇	325°29'	•	•	•
Progressed	•	•	•	•
♄	330°26'	•	•	•
♇	326°13'	•	•	•
Transit	•	•	•	•
☿	•	•	•	335°17'
♂	322°09'	•	•	•
♅	328°38'	•	•	•

President Truman's natal chart relocated to Hiroshima and used as a framework within which to view his natal and progressed planets on the day the atomic bomb was dropped in August of 1945 shows some striking connections. Figures in the table are the sidereal times (as degrees) at which each planet would reach one of the angles shown in the four columns at the head of the table. Planets listed are those reaching an angle within 10 degrees of the sidereal time of Truman's chart relocated to Hiroshima, 329°34'. The sidereal time at the moment the bomb was dropped was 328°38'

President Bush's chart at the time of the Gulf War, but as we shall see, it also repeats a theme found in a particular US chart, for the same date, for the same place–Hiroshima, August 6, 1945 at 8:15 a.m. JST.

7

Prisoners of the Horoscope No More

THOUGH NORMALLY in astrology we think of everyone having both a birth time and a birth place, as we have seen there is a sense in which we are born everywhere at once, with the world as our horoscope. Traveling from one place to another, or perhaps interacting with people in some part of the world distant from our usual residence, brings us into connection with parts of ourselves that we may have ignored or suppressed, forcing us to face these hidden facets of our psyches and deal with them. Even in this day and age of easy international travel, however, relatively few people will have the opportunity to experience more than one or two changes of residence significant enough to alter their experience of their planetary lines in a noticeable way. In the normal course of events, even those who travel a great deal often have the option of ignoring, at least for a time, the effect of a shadowed planet engaging their attention on a journey that takes them through an important planetary line. This is not to say that such experiences are not important, since quite often the thing that is memorable about our experiences in distant locales serves to guide our response when later on some other astrological mechanism such as an important progression or transit, or perhaps a relationship, again brings that hidden part of ourselves out into the open. The recorded experiences of Astro*Carto*Graphy users tell us that people tend to remember even brief journeys through their Pluto lines, especially, for instance, when these bring them face to face with their own mortality in one way or another. Similar statements can be made for Mars and, on a lesser basis, Saturn, as all of these planets are more immediate and demanding in their action than some of the other planets, which often require longer stays in order to reach their peak.

One step up from the life of the ordinary person is the experience of those who have international dealings on a regular basis, but most particularly those who, like American presidents, not only must live lives that are international in scope but are also themselves the focus of attention from people and nations all over the world. In these cases, all parts of the world horoscope are strummed like a zither day in and day out, making them good examples of the way in which the lines on an ACG map work. Even more interesting than events in the lives of heads of state are the experiences of entire nations, something which was brought into sharp focus some years ago with the publication of a book called *The True Horoscope of the United States*[1], not long before Astro*Carto*Graphy was brought before the public. Its author, Helen Boyd, contended that the Declaration of Independence on July 4, 1776, the traditional basis for U.S. Charts, was less fundamental (or, as astrologers say, less radical) than the "Declaration of the Causes and Necessities of Taking Up Arms" issued by the Second Continental Congress on July 6, 1775 (along with the "Olive Branch Petition"), spelling out the reasons for the open hostilities that had been taking place between the North American colonies and Great Britain since the Battles of Lexington and Concord on April 19, 1775. Through the use of historical records, Boyd pinpointed a span of time when she felt this declaration might have been passed, and then with assistance from Roy Firebrace arrived at a speculative chart for July 6, 1775, 11:00 A.M. LMT, in Philadelphia.

Though endless arguments can be offered as to why a particular national chart should be more or less radical than any other, the bulk of the proofs for most charts seems to depend on the political beliefs or patriotic fervor of the adherents or detractors of a particular chart. In contrast to this, the main argument for the Boyd chart is astrological, as it provides sharp and pertinent symbolism for a variety of events, and through the use of a variety of techniques. Moreover, this chart also shows the same kind of sharp symbolism when the geographical techniques of Astro*Carto*Graphy are used, particularly where the idea of "war zones" is concerned.[2]

As Firebrace showed in Boyd's book, this chart actually times at least one of the July 4, 1776 contenders, any one which is more historically possible than the well-known "Gemini-rising" chart for circa 2:00 A.M. LMT. Firebrace's example used a technique called the Progressed Sidereal Solar Return that, while not well known, seems methodologically sound. The essence of the technique is the notion that any solar return (the return of the Sun to its natal place, something which occurs each year around the birthday) becomes, by progression, the solar return for the following year. Because of the fact that the length of the year is about one-quarter day beyond 365 days, the time for a solar return each year will average to about six hours later than the one for the year before, though this varies according to the time of year and other factors. As Firebrace showed, progressing the Boyd chart to July 4, 1776 (two days short of its solar return), yields the same angles as a July 4, 1776 chart set for about 5:00 P.M. LMT—within the time range of the so-called Sibly chart for the Declaration of Independence—thus relating the Sibly chart to the Boyd chart in an interesting way, with the Sibly angles representing a progression and its planets representing a transit. Also interesting is that this progression has the Boyd natal Mars on the Midheaven (with natal Saturn not far off) and the Boyd natal Jupiter setting on the date the declaration was signed.

These are interesting preliminary justifications for the chart, but more telling and more pertinent to our subject here would be any relation Mars and Pluto have to places where the United States has used military force. In the case of Mars lines highlighting war zones for American presidents, we have a simple equation that doesn't depend on what we think of a particular

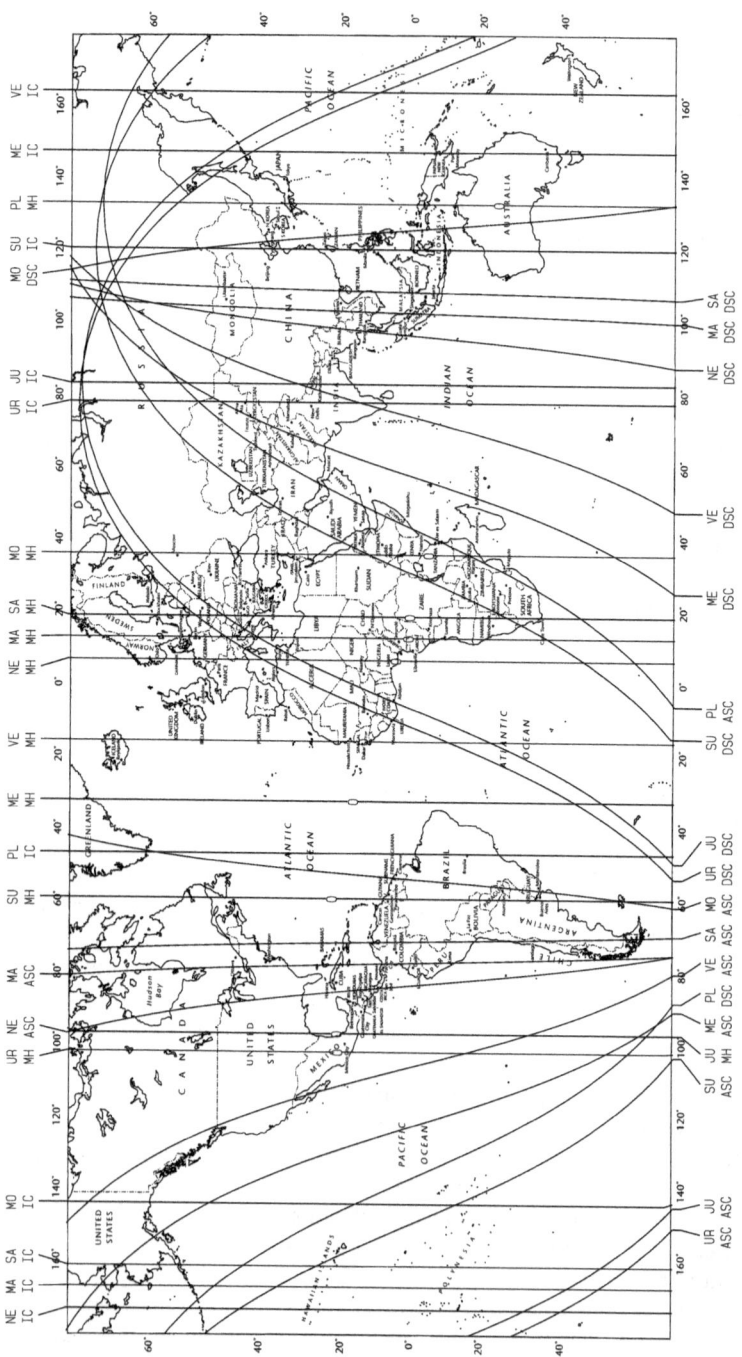

Figure 16 - An Alternative Map for the United States of America (Boyd)

president or his politics. Instead we know that American presidents are often called upon to make war, and that such wars will tend to occur on their Mars lines. So, too, it should be for nations, and particularly for one so involved in international affairs as America has been since the beginning.

As we can see from the map (Figure 16), Mars was near the Ascendant directly over both Richmond (the Confederate capital) and Washington at the time when the 1775 Declaration was signed, the two foci of the most savage and costly war the US has ever fought—the American Civil War. The Mars rising is of course a good indicator of the subject of the original declaration itself. However, almost ninety years later, the progressed Midheaven conjoined that Mars, thus activating the Martian potential for the area shown in the natal set-up. Moreover, the progressed Midheaven conjoined the natal Saturn, which is only six degrees further along, not long after. This aspect was strong during the whole Reconstruction era, which saw the highly political and usurpatory attempt to impeach Andrew Johnson, as well as an attempt to remake completely the political and social culture of the South by a group of radical Northern Republicans in Congress. Obviously one should look to times when these two planets progress to angles at Washington as periods in which the nation will be divided against itself in some fundamental way.

Having pointed out the involvement of both the natal and progressed Mars in the American Civil War, let us go on to consider those areas it touches in the rest of the world. Though not all U.S. wars involved Mars lines, many major conflicts did. The Mars Midheaven line on the ACG map, as one can see, goes directly through Berlin and through Tripoli. The latter city has been enshrined in the lyrics of "The Marine Corps Hymn," which begins: "From the Halls of Montezuma, to the shores of Tripoli . . ." This refers to one of America's first uses of its military as an arm of its foreign policy, aside from its early struggles with Great Britain (the War of 1812) and with France, mainly over economic issues. The pirates of the Barbary States along the northern coast of Africa had been harassing nations on the high seas for hundreds of years by the time the ruler of Tripolitania, Pasha Yusuf Karamanli, declared war on the United States for having had the audacity to take firm action to halt such activity. The U.S. reply was the First Barbary War from 1801 to 1805, which included the fabled Marine raid on Tripoli, resulting in the defeat of the pirates. Of note in this regard is the April 1986 air raid on Libya, intended to destroy a terrorist training camp as well as to kill the Libyan leader Muammar al-Qaddafi (in retaliation for a bombing of a discotheque in Berlin that had resulted in the death of a U.S. serviceman), as well as a 1989 skirmish in the air over the Mediterranean. Both these incidents were instrumental in at least toning down terrorist acts that were held to have been sponsored by Libya for many years previously.

This same Mars Midheaven line also passes near Berlin (which is actually between the Neptune and Saturn Midheaven lines), the source of two world wars in which American troops have been instrumental to Allied victories. Though U.S. relations with Germany have been very strong and cordial since the end of the Second World War, the presence of that Mars indicates how tension between Washington and Berlin is always a potential in the future. In fact, as the U.S. Mars, Saturn, and Neptune Midheaven lines cover all of Europe, this does not bode well for relations between the United States and its NATO allies with the end of the Cold War. Having no common enemy, these countries now face tricky problems of economic competition and political cooperation that would seem to require more harmony than one usually finds under a Mars line.

Also of interest is the fact that the Mars and Saturn Descendant lines go through Vietnam, flanking both Ho Chi Minh City (formerly Saigon) and Hanoi. It would be difficult to think of anything more fitting as a symbol of American entanglement in Vietnam than Mars and Saturn on the Descendant, emphasizing the 1st/7th-house axis in the same way as another divisive U.S. war. The Vietnam conflict in fact resulted in a kind of polarization similar to that present in the Civil War, even if on a lesser scale. For many years, an important line in American politics divided those who supported the war from those who had not, as well as those who had fought in other wars from those who refused to fight in this one. At least as long as the "boomer" generation (those born from about 1946 to 1955) remains active in American political life, this line will continue to be important.

Despite the obvious involvement of Mars lines in U.S. military engagements, perhaps the most dramatic line on the map does not involve Mars, but is instead the Pluto Midheaven line which goes right through Hiroshima. Hiroshima is at a longitude of 132E27 and the national Pluto is at 133E31—less than a degree of orb. Thus at the time when the Second Continental Congress signed its 1775 Declaration, the planet of force majeure was on the Midheaven at a place where it would become activated 170 years later.[3]

Of course it was only discovered in 1930, which may, according to one astrological school of thought, mean that the consciousness of those things Pluto stands for only came to public attention around that time. We can, in fact, date the change of the United States of America from what it was to what it has become as having begun in about 1930, in the depths of the Great Depression, and the basic symbol of that change was the atomic bombing of Hiroshima. When the atomic bomb was dropped on that city in August 1945, the innocence that had been part of the national myth was gone, and there is still argument among historians about how necessary the act was in order to end the war. Before that the United States could say that it had been on the "right" side, and though it certainly was in the war itself, the question of whether it went too far in demonstrating its might will probably not be answered even by future generations.

This Pluto line is, of course, all the more interesting because, as we pointed out in the previous chapter, the man who ordered the dropping of the bombs on Hiroshima and Nagasaki, Harry S. Truman, had Pluto and Saturn rising for those locations at the time of his birth, with progressions and transits etching that symbolism sharply into the scarred ground around the two cities. Thus the coming into being of consciousness through Pluto is symbolized by the U.S. chart and by Harry Truman's chart. When Pluto came to call, the United States of America matured as a nation with the realization that it could indeed do harm. It is interesting also to note that in 1968 the progressed Sun of the natal U.S. horoscope, which began its journey in the 10th house, had progressed to a conjunction with natal Pluto, down in the 4th. This was in the middle of a period that showed great evidence of national disillusion, with anti-war riots and the growth of a so-called counterculture.

This movement was perhaps in part a reaction to the Pluto factor. Both authors grew up in the America of the 1950s, which, for all the bucolic splendor bestowed upon it by those nostalgic for the quiet days of the Eisenhower Presidency, held a quiet terror for the American school child, who was made highly aware, almost on a daily basis, of what to do in case of nuclear attack. It is hardly surprising that the generation which learned that they would have to crawl under their school desks, or jump into a handy ditch (and at all costs not look at the flash) as Soviet missiles destroyed their home towns might tend to have a fixation on this issue, a fixation would could emerge as political activity at the time when the U.S. Pluto was activated. Even with the end of the Cold War, the threat of nuclear weaponry continues as a rather formidable reality in our present world, and as a very basic reality in the national consciousness of both the United States and Japan.

Those who might be inclined to challenge the reality of this interpretation of Pluto in the Boyd chart as both horoscope and ACG map should consider the following interesting fact, which mirrors what we saw in President Truman's chart: If you progress the Mars Midheaven line, which was over Berlin in the natal ACG map, it will move eastward across the map at a rate of approximately three-quarters of a degree a year, touching points east of Berlin as it goes. In 1945, at the time of the bombing of Hiroshima, this progressed Mars was in fact right over the Midheaven in Hiroshima and was therefore within orb of conjunction with the Pluto line. If "right over" sounds a bit much, consider the following. Mars had progressed to a longitude of 132E31, keeping in mind that Hiroshima is at 132E27—four seconds of arc difference. And the national Pluto is 133E31, less than a degree away from both of those. Certainly there is a significance there for those who will see, and Figure 17 illustrates it clearly.

In line with this, consider that a conjunction of transiting Saturn and Neptune was close to the Moon of the Boyd chart during much of the McCarthy era, with all its anti-Communist hysteria. Note that the U.S. Moon

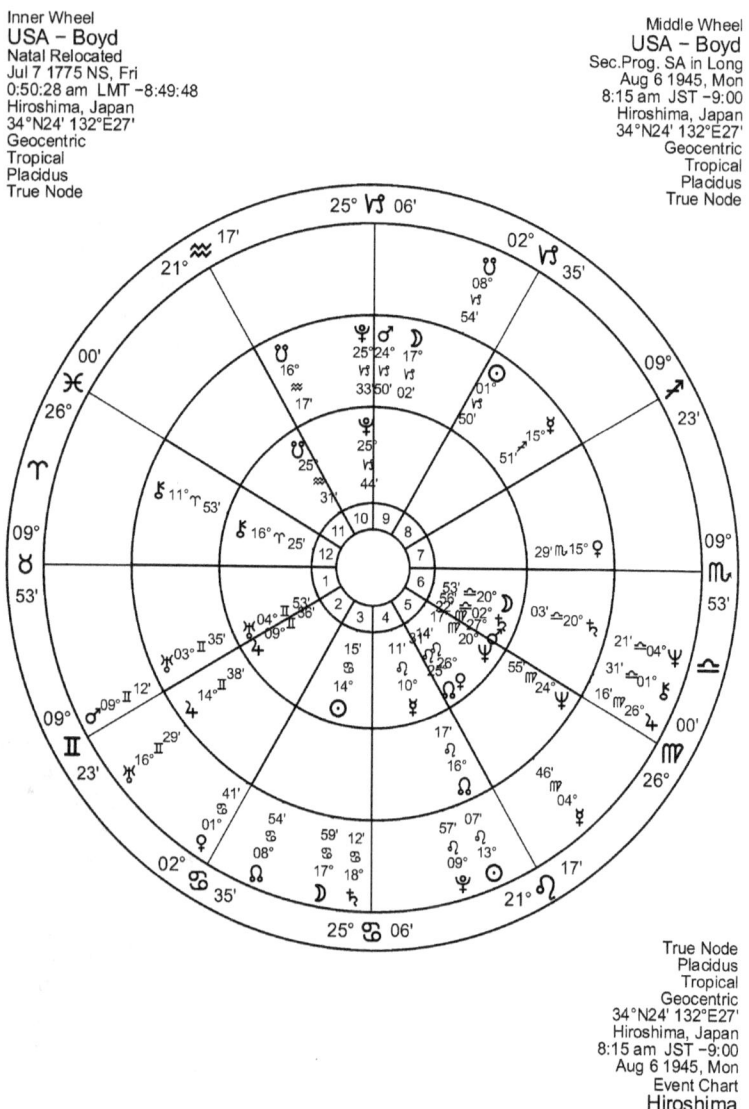

Figure 17 - The Boyd Chart: Mise-en-scène for a Martian Progression

for the Boyd chart is on the Midheaven at Moscow in the ACG map, locating very well the source and object of the national paranoia that tainted the times overseen by the Saturn and Neptune transit: the Russians. The Moon, of course, represents the way in which one is sensitized to incoming information, one's feelings, uncertainties, and unconscious mind. It is almost as if the Soviet Communist government of Russia became sort of a shadow image of the United States itself, a bogeyman to a degree that was almost unbelievable and incomprehensible outside of the United States, just as a negative lunar image often becomes for an individual under the stress of transits.

These are only a few examples of the way in which this chart seems to reflect the national psyche of the United States, but they serve to make the point that Boyd's proposed time at the very least deserves closer consideration. In a larger sense, both this chart and the fascinating connections between the charts of U.S. presidents and the geographical areas in which their aggressive urges merge with the needs of the nation they serve make a point that parallels the one made by Astro*Carto*Graphy itself. In the case of Astro*Carto*Graphy, we see that the scope of astrology extends well beyond the place of birth, just as surely as it extends beyond the time of birth through progressions and transits. The idea was already inherent in the older idea of the locality chart, but it has been made much clearer through the mapping of key elements of the individual horoscope across the world through the development of Astro*Carto*Graphy.

In a similar way, while mundane astrology has always held that nations acted and interacted, in a sense, just like individuals, this has not always been easy to see from inside the land-locked traditional birth chart. A nation is a citizen of the world, so the reach of even the smallest country extends far beyond its borders. Thus it makes good sense to consider a national chart as it applies to the world as a whole, alongside the more traditional modes of analysis based on a chart set for a national capital or other crucial location. So whether we are dealing with nations, or presidents, or individuals such as those we interact with every day, we now know that all are citizens of the world and not just prisoners of the birth place. This brings us to what one might call the admonition of Astro*Carto*Graphy itself (with apologies to Robert Browning and Andrea del Sarto):

A horoscope's reach should exceed the birthplace's grasp,
Or what are the heavens for?

PART TWO

Your Planets and Their Lines: Natal Astro*Carto*Graphy

Introduction

Zen and the Art of (Not) Cookbooking

Each year a high-school chemistry teacher of our acquaintance goes through a ritual, a rite of passage for his young pupils meant to teach them that knowledge without understanding is folly—and can at times be downright dangerous. His class is taught in an old-fashioned laboratory room with big slab tables replete with plumbing for Bunsen burners and locked drawers full of all kinds of toxic chemicals. Lab day is once a week, and when it comes around, he begins the lab session by admonishing his students, "Don't cookbook it!" The meaning is simple: read about the experiment in the laboratory manual before you do it, rather than consulting the book as you complete each step.

For most of the year, his warning makes little difference, but when springtime rolls around, a particular experiment is called for that illustrates the truth of what he has been telling the students all along. "Don't cookbook," he says once more, but this time emphasizes firmly that anyone who does so will end up at one point with a test tube full of chemicals-with a rubber stopper in it—clamped firmly over a Bunsen burner on a high flame. The stopper is necessary in order to keep the chemicals from spilling before you place them over the flame, but it should be removed before the heating process starts—as the lab manual nicely informs you overleaf from the instructions to get the burner going. "Anyone who cookbooks this experiment," he says, "is going to blow up that test tube. As many times as I've had classes do this, it never fails. Twenty minutes into the experiment, bam-bam-bam, test tubes start going all over the room!" And sure enough they do in each class where he tells that story each spring.

And what, the reader might ask, has this to do with Astro*Carto*Graphy? Nothing as such, except for the admonition not to cookbook the section that follows, which is a series of essays by Jim Lewis about the fundamental psychological natures of the planets. Surely enough this information is intended to be applied, as it can be with either an ACG map or a simple relocated horoscope. But before applying it, you must understand it, which means this should be read only after you've gone through the book as a whole in order to understand the context in which the things that follow are said. Having done that, you'll be able to go with the flow of these planetary pieces, rather than simply following them from page to page.

Bon appetit!

8

The Sun: Can Anyone Really be a Star?

OBVIOUSLY, the "star-consciousness" engendered by a strong Sun does not work well for everyone, so if you are a person who is normally shy, retiring, and likes the background, this area may present its potentials to you in the form of inner struggles around love and self-image or in the unpleasant form of domineering and egocentric individuals. Though Aquarius, Pisces, and Virgo types may have more problems here than other people, anyone has the energy to grow and develop the charisma and leadership that lies within, even when this must be done in a public context of some sort.

For Women Only: Since women are not always comfortable assuming authority and power, and in fact may even be discouraged from doing so, Sun zones like this one can seem problematical at the beginning for you, unless you are already very self-assured. A tendency to attract domineering men to you can give way to the discovery of power within yourself, even though you may resist this at first. Events essentially outside your control can force you to accept leadership, and even though at first you may find this unpleasant, you can grow to like the role of "star" as you get used to the perks and rewards. While a more passive and dramatic role, that of "damsel in distress," can attract many gallant knights to your side, they are likely to find themselves unsatisfied the closer they come to the real you, at which point they will gallop off into the sunset, leaving you to cope with the problem of calling forth your own inner heroism—the real challenge of a Sun line.

For Men Only: As a man, you can find this zone particularly congenial, since you are inclined to model your identity after your father, to take control, and to exhibit masculine authoritative power. However, you need to beware of being overbearing and egotistical, of treating women as inferiors and displaying pomposity and arrogance, while at the same suppressing even the positive manifestations of your own feminine side. Despite these rough edges, which must be tended to if there is to be a balance, this is a positive zone for most men, who can find themselves reaching powerful positions and generally enjoying great success here. The young may find romantic appetites extremely demanding here, something which can be taken as evidence of the need to come to terms with the feminine, since the intensity of such needs points to the suppression of this side of your psyche.

THE SUN: CAN ANYONE REALLY BE A STAR?

If You're Just Passing Through...

During a short stay in any zone where you have a Sun line, expect lots of fun and an increase in your appetites, along with many opportunities to indulge yourself in games, amusements, and glamour. Anyone traveling with you may find you a little overbearing, and your budget probably will go right out the window. Just as quickly as your self-image improves, you will find yourself demanding more expensive and exotic clothes, surroundings, and people. Since you and everyone else will tend to think of you as a little more important and powerful than usual, you're either likely to be treated like a celebrity or to find yourself surrounded by them. For this reason this is an excellent zone in which to develop talents, particularly artistic ones. A great place for a vacation, but bring lots and lots of money.

Long-Distance Lines

Even if you don't travel or reside under your Sun line, since this part of the world is inevitably associated with your quest for selfhood, you may relate to mythological or cultural images from this locale in a highly personal manner. Moreover, people or other concerns connected to this place can have transformative importance for your self-image and concept of identity.

Psychological Interpretation of the Sun:
The Celebrity, You

This is your "celebrity" zone, where you can come to express the Midas touch of the Sun. A masculine, egoic consciousness prevails within you here, as the universe seems malleable, laid out before you as if to be acted on by your energy and will. The power of your logic, the strength of your inner motivation, and your ability to bring order to chaos are all expanded. Along with this comes a dynamic and vigorous drive toward self-actualization, as your life processes become more directed, creating an identity that is acutely aware of its own selfhood. This newly-revealed identity is an autonomous, outer-directed, and often extroverted "I am" that sees its own existence and function as the center of the universe. Your direction is molded mostly by inner processes and is less affected by environment and social pressure, so you seem more free from both past and future, existing uniquely and in a high state of self-awareness in the here and now. You expect others to pay attention to you at this location, and indeed they do, to the point that you might find yourself followed about like an important personage, treated to others' generosity as they identify strongly with your creations—even including your children. This is the best locale in which to sell or exhibit creative works—writers easily find a publisher here, and even those with more obscure creative seeds to plant can find them in full flower. If other planets' influences are coupled with the Sun, you could become an extremely powerful, famous (or infamous) symbol of the affairs governed by those other planets, so try to understand carefully just exactly what they mean. By itself, the Sun often demands that you follow a glittering, domineering, and sometimes overbearing style of life. Pride, glamour, and an appetite for the roar of the crowd often conceal an inner incompleteness and self-rejection that demands others' approval as compensation.

Stages and Myth of the Sun:
Heroes Tall and Small

In the early stages of manifesting the energy of your Sun line, you may exhibit the boasting, arrogant self-importance, and prideful ostentation of the vain narcissist, or you may attract to yourself (or even follow) others who have these traits. A solar zone focuses consciousness on a battle with basic feelings of inferiority, so if you have never yet seen yourself in a "heroic" role, then here you may go through a deep, inner preparatory struggle first, one in which you will painfully reject a childish, dependent, immature identity. A later stage of awareness of this planet's power (usually after the age of thirty) focuses on the Quest, or inner, mythic journey. This journey is at best the genuine quest to perform a deed or understand a personal mystery, the accomplishment of which will define an unchangeable foundation of selfhood and power. Pride is the catalyst of this change, so some of the confrontations engendered by youthful overpridefulness of the Sun and a tendency to adopt pompous, officious roles meant to mask a wounded immaturity, later form a strong foundation for a mature inner dignity that grants you the capacity to control your moods and feelings. In earlier stages, you may feel that fixing the kitchen faucet is a feat for which you deserve a Presidential Commendation, but this imperial myopia soon encounters reactions that broaden it to a universal appreciation of your own and others' deepest, immutable power and dignity. In maturity, the solar consciousness exhibits a glowing, fatherly leadership, a creative, self-fulfilled guiding light and energizing influence to all whom you affect, and you will very likely affect many at this location. You speak with authority, and humor at this place, as you develop self-assurance, loyalty, intelligence—and even, perhaps, find fame.

The Practical Side of the Sun:
If You're in Charge, They Can't Order You Around

On a practical level, this zone is one in which men often become fathers and where they find success as a self-made hero (through fighting city hall, for example), as an artist, or as a producer. Though plenty of love comes your way, you may simply take it as your due, and thus not return it in equal measure. You certainly can make things happen here, as you find yourself ready to manipulate the local environment, both material and spiritual, in order to succeed, especially in any business that demands presence, a public image, and powerful dignity. Authority is a key concept for you to understand and work with here, since not doing so invites the danger of insensitivity to others and overwork for yourself, especially if you have not yet wholly integrated your mature identity. If you find yourself fascinated by movie stars, royalty, or powerful leaders, this shows you have not yet accepted your own "Sun" potential; in this case, a Sun zone may hold some critical and bittersweet lessons for you. Pay particular attention to your thoughts about and concerns with parents and authority, and be aware that disappointments in love and leadership concerns point the way to a truer sense of your own selfhood. Music and art may be important themes here, especially if Libra is strong in your horoscope, while a priestly role in religion may dominate if Cancer, Sagittarius, or Pisces is powerful. This is a good area for health, as you can find rehabilitation from old health problems and a vibrant vitality that prevents new ones from happening. Awards, titles, and degrees are likely to be bestowed upon you, as everyone seems to be aware that you are "somebody." At the same time, but only if you give some attention to this side of yourself, inner spiritual experiences can advance a deep sense of personal integration and identity. Gambling, games, and amusements take on new importance, perhaps even professionally, so it would serve you well to be very aware of your personal chart potentials in this regard—you can win big, but you can lose big as well.

Sun on Ascendant:
If You're Not at Center Stage, Will Anyone See You?

This could easily be a "hot" location for you, as the general matters usually associated with the Sun specifically act themselves out through your personality and through the direct effect you have on other people. You are basically attempting to discover who you are here, but you are inclined to define your self image mainly by contrasting it to those around you, a tendency that may compel you to adopt, try out, and then discard numerous insubstantial identities, each of which exists only in relation to particular people. This is not likely to be apparent to many around you, however, as you tend to project pride, dignity, vanity, and even a bit of arrogance, attracting followers and hangers-on with your zestful personality and irresistible charisma. Your relationship with your father may lie deep beneath this personal quest for identity, as you consciously or otherwise seek to imitate the power that he exercised over you in your relationships with others. Work succeeds in areas that attract others' attention: artwork, theater, performance, or as a guide to personal transformation in the lives of others.

You may be assigned the role of "guru" by admiring friends, due to the leadership, audacity, courage, and nobility of character you manifest here as you seek to become what everyone admires and desires above all else. A profession that puts you before the public is thus likely to attract your attention, as you feel quite self-confident, impulsive and extroverted, seeing yourself as an energetic achiever. Children (of all ages) find you irresistible, and you do everything you can to encourage their unqualified admiration as one of assuring that you have a following of some sort. You like to see yourself as "special" in this locality, and several grades better than the ordinary, so there is danger of affectation, theatricality, and vanity adding a slick veneer to your public persona that may put off those who would rather know something about the real you. In any event, since those around you give you complete permission to succeed, you are constantly subject to the dangers as well as the glories of leadership. If you pay too much attention to the glories and ignore the dangers, you could find that often, people who satisfy their unfulfilled identities in hero worship can later become the most unforgiving of persecutors when the hero fails to deliver all that was hoped for. Still, life can seem like a party with you as the guest of honor in this locale, and the "prima donna complex" that develops seems justified by your power, humor, poise, and joyful influence.

Sun on Midheaven:
Listening to Others Fuels Your Fires

In this location, the general effects and concerns of the Sun specifically act themselves out in career ambitions and in the social arena. The growth, change, and redirection of your inner processes are apt to be motivated by how you feel others see you in work and social spheres, and by how they react to your emerging sense of public dignity and charisma. You find yourself on an inner journey to prideful selfhood, urged on by an image of yourself as socially admired and appreciated, awarded, and praised in some enviable field. Because you expect to be looked up to by others, you are likely to be preferred in work situations, especially those involving promotion or public relations, and either the performing or creative arts; working in an obscure, "ordinary," or anonymous profession is not likely to be too appealing to you unless you can figure some way to be a "star" to those around you. What people think of you is overly important to you here, spurring you on to achieve higher social status; but while your sensitivity and pride motivate you to accomplishment, too much concern with appearances could interfere with joyful, spontaneous creativity, and self-expression. Striving is rewarded with at least the trappings of success, so that here more than anywhere else you are likely to find fame.

But the danger ever present under a Sun line of any kind is narcissism, which could lead you to surrender the true impulses of self-expression to empty acclaim and plastic celebrity status—the big frog in the small pond. An addiction to hollow applause could conceal a ragged self-image disguised in a splendiferous royal costume, as you try too hard to be all things to all people. Underlying self-actualization in this locale is your relationship with your father. This you must come to terms with, lest you become driven by fear that no one will want to care for or protect you in time of need and that everyone's regard for you is merely superficial. After donning various disguises and social roles, particularly in the early stages of living here, you can pursue a successful quest for complete self-discovery and mastery, and could even assume the role of guide and teacher-by-example to others seeking their own true identities through a deeper self-knowledge.

Sun on Descendant:
The Road to Yourself is Through Others

In a location at which the Sun sets (and thus would lie on the cusp of the 7th house in a traditional chart), its energies manifest through other people, and they will be most evident in your relationships and marriage. The Sun's lordly, domineering, and authoritative nature speaks through interactions on social and personal planes. When at their best in this location, your energy, self-acceptance, and inner integrity allow you to exert a guiding influence over others, and people may actually be attracted to you as a sort of guru. You exude an air of authority and purposefulness that when properly expressed can help others to sift through the complexities of their life concerns and set priorities. Should you resist accepting this leadership role, you may instead attract arrogant and controlling types, surrendering your own power and authority to them. If you are properly aware of your potential at this location, however, such "surrender" actually can represent an early, immature stage of coming to recognize and assert your own self-determination and charisma in a positive way. Relationships dominate here, as marriage, or in fact any connection with another person becomes a glittering arena for self-discovery, change, and maturation. With relationship and partnership concerns taking up so much of your time and energy, the battle for selfhood is largely fought in the context of other people.

Until you can learn to see and understand the dynamic inner reserves of your power, and incorporate these reserves into your conscious personality, you may feel a little out of control. Problems you experience with everyone from roommates to life mates often merely reflect your own inner situation, as you try just a little bit too hard to seem generous, outgoing, vain, and "on top of things" at times when you really are not. If you become involved in a marriage, you may enter into it with the thought that through it you can either stimulate your own inner creativity, or support the creative aspirations of your mate. Since you tend to project an air of nobility, honor, and leadership onto others, you will find yourself urging more than a few to take their first steps on the road to psychological maturity, giving you a kind of personal satisfaction that could border on the vicarious, as you take their triumphs for your own while downplaying their tragedies. Because of your inspirational gift, artistic people are likely to be attracted to you, something which should be taken as an opportunity, since their volatile personalities can help you to understand the processes of competition, sexuality, and relationship better than you might have before. If you happen to be involved in sales, the arts, medicine, or other alternative modes of healing, you will find this area enhances your abilities.

Sun on Imum Coeli:
Pride In Your Origins

With the Sun at its "midnight" position, its principles play themselves out on an inward level, allowing you to accept yourself and your power in the world with ease and grace. Gradually at first, perhaps almost invisibly, you experience a deep, inward renovation of soul and purpose. At the very base of your self-definition you can find an inner image of who you are that was derived from parents and from other influences in your early environment. It is this inner context—a matrix shaped from traditions, family, ethnic identity, and regional loyalties—from which you see yourself operating. This personal sense of who you are can be restructured, renewed, and ultimately transcended altogether, in much the same way a child grows beyond his or her family to become a mature, self-defined individual. As you are doing this, you may find the need to build on your heritage, or to rediscover it, as an interest in genealogy, pride in family, and research into your personal past become allegories for a profound quest to understand yourself at the most basic inner level.

This zone is excellent if you are either seeking retirement from the workaday world or founding a family, as you naturally take to the duties of running a household. A profound sense of personal responsibility to family, and to tradition evolves within you, as a protective fondness for the roots from which you came strengthens your own identity. Family strife tends to disappear here, or to at least be greatly alleviated, especially if others can acknowledge your talent for leadership, and your creativity in solving problems brings security for yourself and for those you love. Property acquired here can easily increase in value, or at least prestige, so this can be a superb location in which to build your dream home. In fact, any construction you undertake would have an inner meaning that would manifest itself in the outer world, making it doubly satisfying to you and your family. Finally, this is also a good place for self-rehabilitation in the health of body, mind, and spirit, and it is a prime area for the ailing to take on the task of energizing themselves in their battle for wholeness and wellness. Vitality is enhanced at its deepest levels, and thus can lead eventually to providing you with the energy and drive to become a pillar of the community.

Sun with Moon:
Parental Issues Inspire Self-Discovery

The joining of the two most potent indicators of the masculine and feminine elements of a person's nature pinpoints an area of the world in which the concepts of male and female are related, and one where your sexual or social identity itself may reach some sort of crossroads. Men may for the first time find themselves getting in touch with the full power of their nurturing instincts as they feel a "mothering," gentle, and supporting personality flowering within them; women may find opportunities to act on long-held dreams and career desires, especially if these involve demonstrating individuality in the public arena. Either sex may become parents here, and in any case you will become aware of the interaction of your family "karma" or inheritance as it alternately conflicts with and then supports your ego and its needs. Shallow egocentricity could result from this, or perhaps an impulse to rebel against authority that masks overcompensation for feelings of inadequacy while at the same time expressing resentment that the only approved behavior is one that allows little latitude for individuality.

Sexual and personal polarities are intensified, making it hard to relate to the opposite sex except by plodding along in the rut of conventional, marital gender cliches, particularly those patterned after one's parents. The need for approval by others (parents included) becomes very powerful in this locality, and while you seem to be able to attract situations that feed this need, still you feel as if you are not as much in control of them as you would like to be. You may become acutely aware here of a social role that seems to have been ordained for you, though you will probably resent its inevitability, feeling (correctly) that it ignores and suppresses your individuality. This is not an area in which you can grapple with truly cosmic issues, as your life concerns seem very ordinary—at times to the point of boredom—due to their involvement with conventional values and what others think. The best opportunity you can find in being here is to discover how you can integrate selfhood and social position. Until that is done, however, you may attract, seek, or act out dependent roles or perhaps engage in shallow authoritarianism. The biggest challenge you face here is that such negative tendencies are likely to be supported wholeheartedly by your social milieu, which doesn't want to deal with real issues any more than you do.

Sun with Mercury:
I Think, Therefore I'm Here

This influence seems to suggest success in smaller things: you will find that your will, creativity, and leadership find easy self-expression in education, work, and neighborhood concerns, particularly if this is the only influence affecting this locality. Unlike some other Sun lines, here you are likely to be unpretentious for the most part, and able to succeed at things that are useful, rather than those with a lot of snob appeal. Aptitude, talents, and skills can be developed to a high degree here, as will directs self in a way that encourages the development of control over technique. Because of this, habits are formed that could lead to real accomplishment, and thus your work is apt to be praised for its effectiveness. Vocational, writing, conversation, and community concerns receive much attention as you find many new opportunities for their expression, so that recognition comes to you for innovations relating to any form of journalism, writing, or media work. Practical, adult-level thought predominates, of the directed sort that also contributes to learning and using science and math. If this influence is the only one operating, it suggests that life can easily become rather theoretical and abstract, and that underlying all your practicality and technical ability may be an immature "eternal youth" syndrome that leaves you content to deal with the real world vicariously, as you engage your intellect through artistic and bookish pursuits.

Others see you as bright and flexible, with a youthful outlook that makes you a rising contributor to society. Your Sun sign is very important at this locale, and you may be able to find a profession or undergo education that enables you to express its best occupational potentials. The key to utilizing this energy is the application of the inner self to some practical and creative business. From ideas and training that are undertaken here, you may find your life's calling, or at least some new and rewarding work, including a high possibility of self-employment. Unless other factors intrude, this is not an area where you will have to deal with big issues, but your success is highly likely in day-to-day concerns, as your will gradually creates the situation you desire in practical terms. Roles as liaison, agent, facilitator, and community organizer are suggested.

Sun with Venus:
Your Inner Cinderella

Here you project peace, harmony, and love to those around you, making you a stabilizing influence in your milieu, something that makes you very attractive to others. You become very sensitive to art and fashion, and may succeed in some creative vocation, if your talents permit. On an inner level, these planets suggest the balancing and harmonizing of ego and will, a process which serves to symbolize, for those around you, hope for unity and peace, and for improvement of life for future generations. The Sun and Venus together symbolize a "royal wedding," and while you probably will not marry into an aristocratic family (there are, after all, only so many to go around!), in this locale you are apt to be in love with love, craving friendship and status in high society, which you demonstrate daily with a demeanor that is cheerful, considerate, fashionably mannerly, and even vain. As you project elegance and nobility, you could earn rewards and recognition for your taste and refinement, especially in creative activities. People seem inclined to give you things, to invite you out, and otherwise to encourage you socially in various ways.

If you have no influences here from the "heavier" outer planets, the problems you experience may revolve around an unfortunate tendency toward shallowness and vapidity—you are likely to be sought after and admired like a '30's chorus girl—a sex object desired for your beauty, rather than for your personality or humanity. While marrying "well" is a distinct possibility here, you should question whether that really is all you want out of life. Love affairs in this locality seem to make you feel better about yourself, as you find yourself acting out the role of Cinderella or Prince Charming over and over again. You may have also an inclination toward consumerism and acquisitiveness, which can make you at least mildly obsessed with money and goods. Perhaps the best way to avoid the pitfalls of this almost too pleasant and harmonious area is through working in the arts. Success here does not stem from your being a totally exceptional and gifted human being, so much as it comes from the outer trappings which lead others to think this is what you are. See yourself as interpreter, rather than originator, of the beauty that others constantly remind you that you can project.

Sun with Mars:
It's Tough to be a Hero

In this locality, the "macho" expression of a somewhat masculine self-image becomes a matter of personal pride. Your presence is seen as an exaggerated materialization of all things usually identified with the masculine: combativeness, sexuality, derring-do, and boisterous and courageous vitality. Excesses of energy and sexuality can burn you out here, as you tend toward hyperactivity in all things. Though appearing to others as volatile and erratic, you still appear to get a tremendous amount of work done. You admire and project the essence of masculinity, including an arrogant pride in your battle scars. Others are likely to look upon you with some awe and not a little fear, as you can be quick to anger, ruthless, harsh and, in extreme cases, driven by the narrow view that everyone around you is either a competitor or an enemy.

The problem with this location is that society works to suppress the unmitigated projection of such raw energy, except in a few circumscribed areas: the military, athletics, and in masculine-identified professions. So while these may go well in this locale, you are apt to experience constant friction with authority over what you see as your territorial rights, or insults to your pride and honor. With your myopically personal view of things, you easily attract attacks from others, and are liable to develop (you may have to) a Spartan love of adventure, physical work, sex, and contest. Anger and vindictiveness are the main feelings of which you are more or less constantly aware, as other, softer emotions are likely to be suppressed. In general, you tend to exclude nurturing and supportive feelings, whether your own or others, from your life. The constant stress and tension you impose on yourself can wear down your health, however, and a tendency toward accident-proneness may complicate the picture. Your manners are likely to become more coarse here, and though your sexual passions intensify, they do so at the expense of love and affection, and they are instead rigidly governed by narrow sexual roles and stereotypes. At the extremes, you may find yourself prone to seek the destruction of anything you cannot master, though this particular Sun-Mars problem can be diminished if it is given expression in arduous work or athletic competition.

Sun with Jupiter:
Preponderance of the Great

In this locality, your tendency toward cheerful, outgoing self-promotion finds few barriers to its appetite for expansion in society, empowering you to seek, prize, and probably attain a kind of bourgeois success and prosperity, provided that you unquestioningly accept whatever the powers-that-be deem to be correct behavior. Underlying your benevolent disposition is a belief that the status quo is basically justified, and this faith, self-confidence, and belief in the rightness of things as they are rewarded by privilege, tangible success, honors, advancement, and preferment. In keeping with this view that the place you find yourself in is the best of all possible worlds, you may tend more to the right politically, to the conservative where religion is concerned, and may find yourself admiring, in some area of your life, a vested authority which you see as there almost by Divine Right. You may find yourself in an admired position supported by academic, religious, or corporate privilege, but even if not, faith in yourself and the equity of the universe makes you an excellent salesperson, promoter, businessperson, publisher, or entrepreneur. There will be times, however, when foolish optimism and naive imprudence cause reverses, and gambling, extravagance and speculations are definitely temptations to watch for. Sexual and creative appetites are given second place, as they are replaced by the drive for honor and approval by society, and a quest for the recognition that society bestows on those who contribute without disrupting.

If you are naturally an introverted type, you may take less enthusiastically to this climate of self-congratulatory promotion, and, perhaps feeling unequal to its demands may take refuge in overeating, other forms of indulgence, or complacency. Despite this, the near-miraculous luck and the status which seem to be your lot in life at this locality make it easy to give in to external social pressure. In this very fortunate place, opportunities offer themselves on a regular basis, and "quality" people make your advancement easier by their patronage. Careers in law, music, publishing, medicine, religion, politics, self-improvement, promotion, or any highly paid profession should succeed here relatively easily, as you become the admired pillar of your community and a self-identified force for social good. A strong flavor of internationalism and scholarship is also associated with Sun-Jupiter, so you could find yourself associating with a brilliant and cosmopolitan circle of friends and admirers who keep you informed of the latest intellectual fashions.

Sun with Saturn:
Executive Authority

This area is one in which conflicts and problems may come to the forefront, as Sun and Saturn essentially are opposites. These conflicts often are centered on society, so you may find yourself rebelling and struggling with authorities, but such rebellion actually reflects a deep inner process through which you begin to accept the limitations of selfhood. The relationship of child versus father is painfully evident here as the ego seeks to master controlled expression in an atmosphere of routine, repression, and discipline that may hark back to your actual relationship with your more restrictive parent. Yet learning your limits is an important part of growth to a mature and effective adulthood; the spirit thinks itself immortal until it discovers the price of its enchainment to the flesh, but this discovery compels it to strive for self-discipline and self-control by efficiently channeling and conserving its energy.

You project a serious, powerful image here, one full of self-restraint and a sense of autonomy, as you take sole responsibility for your own personal and emotional support. You could develop a Saturnian fear that you must work ceaselessly for your own preservation, something which tends to make life into a job that while tedious merits close and careful attention. Fear of love, guilt about unexpressed thoughts and feelings, and even prudery well up within you here, and the skeptical, abstemious life you lead lowers your expectations and arms you inwardly to endure hardships, which, surely enough, come. You feel the need to live a well-ordered, moral life, replete with patience and prudence and other Victorian virtues, as you resist any outward change. It is difficult to make a favorable impression on others in most respects here, except for the benefits that come from your dependability and tolerance of adversity; love, spontaneity, and most affectionate, creative qualities recede well into the background. A general sense of being ill at ease within yourself may incline you toward self-denial, religious practices that promise to expiate guilt, or a Utopian idealism that secretly seems to weigh against your need for isolation and alienation. Drawn to serious ideas and studies, you forfeit others' admiration in order to deal with the business and material concerns constantly impinging on your awareness. Hard work takes up much of your time, yet yields its rewards grudgingly, and you may find yourself veering from the extremes of poverty and, occasionally, affluence. You have a need to conserve life energy as much as possible, so longevity can be a benefit if you stay here for any length of time, though at the same time your health rarely will be really robust.

Sun with Uranus:
Idealists Know Best–Just Ask One

Those dull, lackluster moments of boredom we all encounter in life are likely to be quite rare for you in this location, as change, creativity, and individualism cause everything you experience to take on intense color, and provide you with the breathtaking excitement of a roller-coaster. The fundamental principles you have a need to act out here are social idealism and ideological "purity," implicit in which there is usually a rejection of the material—a desire that ego and humanity exist in a world of unadulterated ideal and rational, light-permeated understanding. Though you may take on the role of the opinionated radical, pitting yourself against mainstream society in some just though unpopular cause, if you look beneath the surface you may find that such principled rebellion is actually motivated by a thinly disguised disgust for the material. In line with this, you seem repelled by cloying emotional attachment, and feel contempt for the acquisitive, unconscious, irrational aspects of humanity, which you see as primitive, mindless, and frightening.

Impelled by these attitudes, you recruit and inspire others to organize under the banner of your ideals, and so may have a profound effect upon your milieu. Abstract ideas become closely involved with your identity, resulting in a divine discontent that spurs you to experiment with the impossible and to urge society itself to head in the same direction. Everyone will soon know who you are in this location, as you are likely to become a focus of controversy through your eccentric, charismatic, willful, arrogant, and independent behavior. Your ideas (and the trouble they get you into) serve to brilliantly illustrate your own genius and individuality. Aspire to leadership of a purposefully Utopian, ideologically based movement if you must, but keep your sense of humor about it all— giggle, don't scowl, at the emperor's new clothes.

Constancy is elusive, however, and rapidly fluctuating events demand from you a recognition that selfhood is a process rather than a definable entity. You tend to take yourself a bit too seriously, rejecting attachments in an autocratic, impulsive, and rather inconsiderate fashion. However, some attention given to timing will enable you to enjoy a miraculous existence, complete with rewards that you probably don't much want or even care about. Words such as "hippie" and "Bohemian" were coined to categorize the type of personality you embody here, and in playing the part you cast your successes away after brief enjoyment, fearing the attachments they can bring. The establishment knows there is something dangerous about you, but you change too quickly for them to do much about it.

Sun with Neptune:
The Perils of Creative Martyrdom

Though you may seem a little mad to some, and perhaps tend to be ignored because of it, you go right on living out your life in accordance with the principles, rhythms, and inspirations no one but you seems able to perceive in this potent location. Your quest for selfhood is gained (ironically) through total surrender of the ego, though there are stages on the way to your goal that can get you off track if you fall prey to self-deception, illusions, and disappointment. Those who are artists, musicians, poets, or who tend toward the religious and romantic may find this climate intensely inspirational, especially if they can find some external source to provide the illuminations they are prone to receive here. Others may make their lives rewarding by working in institutions, serving society's dispossessed. But the less mature turn to escapism, allowing an overly potent imagination to lead them into perilous realms of cultism, unrealistic spirituality, initiative-defeating communal situations, drug dependencies, and lifestyles that sap creativity and health. This can be a place of illuminated imagination where a spiritual path is found, and where life-altering vision and enlightenment elevate you to extraordinary awareness. However, an inevitable attachment to ego can easily bring you down to unwelcome reality, complete with disgrace and disillusionment, exploitation, and compromise. At that point, true awareness begins, and unselfishness begins to flower from the depths of your illusions.

Ego is weak here, and your personal relationships will tend to have an element of victimization and mutual dependency, as you believe you can reform others through caring and self-sacrifice—though this is true only if you can avoid false humility and delusions of grandeur. You are possessed of true psychic ability here, though it may be difficult to govern. Intuition sustains success in business in some cases, tuning you in to what the public wants next, but success has its own problems, as it stimulates a messianic impulse that inspires you to fictionalize yourself as a savior, only to find that the world is quite consistent in its treatment of "Imitators of Christ." Like the martyr, you may find your true self at the moment of betrayal, when you have lost all faith and hope. Most positively, you can emerge with a knowledge of survival through loss of self and can be a guide and a lighthouse for others, lost in the seas of self-surrender. This may be best done in absentia, however, possibly through art, writing, or distant but inspiring example.

Sun with Pluto:
The Midwife of Change

Here you alone may challenge and pit yourself against the values and institutions of society, motivated by an unconscious inner realization of what will result: society will strike back, often cruelly and unfairly, and thus define for you a lifelong role of rebel and malcontent, as it furnishes you with the proven inner endurance and strength to effectively embody that role. Society, committed to "material security," has a hard time recognizing its own need for intense evolution and change, so people such as yourself are unfairly chosen to act out the suppressed urges of the group as a whole and to be scapegoats when they cause disruption for doing this. In this location, people tend to feel threatened by you, as your intensity and solitude represent the process of change and evolution that leads to death, a subject most would rather avoid. At best, you can help people through crises and be a conscious "midwife of change," emerging as a symbol of evolution and rebellion in its positive manifestation—but this happens only after you have learned a lot about yourself and stopped blaming others for the universal changes that involve you here. Until then, you may have to deal continually with people who seem manipulative, ruthless, power crazed, possessive, envious, and spiteful; betrayal and unfair domination are themes that all too often occur in relationships.

You could here exemplify the lonely genius, creating wonders which others will not appreciate for decades. You may identify with the catabolic element in humanity, and extreme individualism may result in petty criminality, defiance of authority, passion, and an overwhelming need for recognition that often takes the form of intense sexual needs. Inwardly, you can experience a total conversion of self, a new beginning, a transcendence of the needs for relationship and material attachment. Your pride can make you indomitable, aloof, rebellious, and antagonistic. Life at times seems cruelly fateful and ready to take away whatever you have gained, until your very self is seen as the only permanence. The usual vanity that enables one to ignore mortality is shorn away here, so you are intense, serious, and your life is one of inner crises and lonely struggles against absolutes. A creative self can be born from the ashes of the old personality.

9

The Moon: Why Is Everyone So Emotional?

THIS LOCATION can be especially critical for men, those who have a strong dose of masculine identity, or the self-consciously "superior." People who cannot get in touch with their feelings will project them onto others and thus find themselves embroiled in a constant struggle over emotion and possessiveness. If you see yourself as independent, spiritual, and generally superior to the flesh and its temptations, then this zone will pose real problems for you, although you may insist these are the result of other people's failure to rise above their own pettiness.

For Women Only: As a woman, you will find this zone easier for you than many others. Most women have been trained to take care of self and others emotionally, and here such skills are put to the test, quite possibly through motherhood. A nurturing role in society awaits you, and weaker, dependent people, children, and the walking wounded from life's wars will flock to your calm, nurturing presence. Still, you feel needs powerfully, and relationships are likely to be very intense, volatile, and ever-changing. You are truly progressing when you realize that you don't need to care for weak, dependent people in order to feel useful and valuable.

For Men Only: As a man, you will find this area particularly challenging. You can easily become stuck at the earliest stages of Moon awareness noted above, with Woman (or a thinly disguised symbol thereof) constituting the "reigning need" without which you feel you cannot exist. Goaded by desire, you will seek to attach yourself, often to whomever or whatever first makes itself available, in an effort to regain or maintain your autonomy and independence. Since society encourages men to ignore their feelings, if you have bought into this, your journey of self-discovery in this locale will be a lonely one; but the intensity and insatiability of your desire eventually will force you to seek fulfillment within yourself, most likely through parenting.

If You're Just Passing Through...

A short stay in this zone will immerse you in human interest concerns, day-to-day dramas, and emotional storms. Because your appetites (all of them) are intensified, their gratification is all the more rewarding—and the body and its pleasures take on new meaning for you in particular, and gourmets of all kinds will find opportunities for indulgence. You will want to care for or be taken care of by others, so nurturing women (especially mothers), family, and domestic concerns dominate. It's hard to pass through this zone without getting embroiled with other people in unusual ways, but you feel closer to your humanity, humbled and ennobled by the struggles you end up sharing with others.

Long-Distance Lines

Even if you can't travel to the areas where your Moon is strong, you will find yourself better able to care for your own needs as a result of interactions with people from here, so that you may find a sense of family associated with this part of the world, not to mention being attracted to religious doctrines that are strong here. Pay attention to information and travelers emanating from these world zones, as they bear messages telling you what you truly need in order to feel secure and safe in this world. If you relate strongly to your ethnic or national background, Moon lines may well pass through that part of the world. Some maternal figure (probably a relative) who lives here may have exemplified an early ideal of the perfect, nurturing mother role in you, a role which you either attempt to live out yourself or to seek in someone else.

Psychological Interpretation of the Moon:
A World Line Named "Desire"

This is your most intense "feeling" zone, as living here puts you in touch with your deepest and most significant needs. You may view existence at this place as a constant struggle between a need to find the independence of pure, spiritual expression and a need to attach yourself more firmly to the physical world, with its attendant requirements of security, nurturing, supportive surroundings, and awareness and sensitivity to environmental influences. In this location, you become more attuned to the latter half of the equation, so that life is surrendered to sensation, feeling, vulnerability, needs, and attachment. The gratification of appetites becomes the central focus of your existence, as needs seem more intense than in other places, and the senses perceive everything more strongly than elsewhere. Because of this, your appetites guide your destiny, as you find you are drawn to people, seeking their approval in an effort to replace any pieces you sense are missing in your psyche. On a physical level, erotic urges can be insatiable, and even compulsive.

You have an almost naive emotional reaction to every event and affect, and immerse yourself completely in everyday reality—like a child watching a movie, you are hypnotized by the play of sensations and forms outside you. You become especially reactive to other people's awareness of you, unable to ignore their attention or interest, both craving the feeling such attention gives you and resenting your dependence upon it. Yet, just as no seed can grow apart from the earth, this entanglement in sensation inevitably fertilizes your spiritual potential; the incredible magnetism exerted by people, things, and situations acts to draw you to complete involvement outside yourself, leading you to engage in parenting, creativity, or other relatively other-oriented means of actualizing your possibilities. The tides of attraction are so strong here that you cannot remain aloof and thus may be pulled toward a fertile marriage with material reality. The myth that dominates a lunar line is that of the child who is the father (or mother) of the man (or woman), a union of opposites motivated by the mortality of the flesh to which spirit is wed and the untamable desire of the spirit to live beyond the durability of its bodily prison. And, just as the child is unaware of its identity as a child while it is directed entirely toward trying to become like its parent, at this location, what you want to be (or think you want to be) becomes the center of attraction, something quite different from the focus on what you really are (or think you really are) found under a Sun line.

Stages and Myth of the Moon:
Children Come in All Ages, Sizes, and Shapes

In the earliest stages of Moon consciousness, the child inside you dominates, as an acute awareness of personal incompleteness and a need to be cared for are fueled by the apprehension that you would perish if left alone. Hunger is the feeling of the unformed lunar consciousness, that aching void within which stems from the umbilicus, the place where mother was "taken" from us. In this almost primordial stage of Moon consciousness (often the only one that some people ever learn), appetites are so deep and unfulfilled that they almost threaten to devour their objects. This childlike dependency leads eventually to assuming the role of parent within oneself—from the vantage point of the child, one switches roles and begins to act as the parent, the nurturer, provider, and mother-to-the-world, as well as to seek a "parent" in the outer world. This can result in the kind of attachments one enjoys with close relatives, those that spring from an unconditional awareness that you and the other person are in life together, for better or worse. The development of this type of interdependency acknowledges that there are other entities in the world, and thus we begin to make some personal progress in emerging from ourselves. Finally, the Moon matures as the ultimate nurturing parent—the person who can by his or her mere presence make others feel secure, protected, loved unconditionally, and safe in a supportive and growth-sustaining world. Since all these aspects of Moon consciousness depend on interactions with others, it is in the area of human relationships that most of this awareness is acted out, and it is through such relationships that the different stages are first defined and then, eventually, assimilated. The tortured pangs of unfulfilled needs lead to the ability to fill those needs not only for oneself, but for others as well.

The Practical Side of the Moon:
The Tears and the Laughter

On a more practical level, this area is one in which you become very much involved in every thing and every person around you. Strong domestic, religious, devotional, nostalgic, and sentimental impulses that can lead to a xenophobic conservatism motivate you here. You are the center of attention for certain, but in a way that may make you feel self-conscious, exposed, and sympathetic to the point of exhaustion to the multicolored spectrum of emotions you perceive in others. Psychic abilities are highlighted, and you may be easily influenced, like a child who is unable to say "No." Because of your heightened emotional sensitivity, you seem to need love so intensely that you experience frequent crises relating to this area of your life. Romance here thus tends to become one-sided and impermanent, at least until you learn to nurture and care for yourself emotionally.

Your relationship with your mother comes to the fore at this location (though too often it is reenacted in marriage), and this makes you feel your instincts and desires all the more strongly. Perhaps because of this, you will tend to seek security more than you otherwise might, and may find yourself prone to tears and laughter at the slightest provocation. You also may find yourself playing the consumer under your Moon line, desperately trying to fill an empty void of incompleteness that you can't help feeling here. Since you react with a naive emotionality to every affect, you sense yourself as being much too close to every human situation in which you become involved, and may thereby develop an unpretentious mien as you take on varied characteristics adopted from many different people.

Life can seem much like a soap opera, due to the dominance of domestic concerns and the feeling of kinship and family with any and all humans you come in contact with. This is not an area to go to in order to feel superior, as you will find yourself much too aware of the needs that bind you and all people together to be able to place yourself above them. This can result in you gravitating toward a humble, working-class reality, with its variegated feelings and frequent domestic and human-interest crises. The Moon is the "infinite capacity for perception," and here, your feelings guide your destiny.

Fields in which others are cared for are likely to be the most interesting and productive occupations for you in this place: parenting, cooking and restaurant work, helping professions, counseling, or acting as an interpreter or agent. Success is also likely in gynecology, midwifery, nursing, baking, real estate, or sales and public concerns in general. Feelings are at the bottom of most of your health complaints, which frequently center in allergies, the gastrointestinal tract, breasts, and female organs.

If you find yourself attracted to and involved with take-charge maternal types, this may show that you have not accepted your own potential for nurturing, domesticity, or for caring for yourself and others. Work out life routines that enable you to experience and satisfy your emotional needs; working with others defines these needs and enables you to find in yourself a safe haven, and the capacity for self-sustenance.

Moon on Ascendant:
You Are What You Feel

Your self-image and your self-concept will be the focal point through which the general and particular characteristics of the Moon are most apt to manifest in this area, and the identification with your mother is strong, as is the urge to become a parent yourself. It is difficult not to yield to temptation, and since you are inclined toward being shy, retiring, vulnerable, sympathetic, and needful, you could end up molding your personality so as to please or impress others. This tendency to identify with either your own or others' needs (as your emotions tend to rule your intellect under a Moon line) means you are likely to become very easily entangled in everyone's affairs. Ideally, however, you will become the homebody, patterning your persona after the best and most positive manifestations of the nurturing mother image. You are deeply affected by events and conditions around you, and though this may make you seem timid on the surface, when operating from the depths of your feeling (which is much of the time), you can be surprisingly unrestrained, even powerful, and can express yourself with an intensity that surprises others.

Constantly swimming with the sensitive currents stirred by those around you and trying to become what you think others want you to be will only make you more painfully aware of their opinions and feelings about you. Adaptation is a key to emotional survival for you under this line, but at some point it must be adaptation to some inner standard of your own,. Successful self-definition for you under this Moon line is best arrived at through introspection, reflection, intuition, and sensitivity, while your tendency to attract and to nurture others by taking on their own emotional coloring can work either for or against you. Negative manifestations to watch for in this respect include weight gain, moodiness, instability, unreliability, and procrastination. This preoccupation with others' needs, and the problems it entails, can be used to justify a personal backlash of sorts, as you begin to restrict the dynamic personal potential you should be exploring, living a safe, conventional existence instead. The way out is the one most difficult under any Moon line, which is to take personal control of your life instead of just going with the flow around you.

Moon on Midheaven:
My Public Needs Me

Your strongest characteristic in this location is likely to be your emotional attachment to your status, as you seem to crave social acceptance, gearing everything you do toward the attainment of "success" of some kind, perhaps thereby attracting the attention of those of higher rank. All of this can affect your image in society, your career, and your relationship with the social milieu of which you are a part. A definite tilt toward your nurturing instincts reveals itself in your job, so that helping professions, a preoccupation with domestic concerns, and an attraction to public service (perhaps including populist-type politics) are all possibilities here, as is an interest in professions concerned with food service, real estate, and fields related to these. In line with this, you may find your relationship with your mother (or people like her) deepening. This urge to nurture and protect others is acted out in other ways, so that underdogs (whether two-legged or four-legged) may follow you about in needful confusion. Sensitively tuned to public opinion, you are propelled by a need for approval and acclaim that could well motivate a successful public career. Still, beneath your vulnerable, self-sacrificing public spiritedness, there is an underlying self-conscious need for attention, which surely enough comes— usually from an employer, the socially powerful, or the politically important. Relationship is both a key to success and the source of your greatest problems here, since while your influence with others can bring you the status you crave, your stability and emotional security also remain dependent upon others, and thus elusive.

Moon on Descendant:
Seeing Yourself in Others

This particular location is one in which you may see all the best and worst characteristics of the Moon exemplified in other people, and most especially in those in emotional partnership with you. They may seem so clinging, emotional, and sentimental, that you wonder what keeps drawing such people to you. Simply stated, the source of the problem is your reluctance to develop your own ability to care for yourself and others or even to acknowledge the existence or importance of such issues in your life. If you look beneath the surface and examine your innermost thoughts, you will probably find that you have an unconscious craving for relationship and reliance on others, particularly in order to obtain emotional support; this in turn serves to attract people of a like mind to you, producing a whole range of emotional involvements, tangled feelings, and labyrinthine relationships, all of which can make you feel out of control and pulled under by emotional whirlpools. You could find yourself talked about all the time, as others become entangled in affairs of yours they have no business in, especially marital and legal ones. Marriage is a distinct possibility here, but it is most likely to occur due to another's initiative. If you don't act to take charge of your own life and your own feelings, you may find the less favorable side of the Moon's "personality" dominating in this locale. The best way to direct this influence into positive channels is through conscious involvement in the helping professions. You probably will get your needs mixed up with others' anyway, so you might as well at least try to do it in a somewhat controlled setting. Life for you in general is likely to be unstable and perhaps a trifle Bohemian, but in time you learn to fend for yourself and to seek the advantages that your charisma and attractiveness promise.

Moon on Imum Coeli:
We're All in This Together

Your personal Moon here will show itself largely on an inner plane, as you react to circumstances and situations that require you to come to terms with your family and your ancestral background. For most people, family, race, ethnicity, or nationality are used to define self more or less automatically by furnishing a set of values and judgments that are never questioned. This, however, does not work for you in this location, as you find that you must come to terms with a personal instability and uncertainty about these things, arising from an adaptability and flexibility that allows you to tap into—or at least to understand—the family backgrounds of others. You feel a deep longing for "roots," one so deep that it may never be fulfilled, at least not from external sources. But if you look beyond narrow, personal self-definitions and try to see yourself as a citizen of a human tribe held together by its common needs, you will at least begin to feel this need can be fulfilled. More practically, as a result of this, family matters, property concerns, and homemaking may take up a good deal more of your time and energy than you are used to. Any comfortable feeling of belonging, however, is balanced by a constant fear of loss of security; moves are almost constant, as you search for privacy and a way of controlling your personal environment. You want to feel at home and in command, but unpredictable things keep happening, and people keep intruding into your life unexpectedly. You can blend into any environment under this line, and seem to belong where you are despite the ceaseless changes around you. Above all, personal, home, and family matters are charged with emotion.

Moon with Mercury:
The Wandering Mind

This is an interesting combination in which your sensitivity, feelings, and appetites are linked with your mind, your work concerns, and your function and place in the world. This could be the battleground where you take up the struggle between your past conditioning in regard to such matters as family loyalties and practical career concerns and try to make a stand for freedom of thought. In breaking away from habitual patterns, you have the urge to reach out for more sensation, for you find yourself experiencing what may be an unfamiliar craving to know and experience things first hand. The result of this can be a kind of mental wanderlust, as you move your mind from thought to thought, project to project, ceaselessly seeking the sensation behind the next corner, over the next hill.

Your mental abilities, ideas, speech, common sense and physical coordination all take center stage here, as you develop the qualities of precocity, restlessness, impatience, and mental nervousness, perhaps finding that you have a quick grasp of opportunities and ideas that may gain you public attention. Others find you bright and impressionable, and your awareness and your lively, shrewd intelligence guarantee that you can make a living by your wits, while also promising accomplishment in scholarly areas, trade, or commerce. You can become popular for your lightning-fast repartee and perceptual acuity, but your tendency to gossip could get you in a bit of trouble.

Morals could be a little too flexible under this influence as well, especially where money is concerned, so either talking too much or spending too much (especially if it happens to be other people's money) can get you and others into trouble. The mind is like a sponge, absorbing everything with which it comes into contact, though its retentiveness is balanced by a lack of discrimination, direction, and concentration. The mental processes that help you to synthesize new ideas and concepts from the old work well here, as do linguistic and verbal skills, so you may want to seek out opportunities that challenge these parts of your brain. You won't have to look far, as life here is full of quick changes, new people, and plenty of turbulence in your work life and career, while business, journalism, and mental or office work are among the many successful employment possibilities.

This is a perfect locale for a job interview of any type, as both your personality and your skills will shine here, and it is also a good place for real estate, trading, studiousness, genealogy, and developing your talents and capacities. Defense of the underdog may be your lot in life under this combination line, but you are certainly more than up to the challenge. Want to relax? If so, then try another place!

Moon with Venus:
"Life is a Cabaret"

Under the influence of the two most feminine of planets, a world of beautiful people, high social life, fashion, baubles, bangles, and beads beckons you. All the archetypes of woman—mother, beauty, friendship and love, self-esteem, and appetites—dominate your attention and time here, as life takes an elegant, sociable direction. Raising your self-esteem in order to attract love could well come to be a preoccupation for you here, and along the way you may have to explore romantic cravings on the one side as you sample the "beautiful people" syndrome on the other. The attraction you develop here to worldly things such as monetary success can be more than sufficient to challenge any natural idealism you are prone to. Since you want to rise into the "right" social circles, as well as immersing yourself in sentimental domestic and romantic relationships, you may find that the intensity of your appetite can detract your attention away from pursuing any greater ambitions. Still, there is no doubt that this can be a pleasant, comfortable locale, full of glamorous and exciting social pleasures.

Obviously, laziness, weight gain, and self-indulgence are dangers here as voluptuous, epicurean, and sensualistic excesses are the perils inherent in the atmosphere of polish, taste, and elegance. For the same reason, there is little pressure under this line to accomplish much of substance, or to deal with cosmic ideas. On the other hand, you can expect some degree of professional success if you work in any area that deals with art, beauty, or women, as you can hone any talents you have for catering to the fashionable needs, tastes, and concerns of others. Relationships tend toward "sisterhood" rather than manly camaraderie, regardless of the sex of those involved, with the other person usually taking the initiative, and introducing you to things that tend toward refinement and cultivated tastes. You could actually become more attractive here, in part because that's the way you feel, so that sex and romance are likely to be more readily available to you than in other places, though they might tend to be more superficial and less passionate than elsewhere. You are popular, find a good relationship, and develop a steady, calm, diplomatic, unruffled attitude toward the intrigue in your social circles.

For Women Only: This area is quite congenial for you, so you can rise quickly in the social departments usually reserved for women. The only problem is that you do not seem to need the male component in your life much, and thus may spend a lot of time with "the girls" in the coffee shop or at the hairdresser, and may as a result retain a certain adolescent girlishness that tends to put off the opposite sex. Still, this can be a very pleasant area if you are involved with art or fashion, and you will have ample room to grow and express yourself. Motherhood is a very strong likelihood here. It is among the most astrologically fertile places for you.

For Men Only: Clearly, this area may pose some problems for most men, though it is quite likely that a lot of the feminine aspects of this planetary combination will be acted out in your relationships in some way or another. The bonds you form tend to be strongly desired and a bit on the dependent side, and they are often with ultra-feminine women whose natures may conform closely with the description in the paragraphs above. You, on the other hand, may act out the role of a matinee idol, a pampered and tasteful

Romeo, and though you may enjoy women and their company more here than elsewhere, it may be difficult for you to get motivated to do more than dine and dance with them. Attachments you have to women (including your mother) may be hard to break here. In general, the gratification of your appetites and a strong awareness of your appearance can turn you away from more important life goals.

Moon with Mars:
Feeling More Than a Little Upset

Society does not do much to encourage expression of aggressive, angry, physically confrontational, and emotional reactions. In polite and civilized society, these are considered not to exist or they are expected either to be suppressed or channelled into "constructive" activities such as sporting competition, war, or environmental exploitation. In this locality, such sublimation is apt to be very difficult for you, as you are generally more irascible, temperamental, reckless, outspoken, defensive, and irritable than usual (unless there is already a heavy Mars emphasis in your chart). This state of mind does not come upon you without good reason, of course—under this line you tend to gravitate to aggressive people and can't stand by idly while they trample on your prerogatives. Going around with the proverbial chip on your shoulder will indeed attract more than enough people ready and willing to knock it off for you. As you discover your fighting spirit and your fondness for controversy, you can take some pleasure in the quarreling, domestic uproar, and sensitive pride that seem to surround you. More positively, the shy can become bold and daring under the influence of Moon and Mars, but you do need to keep in mind that the risks you gladly take may come to naught if you don't mix a little common sense in with them.

Also be aware that you may experience conflicts involving your own needs for security, the loyalty of others, your attachment to family members, and your own pride. The home itself is under pressure, so that, in addition to the interpersonal crises mentioned above, there is also danger of fire, attack, and injury, especially for those who are not able to feel and express anger and belligerence directly. Outspoken and daring feistiness underlie a distrust and rejection of the dependent aspects of self. A boasting, bullying demeanor can be the result of your own reluctance to admit your own needs for others' affection and sustenance.

For Women Only: As a woman, you'll find this zone one of special problems for you. Women are not usually socialized to be comfortable with their aggressive, assertive tendencies and thus may instead attach themselves to men whose overt masculinity is usually in direct proportion to the suppression of their own. Any such tendency will be exaggerated in this locale, especially in the beginning stages of Mars consciousness. If you understand the lessons Mars has to teach, you can learn to take control of your own masculine energy and to feel more at home with anger, sex, assertion, and self-expression. You may have to undertake integration of your masculinity directly, through assertiveness training, martial arts, or vigorous physical activity. The result of such an effort will be a wider, more mature personality, increased personal power, and the valuable gift of personal autonomy.

For Men Only: As a man, this area poses particular problems for you, as it is too easy to reject your own needs for attachment and affection and then blame the associated problems on women. This blame will tend to fall on those closest to you, whom you will probably view in an unfavorable light, and perhaps respond to in coarse, locker-room terms. Your tendency to denigrate femininity in general will appear fairly transparent to objective observers, however. These problems with women will only be compounded by selecting as companions only those who have a low feeling of self-esteem and who admire your macho posturing as expressive of their own self-contempt. Barroom-style, Hemingwayesque braggadocio wears pretty thin after a while, as will your air of adolescent boyish inexperience, overlain by noisy egotism. Still, courage, daring, and entrepreneurial ability are expanded here, and you may be willing to risk everything in order to prove a point to yourself and others.

Moon with Jupiter:
Wish Upon a Star

As long as you aren't disturbed by fluctuations in the material aspects of life, this area can be one of the best possible, as here you will find fulfillment of your potentials encouraged by the public and personal environment. Loved and admired, you tend to be surrounded with the best in social and material pleasures, and you are likely to be universally regarded, and preferred by those in authority, yet still loved by those with less status than yourself. Advancement comes easily as money and honor accrue to you and your family members, who also prosper in the congenial surroundings of bourgeois comfort.

Your humor and intellect attract to your side people who provide generous favors and opportunities for advancement. The cultured, academic, and exotic air that surrounds you here, promises to be enhanced by additional opportunities that come to you from faraway places, whether through other people from those locales or through travel originating here. The fact that your capacity for enjoyment of the best in food and drink are enhanced here points to one of the real problems you'll be faced with under a Moon-Jupiter line—having too much of a good thing, overindulgence, and a subsequent loss of interest in accomplishment. In general, your good nature and your bemusement at life's curiosities point to an unusually happy life at this location, though a life in which the abundance of good fortune is balanced from time to time by reverses you suffer due to a slackening of ambition and motivation. Feelings of security and well-being put minimal demands on self, and laughter and pleasure are balanced by feelings of righteousness and social usefulness, possibly edged with a "do-gooder mentality."

Religious devotion can be an important issue under this line, and might be shown by an attraction to its more ritualistic forms or by your becoming attached to a teacher or guru. Social successes and skills are easily learned and polished in the cultivated atmosphere prevailing here, and you can do well if you seek to polish your intellect as well, through academic study. You have a sense that all is right with the world, that authority is not to be questioned, and that what you already have (especially as it comes to you from your family and social background) is sufficient to establish yourself as one of the "better" people. Your health is also likely to be particularly good here, except where strong appetites are indulged. Recommended professions for this place include philanthropy, charity, family counseling, academia, civil service, or anything deemed socially desirable and solidly middle class.

Moon with Saturn:
So Who Said Life is Fair?

Life under this kind of planetary line can get pretty serious and no-nonsense. You tend to feel that there is something in your background–perhaps a "family curse" of sorts–that you can never quite overcome, and that this destines you to a life of hard work combined with service to others, and the acceptance of a supporting role in relationships. You're pretty sure that you are not going to measure up to the standards you imagine established authority has set, and a sense of "sin" or karma makes all the hard work, restriction of feelings, and suppression of your own needs seem justified. It's difficult for you to know what you feel, and this leads to an immature lack of self-knowledge and a constant comparison of yourself to others, all of which can lead to depression, isolation, frustration, and melancholy. A certain satisfaction comes to you from remaining in a low station in life, or through dealing with others who have found themselves down and out.

You are inclined to sacrifice your hopes and ideals in order to care for dependent family members or otherwise to take on unavoidable responsibilities–perhaps relating to care of the elderly or infirm. On the more positive side, this area is good for introspection and self-instruction, although you tend to dwell on details and miss the broad view if you don't get at least some feedback from others. You demonstrate a certain personal dignity, a long-suffering stoicism, and a stubborn self-sufficiency, yet your horizons seem narrow here, restricted to rather boring and habitual areas of life. Inner voices seem to say "No" to everything you want to do; a Spartan distaste for abstractions, luxuries, and pleasures makes you a little old-fashioned,

Victorian, dreary, and parsimonious to those around you. Nevertheless, self-control has its advantages, as here you may be best able to abandon injurious habits and overcome flaws in character through will power. Things happen to you here that have you silently swearing, "I'll get even, someday."

Since it is not easy for you to know your feelings, your needs tend to be denied, resulting in cynicism, self-dislike, and perhaps the viewpoint that life is only a task. Authority, for all it oppresses you, is still an object of slavish respect, particularly if "they" set standards you can't possibly attain. Your health may also be poor here, and your personal pride battered by circumstances beyond your control. A lack of ability to view your situation objectively may result in restrictive phobias and a general reliance upon women. Anything that might contribute to putting you in touch with your feeling and nurturing nature can counter such tendencies.

Moon with Uranus:
The Road To Oz

Here you may become the (unconscious?) devotee of an idea meant to liberate people from some real or imagined restriction, or perhaps your name itself comes to stand for a movement, large or small. You can make quite a pest of yourself by encouraging everyone around you to kick over the traces of authoritarianism, old values, and tradition. You find a personal reward in promoting the novel, the revolutionary, and the individualistic, and are likely to develop an ardent attraction to the unusual, the Bohemian, the unconventional, and anything else that you can identify as antiestablishment. Strange and uncontrollable things seem to happen to you here, and your life becomes changeable, exciting, and full of unexpected emotional extremes. Home, finances, and family relationships are in a state of continual upheaval, as are most other areas of your life. Your need to defend the underdog (any old one will do), the downtrodden, and the underprivileged attracts down-and-outers of all kinds to you in profusion. Not surprisingly, authorities of all kinds will find you a threat, thus requiring you to defend your individuality against public pressure to conform. Women especially may experience problems with health.

Inwardly you fight a powerful battle fought between who you always have been (symbolized by family, home, and such attachments) and some powerful idea of who you could be through the self-actualization that comes with liberation from old constraints. Because of this, you seek out and define a new personal meaning, something which can indeed be liberating and helpful if it is not done through pursuit of the eccentric for its own sake. Nothing stands still in your vicinity, as upsets and upheavals occur daily in your restless personal life, fueled by impulsiveness, a fluctuating loyalty to various ideals and ideologies, extremes of erotic imagination, a fascination with the occult, a tendency toward superstition, and a feeling that your personal development can best proceed through being intuitive rather than methodical. The constant state of electric excitement in the air makes the urge for self-discovery so commonplace that you soon might wonder if there is anything left to discover. "Look what we've been missing" is an expression that may quickly exhaust your more conventional friends. Flying before the storm, you are more than ready to try anything once (more often than that might be boring!) in your insatiable desire for individualistic evolution and change.

Moon with Neptune
Sea of Feeling

This combination of planets can be pretty extreme in its effects, even though at the beginning life often seems to have changed only subtly, if at all. The major influence here, though, is one that often leads to a surrender of the ego. You will be strongly drawn to act out, either in your own life or the lives of those you deal with, an idealism so powerful that it demands total renunciation of your identity as it was, abandonment of the urge for self-preservation, and a general relinquishing of any sense of form or structure in life. Total immersion in the rainbow of experience without guidance of purpose or ego results in an overpowering exaggeration of feeling and sensation. Torrential emotions, wild unsubstantiated fears and hysterical elations, phobias, and imaginations may be among the intense and vivid mental experiences of this location. A life of submission, self-sacrifice, perhaps even humiliation and surrender to others' needs could ensue.

The collective unconscious becomes all too accessible to you here, so that dreams, myths, and psychological inner realities become everyday aspects of life. Psychism and sensitivity are greatly expanded, but practical, financial matters may suffer. Relationships tend to involve intrigues that ensnare you, and the subsequent confinement and restriction, voluntary or otherwise, will probably leave you unhappy. For those willing to give up ego and the comforts of the material life, the reward is deepened imagination and tendency toward a life of service that could lead you to find a spiritual guide. People take advantage of you, though, and illusions often are a large part of the "enlightenment" you feel is just around the corner. To survive in this weird and magical climate, you need to learn to deal with the power of humanity's universal, mythological inner mind by assimilating successfully your own past and unconscious feelings and experiences, and by forswearing the pleasures of the ego. The desire to return to the womb may lie beneath your fascination with various religions.

Since you are likely to be too sensitive to live easily or successfully in the day-to-day world of reality, you may withdraw into an artificial reality. This could be an institutional environment (which would include a job in a large corporation along with the more obvious examples such as hospitals) or a pharmaceutical one–addictions and drug abuse can be results of the nervous sensitivity you experience here. Since imagination is strong, artists or those who need to sense exactly what the public needs at a given moment may do well here. More often, though, you feel an insatiable thirst for sensation, and one which could lead to a phony "enlightenment" that thinly masks a moralistic self-dislike. Public ignominy, confinement, and the repeated intrusions of the unknown, the far-out, and the mystical are likely to mark your life here if you allow the negative tendencies of Moon-Neptune too much sway.

Moon with Pluto:
The More You Want, The Less You Get

This location can be quite a problematical one, as a lack of awareness of your fundamental needs and physical desires allows them to build up unfulfilled until they have reached such intimidating proportions that they threaten to overwhelm anyone who might try to satisfy them. This results in an emotional life that moves to the negative extremes of uncontrolled outbursts, alienation, and isolation. As this type of aching, unfulfilled desire you could experience here is largely unredeemable, detachment from the past is one lesson which you must learn, though often such a separation is difficult to accomplish without first going through some intense interpersonal problems, as well as dealing with insecurity, obsession with change, and a roller-coaster ride of sexual desire and feeling. Here is where a partnership with passion urges the butterfly of your innermost soul to emerge reluctantly from its cocoon. Major life changes such as deaths, separations, and tangles with the law, all conspire to keep you agitated, constantly processing emotions and feelings as you develop a stubborn resistance to the flow of events around you.

You expect, and therefore are likely to attract, rejection; growth, while painful, is enforced by the powerful emotions and the intense sexual needs that seem constant in this location. Though antisocial and rebellious within, you resist personal change, preserving your isolation as proof that you are right and that society is all wrong. You may make a final and complete separation from family and roots in this locale—permanent farewells seem so frequent that you come to expect them. Practical matters are in constant flux as well. Rejecting your human needs for comfort and intimacy, you feel superior to the material life and its soft bourgeois comforts. The more you want, the less you get until you accept both a totally unique sense of self and a need for constant change and rigorous inner honesty. Death itself becomes a powerful symbol of change and growth here; a sense of life's impermanence is a tonic, so you may be prone to take risks and to crave and seek out highly-charged experiences. You are apt to be antisocial, charismatic yet alienated, bored by ordinary society, and under constant emotional stress—all this perhaps acting out a forgotten resentment against your mother or family.

10

Mercury: The Taming Power of the Small

MERCURY PROJECTS an influence that is easily assimilated and socially accepted for the most part, so that few people will have problems under these lines—difficulties attend the more socially repressed planets, such as Saturn, but almost everyone engages in the intellectual and communicative activities of Mercury with ease. For those who find feelings and sensation threatening, however, Mercury may encourage an exaggeration of the thinking function, resulting in a scatterbrained changeability, a sarcastic and even cynical outlook, or a heartless, manipulative cruelty. Mercury is democratic, looking at all and sundry under a microscope focused by scientific, objective equality, so that people who like to feel they are superior by reason of birth or accomplishment may not get the type of admiration they seek under a Mercury line.

This locale can be especially good for "success in small things," but it may block more ambitious schemes through a tendency toward provincial thinking, unexpected inconveniences, and communication problems. In other words, while this may be a proper locale for setting up agencies and mechanisms to carry out the details of larger projects, the projects themselves, including the planning, would best be set up elsewhere. *Note: As a traditionally androgynous planet, Mercury shows few if any discernible differences between men and women, so these sections are omitted below.* As with other planets, the pairing of Mercury with Mars *can* be problematic, so that section includes some observations on sex differences.

If You're Just Passing Through...

A short stay in this zone can be busy, stimulating, and a source of new information and fascinating ideas. It's a great place to organize your thoughts about important projects, to do research, writing, and any sort of work that involves manual labor, such as crafts. You should also expect to have many interesting contacts with people, especially youth or those with a youthful outlook, and you should find much enjoyment in activities such as hiking, and exploring. Even a short stay can put you in touch with your own abilities, talents, and perhaps career opportunities, and expand your contact with the world. You could even have an experience with someone who profoundly symbolizes your aspirations, or who perhaps represents the best you see in yourself. Music, literary, and cultural concerns underlie many of your plans and activities here.

Long-Distance Lines

If you can't travel to these areas, they still may be important in your life through other people: relatives, siblings, educational concerns, and any relationship that symbolizes youth or any of the other Mercury qualities described above may be located under your Mercury lines. Agents who reside there may act for you in various capacities to make contacts or accomplish tasks, so that these zones are good for employment of others, brokerage, and particularly for educational concerns or correspondence courses.

Psychological Interpretation of Mercury:
Intellect—Your Key to Success

Your most powerful planet here, Mercury, symbolizes life's second most important function after pure being: the facility and capacity to communicate with the world. This is represented biologically by the twin activities of breathing and digestion, the two means by which the chemical processes of life are refreshed. Less abstractly, it stands for sensory perception and verbal communication, along with the mind's information-processing ability, all of which result in environmental awareness and comprehension. In this zone, you will come to appreciate, understand, and perfect these life processes, as they increase in importance in your life.

Mercury is also a symbol of inner initiation, the recognition of your own nature, so the increased awareness you find in your interaction with the environment will, by way of contrast, highlight and define your own identity. Thus you could become something of a local celebrity as you become publicly involved in various issues, and just as you can make a name for yourself, you may also find a name for yourself, in the sense that a literal change of name (or the way in which you spell or pronounce your old one) could accompany your stay here. Any notoriety you gain here is not the same as "real" fame, however, as Mercury tends to be a localizing influence; rather than dealing with cosmic, grandly social, or super-personal concerns of the sort that might gain you attention in other parts of the world, your interests here lie in the process of communication between you and your neighborhood and close relations. This outreach into the local environment, and the accompanying need to perfect sensory understanding and perception are accomplished through detailing, classifying, attaching labels, and interpreting reality. Mercury is not so creative as it is adept at reorganizing, redefining, and adapting ideas to new needs and deeper understanding. In effect, you become reality's librarian.

Another basic Mercury function is utilization, so under this influence you may be able to identify and put to use the various personal talents, abilities, and resources which have not yet been fully developed. You should find your resourcefulness and innovativeness on the increase as you perfect old talents and recognize abilities that you may not have thought you had, not to mention stimulating latent talents you notice in others. An element of acquisitiveness can also emerge in your nature, as you begin to feel that possessing more material things will give you a better capacity to use your own talents in a directed way. As your need to acquire possessions increases, so your need to find romance decreases, as your adult mind and experience are guided by a youthful Mercury that is largely unaware of such needs, except at a somewhat intellectual level. You may lose weight, seem younger, and generally project a somewhat sexually neutral charisma.

Stages and Myth of Mercury:
Stay Young By Staying Involved

Mercury was of course the messenger of the gods, an ever-young, immaturely androgynous, quick-witted, and adaptable character. In this location you learn resourceful skills that enable you to better link yourself to different activities in the world around you, as well as to form meaningful associations with people through the medium of ideas. At a deeper level, Mercury was mythologically one of the few beings able to exist in the three separate worlds of the gods, mortals, and Hades, and thus it symbolizes a guide for the soul's journey. In this zone, people occasionally have visions of past and future, of past incarnations, life after death, feel they are in touch with "the Akashic Records," or can "hear the silence."

Mercury affects both sexes in much the same way, though its influence expresses itself in different stages: The early stages of the Mercury experience are characterized by a childlike curiosity, a need to ask questions about everything and sometimes by the arid, nervous, intellectualism of the archetypal high school science "nerd." From this develops a view of the world as microcosm and macrocosm—the ability to see the whole reflected in each of its parts—that is the basis of any real and useful knowledge. Using models of the universe discerned in everyday objects and situations, the mind grasps the usefulness and purpose of everything or everyone it touches, becoming a guide for others in their quest for themselves, as well as a valuable resource of knowledge and experience.

In the primitive stages of Mercury's expression, the problem of amorality often must be dealt with. A world seen purely in terms of information and ideas is without feeling or values, and thus without social and personal allegiances. As with a computer, complex questions of right and wrong can reduce to matters of simple arithmetic, and it becomes much too easy to find a convenient rationalization for cunning, expedient behavior. Juvenile delinquency seems associated with Mercury, as is the life of the streets in general. Even if you yourself do not fall into these modes of behavior, such matters could become personally relevant to you, perhaps as a focus of professional involvement, while you live in this locale.

The Practical Side of Mercury:
Becoming by Doing

Mercury can help you come to grips with practical concerns of all kinds. Your mind sharpens, leading to an improvement in communication skills, with eloquent verbal expression becoming a notable characteristic in your conversation as wit, ingenuity, and cleverness shine through to your listeners. These enhanced skills and a greater desire for communicating with others could also show themselves through community involvement and an interest in writing and publishing. Advancing your education is also much easier here than elsewhere, as your expressive and technical talents seem to develop almost effortlessly. Your ability to work efficiently also improves greatly, and thus technical achievements such as inventions and innovations are apt to mark your stay under this line. Work prospers, especially if it is involved with mail order, distribution and transportation, books, informational systems, data processing, detail work of all kinds, agencies, the press, merchandising, libraries, or commerce. If basic secretarial work is your job, you will find that you are better able to organize and maintain efficient office procedures. Craftsmanship and manual skills are also emphasized so that those in most blue-collar jobs should prosper here, including employment related to repair, assembly, light construction, or allied fields. Practical or vocational education, especially if meant to acquire new skills rather than polish old ones, also goes well in this locale. Finally, even your hobbies can be transformed into remunerative occupations here.

Mercury areas are usually good for physical health, if there are no other contradictory influences, though the more sedate and peace-loving person may at times feel exhausted by the constant changes and barrage of sensory stimuli to the nervous system. Nervous complaints often surface here, along with allergies, hypersensitivity to noise and other stimuli, and skin problems. Smoking and drug use are not well-tolerated, and your health reacts strongly to adverse environmental influences such as toxins and pollution. When you're feeling down, quiet and security are the best tonic under a Mercury line.

Since Mercury's influence is easily accepted and assimilated by most people, projection of its qualities onto others is less common than in the case of other planets. Some (particularly women who have been trained to feel that thinking is a man's concern) may find themselves attracted to brainy and intellectual types, though this is actually an indication that your own capacity and inclination for cerebral activity are emerging into consciousness. Relationships are often taken up with younger people, perhaps Gemini or Virgo types, reflecting a more youthful attitude toward self and life in general.

Mercury on Ascendant:
How to Stay Young Forever

This position of Mercury will manifest most obviously and powerfully in your self-definition and image. You'll define yourself through your mind and/or your work, become known for your profession, mental abilities, repartee, manual or conversational skills, craftsmanship, expressiveness, versatility, and adaptability. You seem younger here, gaining grace, motility, and coordinative skills, and if you suffer from a physical handicap, this is a better than average place for successful rehabilitation and therapy. Your youthful image may "rub off" on others as well, so that in this locale people seem to respond to you by acting younger, more mobile, and more versatile when you are around. Your ideas become widely circulated, since you are not only willing to say what you think, but can say it in an interesting, unusual, yet uncontroversial way.

Self-definition and self-understanding bloom here, as life experiences contribute to a growing awareness of self, and an appreciation of your talents and abilities. Your mind devotes itself to uncovering the essential meaning of your life, and to solidifying your identity and self-concept in a way that could well create a new "you" quite different from the way you were elsewhere. Just as you are able to integrate the various aspects of your mind and personality, your role in society increasingly is one of coordinator, facilitator, and connecting medium for disparate external forces and people. The problems you experience may stem from a tendency to postpone commitments and to look upon each experience as temporary until the ideal situation comes along. If you let yourself become a perpetual student, you may never get around to graduating or putting any of the knowledge and experience you gain under this influence to long-term use.

Though you tend to say what you think under this influence, you always reserve the right to change your mind. Outspoken, eloquent, yet always bordering on being an intellectual dilettante, you demonstrate charm and charisma on the outside, while within yourself you attempt to discover the true form and meaning of your identity and purpose.

Mercury on Midheaven:
Gamesmanship

Your career and your quest for status in society are the focus of Mercury under this line. Under most circumstances, you can find work easily, especially in business, commerce, and the other work areas mentioned above. Any education you undertake usually has an ambitious purpose behind it, and as you concentrate on creating a good public image for yourself through advertising your new skills, you may become something of an intellectual social climber. Literary work, teaching, educational concerns, crafts, and even hobbies all prosper here, with all of them serving your ambitions well. Your sense of competition is keen here, though somewhat impersonal, and it leads you to pursue success as a sort of game. Your mind, your verbal powers, and your newly-developing social and diplomatic skills are among your best tools with which to advance social success, and your ability to express yourself could even lead to opportunities to participate in politics and community affairs. But writing is the most powerful of your emerging talents and abilities under this line, so publication (and certainly acceptance) of your ideas could well be a means by which you can attain even greater success and social status. Books, articles, and research succeed here, especially if they promote new ideas, new theories, or just new ways of thinking. With your name bandied about a lot, you are apt to feel a growing sense of social responsibility mingled with a sense of social gamesmanship that keeps you ever mindful of what you must do in order to keep up with the Joneses. You quickly learn the rules for success here, and can play them with skill, despite a lack of attachment to the results. You also watch the game from the sidelines as other play it, viewing it with cool, rational fascination. In the worlds of academia and employment in particular, you soon learn how to get your name and ideas onto the right people's desks and prosperity follows.

Mercury on Descendant:
Intellectual Companionship

Mercury here can sharpen your counseling skills to professional levels as you gain the ability to urge others to fulfill their potentials, acting as a catalyst to help them recognize their own talents and aptitudes. Young people are particularly drawn to you here, and you may succeed in guiding them to personal fulfillment. Your mind and your knowledge expand through being stimulated by the people and ideas you encountered under this line. Flexibility and a more liberal outlook result from meetings with potential teachers, guides, or intellectual mentors, so this zone is excellent for education, teaching, or any other academic pursuits. Relationships, which tend to be fluid and unstable here, are often with people younger than you, and your contact with them easily shifts the focus of your rapidly evolving self-definition. A situation in which you define yourself as some other person's partner, student, or protege would reflect these tendencies. As this location is excellent for business, work requiring contracts, partnerships, or debate and other verbal skills are all very good options to consider. Self-promotion succeeds with relatively minor effort, though your own enthusiasm for same can make you prone to a carnival-like hard sell of questionable ethicality. While sexual relationships may lose a little of their intensity and passion here, communication is enhanced in any sort of partnership or connection. You may come to reflect prevailing ideas more than is usual for you, moderating your opinions in the light of others' input. This can indicate either flexibility or opportunism, and only you can determine the difference by your own actions. Your business skills improve, and careers in advertising, sales, journalism, publicity, career counseling, publishing, or as any kind of agent, should prosper under this influence.

Mercury on Imum Coeli:
Understanding the Past

Areas that concern the home, the family, and your sense of personal roots and origins are the focus of Mercurial energies under this line. The past—your own, and that of your family, race, ethnicity, or region—can become a means of self-identification and definition, sparking a fascination with research into genealogy, and other means of exploring the forgotten past. This in turn leads to a renewed sense of your own identity. The inner personal factors which relate to your family and heritage can be organized into a coherent personal myth here, one that serves to structure the mind more efficiently as the mythology and symbolism inherent in the past allows you a more thorough comprehension and utilization of the present. You become sensitive to how the past has conditioned you, especially in private study and introspection, and so are able to modify its effects. The "archaeology of self" is also plumbed, perhaps, through psychoanalysis and similar introspective modes of therapy.

Your personal allegiance to family, nation, and religious tradition may deepen here, so that your identification with these things becomes a more integral part of your psyche. Moreover, what you do here may itself make a mark in your family history. Because of your constant probing and questioning of your family background, the home situation remains fluid and flexible, and is perhaps unsettled much of the time. Intuition also increases under this line in many instances, as your instinctive awareness of your past enables you to see the more universal patterns in it, which can, in a sense, give you some knowledge of the future and a better insight into the present. Seeing yourself and your family's past as a microcosm that reflects a larger truth thus enhances your knowledge of the world and its future. Finally, you may undertake a quest through education or travel, or intellectual exploration that later in life distinguishes you and constitutes a fundamental part of the identity through which the world knows you.

Mercury with Venus:
The Taming Power of the Small

Under this pleasant line, you are able to define and recreate the beauty within by pursuing and perfecting art, creative writing, and creative communication. This place can well be an area of social accomplishment for you, as it stimulates personal grace and the development of persuasive skills that you can utilize in your work or profession. You find it natural to act as a peacemaker, diplomat, and facilitator, and do so in a personally pleasant and charming fashion that befriends former enemies and charms those already your friends. Education, schooling, and childhood are happy and productive here, as you learn easily, especially in artistic or creative fields. An automatic ease and delicacy of verbal expression lend themselves well to efforts at creative writing, such as poetry or lyrical prose, but this can also help you in more practically, descriptive technical writing, advertising, or translation.

Your instinctive appreciation of fine things, art, and elegance is allied with an ability to get along with almost anyone. Work in education goes well here, largely due to this capacity to get along with most people, no matter what their status relative to your own, and profit should accrue to you through business or commerce—particularly craftsmanship, arts, or any profession that requires good spoken or written expression. Commercial art, graphics, and hobbies in which elegant but useful articles are created, can be profitable under this influence. Since your mind is calm and clear for the most part here, if you naturally tend to be hypersensitive, you may find your anxiety moderated somewhat. In fact, you may almost have to work at it in order to be depressed or ill here, partly because of the affectionate support of almost everyone you meet. A tactful, diplomatic role for you is indicated overall, due to the combination of your talents in communication and your instincts for charity and kindness. But writing is most apt to be your labor of love, and if you decide to go ahead with the Great American Novel here, you can make real progress in such a creative endeavor, due to the inspiration you find from intellectual companionship and the fond encouragement of friends.

Mercury with Mars
Trippingly Over Your Tongue

A chronic case of "foot-in-mouth disease" guarantees that life will rarely be quiet in this locality and that many changes in self-awareness you experience here are the result of an ample number of lessons in the virtues of silence. Controversy seems to accompany everything you say, though introspection will reveal that people are only reacting to the chip you're carrying on your shoulder and to an obvious, if not always intentional, arrogance supported by boastful, and provocative words that are anything but diplomatic and tactful. Still, you are able to attain your goals by putting real muscle into ideas, proving over and over again that the pen is mightier than the sword, at least as long as it is well-guided.

This is a good area in which to find and enjoy any form of active and strenuous work, from simple manual labor to competitive activity such as sports. Even simple jobs can challenge you by being made into Herculean tasks, and such physical exertion is also beneficial in dissipating some of the belligerence and irritability that you may feel here. Socially, though, you could have quite a few problems, as these planets together can make you present a rude, coarse, perhaps even malicious demeanor to others. On the other hand, when their effects are internalized, you may be subject to nerves, allergies, or repeated infection. Injuries caused by rash and precipitate action, particularly in driving, travel, or the use of machinery, also can result from such bottled-up resentments. Your sensitivity at times can make you seem adolescent, awkward, and painfully reactive, even though verbally you can be quite formidable.

You can develop skill and dexterity in the manual arts, so if you already have some talent for carpentry, a craft, or other skilled labor, this zone can be more constructive than problematical for you. Your competitive instincts are sharpened considerably, as you gain a talent for shrewd self-promotion and advertising, and you'll enjoy many opportunities to prove yourself as long as you are careful not to alienate others by furthering your interests in an overbearing way. On the down side, details tend to overwhelm you, which can lead to intolerance for criticism if you don't find a more disciplined way to handle the situation. Sexual exploitation of others, a tendency to overwork, and even the temptation to indulge in criminality are other problems that can manifest here, so the area is best avoided by those not already self-possessed and calm. While living here, cultivating cautious, tolerant friends can act as a check on your impetuosity.

For Women Only: You'll find this area particularly risky and challenging; men won't much like your independence nor the sardonic way in which you assert it. There is even an increased risk of attack, accident, or health problems, though the area can be congenial if you are willing to add a dash of aggression to the usual female roles and put up with a greater number of personal confrontations than you might expect elsewhere.

For Men Only: This area can be somewhat problematic due to the repeated problems you experience with competition and exposure to accidents and to others' ill will. However, it is a good place for such masculine occupations as those listed above, in addition to engineering, entrepreneurial activities, athletics, and any strenuous vocation which can act to channel the overabundance of energy present here. A little effort at moderation will make you ambitious, shrewd, and assertive rather than opportunistic, manipulative, and pushy.

Mercury with Jupiter:
The Big Power of Little Ideas

Culture, the exchange of information, an interest in language itself, communication in general, and the organization of people in order to meet specific goals emerge as primary and important here. The depth and breadth of your intelligence may actually improve in a noticeable way, and you acquire an air of integrity, authority, and experience that ensures your acceptance while granting you a vital and important role in society. The organization and planning that must accompany any activity are your forte; clear, dependable judgment as well as a reasoned, liberal humanism propel you into decision-making roles in work and community. Big ideas can be put into operation, and business especially does well here, as do academic concerns and promotions.

Occupations especially favored under this line are those involving mail order, publishing, anything that deals with communication or ideas, import-export, travel, concerns with foreign countries, cultures or languages, commerce, writing, advertising, media, administration, community work, government, and libraries. Even for people whose lives up to now have been dominated by sense and physicality, this is an excellent area for education and personal advancement, as you easily soak up whatever culture and the arts have to offer, showing your new status with an air of worldliness, humor, and irreverence. You extend your personal reach by meeting people of varied ideologies, ideas, and backgrounds, many of whom may come from abroad. Your ideas are sought after by others and can even see publication if you make the effort. In fact, this is probably the best zone for writers or communicators of any sort, as well as for those involved in commercial, academic, or similar interests. The dangers to be found in this mostly positive Mercury-Jupiter include tendencies to exaggerate, to oversimplify complicated problems, or to engage in intellectual arrogance. You may seem the absentminded professor to some, so important and plentiful are the ideas that cross through your mind here, and you tend toward a simple lifestyle which places a higher value on ideas than on things. People for whom culture and education have seemed inaccessible rise socially here, and work or business interests can succeed spectacularly.

Mercury with Saturn:
The Alchemy of Drudgery

Here you can refine, crystallize, and reduce knowledge and self-concepts to their essentials. What is illusion or what has been acquired from other people in a more or less habitual way is separated quickly from your personal history and identity. Powers of concentration increase as your mind turns in upon itself, and the truths you slowly acquire here are dependable and durable. You prefer unadorned meaning over meaningless form, refusing to take on the patina of culture and dilettantism that others may seek to acquire. Your studies here tend to be tedious explorations into the technical, and the detailed; restrained organization and practicality dominate, and as your surroundings may be rather uncongenial, work is hard and your relationships often clouded with suspicion and doubt. You may fear that your own abilities and intelligence are inadequate here, and thus will compensate by working harder and by relying on the approval of authorities. You trust less in your senses than in accepted interpretations of reality, so knowledge and communication are restricted to dealing with the essential and the real.

Even though you tend to become bogged down in details, you still can develop exacting craftsmanship as well as scientific and accounting skills. Copious note-taking and painstaking research often produce less than you hope for, at least in the short run, but patience and a willingness to commit yourself over the long term can pay off. Imagination (both yours and those around you) tends to be barren, so you are not likely to be highly creative. However, success can come through perseverance, as well as from rather venal types of commerce or small-time wheeling and dealing. Your writing and verbal expression tend to the inarticulate, sluggish, or antiquated. People who need strict routine may find it here, but the mental myopia and rigid adherence to limited opinions of this locale make it too dreary, puritanical, and anxious for most. Health and mood may be depressed here, small complaints can become chronic, and behind most difficulties lies a disbelief in your own powers—a belief which seems borne out by experience. Just as the ancient alchemists tried over and over to convert lead into gold, you labor at inner transformation here, and in fact you can be transformed by the self-imposed rigors of the discipline of Mercury and Saturn.

Mercury with Uranus:
Fidgets, Widgets, and Social Dynamite

In this locality, your mind seems just slightly ahead of its time, drawn to theories and social concepts that are yet to be understood by the mainstream of society. Individualistic ideas and perceptions, undistorted by what "everybody knows," are social dynamite, so not surprisingly you and your iconoclastic mentality that delights in exploding others' myths and illusions with its brilliant logic and irreverent wit don't get along too well with authorities. Your mind becomes articulate, innovative, and inspirational, and you find that you easily see through the sham of unquestioned social beliefs. In no time at all you can find yourself at the forefront (but far ahead of the main body) of scientific opinion, espousing ideas as unpopular as pure materialism, astrology, metaphysics, or any highly individualistic world view. You demand freedom from stereotype, and see the path to truth as personally unique and lonely. Eschewing a dualistic world view, you are comfortable with ideas that others might see as paradoxical or contradictory, but this is only because your sharp mind is able to form lightning-fast associations between seemingly disparate concepts. In the face of the inevitable social criticism that comes to Mercury-Uranus, you remain clear, willful, cool, decisive, and superior. You are instinctively political in your materialistic analysis of reality, but your vision is very personal as well, forging a strong link between you and the ideals and political ideologies of your milieu.

On less lofty levels, your occupation becomes the locus of much personal change, inner turmoil, and growth. Working for others is difficult under this line, so self-employment may eventually be sought. You are clever, innovative, handy and resistant to routine, qualities which seem to suit you better for working for yourself than for others. Work situations are likely to change frequently, in part because they become intimately connected to your political awareness, thereby making them a source of conflict between old and new. Your realistic view of things is unclouded by feelings (and others may in fact see you as cold), which allows your individuality to emerge distinctly in your work, especially through nonconforming craftsmanship and technical creativity. Unusual health problems at this location (often caused by reactions to environmental agents or influences) may defy conventional attempts at diagnosis.

Mercury with Neptune:
Dream-Sayer for the Millions

Your mind can take your little daily concerns and inflate them to what seem like cosmic levels in this locale. Your moods tend to be erratic and your ideas are spacey and easily influenced (albeit temporarily) by others' input. However, you are open to idealism as your vivid and offbeat imagination is very sensitive to social moods, something which indicates that you can affect society in a subtle, almost unconscious, way through your ideas. Writers of fantasy, artists, those who work in institutions and service professions—or in the creation and distribution of social illusion, such as advertising, movies, graphics, and photograph—all find imaginative inspiration here. Under such an influence, however, it often is hard to keep your feet on the ground, and your relationships and career plans seem to exist mostly in the rosy glow of hope. People tend to take advantage of you, and you may experience addiction or health crises in trying to deal with your feelings about this. Other ailments can be caused by allergies, an increased sensitivity to environmental influence, or drugs. Your thinking processes become cloudy, and your highly suggestible, or even neurotic, frame of mind often attracts what it fears the most. Your tendency to find your everyday environments full of intrigue and conspiracy, can cause society to intervene negatively and frequently in your everyday life.

All in all, the reality around you rarely measures up to your fuzzy expectations born of an inveterate idealism that keeps you forever comparing what is to what ought to be. Escape on the outside through running away from responsibility, or on the inside by wallowing in neurosis can in rare cases result from the disorganized thinking processes and occult or mystical obsessions common to those under Neptune's sway. For all these disadvantages, you actually may lead a kind of charmed life here as your intuition gives you a view of the road around the next corner, and you instinctively sidestep problems that might devastate one less tuned in than you. Conventional guidelines for life dissolve here, and the lines between imagination and reality blur, while awareness of nuances and subtleties increases. It is too easy for you to give in to a need to exemplify some social myth or another, so be careful not to feed others' need for a scapegoat or martyr.

Mercury-Pluto
The World in a Grain of Sand

It is hard to imagine what the lighthearted messenger of the gods and the darkling lord of the underworld have in common, and since mentality and mortality are difficult concepts to link, so this zone may indeed be one of conflicts. Life areas of career, health, and day-to-day concerns in the community may feature continual intrusions of dark forces, so that if your normal existence doesn't put you in touch with absolutes, with conflicts and struggles over power, sex, life, and death, it may be subject to drastic changes. The most attuned and self-controlled can use this energy to see the universe as a hologram, and by directing their attention to any part, can receive knowledge of the whole. In this way, the family and cultural patterns that govern you can be uncovered, grasped, and redirected while here. Esoterically, this suggests access to the Akashic Records and a link to universal knowledge which can give you great power and insight. In the process of challenging these patterns, you experience continuous transformations of attitudes and changes of ideals. The impossibility of compromise with critics and adversaries makes this an area where it is terribly difficult to keep your life in order for very long.

Language and speech difficulties can manifest here, for while you may speak and hear well enough, it can at times seem impossible to get any meaningful knowledge out of the information you take in. Sometimes a fear of harsh reality underlies your inability to communicate meaningfully. Your mind is attracted to forbiddingly technical or socially disapproved areas of thought, and research into these may require a new symbolic language, or the synthesis of data in new and daring ways. You should beware, however, of becoming immersed in interesting details that have little to do with the whole, leaving you lost in blind alleys of research, accomplishing little. Your ideas will not, in most cases, make you popular despite their novelty, and you may even be persecuted for expressing them. Your best talent is for looking beneath the surface and extracting the universal kernel of truth that lies beneath the trash heap of contradictions and confusion. Here, the seeds of total inner transformation may be planted unobtrusively in your consciousness through the acquisition of some seeming innocent bit of knowledge.

11

Venus: Is There More to Life Than Happiness?

THE IDEA of a Venus zone, with that planet's emphasis on pleasure, enjoyment, and particularly romance, will have a lot of allure for most people. All these things can be available to you under Venus, especially if no other planets are involved and if the place Venus holds in your chart doesn't unduly stress either its positive or negative qualities. On the other hand, this place may tend to bore people who are strongly motivated, active types or those who find the darker side of life and their own psyches fascinating and important. Moreover, if you are already a rather lazy, unmotivated type, being in this zone may exacerbate those tendencies, leaving you with little reason to grow beyond yourself.

For Women Only: This zone is an especially congenial one for you, as you are likely to feel better about yourself and appear more attractive to others, so that you can succeed in making relationships the center of your life here if that is what you're looking for. The darker side of Venus at this place is that by becoming another's wife, mother, or symbol of beauty, you may be giving up a true sense of yourself apart from someone else's needs and evaluation. You tend to accumulate material possessions, excel in domestic concerns such as sewing and baking, retain an inner beauty and attractiveness, and get along well with other women, with whom you can develop special and deep bonds. Venus emphasizes the "beautiful plaything" image of woman, as opposed to the nurturing, maternal power of the Moon (the capacity to attract and to seek security), so these parts of your personality are magnified in this locale.

For Men Only: Living in this zone poses special problems for you. Men in our society are not trained to think of themselves as beautiful, and for them the Venusian concepts of peace, harmony, love, and beauty are supposed to be sought outside of themselves, usually in women and in a romantic setting. While this means that in this locale you will be presented with ample opportunities to enjoy such pleasures, it is uncomfortable and threatening to a male ego to depend on externals for anything. What starts with the intoxication of unlimited credit at the candy store may end up feeling to you like an addiction to the pursuit of a lifestyle that is governed more by images than realities. It is critical here that you try to internalize Venus—to accept that there is beauty within yourself, not just in your mate, possessions, or bank account, each of which turns out to be inadequate and reliable after you have come to depend on it for self-validation. But before this internalization of your own beauty can occur, the perfect feminine image must be recognized, related to, and assimilated.

If You're Just Passing Through...

This is an ideal zone for a vacation, romantic interlude, or an investment. Love is likely to be a constant preoccupation while you're here, along with your own appearance—which can be improved under this planetary line. The acquisition or appreciation of beautiful things such as objects of art makes this place perfect for relaxation, enjoyment, and enhancement of self-image in every way. Someone you meet here could well become a major love interest, but even if you don't meet Mr. or Ms. Right, you still could come across someone who at least exemplifies some of the qualities your ideal love has. While those who are aesthetically aware find objects and experiences to treasure, those with a more practical bent can find many lucrative opportunities. The key word for this zone is pleasure, making it the perfect locale for leaving your cares behind and reaping some of the rewards of your labors.

Long-Distance Lines

This then is a hot spot for the development of the qualities of sociability, grace, cooperation, and personal attractiveness. Even if you can't journey to or live in this area, you should find that your dealings with it emphasize cultural concerns and that the relationships you develop with people from this area are centered around these same things. Your perfected female image (known as the "anima") would probably be encountered here in person, but from a distance you might still come across it in artwork, a book, or a movie from this area. In the same vein, people frequently marry those who were born somewhere on their Venus lines. Dealings with this part of the world will serve to develop personal qualities of sympathy, your ability to relate, creativity, your aesthetic sense, and, finally, a positive self-image and appreciation.

Psychological Interpretation of Venus:
The World Loves A Lover

The planet of love, marriage, art, relatedness, and interdependence, makes this zone strongly beneficial for most people, as it is a place where these pleasant matters will predominate in your life experience. A deepened need for peace, happiness, and harmony, and a nostalgia for the wonderful (often associated with childhood), impels you to develop yourself into the image of your desire. Worshipping this perhaps unattainable aesthetic ideal, you strive to perfect yourself, and may soon come to realize, perhaps after disappointment, that much of the beauty you have idealized in others actually came from within. Mystically, Venus has a life-giving force, and under its influence you breathe vitality into yourself, motivated by the longings of Eros. Your values and standards evolve as you internalize the beauty you see around you, and it becomes a part of you, now and into the future.

Beneath Romeo and Juliet's dreamy sentimentality lay a very strong and firm commitment to what they loved. If you surrender to the senses as they did, you should do so with the hope of attaining a better understanding of the ideal values that underlie the reality, because it is these that will bring the most lasting benefit to you from living under this line. By opening your heart and your senses, you can develop, for example, real taste and a desire for elegance and affection. The taste for what is refined and pleasurable can become an addiction, however, an idolatry of the beautiful, unless you work to develop the spiritual qualities hidden behind the veil of Venus.

As you would guess, the key Venusian concepts of love and beauty have another dimension beyond their sweet storybook agreeableness. Balance and harmony are the fundamental, underlying archetypes of Venus, for beauty requires instinctive recognition of what seems appropriate and pleasing in form and in harmony with its environment; and love is a feeling of identification with such beauty in its simplest sense. The problem with Venus (or with love, as anyone who has experienced it will testify) is that even harmony must be balanced—love, beauty, sweetness, and light, by being inherently preferable to what is dark and foreboding, invite an overbalance in their favor—and so the psychological impulses toward the less desirable possibilities are neglected and repressed, only to erupt on occasion with frightening force: the demons of possessiveness and jealousy unleashed into the pastel world of Walt Disney.

Stages and Myth of Venus:
The Arrows of Love

The goddess Aphrodite, or Venus, ruled love and beauty, but she had a darker side, too, an irrational vengefulness that unjustifiably and cruelly punished mortals with little provocation. Aside from suggesting the painful side of love, this facet of her personality also warns that residence in the carefree, childlike realm of Venus must be paid for somewhere along the line, at best with increased inner knowledge, or at worst by having to suffer for not developing such knowledge. Narcissism, a consuming love of self, is among Venus's negative aspects, but such self-containment and sterile self-regard is only possible when the outer world is being more kindly, supportive, and pleasant than it ought to be.

The stages of perception for Venus are widely diverse, beginning with a primitive, childish, frivolous, selfish possessiveness that grasps at pretty things and people with unconscious singlemindedness. The inevitable balancing that results leads to an awareness that fairness must be learned and that any relationship (including parenting) requires accommodation, patience, and effort. In the last stage you begin to accept and become comfortable with self as you recognize that you are as deserving a part of the universe as any other; beauty is seen to stem from within and is happily shared with others in an awareness that life is short and that transcendence of mortality can be found through love. Envy, which is usually directed at either inherited physical beauty or wealth, leads you to an awareness that mortality makes all privilege and possessions meaningless unless they are shared. A fully developed Venus consciousness is characterized by both joy and somberness, feelings born of the realization that pleasure, like life, has boundaries.

The Practical Side of Venus:
Shop 'Til You Drop

Now that you've been warned about all the things that might go wrong, it is only fair to mention that the Venus zones like this one are usually some of the most congenial and successful places for anyone. Friendship, mercy, benevolence, children's concerns, conviviality, marriage, romance, and often sex of a particularly pleasant variety enter the life, and the people whom you meet here (the most influential of whom may be women) could become lifelong friends. You develop a childlike trust in happy endings, and you increase in attractiveness, perhaps even becoming popular in a gossipy peer group that reminds you of your teen years. Of course, marriage and relationship become prime concerns, and this is a place where partnerships of any kind, along with your potential for conventional happiness (whatever that might be) are brought to the fore. Marriage is a good possibility here, and all of your relationships serve to deepen your appreciation of yourself.

Money is also apt to be plentiful here, as are the nice things it buys, so you may develop a taste for the good life, becoming something of a gourmet of sensations of all kinds. Some of these sensations are purely personal, including a need for domestic life, but others are more sensual , such as a desire for good things to eat and for other things that you can taste with all the senses. Acquisitiveness is also likely to manifest, as will appreciation of pretty things, people, and pets. This is a good place to store wealth through making wise long-term investments, and often this location is one at which you produce income more easily than anywhere else.

You value things for their pure beauty, so that artistic abilities and appreciation can become central concerns in this zone. Religious images, little dogs, flowers, jewelry and adornments, mirrors, souvenirs, pastels, and luxuries are among the items you might prize most, though your tastes may deepen to include the most refined areas in the arts and music. In fact, you may notice things beginning to pile up around you, as it becomes much easier for you to acquire things than to throw them away. Your artistic abilities improve and you may even achieve recognition for them here.

Of course, many of these positive aspects can be pursued to excess, which may contribute to a very unrealistic view of the world on your part, perhaps resulting in laxity, dependence, and laziness when faced with the realities of everyday life. Shallowness, vanity, and a tendency to wait for others to take care of things are real problems you may have to contend with, as Venus tends to take a passive role. This zone is generally good for health, although overweight certainly can become a problem (too many good things to eat), as can other negative results of excess. If the Venusian influence is entirely projected on to others, you will find that you are surrounded by beautiful people whose presence urges you to perfect yourself.

Venus on Ascendant:
If They Love Me, I Must Be Beautiful

This position of Venus stresses personal self-perfection most among all the possible manifestations of this planet. You may actually become more attractive as you take up activities which improve your physical appearance or you may perhaps learn to express yourself artistically. You easily conceptualize your ideal of physical beauty and seek to emulate it, whether through a greater sensitivity to fashion or by balancing and consciously working to improve your personality by acquiring new abilities or perhaps by moderating excesses that have held you back in the past. In any case, if your efforts can pay off, you will end up attracting the kind of people you have always imagined inaccessible—and this in turn will help you to redefine yourself in a more kindly light.

This is the place at which you can learn to be less hard on yourself, though the life of laziness and self-indulgence that beckons might take you to the opposite extreme of being much too soft on yourself. Part of your desired self-definition here may be on the order of "Hollywood sex kitten," pink bathtubs and all, or (in more gender neutral terms) you want to be valued not for your brains, or even for your personality, but for your looks. Your health may improve (as long as you are aware of the danger of weight gain) and your financial problems are more likely to be those that come from embarrassing excess rather than deficiency; investments you make in valuable possessions and "collectibles" in this locale seem to have been touched by Midas, and thus are quite likely to increase in value.

Relationships are important here, as they are in any Venus zone, and you will tend to define yourself by whom you are involved with, perhaps aiming for relationships that others might envy—especially those with physically attractive people. You can deal with problems of possessiveness here by making an effort to integrate the personalities of those you love and admire into your own, which certainly is preferable to trying to restrict these people socially. You generally will have a pacifying influence on your environment, and often find yourself playing the role of peacemaker or diplomat, arbitrator or mediator. People instinctively try to moderate their feelings in your presence. Artistic accomplishment is personally important here, and learning some form of artistic expression can prove a turning-point in your life. It is a fun location, where pleasure and financial success abound, along with a sense of playfulness and beauty.

Venus on Midheaven:
Zen and the Art of Consuming

Venus on the line that corresponds to your 10th house cusp in this location tends to stress the monetary, social, and public images associated with this planet. You come to be identified by society with what you possess, so that earning and keeping money can become a major preoccupation, as can the enjoyment of conspicuous consumption and the general temptation to live beyond your means in order to create a favorable image for the world to see. If you can rein these tendencies in and make them work for you, rather than against you, you can find real success here, as this is one of the world's best locations for you to achieve recognition for your creative powers and abilities. With a minimum of effort, you can come to be seen as someone who has made it into the best circles with style.

Art or aesthetics is likely to figure into your vocation in some important way. It might, for example, involve gardening, flowers and plants, ornaments, fashion, or decoration, as well as finances or investment connected with "collectibles" of one kind or another. Things you acquire here tend to appreciate in value, but this is no accident since you seem to have the taste to know what is worthwhile and what is worthless. Your image in society may be that of a rather fashionable, indulgent, person who is adept in the social graces. The "beautiful people" who grace your home or hang out with you in trendy spots, have a hedonistic, self-indulgent aura about them, which lends panache to your quest for enviable social advantage. Some of the modes of behavior you perfect now may be rather impractical, but that doesn't mean they can't be profitable.

Other people see you as you like to see yourself, and you are known by all for how you go about getting what you want. Lifestyle is important to you here so you enjoy more, and enjoy it more often and more obviously than most people. Relationship may also figure into your occupation—on one hand you could be known as "so-and-so's spouse," or, alternatively, you might work in counseling, legal areas, or mediation that directly involves the relationships of others. If you do not enjoy luxury in a public fashion, perhaps it will figure into your profession in some way. Some personalities may here succumb to the temptations of indolence and laziness, however, so that though you are "known for your lifestyle" and your friendly relations with large sums of cash, these things could be conspicuously absent or, if present, flowing to you from other people.

Venus on Descendant:
The Marrying Maiden

The overriding concern accompanying a setting Venus is how best to come to terms with self and how best to learn to experience your potential for beauty, love, and artistic creation. Here you are inclined to act out these concerns through another person, particularly in a long-term relationship or marriage. Though you are able to get in touch with your own inner beauty, it probably will be through love and attachment to someone else, whom you see as beautiful. People with whom you deal here are often either artistic types, dancers, painters, etc., or physically attractive people who exemplify the themes of peace, art, and beauty. It is probably the most likely location for marriage, especially for women, though those whom you attract tend to the beautiful-but-lazy type, and thus might not make the best mates. Still, you are proud of your lovers and their appearance, and through them may be willing to live out your own fantasies vicariously. Others respond to your Venusian demeanor by becoming more gracious, attractive, diplomatic, and elegant.

As you acquire somewhat of a skill in human relations, you may succeed here as a counselor, lawyer, negotiator, and should do well in any other role in which social interaction is fostered and encouraged. You social skills and your charm also improve and you find they are more highly valued by others here than elsewhere. If you are the type who likes to be up at four in the morning ready to go fishing or hiking, you'll find that the life of action is quickly abandoned for one of ease and beauty. While pursuing life's pleasures tends to get you involved in other people, you may find that you're tempted to live through their experiences rather than have new ones of your own.

This generally should be a happy and pleasant zone, especially if you are content to live for others. You have a calming, harmonizing effect on your social milieu. You may end up willingly doing most of the work of holding together relationships and making them work, and you seem to derive a sense of identity and purpose from seeing other people happy. Your personality, under the influence of these relationships, becomes more temperate, affable, languid, sensual, and aesthetic, but your belief in the justice and fairness of the universe may be challenged from time to time as you are forced to recognize others' identities and conflicting needs.

Venus on Imum Coeli:
Country Gardens

The position of Venus in this location stresses the enjoyment and perfection of a nurturing home atmosphere either in actual, external terms or perhaps by making you feel more "at home" with yourself, at peace with who you are and where you came from. Here, coming to terms with your experience of childhood is critical, and you may attempt to relive it if it was happy, or perhaps create a more nurturing and supportive environment for others and for yourself if it was not. Your attitude toward home, family, origins, and background—your past "karma"—is central to any self-perfecting activity you undertake in this locale. While a striving for self-perfection might well be acted out through children (who take on more importance here for you than they might elsewhere), it also suggests a deep reformulation of your inner image, the result of which is a more moderate, harmonious, and kindly feeling toward yourself.

You tend to be more interested in home improvement under this Venus line, and will probably take the old saying, "a house is not a home" to heart as you work to make your own place of abode a wonderful and welcoming environment. You will probably be most satisfied living in a rural area, or at least a place growing lushly with gardens full of colorful flowers and attractive leafy plants. As you seek luxury and contentment in your home environment, it can become something of a social center, and your domestic abilities flower, as you find yourself more interested in sewing, baking, decoration, gardening, even light farming. Before you know it, your home becomes your favorite place, the one in which you look best and feel most content. Children ("Are all of these ours?"), pets, livestock, bric-a-brac, and possessions seem to accumulate of their own accord around you, as your appreciation and affection for your family, your loving friends, and the place where you live deepens from day to day. If you're not already a parent, this is a good place in which to become one; and if you are already a parent, the temptation to add to the litter comes with this territory. Though investments in objects of art may pay off in general under a Venus line, land bought at this locale is very likely to increase in value. By surrounding yourself with beauty, you are able to internalize it and to feel better about yourself, which is a marvelous way of obtaining the peace and security you crave here. If you have not already found it, you may experience real, true, lasting love for the first time in this place, something which can help to establish a feeling of contentment and harmony that lasts you for the rest of your life.

Venus with Mars:
Who Cares What the Neighbors Think?

Your awareness of sexual polarities increases under this traditionally hot and passionate combination, so you are likely to identify (and be identified by others) more strongly with your gender, while at the same time the environment you cultivate comes to symbolize the opposite of that identity to an excessive degree. This fosters an awareness in you of the attributes of the opposite sex that you find most alien and threatening. Sex itself is seen in a new light (and one that is not always flattering) as the family and romantic aspects of your relationships seem to recede in this climate, leaving your sexual interest as an openly honest, intense biological urge. In this zone, conventional boy-meets-girl attachments are more likely to lead to the bedroom than to the altar, and in general you seem to have little concern for propriety, what mother might say, or what the neighbors think. Indiscretion and impatience dominate, and you rely on trial and error, seeking endless variety in sexual matters and in other life concerns as well. This may be a good locale for graceful sports such as gymnastics, or for athletic arts such as dance, as the preoccupation with physicality that sparks you sexually makes your body and its attractiveness of unusual concern to you.

Not surprisingly, all the attention you feel ready to devote to sexual matters bears results: high spirits inspire a constant pursuit of the pleasures of the flesh, and you find yourself attracted to hyper-masculine or ultra-feminine types that might repel you somewhere else. Sensitivity is the key to climbing out of the morass of emotional wreckage and immature relationships this kind of life can create, but long before you develop this, you are likely to have ample opportunities to experiment, and your appetites may invite you to explore erotic areas you usually avoid except in your fantasy life. Abstractly, you can deal here with the binding of the spirit to the flesh, or to efforts at self-perfection, and the attributes you develop through doing this are those associated with sexuality, polarity, and gender. Parenthood is accented here—quite possibly as a symbol of raising the opposite-sex nature to consciousness and assimilating it into your life and awareness. Many seeds are sown under this combination, in wider life concerns as well as in biological areas—and all will mature, in time.

Venus with Jupiter:
Too Much Fun?

Culture and beauty become matters for you to study and to emulate, as you glorify art for style's sake, often within a wealthy, fashionable, cultured and bourgeois social milieu. You prize your friends most for their grace, their social skills, or their refinement, but it all seems a little like a soap opera, heavy on concern for pedestrian feelings, emotionalism, and everyone's prima donna complexes. This location, one of plenty of money, beauty, success, and way too much self-indulgence, could bore you if you are naturally creative, highly motivated, or ambitious, as you might begin to feel a bit like a goose being plumped up just before being ground into the paté. Moreover, your expectations can become inflated all out of realistic proportion, so that no matter how well things go for you (and they usually do go well), you will act the role of the naive stranger in Paradise, grumbling with discontent amid plenty. Women usually react to this zone better than men, taking on the proper genteel air as they become centers of lots of social activity. Impressionability and self-indulgence are the flies in the ointment here as you are inclined to let yourself go, meaning that weight gain (aggravated by an urge not to exercise), and a willingness to be imposed upon are ever-present temptations.

Your motivation may at times be hard to sustain, as your need for conspicuous consumption aims to show the Joneses how well you are keeping up through a round of lavish parties and other social hobnobbing. Your friends tend to be wealthy and indulgent, and marriage and friendship are apt to be very advantageous and socially approved but somehow lacking in passion or challenge. Still, all this popularity and exposure to pleasure and success can have positive results, as the financial benefits of residing under this influence are balanced by a new awareness of to what degree consumption, materialistic status, and your place in society really matter to you. For the truly indulgent, this location is hog heaven, but most people will eventually find themselves yearning for a little stress and challenge.

Venus with Saturn
Diamonds Are a Girl's Best Friend

In this zone, a fear that you are undesirable, needful, and unattractive may have some truth to it, if only because feeling this way on the inside often has the effect of making it difficult for people to get to know you, or to get closer to you. This can be a very challenging place for people who depend heavily on their relationships, as a pattern of rejection can develop here that only reinforces the insistent feelings that happiness and contentment in relationship may never be attained. In an attempt to overcompensate for these feelings of affectional difficulty, some fashion for themselves a jaded and sophisticated mask or, just as frequently, pursue a highly material course in life, a course often connected in some way with an important relationship. Ultimately, you might surrender any hopes you have that you can achieve love or security. Friends disappoint you, and love and social concerns do not measure up to expectations. Concepts of femininity inside yourself and in the outside world are likely to be denigrated as well.

You may find yourself deeply involved with or attracted to people and situations that others find burdensome or disagreeable. This can include elements of the "low life," or even in extreme cases a taste for humiliation. More often, though, you simply sacrifice emotional fulfillment to the gods of duty and security, and, as is often the case in any zone influenced by Saturn, even though you are aware of your own lack of satisfaction in this regard, it is difficult for you to leave or change, as you feel there is something virtuous in the suffering.

On the positive side, prudence, discipline, and self-control can be developed here which makes the area a good one for learning and doing detailed craftswork or other painstaking artistic practices, as well as to overcome any of your bad habits. Older people (or sometimes those very much younger than you) seem more attractive to you here than elsewhere, and you find yourself with a growing respect for age and experience, along with a need and capacity to express your feelings and emotions in a tangible form that compensates for the cool, unfulfilling emotional life which marks this zone. Through such difficulties, you always manage to take care of yourself, but still this zone is one of depressed financial opportunities, low self-esteem, and relational problems.

For Women Only: You may find this zone to be particularly difficult, as most women rely on success in the art of relationship for much of their self-esteem—something that proceeds poorly in this locale. Venus symbolizes your attitude toward your own femininity, your attractiveness (not only physical), and your ability to relate, cooperate, and experience happiness. When that planet is combined with Saturn, these concerns are liable to meet with much frustration and delay, with the result that you may be tempted to seek a "sugar daddy" or to drive yourself mercilessly in order to attain material success. Though you may be admired and envied, it doesn't sink in, and only through deep introspection and honesty can you feel comfortable with yourself here.

For Men Only: This influence will most likely manifest in the women you deal with, but it is far too easy for you to see your own problems in their personalities. You may be drawn to a marriage of convenience, or perhaps just give up on developing a relationship altogether, preferring the company of other men and relating to women only as sexual needs and emotional or domestic inabilities require. However in choosing and using women in this way, you will tend to settle on those who bring out your deepest fears and inadequacies. Yet you are liable to take defeats in relationship easily, if only because they confirm your fears about your undesirability. By giving in to such fears, you run the risk of social isolation and alienation, possibly substituting insensate ambition or materialistic greed for personal satisfaction.

Venus with Uranus:
Flower Power

In this zone, you seem to experience a continual conflict between your need for independence, the pursuit of your outspoken idealistic and social objectives, and your need for relationship, stability, harmony, happiness, and peace. The part of your life that centers around relationships is apt to be unsettled, often as an expression of an ambivalent motivation; while you greatly desire companionship and attachment, you want at the same time to preserve your career and experience full social independence. Your social life in general moves along very quickly here; it is colorful, scintillating with contrast, excitement, and unconventionality. Your friends tend to be of a Bohemian persuasion, and "hippie" types, as the famous, creative, and unconventional come and go in your life as if characters in a stage play. You express your rebelliousness and nonconformity in your strange diet, quirky mannerisms, garish but stylish dress, choice of sometimes bizarre companions, and in your rejection of sexual and gender stereotypes. Other people think you are an interesting and offbeat person, usually finding themselves either strongly attracted to you or repulsed by you and the ideas you espouse. Your lifestyle becomes avant garde, anti-puritanical, eccentric, and perhaps artistic. With your exciting and unusual friends, you speak of the need for utopian social reform of one kind or another, based on a philosophy that may also be expressed through taking up life in a communitarian subculture.

Personal relationships tend to be particularly unconventional and tumultuous here, as well as all too brief. Your erotic urges are strong, but they are often nonmonogamous and polymorphous, as you may seek unconventional modes of expressing your sexuality. By such means you are able to see yourself as the mirror of others' unfulfilled ideals, whether this is really so or not. Whirlwind, once-in-a-lifetime storybook romances enrapture you one after another, in rapid succession, and though this inconstancy might be due mainly to your unwillingness to commit to anything over a long term, you may feel it is due to the fickleness and emotional coolness of others. Your ideals are projected onto your beloved, and thus you rebel when he or she demands recognition of his or her personality, apart from your demands and imaginings.

Venus with Neptune:
The Impossible Dream

Dreaminess, romanticism, and escapism mark your life and your feelings in this area; your impulses to relationship and your potential for conventional happiness and pleasure are defined by your illusions, your romantic point of view, and your deeply subjective orientation. You indulge in a poignant nostalgia for what you remember as the beauty, sensitivity, and freedom of childhood, and you may elevate the idea of achieving the impossible dream to the level of an unachievable obsession. You admire and seek out glamour here, driven by intense feelings and a wistful sentimentality. If you are not absorbed in the goings-on of the celebrities who populate the supermarket tabloids, you could easily be living out the same sort of scandalous soap-opera intrigues in your own life. The subjective obscures the objective, meaning that your beliefs, illusions, and imperfections are projected on the screen of reality and, while wishes may have a way of coming true, the wishes are usually for some sort of self-immolation or love-sacrifice.

You tend to choose your relationships badly, perhaps leading to liaisons with a series of disinterested, lax, weak, or unreliable people who end up disappointing or betraying you. Or perhaps you will find yourself becoming involved with people whom you feel you can reform, only to eventually wake up to the fact that you chose them for their faults and not their virtues. The more troubled or mysterious the person, the more you will be fascinated, so be particularly leery of associating with anyone with social, drinking, or drug problems. The same type of problem may also plague you, as the disappointing and unpleasant reality of life is too easily mitigated by escapism. Love affairs tend to be sordid, as you seem to be attracted to the cockroaches beneath the glitter and the unpleasant reality beneath the glamour. Conflicts in loyalties become impossibly complex, and your social life is often driven by gossip and intrigue. Your own suffering defines the depth of love you are capable of unselfishly giving.

Artistic sensibilities and talents develop here, as you find you are able to recognize nuances in form, color, and beauty—to all of which you respond intensely. Your idealistic yearning for merging your identity with an imagined external reality (or person) can best take artistic, poetic, or musical form here as an expression of your demands that life conform to an ideal of beauty and harmony. These demands raise others' consciousness to potentials higher than their own limited, earthbound lack of vision.

Venus with Pluto:
Partnership with a Passion

In this zone, the normally pleasant, happy, and joyful life areas of love and relationship are gateways to discovering the mysteries of mortality, power, and sex, whether this is what you want them to be or not. Sexual needs tend to be intense and intrusive, always seeming to upset the equanimity of otherwise healthy relationships, and your erotic feelings may attract you to extreme or exotic forms of satisfaction. Your insatiable needs can lead to passionate relationships that swirl your feelings around in a "punk rock" social life, perhaps leaving you time for little else. You have the desire to merge entirely with your loved one, but ambivalent feelings of love/hate, jealousy, and sexual control make sure that any relationship is a scene of constant upheaval driven by subconscious impulses you may be unaware of. Every time you let someone get close to you, it opens up the cellar rooms of the repressed past, at which point the monsters of possessiveness, envy, jealousy, power, and your potential to betray your own love must be dealt with. The themes of love and destruction intertwine as you seek the ideal mate with an almost tragic intensity, finding moderation in anything difficult.

There is a positive side to all this, however, as you can enjoy the deepest levels of love in the merging of your identity with another, but only if you are ruthlessly honest with yourself and your beloved, and allow room for periodic changes and rearrangements in your relationship. Among less happy aspects of your love life in this zone can be alienation, involvement in prostitution, or a celibacy resulting from disillusionment.

The themes of intensity, rebirth, and betrayal can also move into the financial arena, so that extraordinary gains or losses whipsaw your bank account from one extreme to another. Partnerships involving money can be subject to exactly the same problems as romantic liaisons, making them difficult to manage. Again, honesty and directness are the only ways to prevent catastrophe. Your personal values also change, and they may emerge as more mature, tested, and tempered. You both seek and fear peak experiences in your life, as frequent explosions keep most of your social relationships honest and nonillusory. Your desire for "sooner, quicker, faster, more" in the end marries you to passion, as you learn some true facts about life (and death) which shatter your earlier naiveté.

12

Mars: Mary Poppins, Watch Out!

OBVIOUSLY, certain types of people will find an environment heated up by Mars more difficult than others do; those who have adapted well to the ties that bind society and family together and who also value cooperation, harmony, and peace will find this zone very perplexing and problematical. Also, people for whom sexual thoughts must be repressed because the subject is considered sinful or is otherwise psychologically stressful will be disturbed to find it irrepressible, demanding, and omnipresent. More adventuresome, independent, pioneering, and athletic types, at home with their bodies and the biological functions that go with it, might find this zone invigorating, energizing, and one in which new approaches and possibilities are discovered.

For Women Only: You'll find this zone one of special problems for you. Women are not usually socialized to be comfortable with the aggressive, assertive power they can command, and thus often tend instead to attach themselves to men whose overt masculinity is usually in direct proportion to the suppression of their own. Any such tendency as this will be exaggerated in this locale, especially during the initial stages of the development of Mars consciousness. Hopefully you will learn to take control of your own masculine energy and will thus be able to feel more at home with anger, sex, assertion, and self-expression. You may have to undertake integration of your masculinity into your psyche in a directed and conscious way, perhaps through assertiveness training, martial arts, or vigorous physical activity. The result of such integration will be a wider, more mature personality, increased personal power, and the valuable gift of personal autonomy.

For Men Only: Obviously you are more apt to find this zone congenial than most women would, especially if you are comfortable with your masculinity and sexuality. Any sporting or engineering abilities you have will be accented, and if you are boastful of your scars, you will probably acquire quite a few more to brag about during your stay here. You may find yourself hanging out in an exclusively male society—perhaps something like the military, in which female influence is minimal—and you are apt to enjoy the kind of camaraderie to be found in a locker room or at a construction site. The danger you must deal with here is that you will become prone to objectification—using and showing disrespect for all that is feminine. As you reject it more and more in favor of the masculine side of yourself and of everything else, you will come to feel that you are alone among enemies and competitors in a cruel and survival-oriented world; burnout and paranoia are the extreme manifestations of too much masculine energy.

If You're Just Passing Through...

Even a short stay in this zone can galvanize your self-sufficiency, build a fire under your competitive instinct, and stoke up your sexual appetites, especially if men are the objects of your desires. Sports of any kind, but especially the more competitive ones, shine here, so expect to have more energy than usual if you are on vacation and looking for athletic and vigorous pastimes. Cooperation, love, and harmony may be noticeable by their absence, however, and if you're travelling with people you harbor ill feeling for, expect constant confrontation while at this locale. This can also be an accident-prone area, especially for those who do not feel comfortable with sex, competition, maleness, or assertion. This can be an ideal spot for a survivalist vacation in the mountains, but this zone is less suited for social relationships, investment, or business other than the most daring of entrepreneurial ventures.

Long-Distance Lines

Even if you can't travel to the areas touched by your personal Mars lines, they may become important in your life through people who come from there. These people may either antagonize you unpredictably, making you angry and putting you in touch with your passions and competitive spirit, or spur you on to growth and self-realization through continually setting goals that test your mettle. You may associate these goals with hardy pioneer types and adventuresome risk-taking; poor for investment, these zones are good for development of new ideas and personality capacities.

Psychological Interpretation of Mars:
It's Hard Work Being Invincible

Mars' nature assures that the dominant theme in this, your "energy locale," is action and the outward projection of strength, often in the service of some symbolically masculine cause or ideal. Mars power is intense, so it should be respected and used with caution. Such raw, masculine energy is regulated and discouraged by modern society (despite the fact that it is idealized in Westerns and crime movies), so its expression often elicits a hostile reaction. You, on the other hand, tend to think it appropriate in a world you see as peopled with dragons and princesses in need of rescue, and where your ego pushes you into the thick of every battle.

Your physical intelligence develops to a high degree here, and whether through erotic stimulation or other challenge, in a sense you "become a man" (no matter what your sex), learning to take control of your own life and to be responsible for your own destiny—a battle of selfhood which will have to be fought over and over. The idea that all nature is renewed by fire, sex, or war is in keeping with Mars, so you burn many bridges here in this locale and leave childhood and dependency behind forever. Mastering the environment and defending oneself against harm are the two most obvious functions of Mars, inclining you to force yourself onto others, to keep yourself perpetually active, and to destroy anything you cannot master.

Competition is a favored mode of relating to others in this locale, and anyone you can not dominate or master directly you will attempt to overcome covertly. While you are continuously testing yourself, at the same time you are constantly attempting to bridle your passions, and you make decisions and take actions that commit you to the struggle for survival. It may be very difficult to feel close to men especially. Since all are seen as potential competitors, courageous, passionate, and impulsive actions keep you on constant guard, never able to relax. Every life activity seems directed by domination and competition, so that virility, some cruelty, and even violence are expressed, as the exercise of power invigorates you, spurring you on to hunt for action and adventure. You feel at home with pain and danger, both of which are frequent experiences.

Stages and Myth of Mars:
The Defensive Survivalist

Mars' myth of course identifies it as the god of war, and while war is an unpleasant human reality, it is in part a process of natural selection among subgroups of the species, assuring a strong genetic stock. Mars purges and burns away what is no longer needed, just as predators thin herds of deer. On a personal level, in a Martian area you learn to fend for yourself, perhaps under actual military conditions or in response to imagined dangers. The result is a spare, impetuous, athletic, trimmed-down personality, unburdened of its more burdensome features and stimulated to healing and growth by the abrupt removal of some of life's clutter on psychological and material planes.

The early stages of Mars awareness are usually the most difficult, as people who have ignored or repressed their capacities for sexuality, competition, or aggressiveness may find themselves dealing with these aspects of personality in quarrelsome, violent, sexually aggressive, irritating people with whom involvement seems inescapable. A lack of consciousness of Mars' potentials in this zone can lead to injury through either accident or attack. In later stages of awareness you may act out some of the least desirable of Martian attributes, as you tend to be boisterous, crude, leering, annoying, and noisy. You act the obnoxious adolescent, cocky and pugnacious, perhaps to the point of losing friends and alienating almost everyone you know. More mature acceptance of your own Martian power, however brings a cool recognition of the necessity to do constant battle with injustice, and, like a surgeon, to learn how to do good by selective destruction. The need to master the environment through taming rivers and the other chaotic forces of nature makes a useful place for Mars, and the really hard-edged Mars type often fits best into pioneering situations at the edge of a frontier, far from the diplomatic give-and-take of relationship in a complex society. Mars' power is such that society spends a great deal of energy in regulating it, so the closer you are to the urban bourgeois reality in which most people live, the less appropriate is the overexpression of its energy.

The Practical Side of Mars:
Casey Jones, Paul Bunyan, John Henry

On more practical levels, in this zone temper, violence, passion, sex, and other biological urges are more powerful, much the opposite of peace, harmony, or the desire for security. You tend to be opportunistic, so that relationships, even marriage, tend to be contentious rather than cooperative. As Mars is the planet of "machismo," you develop a tendency to daring, courage, adventuresomeness, and risk-taking, though this is often accompanied by a tendency toward pride and a sensitivity to insult. An eternal discontent seems to drive you to explore, to test, and to dominate every aspect of the world around you with zest and energy. Though you can be persuasive, spontaneous, impulsive, and excitable, a coarser element to Mars can also bring out traits such as intolerance, crudeness, and lustfulness.

Professions in which Mars excels are obvious: athletics, military, police work, meat-packing and butchery, heavy industry, construction, metal work, use of tools, engineering, and jobs traditionally associated with men—all of these are good areas in which to express Mars' creative energy and physicality. Such active occupations tend to vent the impetuous and intense energy of this zone into healthy channels. Formalized competition can be helpful in doing the same if you do not work in a Martian occupation, so athletes can expect not only to excel here, but perhaps even can set lifetime records. On the intellectual side, your mind becomes more mathematical, scientific, and materialistic.

The dangers of Mars to personal well being comes from two main sources: injury and burnout, both of which are the result of too much energy spent without rest, a lack of moderation, and a need to go it alone that rejects social cooperation. Physical activity tends to relieve the tensions you experience here, and can help you in guiding the energy of Mars in a useful way.

Mars on Ascendant:
Your Best Friends Won't Tell You

In this locale, Mars manifests most obviously in the hard edge it adds to your personality and the tendency of your relationships to move from the equality of partnership as they become more structured and hierarchical. Here you are apt to encounter quite a few problems in dealing with people, as your aggressiveness and belligerence, consciously acknowledged or not, surface repeatedly in social contexts. You project a macho image, as you seek to compete with almost everyone you encounter, expressing yourself in a more physical way. While often acting rashly, you can at times show real courage in taking on situations that others won't touch. On the other hand, undertaking risky endeavors means that while you will have some spectacular successes, these will be matched by a high rate of failure. In either case will find it difficult to take on these tasks in concert with others.

You often carry around a chip on your shoulder, and woe to anyone who volunteers to knock it off. When you turn that aggressive energy in a positive direction, you can push yourself to the limit, especially in athletic competition, where you demonstrate control and mastery of your physical body. Your appetite for adventure and risk can earn you more than your share of the bumps of life, but also more than your share of rewards. Through daring, bravery, and pushing the limits of pain and endurance, you attract attention. Because of an element of self-dislike that lurks within the intense, unrelenting energy with which you drive yourself, you are able to get wholly involved in what you do, and others who dare to tread the same path you choose usually have to be satisfied with matching their pace to the footsteps you have laid down before them. You seek out and enjoy engaging harsh, demanding, and challenging situations, and as soon as one obstacle is overcome you are on to tackle the next.

Life is rarely dull under this line, and your relationships in particular are the focus of much change, often marking your psyche as painful learning experiences. Closer examination of your own behavior, especially with the guidance of a close friend (if such can be found under a Mars line), will lead you to see how you invite confrontations by your offensive attitude, even when you are sure that others are the ones being belligerent and intractable. Health problems due to overexertion, stress, and accidents can cause a lot of problems here, but if you can master these and the other challenges that present themselves, you can begin to understand and accept the confrontive, sexual, assertive, and angry components of your personality once and for all.

Mars on Midheaven:
Room at the Top

A powerful drive for success and social accomplishment urges you on under this Mars line, a drive that should particularly show itself through athletics and other occupations usually associated with Mars. Any masculine, antagonistic environment spurs you on to new heights of attainment, though (as you'd expect) you will not get where you are headed without encountering the real danger of accidents and injury, or occasionally suffering the consequences of rash, inconsiderate action, and temper flare-ups. As you pursue individual success and break new ground in the outside world, you may also experience changes in your own inner world, as, for example, you may discover or experience your true sexual orientation at this place.

In general, your image of yourself is somewhat more macho here than elsewhere, and you'll be attracted to social atmospheres that are more coarse, masculine, and unrefined than usual for you, unless you have a strong Mars emphasis in your personal natal chart. Breaking the rules and rebelling against authority seem second nature for you, but you must understand that the most important lesson of this locale's experience is that you should learn to establish how you can make personal progress through being self-reliant, autonomous, and independent of social interactions. Your greatest success comes through initiative, courage, and risk-taking, rather than through taking orders, or otherwise trying to fit in. Athletes may find themselves stronger and better able to compete here, setting records as they demonstrate new skills and power acquired through rigorous training.

You tend to overestimate yourself and your abilities, but the occasional failure from doing this doesn't dampen your zeal and enthusiasm for the hard work and competition you thrive on. These failures can be due to conflicts with authorities that lead to violent confrontations; injuries, and accidents, all of which can be avoided if you can add a dash of discipline to control your abundant energy. Overcoming antagonisms that block you and meeting the competition head-on leads you to a deeper sense of yourself and your abilities, as you learn your true power to exist and prosper in a hostile environment that demands taming. Your social image is very much on the order of the quiet directness of a Humphrey Bogart, and at times you may in fact feel that your life script is playing itself out like one of his movies. Sex, childbirth, and marital issues require a great deal of attention here, with the latter two needing discipline, attention, and restraint in order to prosper. Sex alone among these will tend to go well without much urging, and you may even become known socially in some way for your sexuality, perhaps through others seeing you as something of a Casanova.

Mars on Descendant:
It's All Their Fault

In this locale, your relations with other people engage your attention, as they tend to be intense, competitive, and confrontational. The more negative aspects of Mars are apt to become evident here, as you tend to project your own violence and antipathy outward, especially if there is any self-dislike in your makeup. You may see yourself as innocent and loving, and wonder why so many around you are so belligerent. As you become more acclimated to the energy of Mars, you may begin to accept that you are probably denying certain aspects of your own sexual or aggressive identity and unconsciously seeking them out in others. Relationships go so poorly here that you may be forced to rely on yourself, but it's not easy, as competitors instinctively go for your weak spots and take a lack of assertiveness on your part as an invitation to aggression.

For obvious reasons, women particularly will have problems in this area, and marriage is not apt to provide much assurance of safety, since your relationship with your husband may well be the source of the difficulty. This can be overcome through adopting a vigorous and physical lifestyle that will help to work off some of your personal tension, as you need to make sure your energies are balanced before you try to understand, much less deal with, the situation. In this area, the ever-present dangers from Mars of injury and accident can be accompanied by oppression, coercion, and unwelcome sexual advances for all but the most self-assured and inwardly honest. Neither investments nor partnerships seem very good prospects here, and litigation should be avoided at all costs.

Despite all this, your confidence in yourself develops, and if you can get in touch with your anger and sexuality, you may find a powerful new sense of your own ability. The hard sell dominates in an environment in which the world seems (and perhaps is) hostile, putting constant pressure on you. Any professions that deal with violence, fire, sexuality, or interpersonal conflict may act out some of the pressure; success comes only through arduous and consistent effort.

Mars on Imum Coeli:
Domestic Hostility

Manipulative or competitive feelings toward your family, coupled with events and circumstances that change your attitude toward your roots, origins, or home situation could occupy your attention with this placement of Mars. The result of the red planet's intrusion into your life may be a new attitude and a renewed relationship with your family and your past. Marriage and long-standing family ties are often tested here, and whether this comes from external problems or avoidable personality conflicts, you will eventually realize that the results are a new and more pertinent definition of who you are and where you came from.

Family problems politely ignored in other localities will come raging out of the closet here, often resulting in a total change in your relationships with home, family, and property. Childbirth and pregnancy are often attended with challenge and trouble as well. You may find yourself devoting extra time to nursing family members back from physical or emotional injury, find that neighbors are harshly obnoxious, or even learn that your actual dwelling is unsuitable, perhaps being more subject to accident or fire than you had realized. Your home life also could be affected or your home changed in some manner by the military.

The result of all this activity is a reformation of your inner concept of yourself on the deepest levels, as you come to a new definition of who you are and how that relates to your roots through confrontations with the past. For the first time, perhaps, you assimilate the idea of your own perhaps latent belligerent and sexual nature, as your sex image becomes your self-image in some sense. If you want a clue to what is lacking in your understanding of yourself, look to what angers you the most. This is an ideal locale to pioneer a home, carving it out of the wilderness, as you seek to subject yourself to harsh and demanding environments under Mars on the I.C. Though centered on such conquest, force, and challenge, you fear the constant tension can tire you out. All this awareness of the passionate and intense side of your roots and family life serves to ground you in your capacity to change the rest of the world, and you discover your heritage of power, albeit sometimes in surprising and importunate ways.

Mars with Jupiter:
Might Makes Right

This locale is especially good for athletic accomplishment and physical culture, as your competitive nature is sharpened, and your strength and virility expand. This new rush of physical and mental energy is evidenced by a delight in sports, hard outdoor work, contests, adventure, and power. There is a military theme played out here along with the athletic one, so you may find yourself commanding or organizing the energy and skills of others here. Your overconfidence and your tendency to take risks are the pitfalls in such pursuits, but despite this, military success or a symbolic equivalent may come for some in this area.

You may imprudently grasp for power, taking "arms against a sea of troubles," only to find that most of them were created by your own dogmatism and the moral myopia that can be characteristic of this location. Always in a hurry (certainly a source of some imprudence), you expand and evolve all masculine and militant life concerns within your reach, forging ahead with your plans so hastily at times that you have to learn from lots of trial and even more error. A satirical and biting wit, a lack of moderation in your pursuit of sensory pleasure, strong sexual needs, and monetary extravagance define you in this place as a colorful personality who seems to have money to burn, as well as the ability to replenish the large sums thoughtlessly spent—others' as well as your own. It seems impossible to save but easy to borrow, and people instinctively believe in your obviously potent ability to create wealth and energy.

A kind of James Bond, Hemingwayesque he-man image manifests here in one way or another (no matter what your sex)—a gallantry and coolness in the face of danger, along with a lovable coarseness, and a not-so-lovable opportunism springing from an expedient set of morals. Your personality and life concerns may turn toward foreign and exotic places or safari-type adventures as your courage increases, along with an imperialistic, authority-respecting, militant, and vigorous charisma. Your greatest dilemma comes from trying to decide what values and social realities deserve your energetic allegiance, as morally, you tend to see even complex matters in childish, black-and-white terms. You may become something of a bigot, imposing your controversial ideas of the universe on the infidels, with imperialistic, militant, and unquestioning narrow-mindedness. At worst, this may evince as a zealous self-righteousness masked under religious hypocrisy or self-serving sophistry. Daring, adventuresome, and courageous, you make or lose fortunes with equanimity and a thirst for life and adventure.

Mars with Saturn:
Basic Training

This is not a desirable place to live for most, as harsh conditions, a tendency to reject what is supportive and nurturing, and a blockage of masculine energy that leaves you open to victimization and violence all unite to make survival here a day-to-day problem. Physical needs never seem to get taken care of, and your attempts to pursue a particular goal with intense dedication and concentration are often unproductive, frustrating, and barren. Health problems of your own or in someone close to you may require continual self-sacrifice. Unconscious memory or fear of victimization can tie you to dependent persons in such situations and thus restrict you in a way that seems to make it possible for you advance.

Conditions in general are more difficult for you here than in most places and the fact your "basic training" in survival at this locality seems to go on forever may wear you down in time. Violence, cruelty, or sadism are the worst manifestations of this combination, but more often your complaint is likely to be that your days are endlessly dreary and depressing. Crowds, high places, and overexertion can pose physical threats, and injuries that come from any of these sources may lead to chronic problems. Yet, for all these difficulties, this can be an area in which you learn that, through tenacity and brute force, insurmountable obstacles can be overcome. It is a good place for those who engage in the roughest sort of livelihood—miners, laborers and steelworkers for example. Anything feminine, gentle, artistic, or sympathetic is notably absent from this locale, and sexual opportunities are strangely abundant, but only so long as sex remains anonymous and without feeling. Having come through the challenges that mark a Mars-Saturn area, you should emerge with the faith that you can survive any conditions—and so you can.

For Women Only: You probably will find this area quite unpleasant as you are apt to attract a rather brutal, coarse, and unsympathetic mate or begin to act out such a role yourself, especially through an opinionated attitude, a brittle social facade, and even cowardice. Withholding of sex can become a means of asserting your power over those attracted to you, and relationships often evolve into a contest of wills. Still, you feel pride in overcoming the obstacles life throws up for you, triumphing over oppression and coercion (often by just waiting it out), and in seeing that males need you. Your father may hide somewhere at the root of these psychological problems, so you may be able to handle this zone better if you can come to terms with your relationship with him.

For Men Only: You will find this area particularly troublesome. Though you may become sensitive and vulnerable around issues of your maleness, pride, autonomy, and sexual self-image, these are often challenged by overwhelming forces. The result is either a hangdog defeatism, or, just as often, a vengeful bitterness that takes out your suppressed rage on those weaker than yourself. Macho posturing is hard to avoid, and a blind obedience to authority leads you to expect the same from those beneath you in station, just as would be true if you were in the military. Love and sexual performance are areas of acute sensitivity for you here, but you may attempt to disguise this by overcompensating to the point of exhaustion. You have the opportunity to understand issues of will, power over others, social control, and your own male image, but it is hard for you to disentangle yourself from your own problems long enough to learn.

Mars with Uranus:
Don't Tread on Me

In this location, you may undertake the definition, articulation, or implementation of your independence, demanding freedom from coercion and confinement. You cannot be made to do anything that you do not wish to do, but your rebellious and devil-may-care attitude can have perilous consequences, though this probably won't discourage you in the least. You delight in the role of the daredevil and are something of a loner, equating masculinity, independence, and power either with an extremely individualistic lifestyle or with open rebellion against societal norms. You will defend what you see as your rights to the end, expressing little warmth or affection in the process, all of which will leave you operating well outside social support groups. Your sexual needs are apt to be intense and may take unconventional forms since you seem to have no respect for others' property or prerogatives, nor for others' concepts of modesty or propriety.

Inventiveness is accented in this place, so engineers, surgeons, miners, scientists, and those working in technological areas may find their creativity enhanced. Though you live for day-to-day thrills in the adventuresome climate you find here, you face considerable danger of injury, and accidents in the use of guns or machinery, in driving or transportation are possible. Shipwreck, aircraft failures, fires, lightning strikes, and other such sudden, violent disasters are more likely here than in other locales, though they will by no means affect everyone. Despite the danger of constant exposure to unforeseen upheaval, you become daring, insouciant, and disdainful of perils, purposely seeking out areas where angels fear to tread—and surviving despite the long odds. Athletes, mercenary or professional soldiers, explorers, stuntpersons, and heroes may find this climate to their liking, but few others will prove hardy enough to relish the narrow escapes, restlessness, irritability, insomnia, frequent broken bones and contusions, and functional health problems that seem to be the daily fare here. Partnerships and human relationships in general tend to upheaval and unpredictability as well, and an extremely masculine climate prevails, evincing little sympathy, understanding, or cooperation. Yet, for those who need constant adrenaline to add savor to life and who enjoy testing and combative situations, this is a challenging and exciting locality.

Mars with Neptune:
Sex, Drugs...and People Who Like Them

A positive, down-to-earth attitude toward masculinity and sex are critical here, for without them this zone can be a real crazy quilt of possibilities and impossibilities. Ideally, like a hippy, you can manage to live out a more archaic masculine archetype, one in tune with natural and mystical forces and respondent to intuition and inspiration. You rarely will be content to let ambitions and career concerns follow along in commonplace ruts, as you must have some mystery, singularity, and magic to keep you interested. In some cases, you are able to bring such fantasy into reality through wishing and visualization, as well as to influence people (almost against their will) through charisma. Your power over others is implicitly sexual, resulting in an ability to play the role of everyone's sexual fantasy or, alternatively, to see everyone as yours. In either case, extremes of indulgence or asceticism result. In fact, this is probably the most sexually bizarre zone possible, and just about everything erotic you've ever heard of may present weird or unpleasant options to you. You may find yourself enthralled by people you don't really like, and you can revel in unusual practices.

On a more mundane level, you may exhibit unusual imagination and intuition in business and particularly in arts involving motion and energy—dance, gymnastics, ballet, etc.—but usually your aspirations are all out of proportion with reality. The lone exception is likely to be that rare case in which you actually become a symbol for beauty and sex, as TV stars, media athletes, and models occasionally succeed spectacularly here. For those uncomfortable with the masculine archetype (which includes most members of modern society), this location can be fantastically unpleasant: illnesses (including venereal ones), unprovoked attacks from strangers, allergies, victimization by society or its lower elements, problems with parasites (the two- or six-legged varieties), drug habituation, sexual problems, paranoia, and neurosis are some of the less glamorous aspects of this zone. These present you with the evidence of what seems an indefinably hostile environment, in which the forces that attack you are invisible, covert, or unconscious, often stemming from within.

At best, this area may see you defending the underdog through nonviolent means and Gandhian ingenuity, but for the most part you can't count on your allies. Humiliation, defeat, and victimization are too often the result of your effort to implement your ideals.

Mars with Pluto:
Dueling in the Dark

Personal power—its use, abuse, and the effects it has in relationships—is a major concern in this part of the world, where you may encounter extreme situations involving domination and submission that could have you on either end. Anything to do with Mars—sexuality, energy, athletics, force, self-projection, mastery of the environment—cannot be accomplished simply, but involves the deepest and most sensitive areas of your personality in a battle for supremacy over powers that seem almost superhuman in nature. Everything becomes a contest, and a compulsive concern with the masculine image and glorification of the manly ideal reflects a subtle suppression of the sexual nature and its subsequent transmutation into a dangerously inflated quest for power. This is an antisocial location, one in which major life changes occur and new directions are taken, usually as the result of the collapse of previously relied-on structures and relationships. Moral values are seen as superfluous (by you or, often, those around you with whom you have to deal), so the possibility of involvement with criminality is a real one, with you as either the victim or perpetrator. Vengeance, passion, or the establishment of power over another are the driving forces behind this.

Sexuality, if not suppressed altogether, may take some pretty bizarre forms at this place, so passion, when allowed to surface, can be explosive and cathartic. Dramatic alteration in life's directions often accompanies the sexual discoveries or first experiences you find in this area. Childbirth and reproductive concerns are fraught with difficulty, and you focus concern on excretory functions, decomposition, and similar matters as symbols of a death-and-rebirth theme.

In this intense, competitive climate, violence may seem to be the answer to every problem, as you become somewhat more coarse, uncouth, cruel, and indomitable, something which suits you for martial arts or other demanding situations in which rough-and-ready competitiveness is an advantage. The military and intensely demanding athletics are career areas which can focus this otherwise unmanageable energy productively. You are a "man among men" (even if you're a woman), and obsession with power and proving yourself assures you an arduous time in this gloomy, testing, and contentious zone. As a result, you learn to stand on your own and make great strides toward independence and autonomy.

13

Jupiter: Does More Really Mean Better?

PEOPLE WHO value society and its rewards and who aspire to the roles society values will be content in a location where Jupiter is prominent. Jupiter zones are less favorable for strong individualists, as well as the truly creative and independent—those who enjoy the challenge of pitting themselves against authority and the odds, and who espouse their own morality and values. If you have a taste for caviar and your eyes light up when a limousine passes by, this is probably the place for you. You'll love it if you feel you are going someplace in society and if you have a vision and commitment to culture, religion, law, education, or the other professions. It could be unfulfilling, however, if you are not typical of your class or family background, consider yourself self-made, or find the life one sees in TV sitcoms dreadfully boring.

For Women Only: In this zone, you may aspire to political, personal, and social power, though you will have a temptation to project these opportunities onto your mate or partners, providing opportunities for them to rise socially because you feel inadequate to pursue these on your own account. In other words, beware of playing the role of the woman behind the man, unless you are willing to accept it, for your own powers here are extraordinary and can lead to very substantial accomplishment in the highest levels of society: religion, academia, the arts, sports, and politics.

For Men Only: You will probably react to this zone's opportunities for social advancement and improvement of status by making the most of them, furthering your education and technical skills and raising your expectations of yourself a notch or two. The big problem you are likely to experience here is overconfidence, perhaps brought on by a life of intolerant excesses. You tend to slide by without doing your homework thoroughly, relying too much on connections and the power of credentials, and you gravitate toward situations in which you can get by on appearances and favoritism. These dangers aside, this can be a very beneficial zone where success comes to you in sport, profession, career, and social attainments and where you feel good about yourself and what you can do.

If You're Just Passing Through...

This is a very positive zone just to visit, as you can associate with a better class of people and generally attract favorable attention to yourself. This can easily result in you acquiring new social status and power, but it will also make you prone to spend money lavishly. Even if you're not a gambler, don't leave without spending a few dollars on lottery tickets, as this very lucky zone increases both your desire for speculation and your odds of winning. It's also a place for facing and discovering religious truth, successful dealings with authorities, and chance meetings with the powerful and wealthy which could result in you being treated like royalty. Your ideas attract favorable attention, and perhaps even offers for publication.

Long-Distance Lines

Even if you can't travel to this area, it can be significant in your life as a source of sustenance, income, and success. People who come from here can emerge in your life as guides, teachers, mentors, or financial benefactors. Investment in companies or industries based here will tend to prosper, and education (even correspondence courses) derived from resources residing or published under a Jupiter line can establish a cornerstone of lifelong success. You find cultural concerns inviting here, and you may like to read about this zone or find its religion, language, or ethnic roots interesting and important.

Psychological Interpretation of Jupiter:
The Taming Power of the Great

Jupiter's power assures that the central theme of this area is growth through expansion or accretion, so that evolution, deeper participation in experience, and cultural outreach are likely through broadening contact with the world and through associating with a better class of people while you reside here. You feel that you are protected by forces or deities favorable to you, and your belief in this favoritism gives you an optimistic outlook that encourages you to dare the impossible, often exceeding the normal limits of your abilities as you ascend personally and socially. This is where "wishing makes it so," as hope and faith expand; you come to feel deserving of special treatment by the cosmos which, because you expect it, occurs, particularly extraordinary good luck and social or financial advancement, not to mention sponsorship and protection by authorities. Bourgeois values and positive self-evaluation become a notable feature of your character here, as you feel yourself distinguished from the mass of humanity. On the negative side, you can become somewhat righteous, self-satisfied, complacent, or self-important in a way that puts some people off.

The issue of class is very Jupiterian, and you engage in a competition of decency, trying to outdo the Joneses (or maybe the Rockefellers), impressing the world with your attainments, credentials, diplomas, and possessions. The "right" people (especially those in the professions, such as doctors or lawyers) are not to be questioned, and one rises in society through a series of steps up in a very structured and traditional hierarchy. A kind of snobbery inherent in this viewpoint is marked by a contradictory need to feel unique coupled with an unquestioning addiction to fashion and public opinion. People in academic, bureaucratic, administrative, and professional circles rise quickly here, though the attendant temptation to fulfillment of ambition is the abandonment of life's meanings, values, and goals in favor of complacent self-satisfaction.

Stages and Myth of Jupiter:
The Omnipotent Executive

Jupiter's myth is, of course, connected to the god who was chief administrator (chairman of the board?) of Mount Olympus. Jupiter (Zeus), was symbolized as justice, light, and intellect, as opposed to the dark earth god, Saturn (Chronos), or the god of the underworld, Pluto (Hades). The problems of this zone all are echoed in this mythology, as they stem from Jupiter's inherent superiority, which is demonstrated personally as an imperialistic privilege to ride roughshod over the rights of others. Positively, Jupiter's insight grants foresight, psychic powers, innate leadership, superiority, and understanding of the patterns and structures of the universe; negatively, it breeds blind fundamentalism, intolerance, self-righteousness, superstition, bigotry, xenophobia, and a barren morality that condemns what it does not understand.

In its immature stages, Jupiter consciousness is usually marked by some of the above-mentioned excesses—since you have found the "truth" yourself, any other reality or person must accept your higher vision or be seen as an infidel to be forcefully converted. A bragging, boastful bullying could be the result, along with an arrogant, imperialistic self-centeredness, and a feeling that you have the right to dominate anyone else by mere reason of who, and how important, you are. This belief is underlain by an infantile expectation that the world is created by your needs in order to fulfill them. Greater maturity, however, finds you dominating through kindness, becoming the philanthropist, the humanitarian, or the liberal who magnanimously wishes all others to have the opportunity to attain the heights of social acceptance and success that you have attained and who seeks to offer such opportunities to others freely.

Wisdom, exuberance, and humor are the mark of Jupiter in full flower— here is the generous, benevolent, divinely inspired philosopher-king, able to guide the community and humanity as a whole to a realization of its highest visions. The moral guardians of the state—judges, academics, artists, musicians, and religious and charitable leaders—embody this most perfected image of the potentials of this zone and, under its most positive influence, the formulation of ideas and concepts that constitute humanity's cultural heritage and knowledge of the past. This ability to comprehend the future can be grasped and understood, putting you in a powerful social role of leader and guide.

The Practical Side of Jupiter:
Living in the Winner's Circle

The conventional interpretation of good luck centers on the acquisition of an abundance of material goods or social status without expending much effort. If this is what you want in life, then this certainly is the right place to be. Prosperity, success, credibility, honor, academic achievement, and accomplishment are furthered here as your life proceeds almost effortlessly: you move up socially, and find that leisure, nonproductive activity, and bourgeois conformity are frequent rewards of that status. This zone accents humor, education, religion, quality, integrity, prizes, and mental and cultural accomplishments, so it shouldn't be too surprising that you are more optimistic, extroverted, and relaxed here. Health improves (except where you experience problems with overindulgence or sluggish activity), as do magical and healing abilities. In addition to this being a place where you can heal others, any sort of business prospers and succeeds here, as do self-improvement and creativity. Your mind aspires to the lofty, as you try to create patterns that explain the universe. You cultivate the ability to see things in general rather than in a particular context, so that you grasp wholes more easily than details or parts. Music, sports, religion, publishing, media, broadcasting, advertising, promotion, business, import-export, education, the law, finance, medicine, languages, foreign concerns, and travel are all professions that do very well under this influence.

Gambling and speculation are likely to be very successful here, as this zone is one in which you can win (and sometimes lose) large sums of money in such activities. You might want to try your luck at speculation here, or perhaps you could invest in companies whose head offices lie within this zone. But beware of blind optimism, extravagance, or of going into debt simply to impress others, as these things, along with overgenerosity, and snobbishness, are all dangers of this area. Resist comparing yourself too much to others, as you could become caught up in a whirlwind of totally nonessential, fashionable activity that has little enduring value. Notwithstanding these potential hazards, this is one of the most optimistic, successful, and fortunate zones possible, especially for any sort of business or material pursuits.

Jupiter on Ascendant:
The Big Frog

This location emphasizes the sometimes superficial acting out for others of a personal role of success, authority, and power. Or, you may act as an agent to activate these potentials in others' lives, as does a teacher or mentor who guides people to self-fulfillment. Your face or personality could easily become famous here, and people are likely to emulate you or even to follow you as a leader or guru, due to your personal self-confidence and the organizational powers you display. Faith, hope, and optimism are outwardly apparent, having effects on those who deal with you, most of whom will feel elevated, ennobled, or inspired by your presence. A living example of the power of positive thinking, you can even work miracles of faith in the lives of others. Many who have lost direction in life are strongly attracted to you, creating a danger if you take all this attention and preferment too seriously. You could, after all, end up as a pompous, self-important, big frog in a small pond.

Spiritual evolution can be attained here, since your mind grasps universal principles easily. You rapidly emerge as a person of consequence, the essence of establishment values, a pillar of the community, and are liked by people for the joy and exuberance with which you live your life, your generosity, your kindness, and your obvious concern for others' place on the ladder of spiritual evolution. As a teacher, spiritual guide, or financial resource, you can contribute to the expansion and development of individuals and the community, though some extreme individualists and idealists may find the unthinking adulation a little irritating. This is a very good zone in which to improve your own health (unless your main problem is due to an excess of some sort, such as overweight), and here you may feel relief, freedom, and much less stress than usual; you may be identified with some religious group or practice and may seek membership in an organization that enables you to improve your self-image and self-confidence. On the negative side, overconfidence can lead to restlessness, conceit, procrastination, pretentiousness, or fanaticism, so moderation needs to be embraced along with the basic good fortune of this zone.

Jupiter on Midheaven
Meetings with Remarkable People

Socially, this is one of the best places for almost anyone to be: you easily make contact with rich, powerful, and remarkable people, and you are preferred in work situations. Tending to rise socially, you also find this the optimal location for most business and financial matters. Your personal status increases, and along with it the number of people who admire you. You could end up in public office, or at least in a position of power and influence in your own corner of the world. Publicity comes almost too easily to you, so most of your accomplishments receive a lot of very heartening attention and support. Your life's outstanding social triumphs may take place in this location, as you acquire academic degrees, enjoy business accomplishments, and generally gain credentials that make you more sought after wherever you may go.

Success here comes from playing within the system so you should find it most often in situations in which it is the reward for others' admiration and approval. This zone is also positive for success in music and in the helping professions, especially any branch of medicine or counseling, as you exhibit a benevolent care for others. You develop your own personal quality, but also might tend to be a little ostentatious, flaunting your superiority and bourgeois acceptability. You feel a need to belong to all the right clubs and professional societies, or even to organize one yourself, and you may find yourself receiving a "citizen of the year" award for such activities. The problems you experience here are those of success, as you may become insulated and protected from the realities of life and thus lose touch with the majority of humanity; such excesses of pride would usually foreshadow a fall. While this is the best zone for progress in legal, musical, religious, medical, social, business, or publicity concerns, there is always a danger of selling out and abandoning the principles of self-determination, as life here is almost too easy. The socially immature may have to learn some hard lessons in how society is really managed.

Jupiter on Descendant:
How to Win Friends and Influence People

In this location, the position of Jupiter manifests particularly through other people and through relationships of all kinds. Personal salvation for you comes from your teachers, guides, mentors, bosses, or other religious, professional, or social authorities. From them you come to understand the potentials open to you and are furnished with an opportunity for their fullest realization. Often this happens nearly unwillingly, as you might feel the tiniest bit "kept" in this zone. You may not mind much, though, as your surroundings tend to be opulent and the opportunities furnished by your benefactors help you to establish credentials and abilities that benefit you later on in life. You seem to attract effortlessly the influence and assistance of persons in high places, and any time you find yourself in difficulty, whether psychological or material, others come to your aid.

Among your biggest benefactors may be your spouse, as here you can marry the pillar of the community or find business and social options opened up through such an important relationship on every level. Legal concerns, business, and dealings with the public prosper, since this zone is ideal for self-improvement and for marketing of your reputation. You get wide public support and sympathy for every undertaking, but particularly for those involved with business, sales, promotion, the law, education, or the counseling professions. While there is danger of overreliance on mates and partners here, it remains a very positive area in which forces beyond your control seem determined that you will have a fairly easy time of it. Problems arise mainly when you try to do things for yourself, so those who by nature or occupation are already powerfully autonomous and independent will find this area boring and confining. Strong individuals may rebel against the polite, conforming hierarchies that form here. Only those who value the usual rewards that society offers will feel adequately compensated for the subtle loss of self-determinism that usually manifests in this climate.

Jupiter on Imum Coeli
Improving Your Family

This zone particularly emphasizes personal evolution and expansion through commitment to your location, family, or ethnic identity. Moreover, your family, past, and your concept of your background may "improve"—that is, you could elevate your social station through marriage or other family interactions, or increase your own estimation of your family and background through becoming acquainted with previously unknown aspects of your past, roots, heritage, or financial background. Your family develops a tradition, grows a family tree, and learns pride in its traditions and heritage. From this growth of an inner sense of tradition and belonging, you develop a greater sense of inner worth and self-esteem which extends itself eventually into other life areas, with resultant good fortune and expansion of career, personal, and social options. Your true inner self is identified by genealogy and a constant centering of self in the past and tradition; others react to this by gravitating to the security you seem heir to, and to your sense of purpose.

This is an especially satisfying place to reside or retire, as your family life prospers here as nowhere else. You can hope for a secure and respected old age as you become matriarch or patriarch, a pillar of society, and perhaps a successful, though usually conservative, politician. Real estate you acquire increases in value here, and you can make things grow, live off the land, or become a landlord. This is your place on earth, in which the seeds of your potential development find fertilization, and your good fortune enables you to care for less fortunate persons. Founding a sort of extended family is your own way of demonstrating that the order of the universe is reproduced in microcosm in the family. Here in your personal Garden of Eden, you cease to struggle with the outer world as you build inner worth, sharing your success with those closest to you, and pursuing your own religious and social fulfillment. Even short-term residence here can have these effects, changing forever your concept of where you came from and thus where you are going.

Jupiter with Saturn:
The Middle Path

In this zone, moderation, social attainment, and a slow but steady rise to status and accomplishment result from an environment that forces progress on us with both the carrot and the stick; the stick may be first and most obvious, while it may take time (perhaps until after age 29) for the carrot's presence to be felt. You feel a necessity and urgency that operate quite apart from real concerns—a sense that time is quickly running out demands the creation of security, social accomplishment, and perseverance toward objectives that seem inadequate as quickly as they are attained. You feel that you must formulate a material, philosophical, and social basis for your life, and that status and success are major requirements. Your surroundings tend to reinforce an orderly, conscientious, ambitious life, and middle class values, so that events take on an uninspired, practical, purposeful, and balanced nature. Impelled by an orthodox and honorable sense of dignity, you have to work hard for what you get, and while opportunities offer themselves unexpectedly from time to time, you rarely pin all your hopes on them, as in your mind true success comes from plodding routine, duty, and justified advancement.

You work for every scrap of money or advantage you get here, and your savings accrue steadily and predictably. Life may tend to rumble along in a rut but it does so only after you exploit some remarkable opportunities, often centering on productive meetings with powerful people, leaders, politicians, and others who establish direction for society. To your surprise, these people find you interesting and possessed of resources they feel they need.

Though at times you may work long hours for low pay, most jobs likely to interest you are relatively secure, such as civil service or corporate positions linked to retirement plans intended to make your golden years secure. Time is your greatest ally here, so while you may tend to greet new possibilities with anxiety and uncertainty, fearful that any change may constitute loss, your perseverance nearly always assures that you can take control of new situations, albeit slowly. You don't get away with any kind of backsliding or corner cutting, but neither will you lose what is rightly yours if you happen to come up short in one situation or another. A love of stability, careful organization, orthodoxy, sobriety, and narrow-minded materialism echo your concern for your place in society. The more you reach for this bourgeois success, however, the more you might fear that you have missed something.

Jupiter with Uranus:
Kites in the Thunderstorm

In this location, growth, evolution, and personal success are linked to what is unorthodox, politically unusual, and in the avant garde of social or personal reality. Intellectually, this is perhaps the most exciting possible climate, and you will learn to judge for yourself, formulate your own moral and ethical principles, and appear very much the free thinker, liberal, or Bohemian, at least to other people. Offbeat or foreign types of knowledge are the most direct route to great personal fulfillment and will be fruitful areas for employment and financial gain. Astrology, the occult, telepathy, as well as highly technical computer science, or anything that is new and in the intellectual or experimental vanguard attract your interest and can help you to be successful in advancing your prosperity and personal growth. Practitioners of unusual therapies may find this the most congenial possible locale for healing and metaphysics. Seeking to define yourself not by category or type, but as a conceptually unique entity, your relationship to the universe is seen clearly and as totally individual. Your oratorical skills develop to a high degree, your daring ideas often work (much to the surprise of others), and you become the scoffer among the godly, criticizing orthodoxy and inventing your own ideas of universal purpose. It is only in the most abstract, airy, and intellectual realms that you find it possible to hold common ground with others, though in the process you often neglect material concerns, feelings, and humane concerns.

Here, wishing can make it so, as it is a very lucky zone in which you might for example be rescued from money problems by unexpected good fortune. You handle more money than is your custom, and perhaps may defy the odds if you speculate, either through investments or gambling. You learn to think on a broad scale, seeing each part in singular relationship to the whole, an ability which fits you well for an organizational role in business, though you may not easily endure bureaucrats. Self-employment is attractive and profitable here, and, despite the creative genius, artistic capacity, and extraordinary good luck of this zone, its deficiencies lie in repressed feelings, impracticality, constant change, shifting idealism, and impossibility of commitment. You may neglect the material side of life as your personality becomes cerebral and somewhat sterile, like a balloon set free from earth. Middle age can be particularly trying here, as you emphasize youth and new ideas, but security, sense of purpose, belonging, and continuity seem to be elusive.

Jupiter with Neptune:
The Music of the Spheres

In this location, growth, evolution, and personal success are linked to concepts of religion, self-sacrifice for ideals, and humanity's spiritual and communitarian longings. You have a sense that self-sacrifice and sharing of the pain of living are the most meaningful of your humanity, so you may seek a career in a religious or helping profession, or, just as often, in music. Ironically, you can do well by doing good here, since you may be sustained effortlessly and comfortably by the government or some institution, organization, or intellectual establishment in return for your vows of self-sacrifice. Interpretive musicians can act as "channels" here, finding success through materializing collective yearnings. In rare cases, you could become a symbol of some cause or ideal, perhaps sacrificing a lot of your personal and private life in order to act out other people's longings for spiritual and idealistic perfection. More often, you are involved in a profession like medicine, nursing, counseling, or welfare administration, and see service to the disinherited as a true vocation. Ideals and social realities mix well here, and you may find yourself attracted to a community, spiritual leader, or mystical system that reflects this. Monastic life, philosophy, intuition, psychism, and humanism reflect a mind universal in scope, at ease with abstract sociological, historical, and spiritual dimensions—though reluctant to face life's cruel realities skeptically.

You will probably tend toward the nonviolent in your social and political beliefs, as your kind and generous demeanor attracts pets, humble people, and dependents—though you could just as easily attract parasites. Meditation, prayer, psychedelic experience, and contemplation are rewarded, though there is danger of becoming a "gourmet of consciousness," caught up in passing fads and hysterical group delusions. Ego must be sacrificed here for ideals and social position, and success only comes from renunciation and service. Morality and how other people view yours can interfere with your search for higher truth, so material scandals may be caused by your general disregard of life's "earthy" side, embroiling you in unending battles over the trivial, material concerns you tried so hard to avoid, or leaving you gullible, open to fraud and deceit. This is a "hippie" zone, where an archaic idealism, political naivete, and tribal consciousness link people by spiritual rather than material ties.

Jupiter with Pluto:
The Miracle Worker

Life in this location can bring growth, evolution, and personal success, especially when you pursue your dream in opposition to establishment values and link it to concepts of regeneration, rebellion, destruction, and rebirth. God, ethics, and world view are created in your own image, and constant change and renewal are linked to your identity of yourself and your values. This can be a tremendously successful locale in which complete life transformations occur, usually for the better. You could find yourself dealing with large sums of money for people who reside here. You can become famous overnight and find, win, or inherit wealth. You seem protected by guardian angels in times of trial, times which are more frequent than you might desire.

Still, becoming a law unto yourself and creating your own code of ethics may transform you into a lonely individualist, outside the pale of conventional society. As a charismatic leader, priest, or politician, you have the power to stir up feelings in others, and may come to symbolize the idea of growth through destruction and renewal. Your presence may occasion miraculous conversions in others, as you tap mythologies and deep human passions with your intellect, communicating their archetypal mysteries to society as a whole. Faith healing may be central to what you do here, as may any sort of prayer and magic, since your ideas and presence have a catalyzing effects on others' lives. Though your circumstances are frequently violently upset, you advance your position in such times of chaos and find yourself able to gain ground when others retire, move away, or otherwise leave openings for you.

The personal magnetism you display here fits you well for a role as teacher, priest, or politician. It also promises success in publishing, advertising, mass media, and finance, all of which could utilize your instinctive grasp of future popular trends and your ability to embody universal, mythological conceptualizations in your career, and daily work. This influence is so powerful that actual magic can occur in this zone, either to you or, with your conscious recognition of your power, with you as its center. Pluto symbolizes the essence of life itself, so you can see the birth of a totally new self with unthought-of potentials and opportunities.

14

Saturn: It's Tough to Know When You Need Discipline

THIS ZONE can be particularly difficult for those who tend to value imagination, who want happiness and pleasure alone from life, whose relationships are important to them, or who continually delegate the power to run their own lives to others. Saturn is not kind to those with such qualities, or indeed anyone who takes a relaxed and open view of life, as this planet continually demands a deeper awareness by imposing discipline, posing problems, and generally signalling that there is more depth to life than we might like to think. Conversely, those who demand autonomy and power over their own lives, and are fascinated with politics, government, and authority may find this zone almost congenial, though never easy.

For Women Only: Your experience here may harken back to, or in some way attempt to resolve, your relationship with your father, which may be experienced over and over with males with whom you deal. Society does not much encourage an awareness of political and personal power in women, so frequently women in Saturn zones like this one attract powerful men or partners to them and act out (and hopefully learn) their own power potential through relationships. Of course, this leaves you open to a victimization which can occur again and again until you recognize your own capacity for power. Tradition, poor health, family, and other responsibilities may assume the role of tyrant in your life, but be assured that every challenge you experience here points to a need for you to take control of your own destiny.

For Men Only: A man in this zone often finds himself in a battle with established authority, a struggle which may hark back in some symbolic way to his early relationship with his father. Goaded on by insult or indignity, you may undertake to perfect your own powers to overcome external coercion. The whole Saturnian problem of the oppressed becoming the oppressor is particularly relevant in your case, so you should be warned that those who seize power from others will not rest easily, knowing that there will be others as dedicated as they.

If You're Just Passing Through...

If you have been drawn to this zone, it is symbolic of a need for a deeper personal investigation of your darker side and hidden self. Things may not go well here, but problems point out the way you should go in order to insure future realization of your potential. This is a good locale for hard work, but health and emotional levels are depressed, and problems of control intrude into most relationships. There is an intoxication here that comes from the taste of forbidden fruit, however, so challenging authority, demanding your way, and doing things your father would disapprove of makes your stay meaningful, if not altogether pleasurable. If you're here only briefly, most of the effects of this zone probably won't even be felt, but an indefinable element in your experiences here will tempt you to return for more thorough experience later.

Long Distance Lines

Even if you don't travel to these areas, they may represent parts of the world that you fear or dislike. You may feel uncomfortable with ethnic types or religious, racial, or cultural expressions coming from these areas, as they stimulate reflection on parts of your past or your psyche that you would rather not confront. People from these zones push all your buttons, and you often become involved in power conflicts with them. There is a strange fatalism to such places—for all your intense dislike and fear of them, you are at times drawn to them and may find that from them comes some symbol of self, or method of coping with the world that brings you a new level of maturity and self-fulfillment. These areas are poor for all but very long-term investments, though values acquired here tend to be permanent, immune to inflation, or speculation.

Psychological Interpretation of Saturn:
Nose to the Grindstone

This zone works best for those for whom happiness is not enough. No one has better described the experience of this planet of limitation and power than Liz Greene, in the introduction to her epochal book, *Saturn: A New Look at an Old Devil:* "Human beings do not earn free will except through self-discovery, and they do not attempt self-discovery until things have become so painful that they have no other choice." Accordingly, though in this location you will be tested by frustration, from this testing you emerge with knowledge of both your limitations and your actual powers. Conscious beings utilize defeat and restriction as propulsion toward self-development and greater awareness, so that every difficulty you encounter (and there are apt to be many) should be seen as prefiguring an emerging part of your personality that eventually will require exploration and assimilation. Saturn represents the Shadow, the repressed parts of self, memory, and personality which you must come to terms with in order for wholeness to be accomplished. No one can utilize their potential for power in the world without first assimilating this darker side of the self, since its repression requires tremendous psychic energy which, when liberated, can be directed toward creativity.

The spirit is essentially unlimited—anything is imaginable, but material reality (and human bodies) are bound by time and strict physical laws that establish the limits of possibility. Residence in this zone makes you aware of such limitations, in both abstract and specific contexts, and as such confinements are usually the result of either health or economic strictures; it is these concerns that most often become problems. Constant concentration upon limited material reality in turn gives rise to an attitude of essential conservatism—life is seen as a limited quantity, to be economized and frugally stored up. Weak parts of the self are transformed into strengths through this type of lonely toil and dedication, which is motivated by remembrance of insult or insufficiency. Patience and wisdom come after long self-searching, and what is gained here is yours and yours alone, an inner fiber that less afflicted personalities will never appreciate. Disciplined power, constructive material values, realism, resourcefulness, seriousness, self-denial, and control are perfected here, and others are expected to share or confirm your puritanical, melancholy point of view.

Stages and Myth of Saturn:
The God Who Took No Chances

Saturn was a dark, archaic earth god, and so symbolizes our attachment to matter and the earth, something quite out of fashion in our modern, cerebral, technological, information society. Here, where his influence is strong, you may seek religious or material roots, and experience a more direct, primitive level of being. Saturn was also the god of Time, so protective of his own power that he ate his children rather than see them grow to overthrow him, and as such symbolizes the negative aspects of this zone: power lust, entrenchment of authority (you may have to deal with frustrating, unresponsive people who hold unassailable, paternal power over you), blind conservatism, and institutional dehumanization.

Saturn, in its earliest and least developed phase, represents this blind power in both its poles: the absolute autocrat, who is authoritarian, intolerant, tyrannical, and cruel; and the victim, who is powerless and constantly under assault. Experience at one pole usually creates its opposite, as young people victimized by harsh and unresponsive parents will grow themselves to be authoritarian and narrow-minded. Both power and powerlessness corrupt with either tyranny or a defeatist expectation of failure. After longer experience with Saturn, you realize how Time is an ally—

tyrants will age, and water wears away the stone. This capacity to use Time must come, of course, with maturity. If you come close to mastering Saturn, you will shine with its positive qualities: dependability, material success, wisdom, ambition, perseverance, responsibility, prudence, realism, and wry, ironic humor. You know life is not easy, but in recognizing its limitations and its inherent materiality, you are guided to an appreciation of the here and now, the possible and attainable.

Saturn zones seem to have a telescoping effect on time: days, full of toil and often frustration as well, seem long, but decades pass unresisting. Instinctively recognizing that Time is the key to understanding this locale and the problem it poses, you plan years in advance and never question your ability to develop ambitions that require lifelong application. Occasionally tiring of the continual frustration and slow, painful progress, you may plan for years to leave this zone, yet stay on anyway, deriving compensatory satisfaction from seeing Time's plan unfold and learning the power and efficacy of determination, tenacity, and resoluteness.

Practical Concerns of Saturn:
Where Pleasure Seems Trivial

The practical, immediate effects of living in this zone center on overcoming obstacles and acquiring direction and purpose in life. You will learn the hard way what is lacking in your makeup, and periods of hardship, penury, privation, enforced idleness, hunger, delay, miserliness, disappointment, or loneliness can serve to single out your weaknesses and the repressed potentials which must be come to terms with here. Personal power, health, and vitality seem at their lowest ebb, and since other people seem to have all the things you want, you may envy and dislike them. You choose a monkish or Spartan existence, seem older than your years, and find responsibility and duty (often to the elderly or family members) burdensome and overwhelming. Despite all this, you learn to fend for yourself and learn to recognize and compensate for your limitations realistically, whether they be physical, mental, or social. You enjoy hard work and acquire will power, frugality, and orderliness, taking life a day at a time, and thinking less of pleasure or reward, than of humility and doing a good job. Your moods are apt to be depressed, and your thoughts tend to center on weighty subjects: death, materialism, determinism, or fate. You may have a desire to delve into the occult or black arts due to your fascination with the forbidden, as well as a need for self-protection. Dirt, decay, and uncleanliness are often themes in this area, though you can feel an ironic sense of freedom as well. Pleasures here are made all the sweeter by their rarity and, like carnival or Mardi Gras, attractive because they precede deprivations.

In Saturn zones, since your health weaknesses surface, among its lessons is the inescapable fact that the mind's enchainment to the physical body has pain and debilitation as its ultimate end. Bones, joints, skin, and sense organs frequently deteriorate here, and every ache or pain added to the list of deficiencies makes you feel another decade or two older, no matter what your actual age. Your relationships are apt to be based on unequal power, and thus are the seat of much struggle and contest. People are seen essentially as competitors, so your personal ambition leaves little room for cooperation. Work goes best for you in "earthy" fields and in occupations where self-motivation counts. Farming is a good choice here, though you will succeed only with considerable toil; mining, or occupations dealing with crystals, lead, gems, cement, death, mathematics, property, coal, refrigeration, or allied ideas are linked to Saturn and may bring you success if you are willing to undertake long preparation and last through the drudgery.

Saturn on Ascendant:
You Become What You Fear Most

The position Saturn occupies in this location tends to stress your own rise to personal power over your life through taking control of personal habits and affairs. You will seem older and more powerful to others here, and they unquestioningly acknowledge your authority. Responsibilities, especially those attached to property, money, or physical possessions, seem to proliferate, and your life is one long schedule of things to be done. If you are lacking in purpose and direction in life you will usually find them in this locale, though often only after dealing with hardship and unwanted burdens. The constant ambition, stress, and fear of losing status can cause you to age quickly here, and you may secretly feel unequal to the tasks before you, anxious that you are ugly and unwanted into the bargain. Hypochondria may manifest, as well as weight loss, poor health, and a tendency to wear dark colors or to dress more conservatively. Still, this is the "ugly duckling" locale, so you can turn such handicaps into personal advantages, like the great orator Demosthenes, who overcame his stutter by shouting above the surf. Others come to fear the dignity and power that you instinctively develop here, but you may care little for their sentiments, answering all criticism with assertions that you did it your way.

Past failures and skeletons in your closet are rarely forgotten here, so while you can triumph over them by indulging your strict and cold obsession with success, others still may not credit you with much, leaving you to feel unappreciated and unfairly ignored. You also may tend to assume the role of victim here, and you think somehow you are doing others a favor by letting them take advantage of you. Acute sensitivity and self-consciousness may incline you to freeze into introverted silence among strangers, but beneath the personal Victorianism and self-denial, you nurse wounds to the pride that motivate you to control your own fears and others' lives. Though you have good reason to hate the role of authority, someone has to do it, and you eventually realize that no one is more qualified than you.

Saturn on Midheaven:
Nowhere to Go but Up

Your relationship with society, authority, and your career become paramount at this location, as your urges to needs to seek power and control of some sort are directed outward. This leads you to seek fulfillment of personal and political ambition, and in order to do this you are more than willing to pay the price exacted by hard work and the surrender of opportunities for pleasure and relaxation. Others may think of you as the loner or miser but, motivated by buried inferiority fears or the experience of social inferiority, you strive to "make it" by any means available—means not necessarily limited to the ethical. You feel that you must control all aspects of your life and environment, so it is impossible to work for others except in the loosest of structures. While this is not an easy place to be, the success that comes after years of toil is all yours.

As raw nerves inflamed by your feeling of powerlessness are exposed to others' advantages and superiority, you rarely are able to forget the humiliations and rejections you experience on the way. Hurts done to you by others are usually repaid, even if you must wait for years to do it. You should take very seriously the warning that powerlessness and power both corrupt, since you will likely have opportunities to experience both. Your personal limitations must be understood here, though you may have to learn them through suffering the consequences of overextending your ambition. A fall from power is possible if you allow yourself to become the hated tyrant you fear so much; your fate may be harsh indeed when your turn comes. On the other hand, if you learn to control the darker and lower strata of Saturn by imposing on yourself strict and Spartan deprivations you will be able to rise under your own power, owing nothing to anyone, and thus perhaps remain at the top. Although you are apt to make much of independence and autonomy, you secretly relish the idea of established power, and find, oddly, that the powerful and rulers of the world are attracted to you—either as oppressors or as those who offer you opportunities to rule. Society may see you as a symbol of all that is old, respectable, and honorable, or all that is to be feared as dangerously reactionary; in either case, while this is not an easy place to live, it agrees with those for whom ordinary life and success are not enough

Saturn on Descendant:
Fair but Cold

In working out your relationship with others and with the public, you seem to find yourself attracted constantly to social situations in which power is an issue, and you often are subject to unfair oppression and victimization.

Still, such difficulties serve to develop inner strength and, since most people you rely upon tend to either let you down or take advantage of you, you learn to rely on yourself. Misfortune usually comes when cooperation is attempted, especially if you are not on your guard at all times when dealing with partners. Legal concerns should be avoided here at all costs, as they tend to be prolonged and burdensome in the extreme. Marriage is a dutiful, responsible, and practical life option at this locality, as you mostly deal with other people for material reasons rather than for affection. You can become the power behind the throne, and who is rather selective, snobbish, and unpopular at that. Thus, this is a difficult place to develop any kind of public image for yourself, unless it is that of someone who wields authority and power with no apologies. You should look within to plumb insecurities that you use as excuses to attract uncongenial people and to accept poor treatment from them. Weakness and hatred that you bear for parts of yourself are inescapable in this locale, as people who symbolize these traits all too well will always intrude in your life in one way or another.

As in any Saturn area, things tend to improve with time, and relationships that survive this locale will be made of tough stuff indeed. You also can develop a sense of judiciousness, impartiality, and honesty, though you may feel that these are unappreciated more often than not. In career matters, you are likely to find yourself dealing with the dispossessed—the infirm, elderly, or impecunious—and in any case you are constantly reminded of the material extremes existent in society. Beware of cultivating a negative attitude which leads you to find fault with every little thing in your social environment, as though it is easy to dislike the people who surround you, as you may actually be rejecting a part of yourself. Happiness of any sort depends on accepting and understanding the flaws and traits you tend to deplore and denigrate in others.

Saturn on Imum Coeli:
The Inner Desert

This placement of Saturn tends to stress your relationship with your family and with the psychological concepts underlying your origins, your "roots," and your inmost self-definition. You may find yourself tied unwillingly to the past, your family, or its traditions (for example, through being forced to take on the burden of caring for an aging relative), but through such assumption of responsibility you symbolically come to terms with and define the character of your own declining years. Finding yourself tied to such weighty matters connected to your family and your past, inheritance or ownership of property is likely here, though it could take more than its toll on you in effort and drudgery. You can have a sense of bitterness and awareness regarding what you have missed in life but, on the positive side, this area is one in which you can center and focus yourself, finding inexhaustible reserves of inner power from which you can create a self-image that can weather any storm. A close and small circle of truly reliable friends or relatives constitutes the foundation of a sense of security and acceptance for you under this line. Aside from this small group, however, you could find yourself withdrawing from society and even becoming something of a hermit.

The image of the desert is a relevant symbol to keep in mind when living here, as it doesn't rain much anywhere under this line (figuratively speaking) while you're around. Agriculture is not a good occupation to choose here, but you could experience success in minerals and mining, and the value of land that you choose to invest in or live on could gradually increase. Like a Biblical hermit, you can excel in self-denial, mortification (often for the sake of others), and contemplation, as you cultivate an austere self-mastery. More abstractly, this area is one in which your religion and world view put you in touch with an archaic Earth-centered tradition, and you may feel greater attachment to primal, tribal modes of social existence. Isolation seems an important part of your home environment, which may be cut off from the usual forms of social accessibility. Stagnation, reclusiveness, ill health, and loneliness may have to be dealt with, but such privations work to help you identify the limits which you can endure. This is not a particularly good place in which to retire, unless autonomy and isolation appeal to you, unless the idea of a place uniquely your own (largely because no one else wants it) can spur you to self-mastery and empowerment.

Saturn with Uranus:
The Paradox of Compulsive Idealism

In this locale, you may find yourself uncomfortably in the forefront of public crisis, as you act out your own version of the conflict between the individual and the social. Your own principles may involve you in an adversarial role with society, or you may find yourself constantly living in a cross fire between warring factions. On a more personal level, you experience conflicts between habits and principles, and only timing and a good measure of wit can manage to save you from the consequences of a defiant attitude, extreme individualism, and destructive anger. If you seek only trivial pleasures from life, you may find this area a little intense, since your charisma gets you involved with labor movements, revolts, and future shock. You must learn and strive for cooperation, as you may find yourself struggling to attain by foul means what could have been had by fair means, and rarely allowing yourself rest or time off for any reason.

Secretiveness, subtlety, suspicion, and your virtuous self-image tend to alienate those whose alliance could advance your goals. Rather antiauthoritarian and anti-sentimental, you will likely be misunderstood or even ostracized by many who might otherwise be able to help you.

Overreacting against authority is a self-defeating mode of behavior, born of attitude or self-destructive inflexibility. Pioneering instinct and constant dissatisfaction impel you to struggle against any form of coercion from the established order, to which you pose a very real threat. Fascinated by the obscure, the antique, and the heterodox, you skillfully blend the best from future and past, appearing both radical and conservative, though probably rejecting alliance with those at both sides of the political spectrum. Reaching goals you have set for yourself can actually become a problem, as when the time comes to change, you will tend to want to hold on to your success. Learning just exactly how long to hold on, and when to let go, is important.

Your major impulse in this locale is to give your ideals a real, concrete form; you will be required to work rather hard to put your beliefs into action in order to avoid the anxiety and stress you will feel if you don't do this. Any appropriate expression of your principles is apt to be highly organized, carefully thought out, and usually will embody political ideals—often those pertaining to social objectives or partisan causes in some way.

Saturn with Neptune:
A Voice Crying in the Wilderness

This is rarely a congenial locale, as ghosts from the past must be lived with, and your darkest secrets eventually work their way out into the open, where they receive public scrutiny. Pessimistic introversion, loneliness, solitude, and mindless obsession with inconsequentiality are moods you may experience here, and while this area may possibly be congenial for monks, hermits, and others seeking solitude and contemplation, it seems mostly negative (or at the very least greatly challenging) for almost anyone seeking an active, productive life. Career progress is apt to be slow and is often made through subterfuge (though this usually is discovered); reality and imagination seem to become confused, with a resultant tendency to paranoia, illusions, persecution feelings, and wild visions of apocalypse. Yet, despite such inclinations, you yourself may tend to have an almost hypnotic power over others. Rigorous spiritual discipline is one pursuit for which this zone is good, however, and you can advance in spiritual matters, learn or make innovations in musical theory, yoga, or complex social ideas.

Unfortunately, the ideal and the real rarely function well together here, and the friction between the two may lead you to overwork and ensuing periods of ill health, fatigue, addiction, imprisonment, or asceticism. Such experiences may lead you to appreciate your link to the whole universe, by underscoring the commonality of suffering to which the flesh is heir. Your illusions are constantly pierced, and you may be the victim (or even perpetrator, if personal circumstances are trying) of fraud, deceit, or other crimes. Involvement with institutions is hard to avoid, and unless these involve some service career (such as nurse, prison worker, social worker, etc.), they could be involuntary. Self-sacrifice (without even the rewards of others' appreciation) is the one pursuit that is encouraged by this planetary pair, but you may emerge from it with a feeling that it served little purpose beyond the pain of self-denial. Your ego seems in a powerful way, so only those who can forswear its attachments and pleasures will be able to enjoy this locale. Despite all this, you retain a basic feeling of your own self-worth, or are forced to forge such a feeling, perhaps for the first time.

The underlying challenge of this area is to learn to deal with the irrepressible need to act out utopian idealism in the material world and to try to bring your romantic and unrealistic expectations into being in a realistic way. You may be attracted to small community groups in an effort to explore these needs, but your messianic impulses often lead you far beyond these small venues in a world where chaos and disillusion await on the one side while promise and a place in posterity wait on the other.

Saturn with Pluto:
Reluctant Metamorphosis

This is a rather lugubrious locale, so your experiences here will tend to be serious, responsible, and concerned with death, duty, and mortality. You respect anything you see as unassailable authority and revere any body of knowledge or tradition, though your conservative ideas may serve to close off varied options. Finality is an attribute of this locale, so that decisions made here may be more far-reaching than you can conceive. Individualism, dignity, and quiet resistance to injustice are the positive sides of this zone, while the negative contains the possibility of a very real experience of death or mortality, fascination with the morbid and gloomy, mourning, unwanted burdens, suspension of growth, and the enforced recognition of personal powerlessness in the face of tyrannical forces or fate. Here you weigh your own soul and make decisions for the rest of your life, and here the past closes behind you firmly and for good. Dependents and the elderly may pass away, and you are humbled by forces beyond your control in the face of your own frailty and humanity.

Destruction and transformation are important themes here, so that endings will always contain within themselves the seeds of new beginnings. You have a tremendous power in this locale that stems from your intuitive awareness that concepts of death, transformation, and mortality must be incorporated into society for its own good. Often seeking to overthrow some established institution or to transform it to one more responsive to change and growth, you exhibit profound resistance to coercion, and constant inner personal turmoil in this locale. Fascination with archaeology, the past, history, or geology motivates long hours of research and investigation, as the past (as a symbol of deep, primitive instincts and earlier social forms) must be incorporated into your daily life somehow. Discipline and compulsion are in conflict here, and phobias and generalized fears seem to pervade your consciousness at times. You may feel uncomfortable in crowds and thus generally seek isolation and withdrawal. This is a necessary atmosphere for your slow, painful, inner alchemical transformation.

15

Uranus: Can Anyone Change the World?

THE SURPRISING planet Uranus hits you like a tornado, and it can either blow you away to the Oz of a whole new consciousness or, if you try to resist its force, tear you to pieces. Obviously, people akin to its idealistic, cerebral, and nonemotional nature adjust more easily to its changes; strongly materialistic, conforming, social types, who depend on their possessions, stability, family, and other permanent life structures, may suffer most from its influence and thus will find this locale the least congenial. If your eyes light up when you see hippies or punk rockers, if you are fascinated with astrology and New Age thought, if you're used to fighting City Hall (from either a zealously liberal or stodgily conservative point of view), then this zone will prove exhilarating, stimulating, and full of color, contrast, and excitement. On the other hand, if you like the Home Shopping Channel on TV, belong to the mainstream, and see your main accomplishment as security, then this zone will probably be upsetting and uncomfortable, often in the extreme, with much of the security and many of the possessions you rely on proving to be of short duration and durability, leaving you naked and more aware in the world.

For Women Only: Many women don't take easily to Uranus zones, as they feel threatened by the lack of material security and continuity often present here. As an actual or potential mother, there is a bit too much change and upheaval to assure children or the security of a place to raise them with the routine and stability that they need. Health upsets, encounters with aggressive males, and family problems may combine to make this place just a little too exciting for you. The exception is, of course, those who are strong feminists, or others desirous of taking on the system in order to create and exemplify a new way of life. Often the first woman to achieve a "first" in some traditionally male area, or to break ground in some other way does so in a Uranus zone.

For Men Only: You are apt to find this zone more congenial than most women would, especially if you are the independent, mental, and idea-motivated type described above. The main danger for you is identifying so strongly with the gypsy-like existence that emerges in this area that you miss out on the pleasures of committed relationship, home, and property. You could remain an eternal adolescent, always about to find a job or settle down, and find that when youth has passed, you are left empty-handed and disillusioned.

If You're Just Passing Through...

If you're just planning a short stay under a line dominated by this planet, expect changes in rapid succession, many unexpected events, and more than a few unusual people to enliven your stay here. Though you probably won't have much time to get too involved, you could get caught up in some utopian social group, as beneath the surface of your trip here is a desire to recognize and implement your idealism in some way. Your stay will be adventurous and interesting, though your companions may find you inflexible, intolerant of others' ideas, and somewhat inaccessible. It's hard to sleep, and your distraction renders you somewhat accident prone. Dealing with technology, transportation, and media tend to take unexpected turns.

Long-Distance Lines

Even if you cannot travel to or reside in this exciting and colorful zone, the countries and cultures under Uranus in your personal map may come to stand in your mind for liberation, freedom, and change. People who have a profound effect on your thinking and a distinct influence on the form of your ideas may come from these places, or a body of knowledge, religion, or teaching indigenous to an area under a Uranus line might deeply change your world view or self-concept. You may take a stand against an injustice you perceive to stem from this place, or support change and growth there in various ways. Cultural interests in this zone are apt to be intellectual, serving to illuminate future directions for your life path.

Psychological Interpretation of Uranus:
Living Out Idealism

In this zone, you are under the influence of Uranus, planet of electric change and transformation. Newly discovered (1784), this planet symbolizes the growth of individuality, since prior to its discovery people essentially defined themselves by their social function, their positions in various hierarchies, their family, or their nationality. With Uranus, social complexity has evolved to a point at which ideas become important and consequently governments have changed along with this, so they now rule through ideals and abstractions rather than through the power of one person. Residence in this zone, then, sparks the growth of your inner power and enlarges the conceptual framework of ideas that underlies it. Life and self are perceived with nonsentimental nakedness and, with few illusions, you fear nothing, except perhaps enchainment to the material, the monotonous, and the ordinary.

You admire diversity and democracy as your personal pride, charisma, and daring are enhanced; you develop a Promethean iconoclasm, constantly challenging accepted truths both within yourself and in your society at large, a predilection that usually does not endear you to its leaders, or to others who are set in their ways. The emphasis on ideas, spirituality (as opposed to materiality), and anarchistic self-determination makes you somewhat intolerant, rebellious, and nonconforming, however, and coolness, unreliability, and aloofness often betray a deep selfishness disguised as idealism. Still, you see your way clear to do exactly as you please. Perpetually youthful and uncommitted, yet strongly principled and idealistic, you seem to fit into no categories or social patterns, and thus must create your own.

You usually identify someone or something as an enemy here, and while it may be the establishment, a political party, or some other entrenched force, the real root of your dislike probably lies in your own attachment to the physical world and to the dark, earthy, primal forces of sexuality and materiality which intrude intolerably into your brilliant, airy visions and ideals. You identify materiality and the environment as a whole with the commonplace and you rebel against it with the fervor of an adolescent, but what you lack in practicality you can make up for with charisma and the ability to rally others to your causes. Your only identification may be with strongly antisocial groups or ideals. Society can act through you as well, identifying you, perhaps unwillingly on your part, as the symbol of some idea, social force, minority opinion, or nationality. A dissatisfied soul on a perpetual quest for impossible answers, you seem to be on a constant quest to raise others' consciousness, a task not often rewarded or appreciated by those who are the objects of your attention. Magical coincidences are commonplace here, and change is constant.

Stages and Myth of Uranus:
Rebel Without a Cause

The Greek god Uranus was a sky god, and his repulsion to earthy materiality was expressed in his intolerance of his own children, whom he confined to an underground hell. He symbolizes both the human capacity to transform the world through vision and idealism, and the cold, brutal intolerance of the pure ideologue who will destroy all who get in the way of his idealistic vision of the future. Uranus was rendered impotent, symbolizing the barrenness of pure spirit divorced completely from the material. Instead of children, the Uranian person has ideas, and these channel his or her creative force into transforming social movements.

The earliest stages of Uranian awareness will of course see its problematical aspects dominate: underneath the adolescent rebel-without-a-cause superiority, the intolerance, and the rejection of any form of social cohesiveness lies a computer-like coldness and lack of sentimentality. Militant action against an imagined enemy, or membership in an anarchistic or radical fringe group may simply be a way of overcoming an essentially weak will and a lack of a sense of individuality. A little more maturity brings some recognition of the necessity to temper ideals with realism and compromise: technology is the result, in which ideas are put to practical use, hopefully with betterment of life as a result. Again, however, the pure idealism of Uranus can here symbolize "pure" and amoral science of the sort that created the atomic bomb.

In the final stages of Uranian awareness, a humanistic maturity develops in the consciousness that demands opportunities for everyone to develop his or her fullest potential; humanitarianism, philanthropy, and technological improvement of the human condition can result, personified in the idealist who creates a society of self-determination and democratic principles.

At any of these stages, however, it is difficult to acknowledge the transforming power as your own. Thus, most people will become involved in a social movement, either by themselves (as scapegoats or reformers) or as group leaders. Ignorant of the source of power, it is easy for you to be manipulated by it and difficult for you to keep such primeval and powerful energies in check. Appreciation of the power of ideas when they are acted on by groups of humanity is the essential experience of this planetary energy and its zone.

The Practical Side of Uranus:
Putting Ideals to Work

In this zone, freshness and novelty are certain to prevail, but Uranus has innumerable manifestations. Though its keynote is individualism and extremism, within that there are as many expressions as there are individuals. Still, if you are bored with life and would give up anything for a change, you are in the right place here. You can become a new person, change your name, or redefine yourself and your individuality. Swift, unexpected liberation from past patterns and tired old habits happens as Uranian winds blow through your psyche like refreshing arctic air in August, and mediocrity and humdrum monotony are replaced with stormy excitement and emancipation. Life is full of prismatic contrast and interest, full of exploration, adventure, and wanderlust. You do things in extremes, delighting in violating bourgeois attitudes and morality as you forge your identity almost as a contrast to prevailing social opinions. You seek out people who are as outrageously expressive as you are and may find yourself most at home in a communal living situation that supports expressions of your unusual ideas. The establishment thinks you dangerous, and your mere existence offends and threatens authorities of any kind, with predictable results. It's hard not to fight City Hall here, but you can win, at least in the long run, for your ideas, while heterodox, are ahead of your time and, thus, the wave of the future.

Your finances fluctuate wildly here, and their total unpredictability only adds to the general atmosphere of insecurity. You are forced to look within yourself to find the calm eye at the center of the storm that rages around, as this is where painful growth occurs as your unquestioned assumptions of old are discarded in the face of the naked reality of the here and now. Technology is one area to which your iconoclastic creativity can be positively directed, especially anything involving electronics or media. Astrology, New Age healing arts, and unusual therapies are also Uranian, as well as aeronautics, invention, labor relations, some community service positions, and radical politics in general.

Relationships in this area are apt to be tempestuous, as you attract willful and unusual persons. Occasionally, instead of acting out the intense, unpredictable influences of this zone, you repeatedly attract yourself to people who are themselves capricious and unstable. Your health is not likely to be too good in this zone, as your energy patterns and your living situation are too erratic. It's hard to sleep, and nervous fatigue is always one step behind you. Accidents, especially affecting the legs, tend to be frequent. Your self-concept and life will change here, and, though there may be some feeling of loss as the past closes behind you, the excitement and stimulations of this zone, along with its promise of freedom from tradition and social coercion, agitate and animate you to heights you never dreamed possible. You become aware of cycles, cosmic consciousness, and transcendent possibilities all emerging from within yourself.

Uranus on Ascendant:
Disruption's Advocate

In this area, the planet Uranus is likely to manifest most particularly in your health, personal image, and inner journey. Although it is really your own self-concept that is undergoing change, it is easy to let other people identify you with some ideal, or use you as a catalyst to galvanize them into action on their own behalf. You stand out as the epitome of individuality, able to slip through the cracks and do whatever you please. Your influence can inspire people around you to rebellion and resistance against an injustice that was quietly tolerated before you came on the scene, and those who deal with you closely are never the same again, seeing themselves, perhaps for the first time, as individuals, rather than focusing their behavior and thinking on adherence to norms and standards. Other people's opinions of the ideals and causes with which you associate yourself will be strongly influenced by your personality and your ideals in every area of life. You break rules with such a nonchalance that others may come to assume you have some special right to do so, and thus your existence at some point begins to challenge the need for rules at all.

Cool, somewhat aloof, and nonmaterially unemotional, you refuse to be needed, shying away from committed, clinging relationships. In this zone, you can alter your body, appearance, name, personality, ideals, or life path every few years without even being aware to any great degree that you are doing so, and the only thing about you that never changes is change itself. You want others to notice you, and thus may adopt an unusual name, costume, or mannerisms, secretly delighting in their dismay at your little outrages, not really caring whether they approve or not. Likewise, though your presence may kindle others' idealism and commitment and predictably usher in a period of change and social upheaval, you don't often participate yourself. For you, "Truth is a pathless land. Man cannot come to it through any organization, through any creed, through any dogma, priest, ritual, not through any philosophical knowledge or psychological technique" (J. Krishnamurti). Identity becomes your own and others' way of deviating from the paths chosen by the majority.

Uranus on Midheaven:
The Loneliness of the Runner in Circles

The position of Uranus at this location tends to stress your relationship with authorities and government or in your career. Social standing, status, power in society, and your vocation may change and fluctuate radically, and you could go from obscurity to fame (or infamy) and back again. The authority presumed by either persons or institutions is ignored here, as you cast yourself into the role of the social rebel and rescuer, promising to save any and all from unfair oppression, something which inextricably interweaves the fabric of your life with theirs. Everybody seems to talk about you here, either admiring or hating you as you cultivate something of a pompous messiah complex, figuring you have all the answers. No one is neutral it seems, as you become the symbol of a cause, movement, or ideal, or express and embody your own ethnic or national background in a particularly striking way. You have a lot of power to reform or to innovate politically, but you may get bogged down in the ramifications of what you have done, with your personal ambition eclipsed by the causes to which it has attached itself. You remain unaffected by the society whose changes you seek to catalyze, but your personal battle for ideals will almost definitely affect the lives of others in one way or another. Accepting personal responsibility for your society and its ills, you may find yourself repeatedly contending for the underprivileged against entrenched power and authority. You become a militant minority of one, seeking peers to support your battle, , and you alone are willing to take on Goliath if allies do not materialize.

The career areas mentioned above may be quite successful here, especially if your job requires innovation, creativity, and mental skill. Technology is of course indicated in this zone, but also any other occupation that has a future orientation, complexity, or radical artistic basis. As the pioneer of a new idea at this location, you meet with the resistance of the status quo or organized authority. Your bravado and your willingness to take personal risks increases here, as you live spectacularly, unafraid of the consequences of all you stir up.

Uranus on Descendant:
The Only "Normal" Person Here

The general influence of Uranus here is apt to manifest most particularly in your personal relationships, in which you feel detached and unable to relate to others for anything but short periods. Often, this inability to relate is what distinguishes you from "normal" people, and you may feel strangely cursed when everyone whom you attract turns out to be some sort of kook, genius, eccentric, or social rebel. Part of the problem lies in the tendency you exhibit to demand all the power in relationships and yet to reject clinging, dependent people or commitments that impinge on your freedom. You can come to recognize your own power, especially as your relationships seem to fall into the same patterns again and again, and, while you may not at first see the responsibility you hold for influencing these changes, eventually you will be forced to acknowledge it.

Sexuality may dominate your relationships, perhaps often in the form of what you see as others' unreasonable demands on you, though in truth it is you who are asking for what it is hardest for them to give. In a sense this means you end up acting as a catalyst for their own growth and change, but you may get a little tired of hearing people thank you for providing them with a learning experience as they head for the door with their bags. Obviously, this zone might be a good place for you to work as a counselor, especially to those undergoing life transitions and changes—since you are doing this anyway, you might as well get paid for it! If you are inflexible by nature, this zone is apt to present you with real problems: accidents or extraordinary, miraculous, and unexpected events become daily fare, and freakish phenomena happen so often it seems as if you're in a movie. Rationalization and analysis do you little good in handling this, as somewhere deep within you is a streak of negative feelings about yourself that is lighting all the fireworks. Until you deal with it, life in this zone is rarely stable, pleasant, or peaceful, though after you have all those wild Uranian urges tamed, you can be a guide and avatar to those seeking new self-insight, and personal growth from the deepest part of their own innermost selves.

Uranus on Imum Coeli:
Even Black Sheep Have Fun

In this area, the planet Uranus is likely to manifest inwardly rather than outwardly. Some of the more radical and obvious potentials of this zone may be muted for you, but they will still affect you anyway, gradually, from within, and perhaps in the context of your family. The direct rejection of the norms of your family, your racial or ethnic heritage, or your religious traditions is likely. This could occur by you creating a role for yourself never before attempted in your own family or personal environment—and succeeding in it. You are free from attachment to anything other than ideals, so home, personal possessions, and property all seem irrelevant and distant to you, mere things that change continually as you lead your life from one minute to the next, with only the present important. As you are likely to be a catalyst for personal change in others, disruption seems to follow you around, affecting those with whom you come into contact, and forcing them to grow out of outmoded patterns of living.

It is particularly difficult for you to take root here, as any efforts at settling down seem not to work, meaning that you may constantly be on the move from one living arrangement to another. Such upset impels you to seek the true self within, and you become the universal citizen, no less at home in foreign places than in familiar ones, and no more. New life is injected into old forms, especially family ones, and though you may be called the black sheep for your pains, at least everyone has an opinion about you. While the scenery on the stage is constantly shifting, there is such ferment within that eventually you may leave the supporting environment altogether, forging an identity for yourself which defines you by how you differ from others and from your background. In rare cases, being in this place could permanently deflect your life path into a totally new and unexpected direction, as you form within yourself a crystal of indestructible selfhood immune to criticism, coercion, and social pressure. Nevertheless, you may get tired of sleeping on the floor (on the rare occasions that you sleep at all) and living out others' dreams of self-realization.

Uranus with Neptune:
The Woodstock Generation

In this locale, you may find yourself possessed by the fantasy of a social utopia that fulfills your need for inner development and individuality through the outer world. Your idealism is likely to be very strong here, encouraged by the irrepressible hope that somehow society can lead the individual to perfect himself or herself. This type of idealism is founded on a philosophy which believes that humans can free themselves from material aggrandizement, greed, and avarice. As you open yourself to universal visions and ideals here, illumination can occur, and you do best to rely on your own inner voice and avoid the answers it might provide to your questions. In this area you may seek congenial communal situations or find yourself deeply involved in community concerns. Intuition and your instinctive understanding of the arcane improve here, as you find yourself by taking yourself beyond the bounds of ego through meditation and organized mystical disciplines.

You may desperately seek someone to symbolize or embody your ideas, such as a "perfect" relationship, but you can find it only after you've given up hope. Issues of liberty and human dignity come to the fore, and your personal relationship to society tends to reflect important struggles going on in the macrocosm. Earlier value systems are scrapped in favor of utopian consciousness, but it's hard to deal with practical matters with distant, otherworldly personality and world view, so you remain distracted and perplexed as the material side of your life deteriorates. To a very few, true guiding genius and enlightenment can manifest under these planets, especially after a sense of loss and futility has been plumbed. You become a vehicle for social, cosmic, or religious forces, perhaps even those of a kind that can change the world, as you see yourself reflected in the grand scheme of your experience, able to manipulate the whole through your own small part of it. Freedom from conscience and the past allows you cosmic insights or warns against letting yourself fall into either criminality or nonconformity so extreme that it becomes unproductive and pointless.

Uranus with Pluto:
The One-Person Revolution

If you idealize the social awareness and activism of the '60s and yearn for the opportunity to become a one-person movement yourself, then this zone will seem quite congenial. Here, you have the option to transform your milieu by remaining outside of it and to become an example of the idealistically motivated rebel who works to transform outmoded forms and traditions. This kind of consciousness shows little interest in reform per se, but rather concentrates on clearing the slate altogether by exposing the hypocrisy and materialistic sham of the present order so that a new, honest order may emerge. Your life can take on an almost miraculous turn in this locale, as blasts of sudden illumination or conversion can wipe out preconceptions of self and relationships, leaving room for a whole new personality to emerge. You might retreat back into an imagined tribal social order, one in which you presume values were more earthy and sexuality more open; you'd like to see the delicate complexity of social relations blown apart by the dark powers of ancient, pre-social humanity.

On a personal level, you should not expect the new self you seek to be born without considerable pain. The past must be left behind for good, so attachments may be severed in a particularly traumatic manner. This can be for good or ill, however, as there is always the prospect of your becoming an outlaw through severing not just personal ties, but also the bonds that keep most of us committed to and focused on a goal that has some meaning to society at large. Following the absolute law of self can present you with a true, unadorned experience of yourself as you exist apart from the matrix of social attitudes and involvement around you. Since the only way to change the world is to change yourself, you do this repeatedly. Death may be an important player in the drama you act out here, and the social convention that inclines all of us to view ourselves as immortal is thrown aside, perhaps due to the direct experience of the loss of loved ones. You try to shock others, love what is spectacular and drastic, feel lonely, notorious, and isolated, but through your personal journey at this location, you can emerge with a self-reliance and depth that marks you for life as a potent, unique individual.

16

Neptune: Materialists Beware!

THOSE WHO DELIGHT in self-sacrifice, recognize a higher power that guides their lives, and perhaps see themselves as a channel for divine or cosmic energy may find this zone a perfect one in which to develop such awareness along with their psychic, artistic, and intuitive gifts. Musicians seem particularly able to benefit from Neptune, as they are really conduits for and interpreters of the very sort of "vibrations" to which this zone attunes one's sensitivity. On the other hand, people who have to be strongly in control of their lives and environment clearly will find this zone the most difficult of all. If you are ambitious, masculine, materialistic, possessed of a strong sense of self, and tend to see the world in objective, scientific, or causal terms, this zone will present the most challenging problems of your entire life, as all your criteria for evaluating experience will become undependable, deceiving you while inexplicable, weird events leave you doubting your sanity.

For Women Only: As a woman, you stand a slightly better chance to turn these impulses to good account, especially if you study or perform in any of the arts. Still, relationships with men are apt to be problematical, as those men may either act out a dominant and/or parasitical role or, conversely, first worship you as an ideal then become disillusioned when your humanity shows through. You have almost magical or enchanting powers of persuasion here, but you use them against yourself all too easily: reality constantly intrudes, and you find it hard to manage the practical side of your life.

For Men Only: You obviously will have some problems with this zone, for our society trains men to be in control, to master external reality, and to think logically and objectively, none of which is easy here. To survive, you will have to learn a whole new way of feeling and relying on inner vision, as well as accommodate yourself to being rather invisible, and somewhat unconnected to those things and people you would like most to influence. Moreover, since many men cannot acknowledge this Neptunian energy in their own personalities, they instead choose a partner who acts out these chaotic, deceptive, dreamy, and unrealistic attributes. Any use of drugs or intoxicants will most assuredly end up badly here.

If You're Just Passing Through...

A short stay in this locale can put you in touch with your more delicate sensibilities and spiritual aspirations. It's all an illusion, but illusions make the hard reality of life more acceptable, so they can be handled with artistry and subtlety. Perhaps you came here to get in touch briefly with your inner ideals, and to seek out people who exemplify such idealism to you. A feeling of intoxication and hysteria lies just beneath the surface, so if you're trying to get away from who you usually are, you've come to the right place. Still, it's all very confusing, and you can't help feeling you don't really know what's going on. Avoid dealings with authorities, and stick to well-lit places. Your dreams and inner life can be quite spectacular here.

Long-Distance Lines

Even if you do not reside in or visit this location, it may still have its effects upon you. You may imagine it as a childhood fantasy or utopia, though equally likely, it could be a place where you would be taken advantage of, victimized, or totally misunderstood. Cultures in this part of the world speak to you on the deepest levels, especially through music or religious ideas. People from this area tend to confuse and upset you, getting you all excited over things that rarely come to fruition. Occasionally, a spiritual master will come from this zone. Investments are not advised in this area, nor real estate ownership, except possibly for petroleum exploration. But artistic, spiritual, and cultural pursuits allied with the places under this kind of line will bring about powerful personal responses that can transform and uplift you.

Psychological Interpretation of Neptune:
Plugged Into the Cosmic Circuit

You may find it really difficult to live your life under a Neptune line on a superficial, happy-go-lucky, day-to-day level, as you are constantly moved by forces originating so deep within that you have no immediate way to control or understand them. There exists a strange cohesion among social animals: at times they build pyramids and at other times computers. While government may have a limited role in determining these directions, there is also a deeper current that carries us all along, as invisible to us as the water is to the fish. Neptune is the main component in this current, and it communicates to each of us from beneath the waves through cultural expressions like music, fashion, fads, and political movements. Residence in this zone plugs you in, for good or ill, to these inexplicable vibrations. Our communication with matters Neptunian is never conscious, bypassing the ego altogether, so being influenced directly by it often proves dangerous and perhaps destructive to personality, at least as it is idealized in modern society. Living here, you yearn to experience anew the total merging with an exterior, protective, and totally absorptive whole that is felt in the womb. This ego-annihilating commitment to rediscovering Paradise Lost hints at the difficulty of retaining a cohesive identity in the presence of the ecstasy of the surrender of ego to something both larger and totally unlike the self.

Of course, there can be advantages to being so plugged in to the currents and mystical patterns that guide humankind: in business, you can intuit the coming trends and fashions far before most others are aware of them; in music, or other performing arts, you can put your audience in touch with the cosmos, and then bring them safely home again; and in mysticism and religion, you seem to have a direct channel to the universal. But in many cases you may act out the tragedy of the martyr, sacrificing the integration of your ego for an illusion of sacrificing it to a greater end, only to find that your beneficiaries either crucify you or distort your idealism into materialistic and banal forms. Acting out society's unconscious, you are likely to be exploited, harassed, and seen as a dangerous, counterculture, anarchic force or, occasionally, you may be worshipped as a superhuman ideal—the expression of some collective yearning—like a 1940's movie star.

Life comes to be lived almost vicariously, as you seem invisible, unconnected in any relevant fashion to the real world. Your romantic ideals, self-fictionalizations, and vivid, imaginative "might-have-beens" come to substitute for real relationships. Existing relationships, on the other hand, may be marked with paranoid and neurotic fears, as they become clouded by projections—your own unconscious acted out by your partner. You may attract the things you fear the most, and as vulnerable and psychically sensitive as you are, your moods swing in wild excesses of elation and despair. Yet, for those few who manage to act as channels for the Neptunian currents without getting their egos involved, or for those who thrive without a sense of ego or identity, this zone can be one in which the heights of spiritual awareness are reached, where you wander in the bardos, and the division between the self and the not-self dissolves.

Stages and Myth of Neptune:
Reality? What Is Reality?

It is fitting that the god Neptune ruled the sea, as this symbol of life's origins stands also for sleep, dreams, and the human unconscious. Neptune was also associated with earthquakes, and the loss of self and material sustenance that earthquakes occasion seem fitting symbols for this planet of the not-self. All life evolved from the sea, symbolically linking it with a primordial consciousness and a past we all share. The consciousness of sea creatures does one little good on land, however, where hard, cold reality must be dealt with.

Awareness of Neptune does not seem to follow a set evolutionary pattern as much as with other planets. Despite this, in time people learn to adapt to its vagueness, inspiration, and lack of selfhood and usually abandon the more destructive and injurious manifestations. A hysterical, wild intoxication often predominates when one first encounters Neptune, an ecstatic surrender of selfhood to merge with some imagined whole, that later can lead its victims into paranoia, delusion, inflation of the ego, and perhaps insanity or addiction. While all this is going on within, deterioration besets the real world without—poverty, confusion, perplexity, victimization, invalidism, and powerlessness are common. With more maturity or, perhaps, with the right sort of personality, these excesses are avoided, and Neptune's intuition and mysticism enable artistic accomplishment and spiritual evolution of the highest sort. The problem is in telling one stage from another, in distinguishing between self-deception and "real" inspiration, as there are no objective criteria in Neptune's realm, and one's perceptions often are no more real than one's imagination.

The Practical Side of Neptune:
Caught Up in Something You Don't Understand

In daily, prosaic matters, Neptune poses its most difficult challenges: on a personal level, imagination and inspiration are enhanced, so that spiritual pursuits, psychism, and intuition improve. But this is balanced with an inclination to abuse drugs, and a dreamy, fool's-paradise escapism based on an addiction to a glamour and romanticism of the sort that real life rarely supplies. The line between dreams and reality blurs. You get caught up in something you don't understand, and when you finally wake up you may have lost your possessions, your identity, your position in society, or even your reason. This zone exudes a vague, depressive, gray atmosphere.

On social levels, you end up too often the patsy; society sees in you something dangerous and chaotic, so victimization by the law, surveillance, or arrest can befall you despite nonviolent, communitarian idealism. A milder manifestation might be involvement with institutions, in which you are faceless and probably unappreciated, laboring for noble principles. Caring for society's disinherited and rejected is among the few positive applications of this influence, but you eventually tire of "rescuing." A desire to be taken care of can often involve you with utopian visions of a nurturing, all-knowing social structure—notwithstanding the poor records such visions have had in practice. This need to be cared for has a sinister side as well: this zone can see you dealing with hospitals, prisons, asylums, or other institutions—hopefully in the provision of services or idealistic administration.

As mentioned above, there are some professions that seemingly benefit from Neptune's influence: music, the arts, movies, dance, photography, TV work, and any business that requires a knowledge and intuition of fashion and public trends. Glamour, the creation of illusions of beauty and desirability, religion (or demagoguery), professions dealing with chemicals, anesthetics, petroleum, or drugs all can direct some of the imaginative and hypnotic energy of Neptune constructively. You probably need a lot of time alone to handle the subtle, intuitive, and sensitive capacities that develop under Neptune—this might be well, as relationships go particularly poorly here, with other people either taking advantage of you and using you or idealizing you and thus ignoring who you really are. People closest to you appear so vague, haphazard, and disorganized that it is impossible to relate to them. In matters of health, this area is far from ideal: chronic infections, mysterious ailments, psychosomatic disorders, and dysfunction of the immune system leave you open to a host of maladies. Vitality is low and resistance to environmental contaminants poor. Intense reactions to drugs occur, often with long-range consequences.

Neptune on Ascendant:
Confusion Profusion

This is an excellent location for salespeople, because people don't recognize or see you for who you really are, and you come to stand in their minds for some ideal, some unreachable goal or impossible dream. People project their fondest and most unrealistic wishes onto you, assuring an ephemeral popularity. Seen as fascinating, beautiful, and mysterious, you are actually only holding a mirror up to everyone's incompleteness. Your self-image is confused with other people's, and you collude in this game all too willingly, since your own idea of who you are is amorphous, intangible, and constantly in flux. The confusion invites a retreat from the world isolating you, since when you are among people you feel a need for total and complete immersion in the personality of some "other," something which often makes your relationships dependent, masochistic, addictive, or decidedly unequal in the distribution of power. If you do make it in a worldly sense, you likely will do so as a media image, with who you really are remaining invisible beneath the makeup and hype. This presents an acceptable compromise, as you cannot stand scrutiny here; one effective way to deal with everyone's attention is to distract them with a false personality. You may acquire a wild love of luxury, a la Hollywood, another way of expressing the fact that you really have a hard time knowing who you are or where you are going while in this locale.

Your arrival in a social situation (or in someone's life) often signals a period of confusion and relationship to dark inner realities: people feel inspired, propelled by unconscious winds of feeling, and in tune with the cosmic when you're around, but this does little to provide you with any sense of relationship or stability. You may seem to others like a free-form broadcaster of confusion (or occasionally inspiration) and particularly the most logical and in-control types find your presence baffling and disturbing. Health is apt to be poor in this locale and very subject to influence from drugs or environmental allergens. You may be psychic, imaginative, and hypersensitive, and success comes best through music or some other profession that allows universal, cosmic, and superpersonal rhythms and impulses to use you as their instrument.

Neptune on Midheaven:
Messiahs and Martyrs Need Not Apply

In this locale, the general influence of Neptune is most apt to manifest in your relationships with society. You will be strongly inclined to follow a career in a large corporation or serving profession, where you can either lose yourself, so to speak, or sacrifice your time to the needs of others. You should be especially aware of the dangers of being socially victimized by being cast into one of society's many self-defeating roles. Ending up a scapegoat is all too possible here, as are arrests, martyrdom, or scandal. Your appraisal of social trends and patterns is contaminated by wishfulness and illusion, though there is the possibility that a genius-like intuition of future fashions or devotion to some social ideal will bring you a glittering notoriety of the sort one finds in Hollywood and other glamour capitals. But you should remember that in Hollywood there are 10,000 lost souls selling out for every one who makes it to the top, so your wishes for the impossible dream may incline you to waste much of your life in the idle pursuit of unrealizable objectives. You may be gossiped about in the sensational manner of supermarket tabloids, suggesting that you appeal to people out of touch with their own unconscious who see in you some larger-than-life figure with their own faults and unfulfilled dreams magnified to mythological size.

Your relationship with society as a whole poses the most difficult dilemma for you in this locale, however, as you tend to see yourself as either Messiah or martyr in relation to the world around you, when in fact you may not command much serious attention at all. Feelings of confusion, imprisonment, dependency, and victimization dominate, leaving you with uncertainty and a challenged identity. Artistic vocations may proceed well, though, as you are able to tune into others' needs for the fantastic and furnish them with glimpses of worlds that seem far better than the everyday one they are familiar with. Your commitment may fluctuate among various social philosophies, especially nonviolent ones, so that your identity in society often will be seen through your willingness to sacrifice your personal privacy and life goals for some abstract ideal. Through it all, society does not see you for what you really are, and while some will be able to pull the wool over the eyes of the world in this zone, the joke will usually be on you.

Neptune on Descendant:
Can You Get Used to Being Ignored?

Your personal relationships are the prime focus of Neptune in this locale, though it is a rather fuzzy focus at that. Relationships seem to hold promise of the realization of long-held dreams and fantasies here, but rarely fulfill your dramatic expectations, remaining amorphous, disoriented, and little resembling the all-encompassing partnership you seek. Marriage or legal concerns are areas in which you may be taken advantage of by others, but you are drawn into them nevertheless, as they represent a yearning, incomplete part of yourself projected outward. Beneath the problems, which are always too easy to blame on others, lies a lack of commitment on your part. Your instinctive feeling that relationship cannot exist in any real sense reflects your lack of a concrete and crystallized sense of identity, so your entanglements become a means to grant yourself a substantiality in your life that you are lacking in other areas. As a result, it's hard to connect with anyone in a real way, which leaves you with a feeling of lonely frustration. Just when you think you have found a real issue to grasp in order to put your relationship on a firm footing, you find yourself in a struggle, that's much like fighting under water.

In marriage and other close relationships, you resist seeing your partners as they really are, preferring to project your own ideals on them, and you may be drawn to people who fear the truth and prefer to support fallacies. Alcoholism, addiction, or illness may strike you or your mate, deepening the dangerous tendency to mutual dependency. Your relationships will only succeed when you learn to leave plenty of room for your mate to come and go and to be who he or she really is, and thus avoid becoming entangled in the clinging web of codependency.

Professionally, you may find yourself dealing often with society's underprivileged, perhaps as counselor or therapist. Your clients' incompleteness again reflects your own inability to define and objectify your own life path, so while helping them you can help yourself. Health problems seem to occur to many in this zone, as long term, chronic problems fail to respond to treatment, often because they are externally caused by allergens or environmental influences, though identification of such causes is elusive. Relocation may be one means of ameliorating such problems. You need to find a like-minded group of supportive peers to sustain your identity against the barrage of negativity to which it is sometimes subjected.

Neptune on Imum Coeli:
In the Harbor Without an Anchor

Here Neptune is apt to manifest most directly in your living situation, home environment, and relationships within your family. You may experiment with various utopian, monastic, or communitarian living arrangements under this zone, perhaps even feeling that you have found your guru, but nothing materially reliable is apt to emerge from these experiences. Real estate matters don't go well here, and attempts to settle down and relate to some environment as your real home may be continually frustrated. There is a lot of idealism connected to living here, as you see the social structures and ethnic or regional peculiarities of this locale as simpler, romantic, and somehow more pure than what you have experienced elsewhere. Some may fantasize an ideal childhood here, a state of dependency more like a mythical Eden than any real place. Behind these fantasies is a desire to be taken care of and relieved of the responsibility for your own maintenance, the better to pursue unhindered your need for intense inner visions and transfiguring psychic experiences.

Your partners or other companions in living arrangements may find you a confusing and disturbing influence, and for them you tend to come to stand for all that is incomprehensible, uncontrollable, and associated with the unconscious, even though they may not be able to say exactly why. People seem to surrender their wills when you are around, inviting you to rescue them from themselves—a job that will be thankless and unsuccessful for the most part. Whatever is built here is likely to have foundations of sand, except, perhaps, for a deep, spiritual, and inner wisdom which can take root in the flux and turmoil of your personal life. It will be hard to assess the true value of any projects undertaken until you have moved elsewhere; until then, your attempts to ground yourself somewhere, to find your psychic roots, will be subject to the whimsical winds of fantasy, unrealistic expectations, and an almost magical, supernatural confusion. Domestic concerns are apt to become so problematical that you feel forced to eschew any identification with location, family, home, or ancestral environment, and instead come to see yourself as a citizen of the world, united with all beings equally on the deepest level of inner experience.

Neptune with Pluto:
"You Mean Life Doesn't Have a Happy Ending?"

In this locale, the ideals and illusions of life are burned away like morning fog, and much of the phony order of the logical mind upset, with a resultant higher and clearer, though frightening and alienating, vision. Here you feel embittered by having been through the worst, and having seen an immature world view (perhaps one too much the product of Hollywood, media fantasy, or a protected childhood) violently and permanently shattered. Any part of your vision or belief system that survives after the experiences of this stormy locale can be counted on to be real and enduring. Belief itself is seen as a type of neurosis, and self may emerge as the only anchor in a sea of otherwise shifting and unreliable values. Sensitivity diminishes in the face of anxiety, fears, and attacks of conscience during the spiritual housecleaning that is apt to go on here, leaving a feeling of exhaustion, loss of faith, despair, and cynicism, though these will in time be replaced with deeply felt values and a spiritual reality more valuable than the old, outmoded illusions ever could have been.

After this period of purging, you may feel there is little or nothing left to believe in, and it is only at this point that you will be able to find the power to see a cosmic, mystical vision of the world through discovery of your intense inner-based strength. During earlier stages of this process, ennui, boredom, and a feeling that everything is hollow may pervade your psyche, demanding that attention be directed toward an inner voice as external realities and their meanings dim. You may come to realize the existence of more than one level of consciousness, a tremendous discovery granting you the tool by which the subjective and inner beliefs can control and change the outside, objective world. Drugs or meditation can evoke changes in life, and when you experience what to others is madness, the definition of sanity is expanded and, along with it, the world that it defines. Of course, tampering with reality has its perils, and the stakes are high whenever you attempt to grow into consciousness so far beyond that of your milieu. Practicalities are often neglected here in favor of this inner transformation, as you deal daily with mythical spirits and demons, along with other often unwelcome guests from the unconscious, until the idea of sanity itself is transcended. Change may sometimes occur here slowly, without your being aware of it, but it will come nonetheless.

17

Pluto: The Intensity Addict

IT TAKES a special sort of person to enjoy and prosper in this intense and powerful zone. But it is not easy to know who will or won't, as anyone is apt to change radically here—perhaps even transforming from the type who always runs from a crisis into a person who readily confronts the intensity offered by Pluto. Of course, the process of transformation will be more painful if you're the type who normally shies away from the darker side of experience, and generally wants life to be pleasant, ordinary, superficial, social, and stable. If the power of sexuality frightens you and changes or upheaval elicit more fear than anticipation, then this zone may be particularly trying for you, but the depth with which your experience is rewarded may be all the more needed. People attached to their possessions, who feel that money constitutes security, also have problems, as the experiences of this zone force acknowledgment of the impermanence of material reality and how it is underlain by the more powerful laws of energy exchange and equilibrium.

For Women Only: Your close understanding of the birth process immunizes you from some of the more intense and dangerous aspects of this zone, but that doesn't mean you don't experience some of the same power struggles, intensity, and life changes that men do. They simply surprise you less. There is also the possibility that you relate to men who typify all the more negative aspects of this zone, complete with social alienation, cruelty, obsessive sexuality, and dominance. This is not a good area for childbearing, and the fact that you are equipped to handle some of the issues here doesn't make them any more pleasant.

For Men Only: As a man, your tendency may be to relate to the separative nature and the intensity of this zone with a brutal competitiveness, a rebellious, outlaw mentality, perhaps becoming resentful and alienated from society as a result of some real or imagined injustice to which you have been subjected. Often you find yourself in isolation from women or have a tendency to objectify relationships into the purely sexual. Femininity seems alien and absent or can take threatening forms, such as one might find in designing and treacherous relationships; this may extend as well to the broader concepts of cooperation, community, and society, which you tend to deny yourself. Relationships of all kinds center around power, money, and possessions and you learn, rather unwillingly, a new respect for your limits in an unequal society.

If You're Just Passing Through...

On a vacation or short stay, you probably won't have time to develop the deeper and more permanent changes seen under this line, but you might encounter a symbol or person who stands for a self that you may become at some future time. This awareness can be precipitated by exposure to the concept of mortality in some form, which could include sexuality as well as birth or death. This is a likely location for self-renewal, particularly if undertaken consciously, such as in psychoanalysis, or through other types of peak experience. In Pluto's realm, the structures of society and selfhood give way to a more universal order. Do be careful though, especially if the ideas most often linked to Pluto are repugnant to you.

Long Distance Lines

Even if you cannot travel to these zones, they are apt to stand in your mind for absolutes, firsts, lasts, and beginnings. People from these places may arrive as great changes are about to beset your life, or, similarly, you may be a catalyst for change in the lives of those who reside there. The symbols of decay, fermentation, and rebirth may be associated in your mind somehow with this locality, and a total resurrection of personal potentials you thought you had lost may accompany any dealings with it.

Psychological Interpretation of Pluto:
The First Chapter of the Rest of Your Life

If you are tired of three-dimensional reality, the laws of physics, cause and effect, and society, this zone may be congenial for you, as here the odds are continually defied, firsts and lasts in life are encountered, and actual miracles can happen. Most people would rather not think much about death—we live as if we were immortal and feel that death is something that happens to other people, hopefully those we don't know. But awareness of mortality is an important motivation for the quality and energy of life; philosophers have counseled us to live each day as if it were our last, and the power and intensity of the sexual experience stems from its relation to death, as through reproduction the individual is born anew.

Death is the opposite pole from birth, and sex the bridge between the two. Residence in this zone will immerse you in experiences somehow allied to these peak-intensity realities, and images of rebirth, renewal, destruction, eroticism, alienation, rape, and leave-taking are apt to prevail. Exposure to such universal truths poses problems, as much of the world's day-to-day operations (often centered around concepts of property and privilege) is predicated on ideas of immortality and continuity. In touch with absolutes, you tend to see yourself and others as one in five billion, truly equal in mortality, and exposure to (or awareness of) death changes your perspectives on life, leaving you to see it with greater depth and clarity.

The theme of social alienation is prominent here, and you will probably do something to isolate yourself from normal, day-to-day, superficial, and trivial social intercourse, then complain about this self-imposed rejection, lamenting your image of outlaw or social pariah. You should have thought of that when you made yourself a focus of social forces. Total inner transformation of the kind stimulated by this zone demands total isolation and an awareness of the unique and lonely position of the individual as focus of the whole; it's impossible to communicate your self-perceived position in infinity and fate. Withdrawal from family and other unquestioned alliance underlies a war with anything that tries to define or confine you. Such total personal transformation rarely is pleasant, as ferment and death of parts of self must precede new growth. The fields must be burned for new planting.

Stages and Myth of Pluto:
Steps Along the Road to Nothing

Pluto was, of course, the god of the underworld and lord of dead souls. His kidnap of Persephone in the myth adds to the concepts of mortality and finality, those of rebirth, loss of virginity, the imprisoned female, abduction, and birth, and suggests that within the female (and her capacity for childbirth) lies the potential to transcend death, to return from Hades. There is also implication of renewal through peak experience and the erotic, as well as symbolic association with resurrection motifs. Through all the trauma, identity is purged, and a new self emerges, enlarged by the intensity and greater depth it has experienced.

The earlier stages of consciousness of Pluto are apt to center on loss, as it is only through this that the new can be given room to grow. A loved one may leave your life; childhood may be lost through a traumatic or epochal experience, with a resultant resentment against family; virginity and innocence may be lost, creating a resentment against sexuality or perhaps the opposite sex. Social position or status may be lost, with a resultant feeling of alienation and outlaw consciousness—you alone pitted against everyone else. This stage sees a wounded pride and an "I'll get even" mentality that can run the gamut from self-destructive despair to firearms fetishism, with the emphasis on how much you have been wronged.

A more mature outlook centers on acceptance and begins to adapt to the new situation. Depression and pessimism are internalized and gnaw less evidently at the outer personality, but there is a feeling that life will never be the same. Finally, in stages of mature, conscious awareness of the power and nature of this zone, you are able to see the immortality that is afforded by old forms perishing and being replaced with the new. Life's limitations are seen as its motivations, and its losses are seen as a necessary part of the equation of existence. In this stage, true magic is possible, as this alchemy of mortality is Nature's secret of creation; when understood on inner psychological planes, it allows the transcendence of physical laws, along with sentimentality, illusions, even blind hope and faith. The butterfly emerges from the cocoon, and just when hope was abandoned, a miracle occurs, redirecting life with a singleness and purpose only dreamed of before. For those who give up the pleasures of the trivial, nature awards the absolute.

The Practical Side of Pluto:
Flies, Wolves, Dogs, and Money

On more immediate and practical levels, while in this area, you may come into closer contact than before with the central themes of death and rebirth; partnerships may undergo transformation, relationships become intensely competitive, or people close to you might pass away, leaving you with a more intimate and painful grasp of this universal reality. Sex is also apt to become more prominent in your life, and firsts in erotic experience often are encountered here. Socially, power struggle seems the key concept in this zone, and your relationship with society may center on oppression or persecution, with a resultant increase in self-reliance and resentment against authority and "normalcy." If you do not experience these realities directly, they may come to you through other people, and outlaws, criminals, underworld types, and the extremely powerful and unprincipled may enter your life. You may even in some circumstances open yourself to the danger of becoming the victim of violent crime—though this is most often the case only when people repress the other, less extreme expressions of this energy, leaving it no way to manifest outwardly in a way that is beyond your control. All these incommunicable experiences and traumas serve to assure that the rest of your life will be shorn of some of the illusions that most of us live in, and this heightened awareness of reality makes you somewhat unwelcome, not unlike a concentration camp survivor at a cocktail party, as you force others to recognize issues that most would rather forget.

You may also experience obsessions of various kinds here, and when the pressure and stress they place you under has eased, you will wonder at the power they held over you. In this zone, you are stripped to your essence, and in learning a weighty lesson, you acquire a sensual depth, a magnetic charisma that requires you to live in a world more real than most. Your work may deal with these vital issues in some way, as, for example, counseling the recently traumatized or bereaved. Flies, wolves, or dogs are among the symbols of death and decay which may surface frequently as signs of the change going on within. Money, itself a potent symbol of how material reality can acquire a life of its own, often will become a preoccupation or obsession in this area. The acquisition of depth is the overriding purpose of what happens to you here, and any attempts to forestall this will only up the ante. Better to make a study of mortality and to seek understanding of the extremes of human possibility.

Pluto on Ascendant:
Indomitable, and Tired of Proving It

The position of Pluto tends to powerfully evolve your self-concept, as peak-experience and mortality themes work through your own sense of identity, changing and transforming it inexorably. You feel passionately about what moves you, and generally are committed, intensely competitive, and easily affronted, particularly by those in authority. Others see you as hypnotically charismatic, memorable, somehow dangerous, and may associate you with things and ideas they'd rather forget. So you spend a lot of time alone, which alienation has the effect of intensifying sexual needs. You may come to identify yourself with the process of transformation, leading you to enlist in an endless progression of self-improvement courses in the desire to transmute yourself into something entirely different. You yourself will often act as catalyst for change in the lives of others—people who come under your influence may have just survived, or are just about to enter, periods of their lives where great upheaval and chaos occur.

For your own part, you want privacy and isolation, spend a great deal of your time alone, hide some aspect of yourself from others, and seem more private, enigmatic, and mysterious than usual. People see you instinctively as a leader or a menace, and the hidden power within you brings to consciousness repressed rebellion, challenge, rejection of authority, and a desire for change in those you deal with. There is danger here, especially for people who prefer to ignore harsh realities; conversion experiences, near-death encounters, social ostracism, and becoming a scapegoat all are unfortunate possibilities. Phobias and fears develop, especially social ones, and you are all too aware of society's inclination to blame its problems on those who are different.

Intense experiences involving supernatural or archetypal forces challenge you here, yet when all seems lost, you seem to have a miraculous ability to turn the situation around and save the day. The total personal transformation you undergo in this zone may be very physical, and could include changes in appearance through matters as simple as a change in your style of dress, or as complete as alterations of your physique and face via plastic surgery. Issues of possessiveness, jealousy, domination, money, and sexuality become central concerns to you, making it hard to have a simple, pleasant, friendly relationship with anyone. You are indomitable, but may get a little tired of proving it.

Pluto on Midheaven
Looking Out for Number One

The position of Pluto in this locale tends to stress your relationship with society and your milieu. Alienation from society calls forth a power hunger which usually is expressed through an intense battle for personal autonomy and freedom from coercion. You resent most authority, yet at the same time you crave it for yourself, thus leaving you always in danger of becoming a model for the very tyrants you rebel against. For much the same reason you could find yourself engaging in hero worship, flirting with despotism, exploring the extremes of antisocial behavior, and generally doing things that create an image of you in everyone's mind that is larger than life, as you constantly remind others of uncomfortable realities. Your identity (perhaps in the press) may come to stand for some popular or unpopular ideal, as you strive to beating the system or find yourself crushed by it. A magical charisma and hypnotic power assures that you will be talked about and noticed, acting as a focal point of group consciousness, but you must constantly keep in mind the cruelty with which society often relates to the things you focus its attention on—black-and-white, all-or-nothing symbols like sex, money, or death.

People in power may oppress you, but usually only after you have provoked them by championing some popular ideal or otherwise challenging the system. You may be successful and be lavished with praise, or you may fail in a spectacular way and be heaped with calumny, but it's unlikely you'll be ignored. You're totally unique in the eyes of many, and because of this you may find your status in society changes constantly. Issues of war, crime, assassination, espionage, politics, or gangsterism intrude here, as you play for mortally high stakes in your battle for selfhood against alien, hostile social forces. Unfair victimization by organized groups or mobs are often experienced in this type of zone. You learn firsthand the meaning of the cliche "power corrupts," as either victim or perpetrator (or both), and a battle of selfhood fought in the public arena leaves you changed for life, with new values, a different life direction, and an identity transformed in the fires of conflict. Money, sex, and mortality are dominant symbols, and terrific battles for self-preservation are initiated around them under this Pluto line.

Pluto on Descendant:
It's A Jungle Out There

This position of Pluto tends to stress relationships and your public image, both of which are apt to be scenes of great change, upheaval, and self-discovery. You can experience many conflicts here, as you feel that the world, hostile and contentious, almost seems intent on extinguishing you.

You must do battle with the very things and people closest to you, while the outer world withdraws and leaves you alone to defend yourself against the crises, all of which seem to demand some measure of personal change and transformation. Driven by the desperation and fear of being alone, you are drawn to people with whom you form relationships that are either intensely combative or sexual. If you can manage to come out on top in such struggles, you are likely to be free from dependency for the rest of your life, though the marriage or relationship in question may never be the same again. Power needs, competitiveness, and hostility mark the beginning of your evolution here. Experiences that renew you almost to the point that you feel reborn in some sense follow encounters in which your identity, will, and reason are subject to intense pressure. There is considerable danger of injury here, or even of experiences that bring you close to death, the purpose of such experiences being to direct your attention and will inward; much strife can be avoided if you accept a more inward-looking life and do not strive so hard to control and direct the people and situations you encounter. Alienation and destruction in relationships may be the first chapter of the rest of your life, but they may seem at the time like the last.

If you truly tap the potential Pluto offers you here, there is some possibility that you can change world opinion, perhaps by laying your life on the line for some heroic objective; but there is, all in all, too much personal danger lurking in this zone to make it suitable for prolonged residence. You may have to deal directly and even forcefully with issues of violence, including coming to terms with the fact that any human is a potential killer. The ultimate battle of selfhood is here fought with those closest to you, and when you finally break away it will be to a new self-concept far more integrated, whole, and complete within itself. This is not accomplished without stress and contention, but the result can be well worth the effort.

Pluto on Imum Coeli
You Love Your Family, But Can't Like Them

Pluto at this position tends to stress your need to define and in some sense control your relationship with your family, your roots, and your origins. The past, your family tradition, and perhaps your ethnic identity become involved in a battle in which you must establish who you are apart from these often restrictive influences. Your family identity and past can easily be left behind, but a new life apart from them is hard to build, since you must define your own place in the world based on your own concept of self and personal identity. Money, sex, competition, and issues of freedom and individuality are pitted against what tradition expects of you, resulting in continual upheaval and perpetual cataclysm in home, property, real estate, and family concerns. Death often makes its presence known in your life here, though through its force you can come to a new sense of personal meaning as you increase the depth and breadth of your life experience. The ultimate stand you make in the battle of selfhood in this zone is most likely to be fought with your parents, but can also be directed at challenging the symbol of some authority or hitherto unquestioned set of values or traditions. Beneath the outer problems you face lies the need for self-purification, a purging of the past and a settling of ancient karmic accounts and outmoded relationships. Forgotten family history may conceal the pattern your life is following.

A personal view of yourself that you cling to, but which in fact has been outgrown and no longer seems relevant, cannot endure here, so a curious loyalty you seem to feel toward the past actually disguises a real need to leave it behind forever. Obsessed with genealogy as part of this process, you try to find some roots to which you can relate, and subsequently many firsts and lasts in life are here associated with concepts of family, continuity, and inheritance. Motivating much of the introspection that catalyzes the life changes you face are resources and abilities that may have remained dormant in other places. These latent powers, talents, abilities, and personalities make themselves felt in this zone in an almost urgent way, as something in your subconscious urges you to get on with the elimination of the traditional strictures that bind you. Your family and cultural heritage are seen very clearly here, but that can also mean dealing with accumulated family guilt, inherited diseases, or the oppressive attitudes of some family members.

PART THREE

Transits and Progressions:
Cyclo*Carto*Graphy

Introduction: Location is the Key

An ACG map can be viewed dynamically through the use of transits and progressions, just as with any standard horoscope. When using that standard chart, any aspect between a transiting or progressed planet and a natal planet occurs when both either have the same longitude (conjunction) or are separated in longitude by some specific angle (for example, sixty degrees in a sextile). Standard transits and progressions thus happen at fixed moments of time, with the "dynamic" (i.e., either transiting or progressed) planet moving to within whatever orb is allowed, reaching exact aspect, and then moving away from the exact aspect and out of orb. The process, of course, is not always that simple, with the slow-moving planets sometimes forming an aspect to a natal planet two or three times as a result of retrograde motion. Even in this case, all we need to know is when an aspect happens.

The picture is much different when we want to know both when in time and where on the earth two planets will make contact. Since we are dealing with both time and space in Astro*Carto*Graphy, there are only two transit moments similar to what we deal with in the standard horoscope. The first is seen when a dynamic planet has exactly the same longitude and latitude as the natal planet, a comparatively rare event which, when it involves two transiting planets, we would call an eclipse or an occultation. The second, similar to a square and also comparatively rare, is seen when the Ascendant/Descendant lines of two planets cross exactly at the equator. Though neither of these cases is likely to happen too often, they are considered to affect the native no matter where he or she lives, so that they are thought to be more general in their effect than simple line-crossings.

Since in Astro*Carto*Graphy we are not dealing with planetary "points" located in one place in the zodiac, but rather with two sets of planetary lines (the natal and transiting or the natal and progressed), the transits and progressions we are looking for are the times and geographical locations at which those lines cross. A brief study of any of the maps in this book will tell the reader that the lines linked to any two planets will always cross somewhere, and in fact, except in very rare instances (such as those mentioned above), lines for any two planets will always cross at four points somewhere on the earth.

As a practical matter there is no need to know where all these crossings are, since most will fall far away from any land mass or population center. When we are dealing with transits and progressions in an ACG map it is therefore best to center on those places where our own interests and activities are strongest. The comprehensive method of doing this uses a clear overlay in which a map combining both transiting and progressed planets (more about that combination below) is placed over the natal map, allowing easy visual determination of those places highlighted by planetary movements. If, on the other hand, we want to concentrate only on one or two localities, then looking at transits or progressions to the angles of a simple relocated birth chart can tell us quite a lot, except that, since it lacks the additional dimension shown by mapping (particularly the inclusion of latitude along with longitude), it cannot time things as precisely as mapping will.

Though we could use such overlays to look at both transits and progressions involving all planets, the planetary-line "spaghetti" would very quickly become too complex for us to make a sound judgment on anything. Thus, from the standpoint of economy and simplicity, the "Cyclo*Carto*Graphy" overlay considers only the progressions of Sun through Mars and the transits of Jupiter through Pluto. This makes good sense since the progressed inner planets move at rates that are roughly equivalent to the transiting outer planets. The interpretations that follow are written with this viewpoint in mind, though we have more generally denoted the dynamic planet as being "with" the natal planet in order to signal that these readings can, with some modification, be used for more general purposes.

The transits and progressions active when George H. W. Bush led the Gulf War and when Harry Truman ordered the total destruction of Hiroshima and Nagasaki show the value of looking at the total picture as much as possible. Considering transits and progressions along with a person's natal Astro*Carto*Graphy map can complicate interpretation if not handled carefully, but it can also be well worth the effort. Even though transitory, the effects of the planets in this framework can be very powerful.

18

The Sun: Let Your Big Light Shine

THE SUN progressing across an angle of a locality you visit or reside in is a powerful influence that can last as long as two years. During this period you are apt to seem far more outgoing, extroverted, ego-centered, and theatrical than usual, and may find yourself in a public role of some sort, perhaps for the first time, due to the leadership and authority you seem to radiate instinctively. Despite its temporary nature, the progression could mark a positive and major life turning-point during which you discover parenthood, artistic expression, or even perhaps turn yourself toward an artistic vocation.

People in powerful positions seem more inclined to pay attention to you, so that you feel appreciated and "special," reacting to such attention with an opening of your heart that leads to a discovery of your deepest creative instincts. This in the spotlight will seem all the more so if you have felt you were suffering from a lack of recognition. Riding the surge of self-confidence you are likely to feel, now is the time to slay your personal dragons as you prosecute a quest for identity and power. If you can build on the good things that happen to you now, you can set a standard of effectiveness and accomplishment that will keep you on the same track for many years after the solar aspect has moved along. More than any other time in your life, you can now discover your heroic inner self, and you will find the process of self-discovery you are embarked upon is more than aided by the people around you.

Sun to natal Sun is in effect slightly longer, lasting for about three years. Generally the indications are the same as those for the Sun alone, only stronger.

Sun to Natal Moon

Residing here could mark a turning point in your acceptance of your nurturing, parental, and emotional potentials as you find new and important relationships with dependents or younger people becoming central in your life. This in turn can bring about an acceptance and recognition of the importance and nature of your parents' influence on you, and a consequent acceptance of your family background, ethnic heritage, or any other personally relevant tradition. You also begin to recognize your need for other people, as you explore fantasies which at other times might have been ignored or suppressed, becoming more sensitive and more willing to let yourself feel and experience life. Those areas of your life which were formerly marked by a somewhat rebellious attitude, now become the scene of more socially approved behavior, as the responsibilities you seek make society, its support, and others' opinions more important to you than they might have been. Security needs, erotic urges, and feelings of community with people dominate your awareness, as you accept your fundamental interdependence with and attachment to others.

Sun to Natal Mercury

This period, of about a year's duration, marks an important turning-point in life which for most people comes before the age of thirty. Under this aspect you may discover for the first time your ability to use symbols of all kinds as implements of your personal will and desire. It is in this period that the educational process first "clicks" for many, so you may find that you begin to understand the possibility of using resources and information in a way you weren't capable of before. As you explore your newfound capacity to learn, you may acquire important new skills or information, perhaps resulting in some formal recognition for scholastic work well done. Job or educational and community concerns bring you into the public eye, and deeper analysis of the symbolic significance of the events that befall you at this time may reveal an emerging personal myth or theme which can affect you strongly for the rest of your life. Mystical insights or a growing interest in the occult are often products of the insatiable curiosity brought about by this aspect.

Sun to Natal Venus

This period, of about a year's duration, marks an important turning-point which is reached by most people before the age of fifty. It is likely to be the most significant time in your life for the formation of aesthetic tastes, growth in your artistic abilities, and for the bonding which forms important relationships, including your relationship to society as a whole. In everything you do you seem bent on making yourself more accepted socially and approved of in ways that might not have been important to you before. You discover that you have the power to select and cultivate friendships and partnerships with the types of people who truly interest you. Love is of course a strong possibility during this period, as are marriage and parenthood. "Children" born during this period may, however, be of an artistic or abstract sort as well, since your creativity is stimulated in ways you may never have dreamed of before. In many of your new creative endeavors you find you have the potential to reap monetary or social rewards, some of which may permanently alter the course of life.

Sun to Natal Mars

For the two years this aspect is in force, you can reach a new level of realization about your ability to effect change and to implement your will in the world, as you become better able to develop a conscious life plan than you were before. Even though ideally this is a period of self-imposed discipline, often under rigorous and harsh conditions, at times you may feel the need to express your powerful inner energy in a strongly sexual way, or even through aggression. Depending on many factors, such as your maturity, your gender, and your willingness to acknowledge openly your own potential for aggression, this period can either be one of tremendous accomplishment or of constant involvement in seemingly unprovoked attacks, rampant controversy, and accident-proneness. Rejection of domination by others, and a need to embrace risk and the thrill of physical stimulation can lead you into many confrontations with authority, and overall you are apt to surprise yourself with a level of courage, daring, and erotic appetite in yourself that are much greater than you had experienced before. More than anything else, you must strive to understand just what your physical and confrontational limits are, as you are likely to be testing them constantly. Knowing how far you can go helps you cultivate discipline and directed behavior; not knowing simply puts you in jeopardy.

Sun to Natal Jupiter

During the two years' duration of this aspect, you can reach a new level of realization in regard to your ability to promote yourself, as more and more you seek social approval, and generally strive to rise in status by letting others know of your accomplishments. Full of self-confidence and self-assurance, you begin to think better of yourself day by day, and this improved self-image in turn attracts the favorable attention of those in authority. Obviously, some may find your positive thinking and self-boosterism a little hard to take, as you tend to advertise your own wonderfulness at high volume at inappropriate times and also may try to force your own ideas of morality and rectitude onto others as if to ask them to play the heathen to your missionary. If you work at it, however, your renewed self-confidence can take a highly positive form, introducing you to a broader horizon of academic, cultural, and literary concerns. No matter what, though, nearly everything you do is bound to attract attention, and you quickly learn to play others' opinions like a musical instrument, enlisting their support for your inexhaustible quantity of enterprises and promotions. In general, this is a very lucky period that can bring you many personal and financial rewards.

Sun to Natal Saturn

This progressed aspect is a very important and critical time in your life, one that probably subjects you to some rather unpleasant discipline in order to make you aware of your weaknesses and failings. With some care and attention, however, such shortcomings as you have can be turned into strengths during this period, often as a result of your increased psychological sensitivity and your reaction to feelings of powerlessness. Carl Jung suggested that everyone has a "shadow," a subconscious identity comprised of functions and experiences opposed to the conscious talents and abilities from which the outer personality is fashioned. These rejected functions are things that you can't do well, so during this time you often are made aware of what they are, perhaps traumatically enough that you inwardly vow to master them at any cost. It is from such awareness of deficiency that one's power needs arise, so this is also a time to experience the extremes of power and powerlessness in your life. Self-restraint, autonomy, guilt, abstemiousness, patience, and other "virtues" come to the fore in your own behavior, while the world seems all too willing to paternalize, discipline, and punish you for real or imagined transgressions. Through dealing with problems, you learn to mask your insecurities well, and can become adept at manipulating feelings of weakness in others, all of which amounts to a constructive overcompensation for the feelings of inadequacy and sensitivity that plague you at this time.

Sun to Natal Uranus

This period of time, about two years in duration and full of surprises, cam mark a turning-point of lifelong significance in your relationship with society and your own self-image. Outer circumstances or people propel you to explore and express the more nonconformist or even antisocial aspects of your personality. Your sense of individuality is stimulated, as personal freedom becomes a critical issue, and you often find yourself standing alone, espousing unpopular ideals as you inspire others to align themselves with you on the side of principle. Such preoccupations may in turn lead you from groups dedicated to common interests, idealistic causes, or social objectives, but your strict (and even restrictive) adherence to abstract standards of honesty may well mask a discomfort with intimacy, emotions, feelings, and other subjective concerns. To your surprise, you may find yourself designated as the symbol of some cause, popular or unpopular, perhaps bringing about a constant tension between the personal and social spheres of your life. You may be attracted more than usual to the forbiddingly bizarre and technical, these being symbols of the awakening awareness of your own individuality, as you seek to associate yourself with anything and everything that can define you as being anything but a slave to conformity.

Sun to Natal Neptune

Lasting about a year, this aspect helps you to reach a new level of awareness about the links you have in your life with the unconscious, the mythological, and the idealistic. Depending upon how comfortable you are with the ideas and phenomena that are both mysterious and illogical, you will find this time either fascinating and miraculous or frightening and bizarre. Usually under this aspect, early stages of your awareness of the importance of the unconscious will be acted out through projection, so you probably will find yourself surrounded by peculiar, spaced-out, and even unbalanced people. Later, by cultivating an awareness that there is a place in everyone that touches the unconscious, you can discover your own connection to the totality of space and time, and perhaps express the feelings engendered by Sun-Neptune as altruism and self-sacrifice, as you experience a poetic merging of the ego with the cosmos. You have a need for privacy that is greater than usual now, so trying to be "on top of things" will generally not work too well for you. Self-defeating behavior—addiction, defeatism, and too much reliance on intuition rather than factual knowledge—can be a danger now, but it can also bring benefits by helping you to transcend life's banality, to develop a perception of the infinite, and to sharpen the artistic and idealistic aspects of your personality.

Sun to Natal Pluto

This period of time, about two years in duration, requires you to learn to deal meaningfully with concepts such as mortality, birth, death, and regeneration in a way that allows you to redirect yourself toward a more purposeful existence. Pluto is "outlaw consciousness," so a feeling of alienation and competition may begin to permeate relationships where you feel you are being taken for granted, as you try to define yourself in terms contrary to the possessiveness and venality of mainstream society. Any activities that you try to keep hidden now may spill unbidden from their closets, leading to revelations that force you to take a stand in areas of your life where you had been "going along to get along" before. All of this upheaval can be the precursor to a new personality and self-concept which are shorn of many of their old illusions and unnecessary psychological baggage; but it can also lead to farewells that are almost always painful. Ruthless, spiteful, manipulative, and envious people you come across are really only symptoms of the buried and repressed parts of your psyche, so if they seem to dominate this period, this indicates you should pay attention to parts of your heart and mind which urgently require development. This can be an exciting time of firsts and lasts, but it is also a time in which you often feel that you are fighting your battles all by yourself.

19

The Moon: An Emotional Interlude

THOUGH THE Moon progressing to a particular place on your Astro*Carto*Graphy map moves quickly, it is still a powerful influence that lasts about eight months. During this lunar period, your needs and emotions are intensified, as you develop responsiveness, sensitivity, and generally find yourself becoming more involved in the moods and sensations of others. You become aware of the subtle emotional climate of your location and the way in which it relates to the social milieu and to other people's needs and their demands on you. As your appetite for affection, nurturance, and sustenance becomes critical, the accompanying sharpening of desire presages an important stage in the development of your ability to care for yourself and to tend to the needs of others. Instability and restlessness are felt when, goaded by the increased urgency of your desires and the apparent impossibility of their satisfaction, your life changes frequently and unpredictably. You are apt to find yourself increasingly the center of attention now, even though the accentuation of your feelings and needs actually tends to make you somewhat sensitive and shy. This self-consciousness nevertheless can endear you to people, particularly allowing for some success in political concerns and in any other endeavor requiring others' support.

At times, your life may seem to be populated(even overpopulated) by mothers and/or dependent children, as issues of nurturing and support for yourself demand recognition through the projection on events outside you. During this period you'll probably begin to feel a subtle but persistent loss of control, as you sense that others are calling the shots in your life more than you; and because other people's concerns dominate, ambitious, selfish schemes and purely personal plans may have to be postponed until this aspect passes The value of the time lies in gaining a better sense of what you need, along with a greater knowledge of how you can begin to satisfy that in yourself.

Moon to Natal Moon shows similar indications, though much stronger.

Moon to Natal Sun

You may well find yourself temporarily fascinated by, attracted to, and immersed in situations which deal with your concepts of authority, leadership, ego, and pride. Either you will find yourself surrounded by people who express such attributes, or you yourself may become more self-possessed, theatrical, outgoing, and creative. This is not a major life turning-point, as these periods occur every seven years and last for about five months. Nevertheless, this can be a valuable time if you consciously seek to experience your own potential for doing things that require you to stretch the limitations of your abilities, to seek recognition for your personal efforts, and to make progress in your search for self-actualization. This progression could coincide with a "hero-worship" phase, as you project your own potentials on to another; or, negatively, you may find yourself under the thumb of one who vaunts authority, representing a projection of your own insecure relationship with your ego. On a more mature level, this could be a time when romance, speculation, amusement, parties, and social life become central to your existence, as evidence of increased self-esteem and respect for your own emerging selfhood. Your dreams and daydreams, ambitions, and yearnings center on power and authority, the type of leadership and self-confidence that makes others follow and admire.

Moon to Natal Mercury

Under the spell of the planet of feelings passing over the planet of communication, learning, and youth, you may find yourself temporarily fascinated by, attracted to, and immersed in the pursuit of knowledge, practical education, youth affairs, or the problems and interests in your immediate community. Since such periods occur every seven years or so, lasting for about five months, this is not likely to be a really memorable period in your life. Rather than pondering the riddle and muddle of existence, you will find yourself drawn into the immediacy of writing, math, and the acquisition of skills, particularly those relating to a vocational interest or study. You may become fascinated with a class of people you normally avoid—merchants, salesmen, even hustlers, as the teeming life of cities and commerce attracts and intrigues you. Complex and involved areas of study also beckon, though the acquisition of new skills and vocational resources will nearly always be central to the concepts and ideas that fascinate you now. Languages and symbol systems (such as math or computer languages) are easily absorbed, and your mind is impressionable, retentive, even though it can also be easily distracted and led astray. This could also mark a period of travel and general unsettledness, as you are drawn out of old patterns and safe, traditional havens to seek new experience and firsthand knowledge of your environment.

Moon to Natal Venus

As this aspect takes hold, you will find yourself fascinated by, attracted to, and immersed in aesthetic and social concerns, including romance, as well as a more than usual interest in acquiring money. Concerns about relationship, and even marriage, become more important to you, and even in those areas of life where such concerns might be secondary, you find yourself sensitive to and intolerant of disruption and strife. Beauty holds more than mere fascination for you, as you become attracted to all things beautiful, from art to people, and you find your own capacity to attract people to you is enhanced by the fact that you feel more confident than usual about how you look to others, and because of this you may find yourself yearning and daydreaming about love, a wealthy lifestyle, and romantic excess. But while feeling better about how you look might be good for your self-confidence or your fantasy life, it can wreak havoc with your self-control, and you will have to guard against overindulging in both food and goods. Socially, you find it easy to get all caught up in gossip about other people's problems, but while it may be okay to listen to what others say, passing it along is not. Women are liable to play a more important part in your life now, along with elegance, sentiment, glamour, and vanity. This is not an enduring situation—six months will probably be the extent of it—but nevertheless it is a good time to straighten yourself out about your feelings regarding possession, relationship, and perhaps financial attainment. Even if you find thinking too much about such things alien to your nature and very much out of character, you will probably associate with other people who act out the inner feelings you yourself are suppressing.

Moon to Natal Mars

This is an interesting and often contradictory combination, especially for those who by nature (and due to the placement of Mars in their horoscope) are not at ease with those things Mars represents. In general, over the six months or so this is in force, you will find yourself attracted to, and immersed in, matters of a strongly masculine and competitive nature. You are also likely to be drawn to the erotic and assertive aspects of the human psyche, an attraction which can manifest in your being attracted to rough-and-ready "macho" types, and engaging in tense, demanding situations that test you to the limit. The impatience and irritability that well up inside you now can also inspire belligerence in others, so it is best to find a way to vent such assertive energies through hard physical work, athletics, martial arts, or entrepreneurial projects that require all of your attention. Eschewing the finer things in life, you may find yourself yearning for the minimalist simplicity of the outdoors, and if you daydream at all during the time this reality-prone aspect is in force, these fantasies will be about getting away from the crowd and forging out into the unknown by yourself. During this pioneering and independent period, your capacity to fight for and defend yourself is much stronger than any desire you might have to compromise. Relations with women, not to mention your home life, are apt to be disturbed, as you find that others' needs for freedom and autonomy seem to stand in the way of your goals and objectives.

Moon to Natal Jupiter

The sky is the limit for you, at least in your dreams, as the awakening of the planet of excess by the planet of emotion turns you toward a quest for the good feeling that can come from social superiority and status. You yearn for accomplishments that assure others' admiration and their admission that you are a "quality" person, superior, authoritative, and above reproach. As most people relate such social approval to money, you may soon be making endless plans and schemes to strike it rich, hit the big time, and generally outdo the Joneses (who will then be busy keeping up with you). Periods such as this come every seven years or so, and rarely last more than six months, so even though you may feel you can hit the heights for a while, it is doubtful you'll really be able to do so, at least for any sustained period of time. Unfortunately, there is a danger that you might confuse the trappings of authority with power itself, so if you're not careful to keep your priorities in good order, you might at times overstep your bounds. If, on the other hand, you can keep yourself firmly grounded in reality, you can benefit from the need to pursue religious, academic, professional, and cultural concerns, rejecting whatever seems coarse or ordinary in yourself or your life. If you keep your sights set on being the "best" in moral rather than financial terms, you can, in fact, turn this into a deeply religious period in which, with some effort, you gain an intensified spiritual understanding of yourself and the world around you.

Moon to Natal Saturn

In contrast to your need to hit the heights under Moon-Jupiter just to experience the rush of exhilaration, under this progressed aspect, an extreme awareness of your own shortcomings, usually the product of a temporarily accentuated sensitivity and subjectivity, can lead you to seek reassurance of your worth by pursuing real power and authority. During this brief period, you'll be more than usually aware of your intense sensitivity, which in turn causes a heightened awareness of personal difficulties. In fact, problems in your life that under other circumstances you might simply shrug off could cause you to set your sights on making yourself independent and powerful enough that you won't have (or at least think you won't have) such problems in the future. Painfully aware of the situations you fear most, you are able to direct an unusual amount of energy toward overcoming bad habits and carrying out ambitious self-improvement projects. But despite your best efforts, the emotional climate is likely to be pretty gray, so it is hard to avoid feelings of despair, frustration, and powerlessness in the face of the hostile external forces you see all around you. Aware of what you feel you can't do, once you are past this period you can set yourself to learning how to overcome the personal disabilities that are brought to light now.

Moon to Natal Uranus

The bizarre and nonconforming aspects of your life hold a real fascination for you now, and you may find yourself surrounded, at least temporarily, by people who express the unusual and rebellious aspects of your own personality. You have a great yearning for freedom, at least for yourself, since your own urge for intellectual independence can lead you to demand that others conform to unrealistic ideological expectations you lay down for them. While your endless reiteration of the correct party line may be right in some abstract sense, your fervor is more likely to alienate people than to win you supporters. Your yearning for the bliss of unrealistic social utopias, daydreams, ambitions, and idealism center on an urgent need to right what you see as wrong in the world around you and to rebel against repressive and restrictive social constraints. You may find yourself attracted to social outcasts and rebels, as anyone outside "the system" is seen, in a heroic light, as a role model who can show you how to overcome your own compromising adherence to social values which you feel are untrue to your innermost beliefs. Fascinated by unusual ideas, technologies, and people, you are constantly excited and stimulated by the latest and greatest idea that comes along to liberate you from your commonplace and routine existence. While a brief aspect such as this will rarely bring you to a crossroads in your life, it certainly will provide some relief from the humdrum and the mundane.

Moon to Natal Neptune

The hidden, mysterious, and unconscious aspects of existence hold your interest for a brief while during the six months or so this aspect is at its strongest. The commonplace seems hopelessly dreary to you as you seek the spiritual heights and aesthetic extremes of sensitivity and awareness. You may find yourself yearning for an opportunity for self-sacrifice, to do something to right the social wrongs that impress you so deeply as you go about your everyday existence, but such altruism is also mixed with confusion over what is real in you perceptions and what is not. The desire to help others can at times take unsavory forms, especially if you allow yourself to be taken advantage of through taking upon yourself a sense of guilt that opens you to exploitation. You want to rise above it all to a place of spiritual ideal and perfection, but enmeshment in escapism, addiction, and hypersensitivity (whether to toxins in the environment or to parasitical people) are the less than desirable results if you don't exercise some control over your personal situation. You can avoid a lot of trouble by cutting down on your expectations and keeping your feet as firmly on the ground as possible. Artistic, intuitive, psychic, and aesthetic awareness is acutely tuned now, so try not to subject yourself to avoidable unpleasantness, and adhere to strict health regimens to avoid illness.

Moon to Natal Pluto

Under this aspect you can become extraordinarily aware of the potentials of this zone, since they are activated by intense, yet temporary influences. You are attracted to, immersed in, and fascinated by the concepts of birth, death, and regeneration, but even though you may long for complete and total change in life, at the same time you fear abandonment and the limitations of your own mortality. This could be a time of farewells, particularly in short-term relationships, as you are highly aware that sometimes growth can only occur after the old has been shed in order to make way for the new. You seek intensity in your daily life, and find yourself impatient with the trivial nature of your day-to-day concerns. Your awareness of life's impermanence tends to alienate you from the mainstream of society, and thus you may idealize the outlaw, identifying with social scapegoats and heroes. Death itself may be looked at more closely than usual, as a greater awareness of your own mortality can provide a motivation for living life more intensely and honestly. The unconscious mind intrudes frequently in your thoughts and actions, and life's daily dealings can thus take on mythological importance for you, symbolizing cosmic trends and powers. This is a short period—six months long or so—but its intensity and depth of the challenge and isolation it often brings can leave their mark on you.

20

Mercury: Link to the Network

THIS POWERFUL temporary influence can last as long as two years, making you fascinated and preoccupied with anything involving communication, travel, work, ideas, and mental growth. It will more than likely be a very busy and active time, perhaps seeing you overcommitted and heavily scheduled, with emphasis on educational and career concerns. Travel and communication figure prominently in everything you do, and you spend a lot of time mentally integrating an amazing flow of information about your environment that passes through your hands. When you speak, everyone listens, not so much because you have suddenly developed a profound viewpoint or a powerful style of expression, but because you're a critical link, plugged into an information network and the important resources it contains. Your interest in computers and their possibilities should increase, along with your interest in neighborhood concerns and your participation in informational study groups.

Ideas about the world and who you are which have been evolving quietly for the past several years now graduate into practical, usable forms, often becoming marketable skills. The foundations for a new attitude toward and comprehension of the world are developed now, bringing a concomitant increase in your involvement and interdependence with new people, professional societies, etc. Your organizational abilities develop rapidly along with your newly learned vocational skills, interests and hobbies, setting the stage either for promotion if you are an employee or greater commercial success if you are in business for yourself. Television, radio, video, and other media all assume more importance than they had been to you before, often providing a new outlet for the expression of your emerging consciousness.

One interesting sidelight of this progression is often that your phone bills attain new highs. Under most circumstances this is not simply because of an increase in your need to gab the day away (though this too is possible), but rather because your sharpened mind seeks out new personal and intellectual connections that can help you to apply and realize the ideas you are developing in the most efficient and productive manner. You become very aware of both the limitations and possibilities of your private resources, as greater opportunities for their development and utilization manifest at this time.

Mercury to Natal Sun

You may find yourself becoming aware, perhaps for the first time, of a personal myth and "quest" now, usually through a good deal of reading, introspection, and mental self-searching. The results of your thoughts taking this direction could be a more accurate self-image, one dominated by your potentials for leadership and by a better understanding of your authority, pride, and ego. This progressed aspect often represents an important turning point in your life, though a process that takes about a year to be completed. Young people, students, teachers, travel, and new modes of communication and employment tend to figure prominently in this growth toward realization of a new goal in life and the talents that can help you to reach it. The work you do in order to make a living may become more creative in an artistic sense, requiring the development of faculties that may have lain dormant or even completely hidden from view. As you become more aware of the real roots of your identity and selfhood your need for approval from others for what you say and do grows in most areas of your life. Even if you are essentially a modest person, you want to put the mark of individuality and identity on everything you do, thus leading you to express yourself in a more unique and individualistic fashion. The importance of this period of time comes from its usefulness in helping you to identify the inner myth that guides you, and while this may come solely from your own introspection, important clues can also be provided by important people who turn their attention on you. Even when you think you know it all, listen to what others have to say.

Mercury to Natal Moon

As this aspect intrudes mildly on your life, you may become more conscious than you have been of your roots, of your heredity, and of the importance of your home and family in shaping your personality and personal identity. At the same time, however, you will be able to develop a greater understanding of the particular individual needs and desires that mold your character and individuality quite apart from what others say, do, and think about you. Ever more active, talkative, and alert, your restless mind seeks to define and to comprehend the meaning of your past, so that biography, nostalgia, and visits to places and periods important to your family history are likely preoccupations now. You may be more aware than usual of your emotional needs, erotic appetites, and of your need for people, things, or a sense of belonging, and are trying to systematize and order these basically chaotic and overpowering desires in an attempt to understand them. Over the year or so this progression takes to run its course, its most useful purpose is to provide you with symbols, words, and even material reminders (such as souvenirs) of your roots and personal origins. This is a good time to spend time with your mother, if possible, or anyone else who knows much about your past, as the realization you gain about where you came from will figure prominently in your self-definition and your understanding of where you should be heading.

Mercury to Natal Mercury

The period of time that you designated falls within one in which the potentials of this area are particularly emphasized and powerfully accented. While this area is a lifelong center of the events and concerns enumerated above, this particular period of time is perhaps the most important and powerful for these realizations. You are mentally integrating a great deal of information about your environment and acquiring techniques and interests that are of lifelong importance. Skills, physical talents, and coordination can be perfected, understood, educated, and developed, along with a mystical awareness of a highly coordinated and intricate universe. Health, seen here as a smooth interoperation of the body's systems, can also be improved by the understanding and adoption of wholesome regimens. This period of time is a quite important part of your discovery of who you are, introducing you to important symbols of yourself and to an understanding of your mental and physical processes of life. It might best be spent in education or the conscious exploration of as much information as you can process, and your verbal and mental skills will be sharpened for the challenge during these two years. Your job or favorite hobby emerges as an important symbol of who you are and who you are becoming.

Mercury to Natal Venus

Though at this location you will have a lifelong need to cultivate your desires and talents for love, harmony, peace, and artistic expression, for this period, about a year in duration, the accent is on understanding these needs in more depth. For example, you could become interested in explicitly defining the image of your love object. At the same time, you turn your intellectual curiosity toward the mental exploration of your affectional appetites, as well as your aspirations for acquiring money, and the good things it buys. Communication is central to this process, and you could be more involved than usual in correspondence, study, and the reorganization of your thinking, about your personal needs for love, affection, and pleasure in life. This is likely to be a very active and highly social period, one in which you have more opportunities to socialize than time to pursue them. Your work is also an area for change and expansion: you may be presented with chances to be more creative and develop pride and a sense of aesthetics in what you do.

Mercury to Natal Mars

The combative, aggressive, and competitive side of your nature are powerfully accented, and though this period may be more than a bit trying, it is an important time in which to develop your understanding and comprehension of those aspects of your character. You could possibly experience an abstract, intellectual curiosity about the concept of masculinity, a curiosity perhaps focused through your relationship with younger people or your mental interests, hobbies, and pursuits. This combination inclines you to view the world with a system of values that is more male-oriented, macho, and confrontational than may be usual for you, and this tendency may increase the number of arguments, and disputes to which you are party. You become aware of how competition and the threat of coercion can affect you and thus may tend to react by pushing a little harder than usual. This is particularly problematical when driving, traveling in general, and when operating machinery, as your impatience, if unchecked, could prove dangerous. Positively, this period of time (about a year in duration) is excellent for beginning vigorous, challenging enterprises, and your courage and willingness to take risks expand. Your work may become more masculine, dangerous, or physical, and your power of analysis is exercised more often on physical problems and competitive issues than on abstractions or matters dealing with imagination.

Mercury to Natal Jupiter

Under this highly mental and communicative aspect, you develop a fascination and curiosity regarding social power and symbols of status and authority which defines and manipulates these symbols. This important period—about one year in duration—is particularly useful in forming or adjusting your attitudes toward society and the demands it makes on you to conform. Your most powerful experiences now emphasize the importance of status, particularly in your work, your hobbies, and your intellectual interests. You tend to see clearly the "pecking orders" by which some define their place in the world as well as becoming aware of your own position (or lack of same) within them. Your job may put you in touch with a higher social stratum—perhaps through travel, educational, or cultural concerns— so this is apt to be one of the best periods in your life for the acquisition of honors, degrees, credentials, or for taking advantage of other opportunities to rise socially. Your health also may improve generally at this time, and the understanding you gain now of alternative therapies, health regimens, or diet can be important and useful to your future well-being.

Mercury to Natal Saturn

You develop a fascination with and a general need to explore society's power systems, possibly driven by a situation (particularly in a work context) in which you feel you have either too little or too much. You become aware of how pervasive and potentially oppressive inequality is, possibly for the first time realizing how politics, government, or other power structures affect you. This time (about a year in duration) could become a continuing symbol of all your deficiencies and weaknesses and in later life, memories of it might act as a motivational goal to accomplishment and ambition. Out of necessity, you develop systematic, diligent work habits, learning to focus your powers of concentration in a way you may not have done before. Where before now you may have been a bit easygoing and even lackadaisical, strict routine becomes your favored mode of procedure, as the world around you seems driven by reality and dominated by necessity. Feeling somehow oppressed by those who have powers greater than your own, you study and reflect on them, creating mental attitudes that are pragmatic, patient, and based on real experience rather than upon speculation or theory. This zone is naturally one of discipline and self-sacrifice, and at this time such tendencies are focused through work, study, and mental attitude.

Mercury to Natal Uranus

You find yourself becoming more and more fascinated by the bizarre and the nonconforming as you begin to assimilate mental ideas and attitudes that are unusual and may even be socially disapproved. Your mind at this time is attracted to the forbiddingly technical or to studies such as astrology, which fall outside usual academic boundaries. Awakened to exciting new interests, you begin to see how narrow and limiting social restraints on knowledge can be. What starts out perhaps as an abstract study of some phase of knowledge becomes an important, lifelong symbol of your individuality, and events and interests while this progressed aspect is in effect can constitute a new foundation for your intellectual independence and creativity. Young people, creative work assignments, or hard to diagnose health problems point the way toward these highly individual realizations, so that after this period is over (about a year after it began), you may find you have developed the ability to perceive associations between ideas which others see as unrelated. Any effort to redefine yourself at present will likely be cool, intellectual, and unemotional: You study the established political and social system in order to learn how to exercise your freedom and to experience your individuality within it.

Mercury to Natal Neptune

The dreamy, illusory, romantic, and intuitive nature of this zone is apt to affect you strongly at the mental level now, so that you may undertake an intellectual exploration of the most hidden and mysterious aspects of mind and transcendent experience. Young people, your job, or concerns about your health may be the precipitating agency that propels you headlong into bizarre and otherworldly mental experiences, including altered states of consciousness. This period could become a permanent symbol in your life for all that is weird, forbidding, and fantastic. The strong stimulation of your imagination leads you to empathize or identify with anyone or anything society has rejected—whether people, ideas, or behavior patterns. It is important to avoid drugs now, as well as the idea of becoming a codependent or a martyr in order to compensate for the shortcomings of others, since these things will be of no help to you either spiritually or practically. The year or so of this aspect's influence may test your reason and world view, but it also can leave you with an expanded consciousness, more in touch with its intuitive and transcendent resources than it was before. Your philosophy and world view tend toward the transpersonal, resulting in a clouding of the more practical side of your thinking processes by the philosophical, something which can cause work and finances to suffer even as it is enriching your spirit. This can be a time of progress and learning for you, but only if you have the benefit of guidance and advice from friends and loved ones with a more practical view than you have at present.

Mercury to Natal Pluto

You find yourself ready and willing, though not always able, to explore some of the more forbidding aspects of life—birth, death, regeneration, and sexuality. Work, health, and intellectual interests tend to lead you into situations that are bizarre and transforming in their effect on you. This can be an important stage of your life, even though it is only about a year in duration, if you can handle the peak experiences and the intensity all around you. This could also be a time of research as you learn to focus and discipline your mind, particularly when you apply it to understanding archaic, deeply subconscious subjects. The information you gather from such probing tends to set you apart from others, alienating you from those who have not looked so deeply or so searchingly into their own souls. Your attitude toward the world becomes more imbued with awareness of the regeneration and renewal themes that are so central to life; knowledge itself for you becomes a means to transcend the mortality to which the flesh is heir. Mental pursuits at this time can silently sow the seeds of a complete life transformation, as you look beneath appearances and become aware of how life's finiteness, as an ultimate shared reality, motivates all striving and interrelationship.

21

Venus: A Time for Love and Pleasure

VENUS progressing to an angle at any locality is a powerful temporary influence, lasting as long as two years. During the period highlighted by this aspect, social events, parties, affection, love, and relationship will dominate activities in this place, along with a desire for pleasure, ease, luxury, and financial success. You're apt to become the recipient of favors, invitations, gifts, affection, and even proposals for marriage or other relationships more often than usual, and your senses and their satisfaction take on new importance for you, especially if you have been relegated to insignificance in your life. This attraction to beauty in turn attracts others to you, since you exude a happy air of charm, diplomacy, grace, and tact. Social activity may reach a new high for you, particularly the less serious sort—birthday parties and the like—as your circle of friends seems bent on pleasure, hedonism, and self-indulgence. Desire for committed relationship increases, and even inveterate bachelors (of either sex) often begin to see the security of marriage in a new light. Along with this increased interest in marriage, a deeply felt need for children can also develop; even if you don't have any of your own, other people's may become more important in your life. Women figure more prominently in your life now, along with traditionally feminine interests and occupations. While you come across new financial opportunities (perhaps through the acquisition of tangible goods), your new and often insatiable appetite for pleasure leads to the exaggeration of both extravagance and possessiveness during this period. Even if marriage does not come about now, this time can represent a turning point for you, especially as you begin to understand that increased happiness and improved self-esteem are the golden keys that unlock new doors in your life.

Venus to Natal Sun

While being born beautiful is certainly fortunate, during this time you can learn how to make yourself more attractive, whatever your natural looks. Of course being attractive has as much to do with attitude and feelings as with facial features, so the grace and charm that mark your self-expression and become an important factor in the way others see you, do in fact make you more attractive so that you find yourself at the center of much social activity. Romantic relationships which you develop now may focus on people in leadership positions or on artists, performers, or entertainers. You find yourself becoming fond of children, and you cultivate an affectionate, playful world view as part of a general tempering and harmonization of your personality. In many areas of your life the rough edges are smoothed, so that you present a more loving, peaceful demeanor to the world. Your finances are likely to be favorably affected during the period of about a year while this aspect is in effect, though improving finances may encourage any tendency you have toward ostentatious spending and speculative pursuits. Finding a creative outlet in the arts will help you find a way to constructively employ some of the more indulgent and nonproductive aspects of this influence.

Venus to Natal Moon

Your home life, and your relationships with family and relatives improve measurably under the friendly and benevolent joining of these two planets. This is an ideal time to beautify your residence with interior decoration, remodeling, gardening, or other aesthetic improvements, but outer glamorization of the home merely reflects an inner harmony with your environment and a growing affection for those closest to you. You now can learn how to take care of others with style: entertainment, parties, and other social occasions (numerous and often glamorous) are liable to mark the year or so that this influence is in effect, reflecting a newfound sense of self-worth and a willingness to express your love and affection for others. Things can become a little too pleasant for you, however, as this influence tends to enforce a kind of idleness and a pursuit of the material which may prove boring to more ambitious types of personalities. While on the one hand, men are likely to feel their erotic needs intensify, women may retreat into rather banal, trivial relationships. In either case, friendships with women improve in general, as you learn that love can mean care, affection, and harmony as well as passion and intense erotic excitement. Money and possessions are important now; real estate and many durable items purchased now will probably increase in value, though the sentimental attachment you are likely to develop to such things, makes that fact rather irrelevant.

Venus to Natal Mercury

Your capacity for verbal and written communication is increased, and as your mode of expression takes on a new ease and facility, it's a good time to capitalize on the skills of persuasion. This is an important and rather long-lasting influence—about a year's duration—and often marks the time when we establish lifelong standards in these areas. Workplace skills also reflect greater sensitivity and awareness, and day-to-day tasks are performed with ease and carried through with artistic simplicity. Relationships at work improve to the extent that you may find yourself often in the role of peacemaker; others see you as a satisfactory compromiser, someone who is able to restore harmony between warring factions or individuals. The creation of any sort of symbol system—from haiku poetry to computer programs—can be completed now with elegance, efficiency, and it will demonstrate structures that are balanced and harmonious. Your attuned artistic sensibility discovers beauty in your environment as well, and making an effort to develop and train attitudes of aesthetic perception can make your future life more pleasant. Problems are easily solved, and academic studies benefit from improved communications skills. Attitude and mood are optimistic and elevated, so that this generally is an excellent period of time for work and life's day-to-day pursuits.

Venus to Natal Venus

This doubly benefic progressed aspect is a location that will be very helpful to you in most areas of your life. It is an exceptionally good time to reside in the place in question, especially if you are interested in dealing more directly with issues of love, relationship, financial accomplishment, and self-indulgence. This is a powerfully social period in which cooperation, harmony, and peace are striven for in all human relationships. Conflicts and competitive challenges are apt to be minimal, and the greatest danger is that there are so few problems that you become a bit lazy, going with the flow just a little too much. You'll feel closer to most women you know, and will find most of your activities involving them to be pleasant, carefree, and elegant. Self-esteem and personal appearance certainly ought to improve under this aspect and, on the other side of that coin, some important theme in your conceptualization of the "Perfect Other" can be identified now. This could involve something as simple as coming to understand ideals of physical appearance or as complex as becoming aware of the personality type that interests you most. Whatever the case, self-acceptance furthers your quest for idealized love, a quest which could meet with some success at this time.

Venus to Natal Mars

This contact is perfect for the development of grace and style in any athletic, gymnastic, or dance pursuits, but it is also a good time to learn how to get things done in any life area where the cooperation of others is required, or in which aesthetic awareness plays an important part. No matter what your normal tendencies are, you are apt to take greater pleasure in exercise and physical activity, and find erotic pursuits, which are likely to be numerous and gratifying during this period, of more interest to you than usual. You will seem more attractive and interesting to others generally, and thus may find a surprising number of people making known to you their interest in forging a new relationship. Social skills improve as well, largely because any impulses to selfishness and competitiveness are moderated and restrained, and as others find you easy to get along with, yet able to get things done, relational and practical concerns move forward with others' cooperation and support. While this influence is in effect (about a year), the more aggressive and confrontive aspects you might normally have to deal with at this location are mitigated, with the energy normally devoted to such things channeled into a sharpened interest in sex and relationships, and a consequent increase in opportunities for their gratification. You're apt to be drawn to more masculine types (of either gender), and while you participate wholeheartedly in the battle of the sexes, you join the struggle with style and grace, and not rancor.

Venus to Natal Jupiter

Your search for social acceptance, status, and situations in which you can express authority are likely to meet success, especially through the means of an increase in financial well-being. Professional, social, and personal relationships proceed smoothly for the most part, and may constitute a foundation for social advancement and enhanced prestige; you find it easy to meet "important people," especially in the arts, high society, and academia—people who react to you and your aspirations favorably and with encouragement. This period is one in which you can enjoy rewards that come from careful planning in the past, including the maturing of successful investments, and an increase in public aware ness of who you are and what you can do. You are able to administrate and control your personal and social circles in such a way that people are happy to contribute to your success and comply with your desires. Social contacts become greater sources of social and financial gain than they have been in the past, offering knowledge of or opportunities for investment and preferment. The danger lies in things being too easy for you, so you'll have to make a special effort to fight the twin problems of complacency and laxity—if you just kick back and enjoy all the party invitations, you will not be able to use this period to lay the foundations of long-term success and advancement. Extravagance also may result from the decrease in self-control that often accompanies this aspect, especially if you indulge the frankly materialistic values that contribute to financial growth and success at this time. Overall, however, this time should be memorable for its pleasance, as your feelings of fitting in to the social scene, of belonging, and even of your superiority to others in some respects are all accompanied by an irrepressible sense of well-being and joie de vivre.

Venus to Natal Saturn

You may express graceful acceptance of the limitations which usually accompany the angular Saturn at this location and can even find a way to incorporate them positively into your self-image. Social situations seem to prick your most sensitive wounds now, but despite this you can realize a certain pleasure or benefit from such difficulties, bearing them with grace and dignity. Moreover, social opportunities may present themselves precisely because of what you see as your own personal disadvantages and deficiencies, some of which may relate to age differences or spring from perceived inequalities in abilities or experience. However, since the concepts of power and physical beauty seem somehow to be linked now, through dealing with people of divergent age and experience you can come to understand those parts of your own earlier life that were unsatisfactory. Since your best ideas now seem to be derived from a need for personal power, this can alienate potential supporters. Because of this, loyalty is likely to be a real issue for you now, and relationships built with this consideration in mind may prosper while those that ignore it do not. Whether in relationships or other areas of your life, when things go wrong you can turn those defeats to your advantage by accepting them with grace and dignity. Careful investment at this time can yield long-term benefits, though speculation should be avoided (particularly in areas pertaining to recreation, art, or currency). You may find yourself attracted to people of lesser stature and status than you are now—the disempowered, the impoverished, or the isolated—as you see them somehow as symbolizing your acceptance of your own deficiencies.

Venus to Natal Uranus

This period, of about a year's duration, can mark a major turning point in your ability to develop your individuality and personal uniqueness in a way that is neither threatening to your success in the long term nor intimidating to others in the short term. Artistic style, grace, and elegance are imparted to any strongly individualistic self-expressions—especially writing, social concerns, and any dealings you have with groups. You are able to express your ideals pleasingly and diplomatically, making it easy for you to find allies and supporters, no matter how unusual the cause. You may feel the need to change your physical appearance in such a way that it expresses your individuality better, so that the clothes, jewelry, and accessories you wear may in some respects diverge from current fashion in a way that frankly accentuates your distinctiveness. Breaking with routines and seeking new social liaisons can be a positive delight for you now, particularly in the area of investment, where your tendency to wander off the beaten track can bring either enormous windfalls or heartbreaking losses. You may find yourself attracted to rather bizarre and unusual people at this time, perhaps seeing them as somehow embodying the type of individuality you would like to express in your own personality. While this can make relationships forged now quite interesting, a roller coaster variability should be expected in marriage or other long-term commitments. Above all, this is a good time to convince others of the value of your ideals and opinions and to gather social support for unusual personal causes or pet projects.

Venus to Natal Neptune

The aesthetic dimension of this location is particularly emphasized now, so that increased sensitivity or inspiration are likely in any form of artistic expression you engage in, though especially in music. Relationships may also take forms which are different than you are usually accustomed to, as you could find yourself attracted to visionary, artistic, or countercultural types who may give your personal experience a slightly hysterical edge. Despite the ups and downs, however, the love you feel for others, and which they give to you, becomes a deeper, more mystical experience, full of nuance and poetry and wistful, sentimental romance. You become extremely receptive to the subtle, disturbing influences usually found in this zone, but you take a certain pleasure and delight in feeling and responding on such deep levels. Spirituality beckons, often through marriage or relationship, and you seek to live out your romantic fantasies in either rural surroundings, or some exotic milieu that intrigues you with its romantic and mysterious aura. You're easily possessed by idealism here, and while your grasp on reality is a bit tenuous now (due to the difficulty with which you separate factual necessities from your hopes and aspirations) during the year this aspect is in effect you can develop in your character an ability to make others look beyond immediate goals so that they can learn to seek perfection and spiritual gratification.

Venus to Natal Pluto

Processes of change, growth, intense personal development, and rapid evolution in your fundamental views of life and death are likely accomplished through the agency of relationship. While this may mean that stable, important relationships such as marriage can suffer stress, they can also act to spur you on to a realization of who you truly are and what your purpose in the world ought to be. Instead of seeing sex and relationship either as ends in themselves, or in terms of possessiveness and commitment, you must try to become aware of their catalyzing effect on emerging parts of your personality and consciousness. A symbol of such realization emerging within you may be seen in an attraction to rather rebellious, asocial types, or even to outlaws—alienated and unique people who can act out your own potentials before your very eyes. Odd obsessions and unreasonable fixations may plague you from time to time, especially as the numerous breaks with the past you are likely to experience often result in a compulsive need to attach yourself to whatever replacement first offers itself, in an attempt to fill the void. Financial matters in this place reflect the general instability of your life, and easily can become entangled with larger personal issues. During this period, which is apt to last about a year, you are very much in the mood for settling up old accounts and making final and clean breaks with the past, so these things usually can be accomplished with a minimum of trauma and heartbreak.

21

Mars: Stress, Competition, and Energy

THIS IS a powerful influence, and though temporary, it can last as long as three years, years that are marked by aggression, assertion, and competitiveness in your life and relationships. Stress, harassment, provocation, irritation, and annoyance seem to cloud everything you experience, challenging you to rise above pettiness while working to develop your assertive qualities and your capacity to take care of yourself as you take more responsibility for the direction of your own life. You become very active, as life makes continual demands on you to exceed what you thought of as your physical limits; everything is seen as a challenge, often quite accurately, as others single you out for contest and competition.

You find you have the urge to purge your life of nonessentials, including unproductive relationships and possessions. Because of this, social prestige and your ability to enjoy domestic comforts are under fire now, and your relationships, whether to peer groups or individuals, become more contentious and competitive. Temper and erotic appetites are inflamed, giving you the courage, impulsiveness, audaciousness, and daring necessary for their indulgence. A hardy, adventuresome, and reckless feeling develops inside you, perhaps making you more inclined to take risks and spend money. Though all of this may surprise you and your friends, especially if Mars is weakly placed in your horoscope, hints of this emerging power could have been seen many years ago. This is a risky period, so caution in the use of firearms and machinery or in driving should be exercised diligently, something that will take a great deal of effort at times. Attacks can also take inward forms such as fevers, inflammations, and other internal problems. If you can balance this out by developing some certainty about who you are and what you want, though this period may not pass without some real or psychological pain, your capacity to endure it is expanded. You relish the difficult conditions and harsh environments that challenge you at this time, and cultivate a self-image that has a tough, masculine edge to it.

Mars to Natal Sun

The importance of your ego and how others see you will increase, perhaps to the point that you become difficult to cooperate with, somewhat selfish, and strongly goal-oriented. You'll find that you have a lot of energy to expand your increasingly ambitious horizons, and since you feel more competitive, dominant, and critical, others may see you as threatening, provoking, intolerant, and pushy. Particularly if you are a man, your sexual needs could be very demanding for the duration of this influence—about eighteen months—something which has less to do with a desire for love and affection than with a persistent intensification of your basic biological urges. Your manners and demeanor may coarsen somewhat as well, which should make you more prone than usual to vigorous physical activity. In fact, being as active and athletic as your own physical condition allows is highly recommended now as a way to relieve the powerful physical tensions that seem to beset you in your haste to set new life records and higher standards of personal accomplishment. Rashness is on the increase, so accidents, and conflicts with authority quickly follow. Others may think you're becoming cruel, insensitive, and domineering, so that their cooperation often is difficult to gain; and though it may seem easier just to do everything yourself, this attitude greatly limits your effectiveness and thus should be moderated as much as is possible.

Mars to Natal Moon

You are apt to become somewhat irritable, easily annoyed, and reactive during this period, which lasts about eighteen months. Your relationships with women (or your self-esteem, if you are female) may begin to deteriorate, though this doesn't prevent you from acting as the mother hen to anyone in your sphere of influence, perhaps even providing them with a lot more nurturing control and care than they want. If mothering becomes smothering it may stem from the fact that you're under stress, or you could be releasing pent-up anger relating to insult or injuries in the recent past (maybe from your family) and are thus unconsciously acting out your anger on others. However, this can be a good period for confronting directly any who have wronged you—you won't spare their feelings—but be sure only deserving parties are victims of your wrath. You're certainly able to stand up for your rights now, but don't visit the crimes of the fathers on the sons, so to speak, just to prove you can. Your forceful frame of mind fits you best for taking on strenuous, constructive projects that help you to relieve inner pressures, though if home remodeling is undertaken be careful not to throw spouse, house mates, relatives, and neighbors out along with the old carpeting! Carefully review plans such as this with someone who has expertise in what you intend to do, and beware of taking on anything that could result in serious injury if it gets out of hand.

Mars to Natal Mercury

Your concepts, beliefs, and opinions are assailed by others and are sharpened by you in response, as numerous arguments force you to perfect your verbal skills and learn to reduce arguments to their essentials. If you have always been a courteous listener and a compromising diplomat in debate, this period of about eighteen months' duration could be "Milquetoast's revenge," as you learn not only how to force others to see your point of view but learn to take pleasure in their acquiescence to your way of seeing things. You approach your daily tasks, both mental and physical, with great energy and intense interest, so it is important that the work you do be challenging enough to relieve the nervous energy and pressure of this highly-charged period of time. Travel and neighborhood concerns can become the focus of much of your nervous energy and activity, but be careful not to let your impatience and impetuousness put you in dangerous situations in these areas of your life. If you are involved in education, this definitely is a time to excel through hard work and the cultivation of your desire to compete.

Mars to Natal Venus

Friendship and affectionate liaisons tend to be rejected under this aspect in favor of more satisfying physical relationships, and you may find yourself losing patience with unrealistic and romantic people, preferring the company of adventuresome, daring, risk-taking types. Love may not be romantic during this period, but it certainly is passionate, so relationships formed now will thrill you with their intensity and sexuality. You are likely to find yourself more in the company of men than usual, especially strong and assertive types, and traditionally masculine concerns—sports, military matters, arduous physical work—could well form the center of your social life and contacts. You have less concern now than usual in this zone for social graces and less interest in what others might say or think about how you act, as gratification is the most important consideration for you now, while propriety, fairness, and cooperation seem irrelevant. You are more likely to spend your money on indulging your need for interesting experiences than on accumulating possessions, and while this period could deplete your savings, it also provides you a great deal of intense, uncomplicated, and physical satisfaction. Action, adventure, and a more vigorous lifestyle keep you moving throughout the eighteen or so months this aspect is in force.

Mars to Natal Mars

All the concerns enumerated in the introductory paragraphs above will be particularly critical now, so if you are considering a move to a zone in which this aspect prevails, this should be taken as evidence that these potentials are more than ready to be consciously assimilated. You seek to experience intense events involving sexuality, conflict, athletics, or just plain hard physical work, so the warnings about excessive belligerence and rashness mentioned above should be especially heeded during this period.

Your ego is apt to be sensitive and easily provoked, your body stronger and more athletic, and your appearance somewhat coarser, yet still attractive in a powerful, masculine way. You should tend to the formulation of goals, life ambitions, and important short-term objectives, while simultaneously working to suppress any tendencies to be argumentative or overly competitive. While this zone is always one in which assertive and egocentric concerns come to the fore, it is particularly strong in these respects now. If you don't consciously undertake to integrate these potentials internally, external situations will constantly urge you to do so.

Mars to Natal Jupiter

The more problematical aspects of this influence may make you more than usually prone to push your ideas onto others and to feel empowered to judge what is right and wrong in their lives. Even though your beliefs may be under attack at this time, you should look beneath the surface and try to see how a limited world view or unthinking ignorance on your part could have contributed to the misunderstandings that seem to plague you. Your reputation, prestige, and financial status also may be under attack, as antagonists and your own rashness and ill-considered actions produce expensive mistakes, meaning that expenses now may seriously outstrip income. Be particularly prudent in investment now, and anticipate that some of those who ask you to place your cash in their hands could be out to con you, or that entrepreneurial schemes described in rosy, glowing terms could end up as real losers. On the positive side, this period of time is excellent for athletic competition, as your belief in yourself makes winning easier; expect to set lifetime records and to have more stamina and energy than usual. Jogging and similar activities will relieve tension and help you to channel excess energy constructively.

Mars to Natal Saturn

If you are unaware of what your weaknesses and failings are, expect that to be changed soon at this location, as external forces or your own introspection are apt to probe your most sensitive secrets and subject you to a rather unpleasant awareness of what you need to improve in your personality. If you suffer indignity and injury at the hands of others, this can be taken in a somewhat constructive context as arduous discipline to toughen and to harden you. This period is helpful for exploring and recognizing your limits, particularly physical ones, and it is good for hard work, intense, sustained competition, and learning to overcome what may at first seem insurmountable through the determined application of incessant effort. If you must be here during this period, expect it to be rather debilitating, dreary, and depressing, though the dullness is somehow worth it for the sense of power and self-motivation that comes from surmounting impossible obstacles. It is also good for those who already do demanding physical work in manual trades—carpentry, metal working, etc., though you should be aware of an increased danger of injury, incapacitation, or illness at this time. Be sure you are ready for an arduous, adventuresome, and intense experience if you happen to be considering a move here now.

Mars to Natal Uranus

While this locale will always be the scene of upheavals and powerful changes for you, during the eighteen-month period in question, such change is apt to come without much warning, and could perhaps be engendered by fire, violence, or accident. Much of the problem stems from your attitude, as you tend to be more rash, opinionated, and so certain you are right that you'd rather fight than switch—or even listen. An impulsive desire to rebel against any constraints on your freedom makes you hard to get along with, and you should avoid traveling, using machinery, or handling firearms when under the spell of one of the frequent fits of anger you may experience. This is probably a good place to avoid at this time, unless you are ready for hair-raising adventure and exciting, perilous stimulation on an almost daily basis. The adrenaline junkie and daredevil may delight in this climate of intense unpredictability, but most will find it too dangerous, upsetting, and threatening except in limited doses. Those who enjoy the thrills and spills they can find here will emerge from such exploits to relate with a good stock of interesting stories to tell, and the scars to prove they lived through them all.

Mars to Natal Neptune

While this locale is always the scene of nonrational, imaginative, and chaotic intrusions from the unconscious, these are now stimulated to a sometimes distressing degree either by external attack or by internal distress so acute that it seems to threaten rational integrity. Perhaps the best way to deal with the seething, intense feelings set loose at this time is through some marriage of art and action, such as dance, gymnastics, or strenuous training in order to perfect some form of visual or musical artistic expression. If positive steps are not taken to channel these chaotic energies wisely, health and relationship affairs are apt to suffer from the excess of undirected emotionality seething in you, and accidents and illnesses could be the likely result. Drug abuse, allergies, venereal infections, involvement with crime, and delusions of persecution are the most intense (though thankfully rare) expressions of this force, but anyone can expect practical matters to suffer as moods swing from one extreme to another, upsetting the natural balance that helps us do what we need to do. In addition to constructive artistic expression, this period of time can bring political involvement, especially when it involves high ideals and utopian visions, but too often this kind of activity ends up accomplishing little. This period will last quite a while—up to eighteen months—so if you must reside here during this time, selfless activity, spiritual pursuits, and a saint's patience are perhaps the best defenses against the more negative possibilities.

Mars to Natal Pluto

This is a difficult zone to begin with, as explained elsewhere, but during this period, lasting about eighteen months, it is even more so. Powerful upheaval and life changes are occasioned partly by a belligerent, provocative attitude both in you and others, and partly by fate, and it is often difficult to keep arguments from escalating into vendetta. Long forgotten relationships may resurface, demanding that unfinished business surrounding them be resolved. If your work exposes you routinely to danger (such as military, law enforcement, search-and-rescue, etc.) you may find that you exult in the risk, something that should serve as a warning, as a healthy sense of danger may keep you safer and help you do your job better. The purpose of this period of time is to make you aware of your physical mortality to the end of defining a more realistic direction for your life. Shocks, indulgence in erotic intensity, or you yourself becoming more brutal and cruel are external indicators of a great inner change that demands an alteration of your life directions. Expect this period to be intense, and be willing to surrender life interests that have run their course.

23

Jupiter: Full Speed Ahead

THIS IS a powerful temporary influence, lasting about three months, though it can reoccur throughout the year due to retrogradation. During this period, expansiveness, optimism, and increased self-esteem are promoted by external events which offer opportunities for honors, rewards, and recognition. You find yourself dealing significantly with the prospects and problems of conformity and social or cultural regulation at this time, most likely through recognition or reward of your accomplishments by established authorities in your field of endeavor. However, your appetite for success and wealth may exceed the benevolence of even this fortunate influence, and you actually may feel that what has been offered you is either not enough or is not what you wanted. If the latter is a problem, it is quite possible that your real problem is that you feel that accepting recognition limits your future options in some sense.

Objectively, though, business is apt to be excellent, and opportunities proliferate for social advancement and improvement of your financial status, as others seem to see you as somehow deserving of recognition and honor. You exude a sense of leadership born of a confidence that you somehow represent the best in your sphere of influence, and you expect everyone to acknowledge this inherent superiority which you feel now. However, if displayed too openly, such expectations may not sit well with the less trendy and fashion-conscious of your acquaintances. Such negative judgments will not affect you much for now, as you are likely to be too busy enjoying the company of the rich and famous (or what passes for same in your world), as you expand your social circle in order to feed both your ego and ambition. Others' rights and opinions may not seem very important to you right now, as you tend to feel that your way is the only right way and that this "fact" is validated by your association with the right people in the right places. In the midst of your ever-expanding hopes, dreams and ambitions for the future, keep in mind that this influence is short-lived, and try to accumulate durable and real accomplishments. If you cater only to the short-term and don't try to build on present opportunities, all of the glory will fade quickly once the transit passes on.

Jupiter to Natal Sun

Under this particular configuration, you are apt to feel quite optimistic, secure in the knowledge that you can handle any situation, but though you may feel your actions and intentions border on the heroic, you should beware of the kind of "psychic inflation" that leads to overconfidence and overextending yourself. This very fortunate period is one in which you are apt to act the role of the authority, teacher, leader, or entrepreneur, and good luck, often extraordinary in degree, confirms your self-confidence and will to succeed, almost on a daily basis. The only real problem with this influence is that it is short- lived. If you designated a time between April and the end of the year, it operates until year's end; if your time is in the early months of the year, it operates for only about three weeks at the time you designated. When in effect, it should be full speed ahead on personal projects, especially those involving art, personal charisma, or leadership and it is definitely a good time to apply for jobs and positions. Health improves, religious insights are deeply felt, and exposure to cultural influences increases awareness and imparts an air of "class" to your image. Opportunities offered and projects initiated at this time can become the cornerstones of future prosperity, as the world seems intent on recognizing and rewarding you for who you are. Don't let this time pass without making a concerted effort to move several steps up the ladder toward your goals. If you are one of those strong, self-assured individualists who do not find the type of social acceptance that comes with this transit of much value, you should still consider the long-term benefits of riding on the crest of the wave generated by this aspect.

Jupiter to Natal Moon

This is a most fortunate and positive time, one in which opportunities are offered, doors are thrown open, and you are able to rise socially. Powerful feelings and emotions are the driving force behind all of this, as you become more aware of your deepest needs, perhaps because you feel that they are being satisfied now more than ever. Emotional security lets you feel and express deep caring and love for others, which is returned to you manyfold. Family affairs go well as expansiveness and optimism prevail, and you feel highly pleased and very comfortable with who you are, with your roots and your personal origins. Your needs and cravings may increase in power, but seem to have more than the usual chances of being fulfilled; more people may depend on you, as your confidence and contentment attract them. Physical needs increase along with the emotional ones, so that overindulgence in food or drink could be among the few problems encountered here. A subtle attraction to the commonplace which often accompanies this aspect may deceive strong, hardworking individuals into a comfort and complacency quite out of character, but there can be little harm in indulging this, so long as you are ready to get back down to practical basics once the transit has passed.

Jupiter to Natal Mercury

Success and advancement in work and educational areas are featured now, along with opportunities to travel that can bring both material and cultural awards. Studies, research, writing, journalism, business expansion, and any undertaking involving communications should go very well now, perhaps attracting prestige, job advancement, or financial success. Highly suitable for self-promotion, this period is one in which the more positive potentials listed above, and their more cultural and expansive interpretations, will manifest. Influences from foreign sources, along with the assistance of people of influence should make life easier for you, and if you wish to seek new employment, to write or to seek a publisher, to promote or advertise, these matters should go particularly well for you. Exciting new ideas from the four corners of the earth stimulate a new view of the world, as you are made more aware of the importance of your fit into the grand scheme of things. Feelings, sex, and relationship seem less important in the midst of the abundance of ideas that flow during this time.

Jupiter to Natal Venus

Personal pleasures, indulgence in the arts, socializing, and not a small bit of ambition for social advancement drive you during this very pleasant transit. As the planet of abundance aspects the planet of love and harmony, you may find yourself going to more parties or even weddings, than the usual, as the world around you seems full of happy, playful, contented, and nurturing people. Rewards (including increased income) accrue, resulting in a sense of security and success, and even problems that occur now seem to have a silver (or perhaps gold) lining. You are recognized for accomplishments in your career and, in keeping with the new status that seems to go with this, you may seek to spend more than is reasonable on improving your appearance, outdoing the Joneses and "putting on the Ritz." Suddenly, limousines seem a tempting mode of transportation, particularly given the social company you'd like to be keeping. Overindulgence is of course a danger under such beneficent influences, and those who already have weight problems, or who tend to spend too much, will perhaps be the only ones likely to find this a challenging period in some respects. Relationships develop in a positive direction and, if begun at this time, have a good chance to be prosperous and enduringly affectionate. You envision a prosperous future at this time, and you strive to meet people whose support you think can assure it. Whether social or financial, investments you make now have a good chance of prospering significantly over the course of time.

Jupiter to Natal Mars

Some of the more difficult potentials of a zone where the planet of competition, strife, and self-assertion is strong are mitigated, allowing you to make major accomplishments in fields of endeavor which normally might not be favored here. This is a strongly energizing influence, so sports aficionados, competitors, entrepreneurs, and adventurers of all kinds can enjoy outstanding success—as long as they are not driven to *excess* by overconfidence. Athletic or military training, body-building, outdoor work, construction, and practical concerns do especially well now, as aggressive instincts are sharpened and focused in a way that tends to stymie the competition. Perhaps the only problem in dealing with the success that comes your way now lies in your increased potential for being inconsiderate and brash, as winning battle after battle may incline you toward boastfulness, authoritarianism, and domineering pushiness born of overconfidence. Whether you are male or female, you are likely to act somewhat macho, but as this is not a long-lived influence, you can make the most of it by concentrating your energy and assertiveness on some kind of strenuous, demanding, active, and constructive undertaking, including giving some attention to health regimens. Try not to take foolish risks, even though the temptation to do so will always be there. Overwork and getting stressed out should also be avoided. Sexual and erotic appetites are expanded, as high-energy biology can often overwhelm politeness and social restraint. That may be fine for short-term satisfaction, but don't count on building too many long-term relationships unless you are really willing to work at it.

Jupiter to Natal Jupiter

Jupiter transiting Jupiter brings a time that is notable for both success and excess, as though your potentials for increased status and social accomplishment are in high gear, so too is your potential for more snobbery than the average person can handle well. This is a prime time to speculate, and you should always observe the caution to not bet the rent money, since the luck that seems to follow you around now is very fickle and will abandon you at a moment's notice, particularly when accompanied by your good sense. Despite the cautions and precautions to be observed, however, you should be aware that lottery winners and the like often make their fortunes during this short but optimistic period of time. Your desires for status and social approval in all its forms are heightened now, as limousines look somehow more attractive as a mode of transportation and you may begin to worry more about what the neighbors think. Honors, promotions, and recognition which are sought can be won if you invest some effort, and in general you can find yourself traveling with a "better" (though possibly more boring) crowd. Teachers, counselors, and healers who undergo this transit will find ability to inspire and encourage others at a peak now. Salesmen are also likely to be in hog heaven, as positive thinking seems to help them set new standards for others while at the same time setting new records for their own personal earnings. Cultural and educational concerns also prosper, as you seem more worldly, mature, and just plain professional. No matter what your profession or other interests, one thing to beware of under the heady intoxication of this aspect is that you don't sign up for long-term debts which you later realize you can't really afford. The more negative effects of Jupiter to Jupiter are often subtle and long-term, so if you concentrate on reaping rewards (particularly financial) that are obvious, short-term, and don't require future commitment, you can have all the good and none of the bad.

Jupiter to Natal Saturn

Due to the release and relief which Jupiter brings to bear on the usual restraint of Saturn, you are able to make slow but real progress against difficulties which you have faced at this location, and you can possibly turn such liabilities into real and lasting successes. You seem to be on the way up, and while this ascendancy may be short-lived, you can make good use of it in redeeming past mistakes and the restrictions in your life that resulted. People in authority, or others who have some measure of control over your life, may offer you an opportunity which, though perhaps requiring to pay your own way, could increase both your finances and status over the long run. Travel and education open opportunities you've never had before, and new input from old friends or other trusted advisors can help you to follow your ambitions and expand your horizons. If relationships change much now, it is likely to be for the better, and careful growth and expansion is now possible in business and job concerns. All of this is motivated psychologically by subtle but persistent feelings of inadequacy, quite possibly based on dissatisfaction over your social class or your upbringing, but you're able to turn these relatively negative feelings to good account and thus to overcome them to some extent. If you're a strong individualist, this period may see you working more within the system and attuning your ambitions to conform more to the status quo.

Jupiter to Natal Uranus

Excitement, intellectual stimulation, and idealism fill the air as Jupiter touches the planet of surprises and inspired thinking. You tend to take more risks than usual, and one of them could pay off handsomely, since speculation and gambling sometimes succeed quite well during this short period of time. However, don't spend the rent and grocery money, and try to put at least some of your winnings aside. You are able to think in a truly original fashion now, perhaps turning your mind toward inventing or creating something of a technological or intellectual nature. Sudden changes in your life direction which happen now are usually favorable and tend to accentuate your individuality and uniqueness. The more radical and heterodox opinions which you might have kept hidden from others become stronger and are powerfully expressed for all to hear and see, as you feel less constrained by responsibility and more inclined to go to idealistic extremes where politics is concerned. This can be a time of unexpected opportunities involving travel or dealings with people in foreign countries. Your social circle becomes youthful, rebellious, and more than a little kooky in the eyes of some, but as you are less concerned with approval and more concerned with the free flow of interesting ideas you find in such company, you are far from concerned. Involvement with unions, public interest groups, and the like may become more important in your life now, as you become more of an activist, impelled by either the encouragement or apparent complicity of authorities. You adopt a broader world view and a more cultured and worldly set of values.

Jupiter to Natal Neptune

Intense introspection centered on spiritual concerns occupies your attention, and you may spend quite a bit of time alone, seeking to visualize the future and how it might relate to your religious feelings or other inner needs. This period is good for the experience of monastic or communal life or other situations in which ideals and, to some extent, isolation are of paramount importance. Your desire to help others seems more important than personal ambitions or aspirations. Occasionally, long-term injustices can be righted under this aspect, and moral authorities will generally look kindly on you and your projects. There is some danger of optimistic self-deception now, and feelings of exhilaration, hysteria or religious ecstasy, or a desire to sacrifice yourself in some sense for others should be closely questioned lest you succumb to totally false and unrealistic hopes. If you find yourself abusing drugs (prescription or otherwise), it is a sure sign that you are not willing to face some reality in your life, and the "revelations" which seem to emerge from your introspective periods may be nothing more than thinly disguised escapism. Still, spiritual awareness is possible now, and your imagination, intuition, and social insights can be highly inspired and deeply significant.

Jupiter to Natal Pluto

This is apt to be a time that involves you in a battle between the concepts of individualism and authority, and you may be required to formulate and adhere more closely than usual to your own concept of what is right and moral—often in the face of the implicitly superior opposition of a majority. Yet if you are willing to fight, you may be proven right by events that transpire now. This can happen through unusual good luck, due to success in professional activities involving money, publication, speculation, stocks, and bonds, or through being rewarded for long, hitherto unappreciated effort in some area of endeavor. Opportunities for advancement present themselves as a result of someone else's departure or removal, and you may be freed from attachments, relationships, or life interests that are no longer appropriate. This transit presents you with an unusual opportunity to sell possessions at a profit, to rid yourself of oppressive personal situations, and to gain through conflict with the "old order." Power needs and ambitions are sharpened, and conflicts of principle with those who stand for establishment values should be expected. It may be best to avoid direct confrontations with authority now, for while you feel more alone and at odds with society, you also see the advantages in such a posture, and understand that by quietly capitalizing on what others reject, you can come out way ahead. For some, fame, notoriety, or sudden accession to power may occur during this period.

24

Saturn: Responsibility Is the Keynote

THIS POWERFUL temporary influence, can last as long as one year, a period during which responsibility becomes a central issue in your life, and events and situations in your life conspire to force you to take on more of it than you might ordinarily be willing to accept. Increased pressure is put on you by employers, friends, family and most of the other basic environments that shape your life, and though you may begin to fear your abilities are inadequate in the face of such demands, this time can be very important in establishing your capacity to deal with issues essential to your social position, power, and autonomy in society. Restriction and frustrations may force you to trim hopes and aspirations in order to deal with tiresome and dreary day-to-day issues, but this is only part of the learning process. Other people often seem either unsupportive or hostile, but this is mostly when they sense your subtle need for individual power and control in any situation, something which dampens their own desire to cooperate. If you willingly assume the many new responsibilities thrust upon you now, this will simply seem to you a time of hard work that produces slow, satisfying progress toward distant goals. If you do not face up to what you must do, however, misfortune and difficulty—particularly in health, relationship, career, or family matters—may enforce the patterns noted above and restrict your freedom until you are willing to impose some limits on what you can expect to achieve. This influence often manifests itself in the guise of harsh external authorities or through various mechanisms which withhold or withdraw material resources, so dealings in finance and real estate can suffer, and your parents or others acting as surrogates for parental authority can impose limitations on you and require you to undertake difficult tasks in order to receive what you may feel is your due by right. Such tests of endurance and character can later prove essential to the evolving purpose of your life.

Saturn to Natal Sun

At this locality you are likely to experience a time of unusual structuring and self-discipline, when you encounter obstacles to your aspirations that are sufficient to demand rethinking of your personal priorities and goals. Inappropriate ambitions will now be exposed as such and may have to be given up; yet the difficulties encountered under this aspect could create a determination to succeed that can constitute the foundation of a more mature and powerful grasp of who you are and where you are headed in life. In particular, projects and concerns that have personal acclaim, success, or ego gratification as objectives will meet with serious obstacles, and success comes not through lucky breaks so much as through cultivation of an awareness of your limitations and the development of the ability to patiently persevere. Knowing what you cannot do will minimize wasting opportunities that do present themselves and will allow you to concentrate on what you can do, even though such knowledge is often hard won, and less than gratefully accepted. This is a time of responsibility and enforced hard work, so that patience, focus, and self-knowledge are essential. Health may not be at its best, so stress and inadequate nourishment or rest should be avoided as much as possible. Wishes can come true under this transit, but only if you realize that you have the power, determination, and personal responsibility to bring them into reality yourself.

Saturn to Natal Moon

You are likely to feel somewhat restricted, emotionally limited, and even depressed, and you are highly aware of those times when you are subject to high-handed treatment from those in authoritative positions. Such actions injure your most sensitive feelings, leaving you to vow that someday you will even the score. Women especially may find this period of time frustrating and debilitating, especially when responsibilities seem to multiply beyond your capacity to handle them. You should try not to become overly self-critical nor to accept other's judgments of your deficiencies unquestioningly. Even if you can see your faults now all too clearly, that doesn't mean you should waste time despairing over them, nor adding your own mea culpas to the list of your deficiencies compiled by others. Instead, you should take advantage of such problems to develop your will power and control in order to make an effort to build on the things you do well and to improve the things you don't. You can be realistic and firm in your efforts at self-appraisal, which is why where your own abilities are concerned, you should rely on your own judgment more than that of others. Cravings, feelings, and an increased need for nurturing and comfort are not likely to be satisfied to any great degree at present, so turn your thoughts toward making a realistic appraisal of just what place those who normally provide such thing–family and friends–really should have in your life.

Saturn to Natal Mercury

While concerns with work, creative ideas, your own self-definition, and health are apt to predominate during this time, they will do so in an atmosphere of compulsion and necessity, as problems and responsibilities present themselves, demanding to be dealt with. The acquisition of new skills and a better education may in some sense be forced upon you, perhaps requiring serious, dedicated study in forbiddingly technical areas. Such studies progress only with extra effort, however, and though you may feel that in some ways you are not up to the challenge, perseverance can win the day. Health, particularly when it involves your resistance to allergens or infection, may be at a low ebb, and the problem is often exacerbated by stress in work and personal life. The immediate environment may be at fault in this, but battering your head against the wall won't change the architecture much, so you will just have to take extra measures and precautions to keep yourself in trim. Habits of thought may restrict you now more than they usually do, so in some cases it is better to accept discipline in work and study that is imposed on you by others than to try to do everything in your own way. Your inclination toward overly serious thinking and perfectionism may lead you to work long hours to master difficult mental disciplines which others see as useless or pointless, but ultimately these things may prove to be highly practical. This period of time seems tedious and purposeless, but behind the humdrum routine and boring repetitiveness, this transit offers opportunities to master new information and learn new skills.

Saturn to Natal Venus

The social and hedonistic opportunities inherent in this zone under normal conditions are restricted and turned to more practical account. Social concerns and personal relationships, especially marriage, may seem disappointing now, and thus your needs for love and affection may be sublimated in activities that feed your material ambition and your desire to acquire power, money, and influence. This is a poor time to rely on any but the most practical of relationships, and legal concerns may not go well this year. Still, you are able to eliminate those relationships, possessions, and social responsibilities of which you have tired, and those which remain probably are those that can be counted on most to be worthwhile. Whether romantically or otherwise, you may find yourself most attracted to people who are older than you, have a serious demeanor, or who have notable problems of some sort, and you may tend to lose interest in people with whom the sharing of pleasure is all you hold in common—and in fact, enjoyment itself seems less important now than getting ahead and acquiring possessions. If you insist on pursuing a self-indulgent and luxurious lifestyle, you may be constrained by lack of resources or by the disapproval of some external authority. In this somewhat serious period of time, any reassessment of long-term financial and romantic plans is likely to have stability and value as its prime criteria. Like the ant in the fable, you see summer as just extra time in which to get ready for winter.

Saturn to Natal Mars

Much of the boisterousness, zest for living, and risk-taking that could be seen in this locale may be moderated now, or made more difficult by reason of outside pressures and responsibilities. Generally, it's a poor time to begin adventuresome or entrepreneurial projects, though it can be a very good time to lay the groundwork for such projects, do preliminary research, or anticipate the kinds of problems you might face in carrying these plans out. Though this zone is usually good for exercising your personal initiative in a variety of ways, you seem low in energy now and make headway against obstacles only with the greatest of effort. In the same vein, your sex drive may be lower than usual, even though you may find yourself sought after as a sexual "object" in some fashion. Your sense that you're constantly battling against an overly competitive and harsh social climate could incline you to temperamental outbursts, though such fits of pique only mask your insecurity about whether or not you can meet the challenges you face in an adequate way. Men may see this period as particularly frustrating in personal relations of all kind, while women may find themselves dealing with men who are unresponsive, cruel, or unkind. It is best to keep aspirations to a minimum, as this influence can discipline your energy and financial resources well only if you are not involved in too many projects. You may set up situations in which others take out their anger on you, and it will take all your effort to handle such negative feelings in an adult and outward manner. Avoid taking foolish risks , but most especially if they will put you in any physical danger.

Saturn to Natal Jupiter

Any possibilities which you had hoped might bode well for an increase in prosperity will probably not come to fruition, at least just yet, and even if they do advance, they do so slowly, through your own motivation and determination. Business slows down, making this a good period of time to plan future expansions rather than to institute plans already made. In general, quite a few of life's ambitions have to be put on hold now, particularly in the area of religious, cultural, and financial interests. If you're one of those people who get a great deal of gratification in conspicuous consumption will find this period trying and tedious; bills come due, and increasing costs meet decreasing income head on, meaning that even if you are tempted to spend lavishly, you won't likely get the chance. The self-reliant have far less to fear from this transit than those who depend on "going along to get along," and if you happen to fall in the latter category, you should take steps to gain more personal control over your financial life. If you can do this, then when progress toward prosperity resumes, your life can move along in a more streamlined and efficient fashion. Working to become more independent, self-motivated, individualistic, and persevering is thus the best course to pursue, as you learn to temper your enthusiasm and idealism with patience and reason. Long-term plans conceived of now have an excellent chance for success through carefully sustained growth, and you find that their rewards will be well worth waiting for.

Saturn to Natal Saturn

The potentials of this zone are sharply and directly brought into awareness now and you might begin to feel that your purpose for being here at this time is to fully experience and understand the true nature of Saturn. If you happen to be around age 29, this truly can be a turning point in your life, both a farewell to youth and an acceptance of the powers and responsibilities of true adulthood. If you do not consciously make decisions to assume greater responsibility in some major department of your life (most often career and power relationships in society), external situations will tend to eliminate all other possibilities, forcing you to face directly what you have been trying to avoid. At other ages, this aspect will either reiterate or anticipate in a lesser way this major understanding reached at age 29, as you are more or less forced to assess your progress toward personal self-sufficiency and autonomy, and you are made to recognize your abilities and your weaknesses as you cope with new developments that affect your career or social position. An increased awareness of your age, and to some extent your mortality, brings you face to face with those things in your life that will require greater attention and development over the next fourteen years, while also making you admit to yourself what needs to be discarded. This need to take stock of your personal repertoire of skills and needs applies particularly to your self-image in relation to your job, your permanent relationships, your lifestyle, and health matters. Anything that goes wrong this year must be set right by you, and you alone.

Saturn to Natal Uranus

You find yourself strongly concerned with individualism and idealism, if only as a means of resisting the pressures to conform that come from legal, social, and political authorities. You may find yourself reacting powerfully and emotionally when on occasion you, or those you admire, must compromise unalterable principles and ethical necessities for short-term gain. People may not thank you much for your input in such matters, even when they feel that you're right, if only because you are forcing issues they are trying to avoid. Your desire for radical change as a means of personal evolution seems blocked now by habitual defensive patterns you have created in your life, and it may be difficult for you to come to the realization that changing these old habits can not be done any more quickly or easily than changing other people's minds. Though it may seem to take forever, change will come, often suddenly and from an unexpected quarter. However, while you are working hard to buck the forces you feel are restraining your personal freedom, that once you have broken free, you will then need work to create enduring structures that will permit you to "graduate" to a new stage of life. You will at times have to work hard to keep believing in that part of yourself that makes you unique apart from all others, but if you can keep the faith through this tough and tempering transit, you'll have clearly forged that uniqueness into an enduring and central part of your personality.

Saturn to Natal Neptune

For most, both Neptune and Saturn lines are already difficult , so this period of time can be particularly challenging. You should be prepared for confrontation with the realities of these two planets in various ways, but most particularly on a mental level: you may tend to feel depressed, confused and uncertain more than usual now, feelings which should not be taken at face value. Tending to dwell on the negative side of experience, circumstances and your own moods can make you feel powerless and can distract you from the things that really matter. Health may reflect this mental confusion, and it may be difficult to decide whether ephemeral and inexplicable symptoms should be taken to the doctor, or ignored as just hypochondria, though it's safer to take the former course. Habits formed now may "crystallize" some of the negativity of this period, so be particularly leery of establishing habits that might lead to physical dependence—everything from drinking too much alcohol to taking prescription medications which could have risky side-effects if used over long periods. On the positive side, this time is one in which your feet may be more firmly on the ground than usual, since most forms of imagination from pure idealism to misleading delusions are likely to be suppressed both internally and externally now. A sure knowledge of what you *don't* want in life is likely to be the most lasting legacy of this transit, but you may have to spend some time after it has past in rebuilding the knowledge of what you do want. Solitude, music, and the beauty of nature can be consolations now and a source of inspiration which can make this period creative and fruitful.

Saturn to Natal Pluto

While this zone is normally one of personal transformation that can deal with fundamentals that include birth, death, and regeneration, such processes are slowed or inhibited during this time, resulting in a feeling of spiritual blockage and frustration. You feel resistant to implacable change, and a general malaise running through your daily life should not be allowed to obscure the realization that these difficulties are temporary and that change will come, often with shocking rapidity, once this period is over. The problem of coping with the fact of your own mortality may occupy your thoughts now, and external situations (including financial problems) may restrict you and make you all too aware of your limitations. Occasionally, long-forgotten errors or transgressions are brought to light now, and you may have to deal with the authorities or police as well as your conscience in putting these things to rest. However, for those willing to assume new responsibilities, this can be a positive period when your place in the scheme of things is understood more clearly than at most other times, and you can work to create a place for yourself in life which embodies that view.

25

Uranus: Excitement, Change, Nonconformity

THE STRONGEST effect of this transit is about eighteen months. The totally unforeseen—things that you would never seriously consider happening—seems to become almost a daily occurrence now. Though you may somehow feel that your life is altered permanently by events that occur under a Uranian transit, when the dust settles you will probably find that things have returned to the way they were before, although you will have changed somewhat, particularly in your willingness to see the world as a more improbable, exciting, and unpredictable place. Sudden travel, relocation, meetings with strangers, and eventualities which could never have been foreseen intrude on your existence. It goes without saying that if you happen to like lots of change and variation you should find this year exciting and refreshing, but are one of the more habit-bound of earth's creatures, you could find it more than a bit upsetting as it tilts you this way and that out of your safe little groove. These changes should remind you, however, of the vast potential and power of your own uniqueness and to prove to you that it is always possible to overturn the most entrenched and resistant life routines. Any inhibitions you have are likely to be abandoned, and you will also have to re-evaluate self-imposed restrictions that may have held you back. Just as the process of adaptation in nature is often initiated through mutation and radical change (a process which can at times produce a certain percentage of useless abnormalities), every life needs periods like this year in which you are forced to grow and adapt to unforeseen and emergent circumstances. It is likely that most of what happens now simply reflects inner changes that have been seething within you (though artfully repressed) for several years into the past. Now you will be forced to give them free rein to see just what they will produce. At the end of the transit, you will have a better idea of who you truly are, apart from your personality and accomplishments in society, and the knowledge could well surprise you. You will feel more aligned to counterculture ideas and people, as mainstream conformists seem as dangerously inflexible and outdated as the mastodons in the tar pits.

Uranus to Natal Sun

Self-expression undergoes evolution and transformation, as public attention—even notoriety or fame—that comes to you now often forces you to act on the spur of the moment, as if by instinct. You become bolder, even outrageous, in expressing who and what you are, and are less concerned with social opinion and its limitations on your demonstrations of individuality. Your opinions and ideas get caught up with your identity, and both are defended against what may seem others' venality and self-interests (both of which very likely are negative projections of your own problems). Your interest focuses on anything original, anti-establishment, technical, and heterodox, which—along with unforeseen travel to unusual places or meetings with extraordinary people—can make this an exhilarating time. Your true identity, once all your attempts to conform to others' expectations are put aside, shines forth now in almost irritating clarity, and the life structures upon which you have relied heavily change unexpectedly, leaving you more reliant on yourself and your own resources. Old friends may quickly tire of your one-person revolution and move on, but trying to hold onto remnants of the past is hopeless now, and you will eventually understand that some things and people in that past have inhibited your personal growth. Despite the fact that you often embrace and more often cause change, this still can be an upsetting period of your life. Despite this, after it has passed, your sense of who you are will be sharper, clearer, and far more in keeping with your true self.

Uranus to Natal Moon

Unforeseen events can make you very much aware of your needs, dependencies, and emotional attachments, largely because of changes in these life areas. Your public image, your standing in the community, and your family relationships may undergo drastic change, sometimes occasioned either by a need for relocation or upheavals in family patterns and structures. Appetites for variation and adventure increase, and in particular intense but brief romantic affairs betray an awakening of erotic desires which you may have been suppressing up to this point. Perhaps most interesting, you may be put in touch with a philosophy or group whose ideals make you more aware of your needs and capacities for self-nurturing and your ability to take care of others. Your personal needs are at times rationalized by seeing them as related to the larger society in some way, and you could emerge from this period feeling that you have a perfect right to fulfill your desires directly, in all their thunderstorm intensity. Relationships with the opposite sex can be tempestuous, but they are also likely to be exciting now—in particular, women undergoing this transit may rebel against traditional roles associated with gender. Relations between parents and children are also under pressure now, meaning that if family structures don't change to accommodate fuller individual expression, they could be in danger of breaking. It is an unsettled period, so that frequent moves or neighborhood disruptions ensure that home life is far from tranquil; but, at least for now, you probably prefer it that way.

Uranus to Natal Mercury

The many changes likely to happen in your life now center on your work, vocation, the educational goals you pursue to meet these ends, and the maturing of your intellect in general. Your mind is awakened to new horizons of communication and study now, some of which may take in areas of inquiry that may be considered unorthodox among your peers, including forbiddingly technical knowledge, Utopian political theory, and even astrology. Work becomes the scene of changes which even may involve some form of idealistic confrontation. You grow impatient and rebellious against religious and educational institutions, professionals and academics, or others who tend to espouse what "everybody knows." Your own curiosity is extreme, as you become aware that what everybody knows may not be the truth—or at least not an interesting truth. Your mind reaches for new ideas in hopes of discovering that new truth, but also as a way of seeking a key to your own identity, which you will now perceive perhaps for the first time as unique and powerfully individual. Though your insights may well be lost on others now, you strive to develop more powerful communication tools in hopes of converting them to your world view and sharing your new insights. Do not, however, expect too many people to agree with you, and if your thinking has hitherto been overly structured you should expect some resistance against your "re-education" even within yourself. Travel and exposure to new ideas are both very stimulating to you now, as your life becomes more mobile, worldly, and exciting. As a consequence, feelings and attachments, including material concerns, may be left by the wayside for the time being, as ideas are what count most for you now.

Uranus to Natal Venus

Unexpected developments and numerous changes should be expected in your relational and romantic life, with the focus on extraordinary social contacts and fascinating relationships. It's time to kick up your heels as you meet exciting, glamorous, and unusual people who open options in relationship and eroticism for you that you might not have imagined possible up to this time. Your irrepressible desire for novelty and variation may, of course, tend to upset existing relationships, so at some point you may have to consider whether the long-term effects of this transit will be as happy as the short-term effects. Your tendency to seek out unorthodox social situations may have the neighbors whispering for now, but you couldn't care less, since you're having too much fun. Even if you've been rather conservative up to this point, you may find yourself falling in and out of love every twenty minutes and willing to at least consider exploring the furthest boundaries of your personal erotic expression. This will certainly make life more exciting and unpredictable than probably ever before, but it could also give it a hint of scandalous color that's not your usual shade. Your long-term relationships undergo just as much change as the short-term ones, or at least they had better if they are to retain your interest. In particular, the habits and routines of marriage can be challenged now in a way that requires them to be reformed and renewed. Far beyond romance, any kind of partnership is likely to prove unpredictable and could be frequently upset, due as much to the people you choose to relate to as to your own restlessness and instability. Artists and the creatively inclined will be inspired with new ideas and new directions in their work, and anyone may look back on this period as extremely exciting and stimulating.

Uranus to Natal Mars

The excitement and change under this transit may have you living life on the edge in a way you hadn't dared before. Though this can be exhilarating, it can also put you in some very dicey situations, and make you subject to more than a few close shaves. You actually may not be consciously aware of your need to repeatedly tempt fate by pushing your luck and taking unnecessary risks, and while this might make you confident in situations where others might lose their grip, it also represents a loss of control that could make you your own worst enemy. In driving, operating machinery, or engaging in any activity of this type, you should work very hard to impose on yourself an extra margin of caution. Doing so will make your life dynamic and productive; not doing so may simply make you waste all your time cleaning up the resulting messes. Men are particularly affected, and their sexual demands can become quite intense, often taking unconventional forms. Much of your need for excitement may be fueled by suppressed anger, and you should expect yourself to be more competitive, quick-tempered, and irascible now. Finding constructive outlets for that anger, such as physical activity, will put you in better command of yourself and your destiny, not to mention making you a better person to be with. People often fear anger because they fear losing control–but learning how to channel and focus it will make you less fearful of its power. This period is good for pursuits that require courage, daring, and technical expertise, but don't put yourself in peril just to prove how brave you are. Engineers and technicians may overcome problems in a creative and innovative way now, and the excitement of this period results in initiatives toward a new and more powerful sense of self for everyone, no matter what their specialty or interest.

Uranus to Natal Jupiter

You are liable to encounter opportunities that promise to further your prosperity, help you attain success in your chosen endeavors, and bring social acceptance from unexpected quarters. A complete change in social status can occur for you now, involving travel, educational possibilities, or even a drastic (though often temporary) change in financial position upward or downward. This is an exciting and unorthodox time, when new ideas and intellectual stimulation enable you to break with the mainstream and to seek your fortune in an original, individual, and self-determined fashion. You will question conventional wisdom in both your personal and professional life, and can outgrow unquestioning attachments you may have had to social and religious institutions. Your thinking about how the world works is fired by an infusion of idealism, perhaps stemming from an exposure to original thinkers or outrageous nonconformists. Because of this, you come to see your own life's purpose as self-fulfillment and self-actualization, and this in turn promotes a more live-and-let-live philosophy in regard to others. Financially, this period of time is somewhat unpredictable; you might consider playing the lottery more than usual now, as long as you don't bet more than you can easily afford to lose, and you also might feel free to take more risks regarding your job or your social situations. Opportunities involving publication or technology could offer you special opportunities to increase your income; be careful that you don't lose whatever you gain through overconfidence, however. This end of this singularly exciting period should find you way ahead of where you were when it started.

Uranus to Natal Saturn

As this transit proceeds, you will probably find yourself involved in an ideological battle that sets you against either society or, well, yourself. Normally, this Saturn zone moves your thought and action in the direction of conservatism, as you work very hard to build and maintain permanent life structures—though often to the detriment of freedom and individual expression. During this year, however, such structures (and the people who symbolize them) may be totally changed or even destroyed, and those which do endure may in the end seem less suitable to your own needs. This is probably a time of considerable tension and irritability, as it's hard to know where your life is heading, and change is the one certainty in your daily existence. Your career and your position in society may shift, impelled by idealistic considerations, and those whom you consider unquestioned authorities in your life, parents particularly, may see their lives change along with yours. But the major importance of this period is likely to be social, resulting in a redefinition of yourself as more socially relevant than at any other period of time in your life. Somehow, issues of your own growth and liberation seem to parallel those of your society, so attention may focus on you as the representative or exemplar of some larger pattern. You may be called upon to act out important social conflicts in some constructive and creative way, putting you in the position of solving problems which may prove to be of benefit to others. If at times you feel like the proverbial voice crying in the wilderness, you should be assured that at some point that voice will be heard.

Uranus to Natal Uranus

In a sense, your reason for residing here could be to experience the true strength and depth of this potential. Particularly if you happen to be around forty years of age, you shouldn't plan on getting much done in a structured, orderly way this year, since you will likely be catapulted into some experience of maximal emotional intensity that will demand all your attention. What this might be is not really predictable, except that it might be something you would least expect. The structures and patterns of your life suddenly could seem intolerably confining and repressive, and your friends may shake their heads in wonder as you act out the most individualistic and eccentric of all the potentials listed above. If you can, take a sabbatical this year—leave yourself free to be blown by the winds of change toward possibilities and interests you'd never otherwise consider. Your life will likely still be there if you want to come back, and what you experience now may set standards for commitment to idiosyncrasy (if indeed there can be standards in such a situation), and could have important ramifications later. You feel the need to define yourself outside the patterns and structures of society—who you are apart from your career, status, name, or even personality. Particularly if in middle age, near forty, you acutely feel "time's winged chariot drawing near" and suddenly realize that life is a limited quantity; at other ages, you rebel from constraints and seek a more honest and personal expression of who you are than that demanded by authorities, institutions, and other representatives of convention.

Uranus to Natal Neptune

During this transit, idealistic and social issues are likely to take a great deal of your time and energy. Visions of utopia, your hopes for the world, and your feelings of kinship with humanity are focused with intense clarity, so that you feel personally empowered and obligated to implement them in some way. Involvement with an idealistic community, political party, or religious movement is quite possible now, or you could find a spiritual guide, guru, or philosophy to which you are willing to devote a good part of the rest of your life. Such ideals are more easily grasped when felt rather than thought, but now your mind is full of powerful opinions, whose bases, though illogical, may be entirely unquestioned. Implementation of these opinions may tap into collective visions and ideals that are stronger than your own ego, and you can find yourself caught up in something far beyond your control, or even your powers of comprehension, as social movements and the conflicts sparked by them seem to consume you. Your world view is quite original now, and you seem to have the ability to put into words and actions what others only vaguely feel, tapping power that seems to come almost from humanity's unconscious. You might become the spokesperson for some ancient idea or belief or perhaps seek to live life in a community that adheres to such beliefs. Drugs, especially mind-altering ones, can have unusual and powerful effects on you now, so any experimentation with such should be undertaken with great care, if at all.

Uranus to Natal Pluto

The intensely cathartic and critical potentials of Pluto are apt to manifest in a direct and forceful manner for you here. Fueled by a newly-kindled idealism and motivated by a powerful desire for freedom and personal autonomy, you are apt to rebel against anything or anyone that you feel prevents you from becoming who you truly are. This aspect of intense individualism impels you to seek new relationships and a new peer group that will support unquestioningly your rebellion and your search for individual self-expression. Long-held resentments boil to the surface now, and changing circumstances allow you to let go of ideas or people that you long ago outgrew. Rebellion for rebellion's sake seems to be the order of the day for you, everyday, as you associate with elements on the edge of society as a symbol of your own determination to be uncompromisingly true to the deepest standards of individuality. As financial, home, family, and career situations can change drastically, this period could mark the beginning of a new epoch in your life and establish a lifelong pattern of individualism and radical transformation. This is one of the most intense possible times to be in an area that already promises powerful change, so about the only way to avoid cataclysmic upheaval is to consciously surrender self-concepts and future plans to the unknowable processes at work here.

26

Neptune: Go with the Flow

THE EFFECT of the movement of the planet of diffusion, confusion, and imagination to an angle at a particular locality can last as long as two years, bringing with it a profound sense of uncertainty and lack of direction. Though strong, this influence is a subtle one that is about the worst possible for any sort of tangible, concrete, and ego-directed accomplishment. Will and purpose seem diffused, and the world doesn't operate according to rules that follow any rational pattern. Other people seem to look right through the real you, seeing you only as the projected illusion of what they lack, rather than who you really are. None of the structures upon which civilization and society depend—schedules, consistency, predictability—seem to work very well now, and the more attached you are to ideas of who you should be and what the world is, the more trouble you are likely to have. Beware of impulses to rescue the world, as more often than not your altruistic ideals in this regard will be based on a combination of self-dislike and false romanticism. Likewise, beware of an attraction to the sort of charismatic leader who capitalizes on others' sense of sin or guilt, as the threat of victimization hangs heavy in Neptunian air, along with the potential for addiction, as well as for involvement in scandal. However, this transit should not simply be seen as an inevitable exercise in frustration and personal belittlement, but as a transcendent reality, the kind often only accessible in meditation or religious ecstasy, that actually demands recognition underneath the decay that seems to beset you now. If you can go with the flow of this reality, and not resist by trying to be overly rational in situations that call for feeling, your sacrifice of ego and self-concept can be rewarded with a new view of the world that positively sparkles with rich insights. Artistic, musical, and religious inspiration obviously wait for you on the positive side of this Neptunian river.

Neptune to Natal Sun

Your self-expressive and creative side looks inward now, heightening the possibility for intuitive and mystical awareness. This is a time when you will be out in the world exploring the local environment, with your personal quest for meaning demanding extroverted immersion in the world and its problems. Instead you look inward, with a great need for solitude in order to contemplate the tenuous grasp on practical matters that seems to have caught you unaware. Sensitivity and empathy for those experiencing cruelty and injustice are central concerns for you, as these things seem emblematic of your increasing feeling that you yourself are victimized by the world. Artistic abilities increase, especially in music, but a sense of aimlessness and lack of direction make applying your creative insights in a useful way very difficult. You may find that you're attracted to mystical religion, communal living, drugs, or even to work in institutional environments now, but expect these attractions to wane when the temporary influence passes. Where idealism and utopianism increase, gullibility often follows, so beware of attaching yourself to unorthodox gurus or movements until this transit is past.

Neptune to Natal Moon

The emotional, security-seeking, and possessive instincts normally active in this area become more diffuse, and other-worldly, lacking any firm direction. Your feelings are intense and unpredictable now, and your family matters, as well as your hopes to establish personal security in life, seem threatened by feelings that intrude on your life from the least accessible parts of your unconscious. Your sensitivity may increase to an intensity that is hard to handle (this is especially true for men), so confusion and vacillation seem to dominate in the areas of your life in which practical judgment and realistic decisions are called for, including finances and relationship matters. Your tendency to unrestrained excitability and to hypersensitivity to the more mysterious and illogical aspects of life makes it easy to get caught up in the moment, or to be dominated by other people and their ideals. Drugs and alcohol could pose particular problems, but the same things which make you sensitive in a physical sense also make it possible for you to intuit what others want and feel, enabling you to anticipate trends and fashions. In the best of circumstances this can be a particularly difficult period in a zone that tends to ups and downs anyway, and much of it could be spent in some sort of confinement (self-imposed or otherwise), in which you are forced to come to terms with your feelings and attachments to the people and ideas you hold most dear. The more personal aspects of your life are likely to be neglected now as you contemplate an overdrawn, baroque world of fantasy and feeling, full of dragons, maidens in distress, and magic.

Neptune to Natal Mercury

The normally logical, youthful, communication-oriented concerns highlighted by this zone become tangled up in diffusion, confusion, and strangely illogical happenings; work, study, and health concerns encounter mysterious problems that defy analysis, and mobility is challenged by aimlessness and constant, unforeseen impediments. Intuition works better than logic now, and about the only communication that proceeds well is that which is inspirational, poetic, musical, or artistic. Attempts to organize your life will encounter nebulous obstacles, and the best idea is to "go with the flow," allowing your unconscious to give direction to your life through hunches or inspiration. The world of practicality seems to have been taken over by denizens from *The Lord of the Rings*, making it nearly impossible to control or predict the outcome of even the simplest activities. Investments should be avoided, or at least very carefully considered, and business opportunities should be closely scrutinized for deceptive aspects. It's difficult to trust your ears or to rely on most information now, so important decisions should be postponed until such time as this transit begins winding down. Beware especially of matters that seem imbued with mystical importance and subtle "magic," as they are most apt to be falsely perceived. Interest in psychism and mysticism increase, as do your skills in prophecy, dream interpretation, and psychology; the problem is, your insights may see deep and your rendering of them so complicated that no one will understand what you're saying.

Neptune to Natal Venus

The romantic, social, and acquisitive nature of this zone is modified by increased sensitivity, romanticism, and idealism, so that sacrificing your interests for love and feeling new heights (and depths) of relationship are likely. Your artistic receptivity increases, as does awareness of the nuances of color and form, so those who are artists may experience intensely visionary inspiration that takes their creativity to new plateaus. Relationships are fraught with deceptions, however, and your desire to "reform" your lover or spouse, or to sacrifice your own interests for those you love, should be carefully scrutinized for the pitfalls of self-deception, false humility, and hypocrisy. You are also more apt to suffer from the negative effects of religious idealism and escapism, due to the seductive consumerism and venality that can run rampant in this zone under Neptune. You are able to see the beauty in the most commonplace of people and situations, but may at the same time overlook even glaring or exceptional flaws. If possible, avoid legal involvements, partnerships, and marriage now, and expect your life to be peopled with colorful and often disreputable characters. You can enjoy the play, but you don't have to buy the theater.

Neptune to Natal Mars

The aggressive, self-promoting, and assertive aspects of your personality will not manifest as openly or as obviously as they might at other times. Instead, this period of time is one in which you might feel overwhelmed by unseen and enigmatic forces and thus less able than usual to act in your own defense. For men, this can be an extremely disturbing influence, as any initiative you make seems to evaporate under a torrent of frustrating obstacles, and your will is challenged at every turn by circumstances. Illnesses can take hold here that normally would not affect you at all, as your resistance is compromised, leaving you prone to allergies, venereal infections, and chronic, unpleasant irritations. You may be tempted to become entangled in petty criminality, or the use of drugs now, but such ventures turn out even worse than one would expect. An attitude of detachment and a suspension of your need to meet specific goals will help you through this period, and it is generally a poor time to seek completion of projects or personal advancement—which is to say that it's best to limit your ambitions to avoiding conflict and responsibility. You may feel called upon to sacrifice your own self-interest for a cause, or to do something to liberate others from their chains, but success in practical affairs will likely elude you during this period.

Neptune to Natal Jupiter

This locality's expansive, self-promoting, and optimistic aspects become more spiritual, as you take up a search for inner, rather than outer, meaning and accomplishment. Partly this may be because things are not going well in your material and business life—income and prestige may dwindle, and the more structured parts of your life will be reduced to their true value. Any sort of hype or optimistic self-aggrandizement will not work at all well now, possibly because of negative publicity, betrayals, or just bad luck. Yet in reflecting on such setbacks you will find that you can perceive a deeper meaning and purpose to your life, and you may even experience a philosophical, religious, or spiritual breakthrough of some sort. Simplistic religion and world philosophy are abandoned now, as you begin to perceive the depth of unity that binds human consciousness to the cosmos. Idealism guides you, so though business may be bad and money may be tight, you can still find a way to stretch your meager funds in helping others. But your judgment is poor now, what you see as a highway to heaven, paved by inspiration, might be seen by some more pragmatic as a road to hell paved with no more than the best of intentions.

Neptune to Natal Saturn

Stability, hard work, self-knowledge, and pragmatism become servants to illusion now, making it difficult for you to achieve anything of a practical nature for the time being. This is a particularly difficult time, as what structure there is in your life may evaporate, leaving you uncertain, aimless, and unmotivated. Low vitality adds to the difficulties, so any health problems you suffer should definitely be checked out medically. Society itself seems bent on subjecting you to victimization or unfair harassment, something that is only aggravated by your complete lack of insight about exactly what is happening to you, and why. Your instincts now are to spend time alone and to retreat into settings of natural beauty, isolation, or solitude, though this is not likely to happen under most circumstances. You are attracted to those who seem most victimized by society, perhaps since you feel you are in much the same position. Those who do not have a firm grip on their self-identity are likely to undergo the greatest change now, as you find that the props and crutches you have been using to keep yourself standing are firmly planted in Neptunian quicksand. Any stress multiplies the disorientation you feel now, as since it is hard to understand where it is coming from, it is nearly impossible to deal with; ungrounded fears, dread, and hysteria may prevail at this extremely difficult time, but when you come through it, you will realize that there is a depth of life beyond the self and its illusions.

Neptune to Natal Uranus

Human concerns and a utopian vision serve to give your bent for idealism and individuality a more realistic focus, an odd twist for a transit by the planet of illusion. You tend to enjoy solitude in natural surroundings, finding that this gives you a time and space in which to contemplate the universal rhythms and philosophical truth which underlie your quest for personal uniqueness. You are easily caught up in the social currents that swirl around you now, and your own life and personal struggles somehow seem part of larger social problems. Because of this, you may be drawn to some philosophy or religion which strongly prohibits activities or ideas that are actually rather attractive to your inner nature. Since you find it more difficult than usual to stand up for what you believe, you may soon find yourself swept along in an ill-chosen movement that soon becomes more oppressive than inspirational. Gurus and spiritual leaders may promise to relieve you of your need to deal with your identity, but this only works for a little while. Much of what you once believed unquestioningly is likely to be dissipated now, and in its place grows an intuitive and transpersonal sense of belonging to something larger than yourself, though something is equally enigmatic, and just beyond your reach in some way.

Neptune to Natal Neptune

During this transit, you may begin to feel acutely that you have forgotten the ideals you grew up with, and that they have been superseded by those of a newer generation and its values. However, the understanding that the effects of idealism are often ephemeral doesn't keep you from feeling alienated and somehow out of touch. Your need for privacy, solitude, and meditation are heightened now, and sensitivity, intuition, and artistic sensibilities are all enhanced during this time of psychic receptiveness and general impressionability. It is hard to rely on perceptions now, as the ideals underlying your values are going through modification, but you can be artistically inspired, and the inner world seems more real and important than the outer. This is a stage most of your contemporaries will be going through at the same time, so social support from those your own age is important.

Neptune to Natal Pluto

Your tendencies toward isolation and individualism are moderated by an increasing mystical awareness of yourself as part of a larger human consciousness and collective awareness. Concepts of finality, birth, death, and of the destruction of self and ego give way to deeper awareness of the transcendence of the soul and how the laws of universal balance make the perpetuation of this personal ego unnecessary. For those unwilling to accept this sort of mystical redefinition, however, life can deal you some nasty surprises now, and you may find to your dismay that the tricks and stratagems you once used to set yourself apart from the crowd are now being used against you. Your autonomy is challenged, but it's hard to see just exactly who or what is doing the challenging. Paranoid fears tend to surface now, made all the more irrational by the absence of any clearly defined adversary. Friends, financial obligations and practical matters are difficult to pursue now, as a feeling of despair closes in on you if you don't take a more universal view of things.

27

Pluto: The Beginning of the Rest of Your Life

LONG-STANDING inner changes and repressed growth may erupt outward with a force that transforms your life and your self-concept. Attachments, relationships, and possessions are usually the first to undergo change that include separation or abandonment, among other things. People on whom you have relied may pass out of your life at this time, as you discover the limitations of even the deepest commitment and come to realize that a higher law of transformation, birth, and death (literal or figurative) applies to everything and everyone, including those you hold most dear.

If there is something in your life you have tried to keep hidden, you could be in for some nasty shocks, as secrets and clandestine activities rarely remain hidden for long under this transit, and these secrets include those you have tried to keep from yourself, whether consciously or unconsciously. Your self-concept, physical appearance, career, family ties, or major relationships at first undergo what may seem needless disruption, but as the changes proceed (or perhaps after they have been completed), you could realize that they signaled a necessary unburdening of your time, energy, and psyche in order to allow new growth and evolution in your life. The intense, volcanic changes in your outer life are likely to make you uncomfortably aware of pressures from your subconscious mind as hard-to-control emotions boil to the surface in a seemingly irrational way in the course of your day-to-day life. Psychoanalysis, growth therapy, or similar methods of self-exploration may lessen the stress of this process of personal rebirth. The more you resist the process, trying to forestall the inevitable death and evolution of your innermost essence, the more serious your outer problems are likely to be. Oddly enough, loosening your grip on those things you do not want to let go of in your life is the best way to re-establish some control, and how and when to let go is itself a lesson to be learned now.

Pluto to Natal Sun

The self-promoting, expressive, creative energies normally dominant here begin to take unusual forms, and you may make other people uncomfortable by too publicly giving birth to your new self at a time when those around you would rather tend to more trivial pursuits. However, you shouldn't let yourself be affected by such negative feedback, as if you do not undertake reform of your selfhood consciously now, you could be subject to rather intense experiences, coercion, or at least intense confrontations, which await those who do not willingly undertake a necessary psychic housecleaning. You are likely to have unusual charisma and personal power now, with your true identity manifesting for all to see, and freed from others' expectations. In fact, the honesty with which you are forced to live your life serves to point out to others the illusions under which they live theirs. Relationships with parents can terminate or transform, and in the course of this, the security and comfort of your ego and self-image may be violated. This rather upsetting period, once you have lived through it, serves as the cornerstone of a more aware selfhood and a more realistic self-image.

Pluto to Natal Moon

Your needs for security, family, and home are strongly altered by events and by your own personal growth now. Monumental changes in your relationships with family and security structures are possible, as well as permanent separations from people you held dear. This is an emotionally trying period, as your feelings are deep, and since they are often (at least in your estimation) impossible to share, they could serve to make you isolate yourself from other people. Even when you do open up, as your needs at times seem so exaggerated and impossible to satisfy, their expression becomes overwhelmingly insistent, perhaps frightening off those very people who might offer consolation and security. Powerful emotional experiences serve as a way not only to act out your present needs, but also as a means of expressing long-forgotten injuries that have not been healed over time. It is important not to become fearful in the face of the need to express these very deep feelings and long-stored-up resentments—by learning to act them out you begin to take some power over them, even though at times you may fear they have taken you as hostage. You will emerge from this period better able to create your own self-nurturing environment and more mature in your understanding of your needs, but don't expect the process to be easy, fun, or entirely under your control—people build the best seawalls after the greatest storms.

Pluto to Natal Mercury

As with any transit to the planet of communication, your mental abilities, work, and interests in development of skills and techniques are the focus now, as they undergo profound change and evolution under pressure from the planet of transformation. You may find yourself fascinated by an introduction to a forbiddingly technical and bizarre area of thought, perhaps being motivated to spend hours poring over abstruse formulae or obscure, scholarly sources. Such obsessions parallel your unconscious preparation for a major creative event, as you fertilize your mind now with ideas that will only bear fruit far in the future. This doesn't make it any easier for people to understand you, and this in turn can make you feel isolated and alienated. Rebelling against conventional educational structures, you insist on autonomy in pursuing your interests, but since at the same time you are likely to communicate in an unnecessarily abstract fashion, this is likely to result in your at least feeling restricted in your efforts to explore new intellectual territory. You could be less than graceful in expressing your frustration at the lack of response to your enigmatic utterings, and in contrast to your abstractness in some areas, your sharpened tongue and direct wit seem ever ready to perform psychic surgery on your friendships. While your views in those areas you concern yourself with might be heterodox and difficult for some to understand, nevertheless they are probably correct. Have some confidence in this and try to understand that time will remedy what you can not, which is to say that your points will sink in eventually. On more abstract levels, this period is one of inner, almost alchemical transformation, as you explore the limits of your mind, finding that they are deeper and wider than you thought possible. The result of this understanding can be at least the beginning of true self-transformation, the creation of a new identity.

Pluto to Natal Venus

Radical change and transformation come to you mainly in your romantic and social life, often affecting your material concerns as well. This could represent a watershed time in your understanding of your romantic and affectional nature, as you meet people likely to transform your most firmly-held ideas about relationship, sexuality, and eroticism. "Firsts," "lasts," and "mosts" come to you almost daily in these areas of your life, as you seem to move between extremes of possessiveness, obsession, jealousy, frustration, and sublime ecstasy. Though this zone is usually one of the least stressful you can experience, this is far from true now, as you purposefully put yourself through the most exacting and intense emotional experiences possible. Existing relationships enter a period of cathartic growth and change or else are abandoned as being too shallow for your tastes; artistic expression takes on a more somber and serious hue, with trite and trivial themes discarded for those with more immediate impact, including birth, death, abandonment and isolation. This is perhaps the most powerful period of activity you'll ever encounter in a place characterized by a climate of relationship and pleasure. Don't fight the compulsiveness, intensity, and powerful feelings; though it seems impossible, life will someday return to its humdrum normalcy, leaving you with memories of the ecstatic and a glimpse of the eternal.

Pluto to Natal Mars

This zone is rarely the easiest for most people, so the intensity and depth of the feelings and changes engendered by this transit can be quite trying. Your need to fight for the acceptance of what you believe in and to defend the people and things you care for most is activated by external or internal threats and challenge, and the pace is so hectic that you may at times feel as if you're starring in an action movie. Though you have to deal with destruction and violence on some level, this needn't be personally dangerous if you are willing and able to push your physical and emotional limits to their very limits. The tasks you set for yourself now are formidable, so if you can't (or won't) commit to the course of action you must take, it's better to move away from this zone for a time. Tremendous energy wells up from within you, perhaps saved up from all the contests you ever lost or the other frustrations you ever experienced. Finding a way to direct this energy is your most pressing task, as otherwise you will tend to waste it by being irritable and unpleasant to those around you. Women particularly will find this time difficult if they do not rationally assess the importance and valid place of power and strength in their lives. There is no reason you can't acquire personal power and learn a lot during this period, but be ready for all that is written between the lines above. When it's over, you're ready for a miracle, which you'll have had the energy to create.

Pluto to Natal Jupiter

Few people would willingly miss the excitement and stimulation of this particular transit. The world of mortal creatures is ruled by the law of death and rebirth, which decrees that nothing may endure and that all value must be passed on to others in some form; at this time you may benefit from this universal law, acquiring money or value through inheritance in its broadest sense—anything from a legacy to a promotion occasioned by someone else's death or retirement. Your concept of your place in society undergoes radical change—no longer content to be evaluated by others, you begin to create your own rules and ethics and to live by them. Any form of publication, self-advertisement, even speculation or gambling, can succeed far better now than usual, as this is the aspect of the odds-defying long-shot winner. It's not so bad being an outcast when you're convinced you're better than anyone else, and at times it may be hard to convince yourself otherwise, due to the wealth, influential social connections and other resources that seem to come your way. Expect miracles during this most singular of times in this fortunate area, and even if you can't walk on water, you may meet someone who does.

Pluto to Natal Saturn

This serious transit is likely to make you all too aware of your limits and deficiencies as extraordinary events challenge you in your social and personal life. Depending on your reaction to these challenges, you might remember this year either as the time you first learned just how vulnerable and injury-prone your ego can be, or as the time when you transcended those limitations through personal growth. You may well have to deal with some of the basest of human instincts now, as battles for power, victimization of scapegoats, and the sacrifice of individual rights in order to assuage collective needs (and fears) take place around you, perhaps with you as participant. Your resistance to change and toward the acceptance of some limits to your abilities can only be overcome by conscious effort on your part, though the will for this may not be easy to muster. The things you cling to most tenaciously are the very ones taken away, but despite the many personal burdens being sloughed off around you, you will not be liberated from them until you actually let go of them inside yourself. This process is rarely much fun, but it can at least be made easier if you can cultivate the right attitude toward what is happening. In the end, you come out ahead, even in spite of your own resistance. Like when a diseased tooth is extracted, though the wounds and memories of pain and humiliation won't ever be among your most cherished mental possessions, you can face a new day without the unwanted burdens of the past to hold you back.

Pluto to Natal Uranus

External and social forces seem to conspire to force you into a position of alienated individualism, from which you do battle with the unthinking and unfeeling forces of society. You will almost certainly retain and increase your awareness and consciousness in this process (indeed, you can't afford not to), so that you can go beyond the foolish "rebel without a cause" idealism that can prevail at this location. Still, you should beware of anyone who tries to channel your potent social power for his or her own ends now, and you should heed the inner voice that compels you to strike out on your own, leaving the past behind. Those who cannot accept their own individuality and whose lives do not afford them the opportunity to rebel will probably find themselves surrounded by social chaos and upheaval acted out by others. Change is inevitable now, whether from within or without, so to benefit from this intense transit, you must learn to be the master of it, rather than the recipient. For the young, this may be difficult, as a trivial rebellion and dissatisfaction against parents and authority can distract you from a true course. It's open season on your illusions now, and you can only score extra points if you didn't have any in the first place.

Pluto to Natal Neptune

This transit is an astrological event in the life of everyone born after 1940, occurring typically in the mid-twenties, and represents a time when the myopia of youth gives way to the perceptions of how the world "really" works. Modern media, which have taken over much of the education and socialization done by parents and schools in the past, have never been very honest in their reporting of the disappointing aspects of human nature, so in maturity many of us come to realise that real life is much deeper, more real, and less idealized than it seemed when we were children. A similar transit occurring to people in their mid-sixties is associated with recognition of the disillusionment of our mortality, as the proximity of our own demise becomes pretty obvious by this time. In both types of transit, the death of ideals can be a profound disappointment, yet from this mourning can spring a more realistic and vital world view, allowing you to truly savor life—shadows, imperfections and all—released from the vulnerability created by defending unrealistic expectations. Frequent changes of residence are usually part of this rather long process, but as everyone goes through some form of it at about the same age, it is often easier to deal with than other Plutonian transits.

Pluto to Natal Pluto

Pluto strongly aspecting its own place on a local angle means you will have to deal with mortality—friends or relatives may pass away, or you yourself may have a close shave, reminding you that the ego's illusions of eternal life can't last long when the body in which they are housed is transitory. Much of this process has social overtones—the distribution of wealth and the glorification of the efforts of a few at the expense of the many is a way for society to grant advantage to those whose personalities and talents are needed most by humanity at large. Such criteria change, and people who hold too tightly to beliefs and ideals will find themselves alone in a seemingly hostile world. You will have to surrender some of your beliefs now and even perhaps some of your prestige, power, and financial advantage, as a sacrifice to the times and to the needs of society to adapt. You should find that you have the maturity to accept such change and growth as necessary and can now make plans for your own future security with such knowledge in mind. Life without growth and change lacks vitality and eventually becomes a victim of its own inertia. This period assures that this won't happen to you.

AFTERWORD

About Jim Lewis:
Friend, Teacher, Humanitarian

James Lewis Slayden, known to the astrological world by his business name, Jim Lewis, was born on June 5, 1941 at 9:32 a.m. EDT in Yonkers, New York. He died all too young on February 21, 1995 at 3:33 p.m. PST in San Francisco, California, leaving a public legacy as a key founder of the astrological networking organization AFAN and as the creator of Astro*Carto*Graphy, a complete interpretive system for locality maps based on personal birth charts. His professional legacy can be found in the pages in this book, but also in the minds of those fortunate enough to have been certified through his rigorous training seminars. He left a more personal legacy of caring and generosity that can be found in the hearts of those he helped during his life journey as well as in the ongoing work, both charitable and educational, of Continuum, which is the recipient of funds generated through licensed sales of his products. On the following pages, Madalyn-Hillis Dineen tells her own story of Jim the caring friend and careful teacher, and Angel Thompson and Karen McCauley explain the origin and work of Continuum.

"The Higher Soul That Watches Over It"
Jim Lewis, the Teacher and the Man

As an Astro*Carto*Graphy practitioner certified by Jim Lewis, I know very well that the basic principles of the subject as he taught them are accurately and clearly put forth in the pages of this book. I learned these principles from him in September 1992 when I sponsored a Jim Lewis A*C*G certification workshop in Cranford, New Jersey. The story of how this opportunity arose for me is quite illustrative of who Jim Lewis was as a person. At the time, I was the Executive Secretary of the National Council for Geocosmic Research. That group had in its bylaws a provision that allowed for something called a "null" vote, i.e., members who are opposed to an item may vote against it; those not voting are considered to be in favor of the motion. Jim called my office in response to a proposed bylaw change using this procedure that had been recently announced in the NCGR *memberletter*. He told me that he wanted to register his vote in opposition to the amendment, not because he was opposed to it, but because "he did not function well as a rubber stamp." I thought that was one of the funniest things I had ever heard and told him so. We proceeded to have a wonderfully spirited conversation as you might expect would occur between a Gemini Sun (him) and a Gemini rising (me). I asked Jim when he might offer one of his certification workshops in the East and the next thing I knew, I was organizing one with him!

Jim came East in the late winter/early spring of 1992 and we spent a day or two driving around NJ in my car looking for a suitable venue for our workshop, all the while with him regaling me with hilarious anecdotes about his personal A*C*G experiences. He cheerfully bemoaned the fact that he had popularized an astrological tool that had done him absolutely no good personally—all his good lines were in places where no one could live! He also let me know in no uncertain terms that he considered other locality maps, specifically those that showed the lines for aspects to the angles, to be "ripoffs" and that the information they provided was useless. The basis of A*C*G is the importance of planet angularity and parans, not aspects to angles!

During those drives I also learned about his role in the formation of the Association for Astrological Networking (AFAN) with its non-hierarchal structure, and despite my position with NCGR, he encouraged me to run for the AFAN Steering Committee. Not surprisingly, we also found that we shared similar political views, as we both had a passion for social justice. The time spent with Jim in my car was the beginning of what would become one of the more pivotal encounters for me both professionally and personally. Jim was not only a teacher and mentor; he became a cherished friend.

The workshop that Jim and I organized was a resounding success. In fact, Jim later told me that it made more money than any other single workshop he had ever done and attributed this to his Jupiter conjoining my Saturn. Though I'd like to think that it was our great synastry that made it such a winner, I can't help but wonder if the fact that it had never been done in the East before was also a factor.

All of his workshops had the same format. They began on a Friday evening with Jim giving an introduction to the technique, including the concept of shadowed planets. He was a great teacher who could hold an audience's attention for hours at a time. His legendary conversational ability translated well to the more formal classroom setting.

On Saturday, another astrologer (in our case it was Joan Negus) would give a basic introduction to the meaning of the planets and then the rest of the time was all Jim, and therefore entertaining as well as informative. Jim taught from his own extensive experience with the technique, covering all areas of astrological practice including mundane, political, and personal. He paid special attention to the Mars Cycle chart, a valuable mundane tool often overlooked by many astrologers. At the end of the weekend, those who wished to could apply to take the certification exam. Though this was a take-home test, it was no piece of cake. It was rigorous and challenging but fun, kind of like Jim himself. He corrected the exam on a cassette tape, another bonus and another opportunity to receive pearls of wisdom from him.

It was not long after this workshop that my mother was diagnosed with lung, brain, and bone cancer. Shortly before her death, Jim and I were on an AFAN Steering Committee conference call. Noting that I was particularly sad, Jim called me afterward to see what was wrong. Though some other good friends were on that call, no one except Jim was perceptive enough to know that I needed to talk about the fact that my mother was dying slowly in my living room. We had a memorable conversation about death, and what it meant to die well. Not long after that Jim was diagnosed with a brain tumor, a metastasis from cancer in his lungs.

On the heels of that news, my son had a cerebral aneurysm. As a result, a trip I had planned to visit Jim never materialized though we spoke a number of times during his illness. Toward the end, someone called and told me that it would not be long before Jim would leave us and that Jim was no longer accepting phone calls, though he was listening to the messages on his answering machine. So I steeled myself to make that final goodbye phone call. As I began to leave a message, Jim picked up the phone. I told him that I had not meant to disturb him and that I was told that he was no longer picking up the phone. He said that it was true, but that when he heard my voice he picked up the phone because it would be the last time. And it was.

I heard about Jim's death standing in a giant phone booth in the AT&T

building at Epcot Center in Florida. Actually, the entire phone booth was a phone, and it was so novel that my kids urged me to make a phone call. I decided to call Maggie Meister and Lee Lehman, who were maintaining an 800 number for NCGR in their home, and they told me that Jim had passed. I always thought it ironic that I heard about the death of astrology's great communicator via a larger than life telephone.

You may wonder why I consider Jim to be astrology's great communicator. Sure, he was a wonderful speaker. But, more than that, he was the first person to popularize a technique that went beyond Sun signs to the mass market. In fact, a character on the soap opera *One Life to Live* once mentioned that she was going off to have her Astro*Carto*Graphy map read.

In the 20 years since becoming a certified A*C*G interpreter, I have had the privilege of working with many people on their life's journeys, helping them to find good places on our planet to live, to work, to find love, to vacation and to do business. Though I have gone on to explore other tools for locality astrology, including working with midpoint lines and the lines for the transneptunian planets (but never the dreaded aspect lines that Jim so despised), the principles I learned from Jim Lewis back in 1992 still remain the basis of my work.

The inscription on the certificate presented to those who pass the A*C*G reads *Altior incubuit animus sub imagine mundi*, which is the motto of the Italian Geographic Military Corps. It translates to something like "the world beneath is a reflection of the higher soul that watches over it." For me and many of my colleagues, this principle guides our astrological work, so that we can be an instrument of that higher soul as we try to explain the world beneath to our clients. But, on occasion, when I am feeling most inspired and privileged to do the work that I do, I also like to think that Jim's soul is watching over those of us who learned from him.

Madalyn Hillis-Dineen
Brewster, Massachusetts
April, 2012

A*C*G and Continuum

Jim Lewis prided himself on economizing and living simply, so it was quite a surprise to everyone when he died a rich man. His will specified that most assets were to be divided between his favorite charities, family, and friends, but he was also greatly concerned about the welfare of the astrological community. To that end, Jim's will also directed that all royalties received from his intellectual property, such as the sale of Astro*Carto*Graphy maps and booklets, A*C*G reports, and two books, were to be given to the Association for Astrological Networking (AFAN), an organization he was instrumental in creating.

As one of the driving forces behind the emergence of AFAN, Jim wanted AFAN to be the "Astrologer's Union," the umbrella under which all astrologers would find shelter. His goals for AFAN were lofty: to secure the civil rights of astrologers, decriminalize astrology, advance professionalism, and share its resources with the astrology community. If AFAN no longer existed, violated its bylaws, or had no outstanding financial need, the royalties were then to be given to astrologers as scholarships, grants, donations, and gifts.

When Jim designated Angel Thompson as the trustee to distribute these royalties, it was an honor and a great blessing, but also a tremendous responsibility. AFAN's needs were considered first, but there were, and continue to be, astrologers needing support.

It came to Angel's attention that Jim had trained and certified many Astro*Carto*Graphy practitioners whose work he had promised to promote and support. So in Jim's absence why weren't they coming forward to teach the art, science, and technique of Astro*Carto*Graphy? Before Jim died in 1995, he even lamented having no intellectual heir to carry on his work, but his will made no provisions with regard to the future of Astro*Carto*Graphy itself.

One afternoon, while Angel was brainstorming with her friend and colleague Karen McCauley, an idea emerged: Some of Jim's money could be used to support and promote those practitioners he had trained. On August 1, 1995, at 2:04 p.m., PDT, in Venice, California, Karen proclaimed that the name should be "Continuum," and an organization to continue Jim's work was in business.

First, Angel and Karen contacted all the people Jim had trained and tested to see if they wanted to create a network of A*C*G practitioners. Their enthusiasm gave Angel and Karen the vote of confidence they needed to take the next step.

With the help of Ariel Guttman, coauthor of Jim's first book, *The Astro*Carto*Graphy Book of Maps*, Madalyn Hillis-Dineen, Donna Cunningham, Ken Irving, Gregg Howe, Lawrence Walters, and others, Continuum began its work. The task included:

- transcribing Jim's 1993 training seminar,
- creating and making accessible a curriculum to help those involved in independent study,
- reconstructing and updating Jim's original certification test,
- offering A*C*G proficiency testing and certification,
- maintaining a list of certified practitioners and map distributors,
- creating a website (continuumacg.net) featuring Astro*Carto*Graphy and its certified practitioners, supporters, and location/relocation-related authors and publications.

And of course in accordance with Jim's wishes that the royalties from all his intellectual properties be returned to AFAN and the astrological community, over the past 17 years, Continuum has helped AFAN as well as many individual astrologers for ordinary and extraordinary reasons. Whether the money was needed for study or travel, work or recovery, fun or the future, Continuum did its best to help. Jim always did. We could do no less.

Continuum upholds the ideals to which Jim was committed. Administered as a public service without charge, Continuum has made Astro*Carto*Graphy information available to anyone requesting it. At year end, our bank balance reads "zero" as any monies received have been distributed to the astrological community.

Though Continuum has historically donated money to astrologers in need or who selflessly work for the good of the astrological community, after 15 years of service, our yearly income has been reduced to about 2% of the royalties first received in 1995. Naturally, this has drastically restricted our ability to distribute funds to others. But we have continued to support, through advertising, those individuals who have been trained, tested, and certified as Master Astro*Carto*Graphers. We have also publicized the efforts and training offerings of legitimate practitioners or schools working the time-space field of locational astrology.

While we would like to have a more substantial grant program, to do so we would have to find additional sources of income, as Jim's royalties have dwindled to the point of barely paying for the annual costs of maintaining the website. We are truly at a decision point regarding the viability of Continuum's future. It is worth mentioning that proceeds from sales of this new edition of *The Psychology of Astro*Carto*Graphy* will add to our pool of resources.

Continuum encourages all readers to seek out and network with like-minded people, to share their information without reservation or fear, to help others become proficient in A*C*G or other time-space methods, and finally to remember and acknowledge the philosophy and the products that were the intellectual children of Jim Lewis, a great astrologer, teacher, and friend.

We appreciate Ken Irving and Ronnie Dreyer for educating others about Astro*Carto*Graphy, and applaud their reissue of *The Psychology of Astro*Carto*Graphy*.

Angel Thompson,
Trustee, Jim Lewis Slayden Foundation

Karen McCauley,
Continuum Director

Historical and Technical Notes on Astro*Carto*Graphy

by Kenneth Irving

Though Astro*Carto*Graphy is very much a child of the computer age, the fundamental idea which underlies it, planetary angularity, is perhaps one of the oldest concepts in astrology. In their comprehensive survey of twentieth-century research, *Recent Advances in Natal Astrology*, Geoffrey Dean and Arthur Mather found that though astrologers disagreed widely on many other areas of astrology, from zodiacs to house systems, there was a broad consensus among astrologers both ancient and modern on the view that planets are at their greatest strength when either rising, setting, or at upper or lower culmination (points which astrologers refer to collectively as the "angles" of a birth chart). Though opinions do differ with respect to how far and in which direction these power zones extend from the angles, there seems to be general agreement that an area from five to ten degrees on either side of the angles represents the strongest point in a chart for an individual planet. It is the center of this area, the exact point of astronomical rising, that the planetary lines on the ACG map emphasize.[1]

Before going into the technical aspects of the mapping process used by Jim Lewis, let's take a look at some of the history behind it. This is especially important since various urban legends about the real "inventor" of Astro*Carto*Graphy have come to my attention since the first edition of this book appeared. The most persistent idea is that Jim Lewis was only the popularizer of something invented by others, which is not true. There were definitely precedents to Jim's system, but the core of what he did, as shown in this book, was his own.

Before looking at some of those precedents and considering their relationship to Jim's work, a couple of definitions are necessary:

1. *Locality mapping* – The process of plotting on a geographical map the locations at which a planet will rise, set, or culminate (be on the upper and lower meridian) on a specific day at a specific time. We'll call these the "angular locations." "Locality map" is a general and generic term, as there are various ways of defining rising and setting. The two most important use either the two-dimensional location of the planet (i.e., both its zodiacal longitude and its latitude) or only its zodiacal position (i.e., only its longitude, ignoring its distance above or below the ecliptic). Let's call these a two-dimensional locality map and a zodiacal locality map.

2. *Astro*Carto*Graphy* – A process of plotting a two-dimensional locality map combined with an interpretive system outlining the meaning of each

planet at its angular locations. When this is done for a person, each planet's meaning is always looked at *in the context of the birth chart for the original place of birth.*

That point in italics is extremely important, since even though Astro*Carto*Graphy highlights the planetary lines, it treats the chart for the place of birth as primary. In the literature of locality astrology there have always been two fundamental ways of looking at how a locality change relates to the original birth chart. Usually this comes up in the context not of angularity but of houses and house rulers. If I have Jupiter in my 2nd house at one location and Saturn in that house at another location will I be more generous at the one place and more stingy at the other? If I have a wonderful trine between the ruler of my 2nd house and the ruler of my 10th where I was born, but a square between the two house rulers at a location where the signs on those house cusps are entirely different, will my vocation make we wealthy at one place and poor at another? Questions such as these have absolutely no meaning in Astro*Carto*Graphy, but they are central to some other interpretive systems that use locality mapping. The debate about these two quite different ways of looking at the birth chart is more often implied than explicit, which is why I'm making it explicit here. Not understanding the difference between these two approaches leads to a great deal of confusion, and also can obscure the answers to the three questions we need to answer in order to understand the history behind Astro*Carto*Graphy:

1. Where can we find the first complete locality map?
2. Where do we find the first use of a locality map for a personal birth chart?
3. Where can we find some evidence of the role of the birth chart?

The answers I can give to these questions are limited by my resources at hand, but I think that even someone with a more complete library than mine will come to similar conclusions. Jim Lewis came into astrology through helping an astrologer who was working for the personal service department of *American Astrology* magazine. This department offered typewritten natal interpretations and forecasts that were personally written by a staff of freelance astrologers. Through helping his friend type up his interpretations, Jim became interested in astrology, studied it on his own, and eventually became proficient enough to work for *AA*'s personal service department and to take on personal clients. He developed Astro*Carto*Graphy in the mid 1970s, but during his time working for *American Astrology,* he was probably influenced in his thinking on angularity by exposure to the ideas of Cyril Fagan and fellow sidereaIist Donald Bradley, the latter of whom he was acquainted with personally, though Lewis firmly rejected the sidereal zodiac itself.

Geniuses, Idiots, Houses, and Angularity

Fagan and Bradley used the house structure of the horoscope purely as a means to define a planet's relation to the angles of the birth chart. They did not as a rule use houses to compartmentalize topics of life (e.g., the 6th as the house of health, service, and so on), nor did they use house rulers, or transits or progressions to cusps, or similar devices. Consider the following passage in one of Bradley's earliest published post-sidereal works. Even though the subject is the interpretation of sidereal solar and lunar returns, it very succinctly defines the Fagan-Bradley approach to houses in general:

Considerable differences from the customary approach toward delineating "standard" horoscopes exist where solunar returns are concerned. The student must bear these divergencies from habit in mind at all times until he is thoroughly conditioned to the new plane of thinking to which he has elevated himself. First of all, it is not allowable to think in terms of "house rulerships." The chart is used exclusively in the context of the constellations, thereby voiding any such attempt to use the familiar trick of house rulerships to arrive at a conclusion. Such a ruling as this is certainly welcome, as it greatly simplifies the reading of indications. The natures of the planets are innate and inflexible. Use of the "lords" and "ladies" of the various constellations, as well as their "dignities" and "debilities," is permissible, but not as disposers in the chart.[2]

He goes on to define position relative to the angles, via the concept of angular, succedent, and cadent houses, as the fundamental means of determining the "power and importance" of a planet in the return, and then continues:

...All transits are referred to the nativity equated to the locality rather than to the birthplace, unless no change of residence or position has taken place. The "reading" of the birth chart, of course, remains indelible, but so far as transits of the planets are concerned, the cusps of the locality-chart houses are those used to evaluate the effects of transitive indications...

His reference to house cusps has to be taken within the context of his previous use of the house structure as a means of defining angularity, something further emphasized by his preference for the Campanus system, which is based on an astronomical division of the celestial sphere. What Bradley does here is to define a particular view toward angularity, locality, and the "indelible" nature of the birth chart that is very close to what we see in Astro*Carto*Graphy.

This was published in 1948, and several years later, writing in the 1958 *American Astrology Digest* (which would have been published in the fall of

1957), he added a second important ingredient, possibly the first complete mapping of angular planetary lines, complete in the sense of including all of the standard bodies used at that time–Sun and Moon, plus the planets Mercury through Pluto. This was a polar projection for the northern hemisphere showing the positions of all bodies at the time of the solar ingress into sidereal Capricorn, or the "Capsolar" as he styled it. Fourteen similar U.S. maps for the monthly "Caplunar" were also shown.

Again, Bradley was considering only transits, and this time without the involvement of a birth chart, but between the principles laid down in *Solar and Lunar Returns* (and followed in his subsequent columns and articles in *American Astrology*), and these maps we have the basic elements of Astro*Carto*Graphy. The next step came from Cyril Fagan, writing in his "Solunars" column in 1966, but before we get to that, let's consider a statement which long precedes the writings of Bradley and Fagan that we're quoting here, but which clarifies a fundamental idea about the importance of the birth chart itself. This is from Edward L. Johndro, writing in 1929:

...Broadly speaking, genius is genius anywhere; an idiot remains an idiot in any retreat. But these anomalies are the exception, not the rule. The average person is susceptible to the forces of improvement and detriment.

What is meant by a suitable location is one wherein the best promise of the nativity is the most intensified and the detrimental qualities are the most minimized. If the individual's planets–his scheme of "plan its"–are all favorably placed and rayed, which is rarely indeed the case, it is still possible to amplify their effects in one location and suppress them in another and so enlarge or limit his success. If the planetary couplings are most adverse it is still generally possible, except of the hopelessly foolish, idiotic or criminal, to change the relative intensity of different qualities in such a manner as to modify the life tendencies. In the average horoscope, however, there is found such an admixture of good and detrimental qualities that the problem becomes one of calculating a place where the good is brought out and the ill suppressed.[3]

Now with that in mind, consider the following from the January and February 1966 installments of Fagan's "Solunars" column in *American Astrology*. This is probably the first description of the application of locality mapping to a personal birth chart. Fagan is considering the problem of a young woman born June 29, 1940, 9:15 a.m. GMT, 31N35, 105W50:

. . . Should this unhappy girl wish to remedy matters, she should remove sufficiently far away from her place of birth to put her Sun and Venus on the Midheaven; she will then know fame and happiness.

In such cases as this, it is usual for the wise astrologer to recommend that the native (i.e., the owner of the horoscope) should remove sufficiently far away from the place of birth to throw the offending planets into the inactive places and bring the benefics, principally the greater benefic Jupiter, onto an angle. It is well to search for a suitable location whereby any or all of the benefic planets will be brought, by a serious application of science, to one or the other of the four angles . . . But in this instance we are precluded from using the good offices of the natal Jupiter for, as our Hindu brethren would aver, ". . . it is under check . . ." being at birth in conjunction with the greater malefic, Saturn, and not far removed from the Moon itself, the prime significator of her aberrations. So to bring Jupiter to any of the angles, we would also be bringing Saturn and the Moon right into the foreground thus intensifying the trouble and defeating our purpose. It is not always a simple matter to place oneself in a benefic location.

Up to this point he is simply outlining a particular approach to locality astrology that reflects the attitudes and definitions shown in Bradley, and which in any case may have been practiced by others before and since, though using a simple recalculation of a horoscope wheel for a new place of residence. Fagan is, however, considering how to balance the idea of angular benefics against the simple exigencies of either not coming up with a place that is perhaps in the middle of the ocean, or otherwise in hostile territory, or which combines a benefic on one angle with an undesirable planet in another. He then suggests:

The reader should procure a large scale map of the world and of the U.S.A. on Mercator's projection. Having put a small pencil mark on them against the geographical coordinates tabulated below [table omitted here - KI] and joining them by a pencil line he will find that he has a gentle curve revealing all the places between latitude North and South 60°, when Venus or the Sun rose and set at the precise moment of the native's birth; thus enabling her to pick a suitable locality wherein to live; with Venus or the Sun, as she wishes, on the Ascendant or Descendant of her "Locality Chart"; preferably on the Ascendant. For instance, the above tabulation informs us that Venus, at the moment of the native's birth was rising in Latitude N 40° and Longitude W 75°09', which is pretty close to Philadelphia, PA! As Venus enjoys 3°18' of south latitude, the solar and Venusian curves will not lie parallel to one another.

The paragraph following this explains that since the rise and set times given in tables accompanying his discussion are from *The American Ephemeris and Nautical Almanac*, they are for apparent times of these phenomena, as corrected for refraction, etc., and where sunrise, for example, is the first appearance of the cusp of the Sun's disk, as opposed to its center, above the horizon. Fagan notes that proper astrological methodology requires calculation of rise and set geocentrically, and not topocentrically.

So at this point it should be clear that all of the fundamental principles necessary for Astro*Carto*Graphy are in place, including its astronomical basis, the fundamental nature of the birth chart, the use of locality to bring out the desirable qualities of the birth chart while avoiding the undesirable, and the use of locality mapping as an aid to the process. One missing ingredient in what we've looked at so far, the use of a computer to plot the lines and draw the maps, is actually the least important. In fact, when Jim Lewis began to sell his maps and interpretations, all of his calculations were done by hand, and all of his maps were hand-drawn using drafting instruments. It wasn't until 1977 or 1978, several years into his venture, that he teamed with Gregg Howe, of Astro Numeric Service, to provide computerized maps. However, the first computerized map showing planetary lines was likely published in Llewellyn's *Moon Sign Book* for 1966, in a mundane prediction article by Gary Duncan (Neil Block).

Our Questions Answered

All of this would make an interesting book in itself, but in order to get on to some technical matters underlying Astro*Carto*Graphy, we can summarize by saying that during the 20th century the idea that changing locality is a means of changing the *emphasis* on various elements of the birth chart, *but not of changing the birth chart itself,* was a common one for which it is probably difficult to find an origin point. It is a concept that would come easily to a technical astrologer such as Johndro, Bradley, or Fagan. The related idea, that the natal chart is still of primary importance when relocating is a logical necessity, and is often found as a corollary in locality writing.

Where the use of locality mapping is concerned:

- Bradley seems to have priority for the actual technique of mapping the angularity lines of charted planets (i.e., all of those included in a standard horoscope of the time) in order to extend the scope of the chart beyond a single location. Bradley and others who published maps after him (notably Firebrace[4] and Duncan) used the technique solely for mundane work.
- Duncan probably has priority for producing a computerized locality map, though as with Bradley he applied it to mundane, not natal, astrology.
- Fagan has priority for outlining how to apply the mapping technique to natal astrology.

So where does this leave Jim Lewis? Very simply, he has priority for the development of an actual interpretive system, as well as for working out many of the practical problems of the relationship between the fixed birth chart and the fluid picture of a world map of planetary lines. This is an important distinction, because what Jim did required substantial and sustained effort, and it included solving a variety of problems beyond how to plot lines on a map. So dismissing him as a mere popularizer of work done by others is far from the truth. There is a vast difference between the passages quoted above and the work outlined in this book.

Though Bradley apparently pioneered the mapping technique mundane use, and Fagan outlined its application for natal work, nothing comparable to Jim Lewis' original articles on the subject, let alone the comprehensive system he derived from this simple idea, seems to exist in astrological literature before his time. The reader bombarded by an ever-growing number of locality mapping software and interpreters should keep this fact in mind, and should also be aware that very likely none of these products would be available today had Lewis himself not had the energy and pertinacity to develop and learn the subject by drawing such maps by hand, both for his own studies and for client work, for several years before the process was finally computerized. More than that, he carefully considered the ramifications of the relationship between the locality map and the birth chart, both astrologically and philosophically, and developed an interpretive framework that combined the two.

The Mathematics of Locality Mapping

Technically, the culminating (MH) lines on an ACG map represent those places on the earth at which, for a given Greenwich Mean Time, the sidereal time equals the planet's right ascension; the anti-culminating (IC) lines on a map are those places at which the sidereal time equals the planet's right ascension ± 180 degrees. The MH and IC lines are the same for all latitudes from pole to pole, but the rising and setting lines vary from latitude to latitude, based on a standard equation:

ST rise = RA + SA
ST set = RA - SA

where ST indicates sidereal time, RA indicates the planet's right ascension and SA is the planet's "diurnal semi-arc" for a given latitude, derived from the equation:

cos SA = -tan lat x tan dec

with "lat" representing the latitude of the place (positive for the northern hemisphere, negative for the southern), and "dec" indicating the planet's declination; and "cos" and "tan" indicating cosine and tangent. A full ACG calculation plots a planetary line as a set of points from the equator to the planet's colatitude north or south. It does not use astronomical variables such as refraction or dip of the horizon. A careful look at an ACG map can be very instructional, so the reader is invited to examine those in this book and note the following:

- at the equator, rising and setting lines are always exactly 90° on either side of the MH and IC lines.

- the rising and setting lines "peak" at high latitudes. In fact, this happens at the colatitude of a planet, which is found by subtracting the declination from 90°.

This means that each rise/set "line" is actually a continuous, symmetrical curve showing those places around the globe at which a planet is found on the horizon, with the height of that curve (i.e., the distance of its highest point from the equator) equal to the co-latitude for the body in question. Though little interpretive significance can be attached to any of these facts, being aware of them does help to give a general sense that the lines we concern ourselves with on an ACG map are actually part of a larger whole.

The important idea of latitude crossings in Astro*Carto*Graphy may also have originated from Lewis' awareness of Fagan's writings. In a chart drawn for a particular location, these crossings (which are found at latitudes at which any combination of the angular lines of two planets intersect) would be called "paranatellonta," or paran for short, a Greek term popularized by Fagan, which he defined as the simultaneous appearance of two planets or fixed stars on angles of a chart. The paran is much used by Western siderealists, and it is usually interpreted by those who use it as a neutral aspect that simply blends the natures of the two planets. More often than not in regular chart interpretation, a paran is considered to be potential more than actual, as the relationship is thought to be there even when the two planets are not actually on angles at the time of the chart. In other words, what is important is the fact that the two planets *could* be simultaneously on angles at some future date or some other place were the chart either rotated diurnally or viewed from another locale than the birth place.

However, as Lewis used them in the world map setting of Astro*Carto*Graphy, parans are considered to be "actual" in their effect all along the entire latitude at which the lines cross, with an orb on either side of that latitude as well. Crossings are not considered to be quite as strong as the rising, setting, and culminating lines themselves. Thus, underlying the lines plotted on an ACG map is an invisible web of crossings which can be used to enhance the interpretation. This web of connections should not be overemphasized, however, as the core of Astro*Carto*Graphy interpretation is still the focus on those places where rising, setting, and culminating occur.

What orbs to use for these lines—an important consideration—was worked out empirically by Jim Lewis, both through personal observation and by considering feedback from Astro*Carto*Graphy clients. The following orbs were applied:

- natal rise, set, MC, and IC lines: 4-7°
- line crossings: 1-2°
- progressed "Cyclo*Carto*Graphy" rise, set, MC, and IC lines: ±4° alone, exact when contacting natal lines

HISTORICAL AND TECHNICAL NOTES

Aspects, Synastry, and Gauquelin Sectors

A whole range of more advanced techniques is possible with Astro*Carto*Graphy, and in fact anything that can be done with one or more charts can also be done with an ACG map, as long as it can be expressed within the two coordinates of right ascension and declination. Some things astrologers do with their charts are not so easy to apply in this setting, however. One example of a traditional chart tool that cannot be used with an ACG map is standard aspects, as these do not translate easily into this frame of reference. Aspects, after all, are measured along the ecliptic, in the single dimension of longitude, while the planetary lines of Astro*Carto*Graphy are mapped out through the use of two entirely different coordinates related to the celestial equator. A planet's location in right ascension and declination can be translated mathematically into ecliptic terms, but it still requires two dimensions—both longitude and latitude. In order to ponder on how different a one-dimensional aspect is from a two-dimensional aspect, the reader might consider that, if we allow an orb of one degree (pretty tight by astrological standards), Montreal, at 73W34, could be considered as "conjunct" New York (73W57) in geographic longitude. On the other hand, as we can see from a map, the two cities are separated by nearly five degrees of latitude (45N31) versus 40N45) and a great distance in miles.

The closest analogue to ecliptic aspects that can be seen on an ACG map would be the conjunction and the opposition, as any two planets found on either the Midheaven or IC on a map are in a conjunction in right ascension, and would probably be found within orb of a conjunction in longitude in a horoscope for the birth place as well. The same could be said of pairs of planets in which one was on the Midheaven and the other on the IC, which would probably put them within orb of an opposition in longitude in a regular birth chart. However, the "mundane square" which is seen at those locations where Midheaven/IC lines cross rise/set lines, might appear as anything from a conjunction to a square (or no aspect at all) when only longitude is looked at, as in a standard birth chart. Though it is certainly possible to consider planetary positions on a map in terms of longitudes only (and thus, for example, to find a place on earth that might be sextile in longitude to a particular natal planet), it becomes a very complicated matter to represent visually, and also becomes something entirely different from Astro*Carto*Graphy itself. In other words, while all things may be possible astrologically, or map-wise, this does not mean they are either right or necessary.

One largely unexplored use of Astro*Carto*Graphy is that of synastry. In an era when it has become more or less commonplace for people to relocate several times in a life, most of us are likely to have observed the differing effects a change in location often seems to have on two individuals.

People who fall in love and marry in one place may divorce in another, and the reason for the change often can't be traced to obvious local factors such as the climate or the local culture. People change and drift apart, so the conventional wisdom goes, and that is often seen as the end of it. Astrologically, however, one reason for that change could be that some new and perhaps contradictory facets of the individuals in question have been emphasized at the new locality, or perhaps that the underlying dynamics of the synastric contacts have changed.

In considering this and other possibilities, we can look at pairs of ACG maps in either of the following two ways:

1. As two separate charts, by considering the differences in angular planets, line crossings and so forth for each individual between the place of meeting and the place of relocation.

2. Viewing each map's relation to the other in the same way that transits or progressions to a natal map might be viewed in Cyclo*Carto*Graphy.

The first is analogous to casting two standard locality charts and treating them synastrically, and the kinds of contrasts possible in this case should be obvious. For example, suppose a person whose natal chart has Jupiter rising at the place of birth should move to a place at which Saturn is rising and Jupiter is moved far away from the angles. With such an obvious change, the emphasis in both personality and life interests would shift in a noticeable way, with a person who might tend to be on the cheery side becoming more circumspect, and someone who had before sought to associate himself with "the best" in a social sense perhaps becoming more oriented toward authority figures, generally emphasizing power more than social concerns. No matter what the particulars, the contrast between Jupiter and Saturn is such that, all other things being equal, over time this person would change quite a bit in the new locality. Given this, it wouldn't be too much to suppose that a spouse or lover whose chart showed a strong attraction to Jupiter types would tend to be more easily attracted to this person at the Jupiter location than at the Saturn location. A strong bond formed under Jupiter could well last under Saturn, but the nature of the relationship would change. Adjustment would be demanded on both sides, and if either partner couldn't manage this, the relationship itself might begin to falter.

More interesting is a second possibility, which can be looked at fairly easily for a single locality with the "bi-wheel" option on most computer programs—using one chart's planets and house cusps as base chart, with the second chart added in an outer wheel for comparison. When done as an ACG map, the second chart would simply be set for the same sidereal time at Greenwich as the chart it was to be compared with. As an example, consider someone whose natal Venus happens to be conjunct the local Ascendant of someone else, perhaps in a place where both are attending school. Under this classical romance and marriage contact, passions might be fired, and as long as the two remain in the area and the changes brought about by transits and progressions are not too demanding, they should experience a nice time together. On the other hand, suppose they move a great distance to a place at which the Venus person's Saturn is now on the other's Ascendant. Though certain Saturn contacts can be helpful for marriage, Saturn in one person's chart to the lights or angles of the other could easily make the relationship seem a dead bore to the person receiving the Saturn contact, who will very likely also feel himself or herself under heavy pressure from the Saturn person much of the time. At the very least this would make for some problems in the relationship.

More interesting than simple contacts of a planet in one person's chart to another's local angles is the situation in which we consider the complete astrological context of the planet in question, including sign, house position, and aspects. For example, what might be the effect in the example just given if Saturn happened to be a shadowed planet in the second person's chart? In this case, that second person might feel the contact in the same way as a transit of the shadowed Saturn, so that far from simple boredom and restriction, she (using the feminine for the sake of the example) might find that interaction with the first person at this new location now calls up demons from the depths of her psyche, forcing her to face issues in her life and personality that she might rather avoid. Here, while the strongest of relationships could manage to survive and grow, the weakest would surely be in danger of failing, unless the person being transited happens to be just at the proper stage in life to benefit from his or her shadowed planet being brought out into the open. There is a rich field here to be mined for those ready to explore it.

As one final interesting future application of Astro*Carto*Graphy, consider the connection often noted by Jim Lewis between the fundamental premise of his creation and the work of Michel and Francoise Gauquelin. Though Lewis had developed standard "orbs" to use in gaging the effect of planetary lines, the work of the Gauquelins suggests that their statistically derived definition of the angular "power zones" might be used with Astro*Carto*Graphy. A precise definition of these zones takes into account the daily motion of fast-moving planets, but it is an allowable approximation to use the planets' positions at the time of birth only, as we do in both standard birth charts and in ACG maps. If we applied this to a set of lines for an individual planet, it would bring about two major changes in the orbs usually used in ACG work. First of all, the orb would encompass a small area to the west of the line in question and take in a larger area (about three times as large) to the east of the line. Secondly, the orbs for locations where a planet either rose or set would vary with latitude, taking in a greater geographic distance at the equator and a smaller distance in higher latitudes, with the orb for a rise/set line reaching a mathematical vanishing point at the colatitude, the place at which the rise/set line crosses either the Midheaven or IC line. Interpretation in this case would depend less on the elements of standard astrology used in ACG work (such as the differing meanings of each of the angles) and more on a pure blend of the planet's natures.

In such suggested extensions of Astro*Carto*Graphy as these, and in other extensions that might be suggested in the future, the main thing to keep in mind is that the planets (and the planets in two dimensions, not simply ecliptic longitude) should remain central to whatever is proposed. Though Astro*Carto*Graphy has gained the astrological world's attention through the appeal and beauty of its maps, and through its promotion of the idea that we are not limited to our birthplace, its real core is the planets. In that sense, while Jim Lewis' appealing idea has provided us with new vistas, it has also taken us back to basics, back to the planets that are the heart of astrology.

NOTES

All notes and comments are by Kenneth Irving

CHAPTER 1: Space and Time in the Horoscope

1. Noon and midnight are meant to indicate direction only, and thus the quotes. Noon or midnight as times only coincide precisely with upper or lower culmination twice a year.
2. See for example Michel Gauquelin, *Neo-Astrology, A Copernican Revolution,* (London: Penguin Arkana, 1991). Chapter 2 is particularly pertinent in the case of angularity. Françoise Gauquelin's *Psychology of the Planets* makes the case for the connection between personality and the original Gauquelin findings.
3. This abbreviation for Astro*Carto*Graphy will be used at times for the full trademarked term throughout the book, mainly as a way of aiding readability.
4. In preparing the first edition, I couldn't find a source for this, which appeared in quotes in Jim's original. It may refer to the following widely quoted statement from Jung's autobiography: "My life is a story of the self-realization of the unconscious. Everything in the unconscious seeks outward manifestation, and the personality too desires to evolve out of its unconscious conditions and to experience itself as a whole."
This is from page 3 of Jung's *Memories, Dreams, Reflections,* recorded and edited by Aniela Jaffe Collins (New York: Pantheon Books, 1963).
5. From Jung's "Christ, A Symbol of the Self," Chapter V in *Aion, Researches into the Phenomonology of the Self* (*Collected Works* 9ii, paragraph 126): "The psychological rule says that when an inner situation is not made conscious, it happens outside, as fate. That is to say, when the individual remains undivided and does not become conscious of his inner opposite, the world must perforce act out the conflict and be torn into opposing halves."
6. Robert Bly, *A Little Book on the Human Shadow,* page 20 (San Francisco: Element Books, 1988).
7. January 5, 1893, 8:38 p.m. LMT, Gorakhpur, India. Data from *The American Book of Charts.* (San Diego: Astro Computing Services, 1980). Astrodatabank. com's source notes: "*Mercury Hour,* 7/1976, quotes his ashram, the Self Realization Institute."
8. May 29, 1917, 3:00 p.m. EST, Brookline, Massachusetts. From mother, according to Blackwell Database. Astrodatabank notes same data found on page 274 of Doris Kearns Goodwin's *The Fitzgeralds and the Kennedys* (New York: Simon & Schuster, 1984). In publications and lectures Jim may have used a rectified time of 3:17 p.m. EST (making the Pluto line run precisely through Dallas), but the 3:00 p.m. time of record is used in this book.
9. July 26, 1875, Kesswil, Switzerland. According to Blackwell, either Jung or his daughter gave various local times from 7:20 to 7:32 p.m. LMT, around sunset.
10. See Note 1, Chapter 5, "Winds of Neptune, Fires of Mars," for data and sources on Jones.
11. These remarks are true for a birth time of February 27, 1932, 7:56 p.m. BST, London. Neither this nor any of several alternative times seems very reliable.
12. This facetious remark refers not to a Mars line for a timed birth, but rather the primary focus of Reagan's presidency, the Cold War, with its multiple fronts. At the time the first edition of the book was put together, in 1995 and

1996, Reagan's birth time was widely disputed, with several astrological sources claiming knowledge of quite different times, all supposedly from Reagan himself, or from sources close to him. However, according to Reagan's chosen biographer (Edmund Morris in *Dutch: A Memoir of Ronald Reagan*, published in 1999), his birth certificate indicates he was born February 6, 1911 at 4:16 a.m. CST in Tampico, Illinois.

A typical reaction by critics to Morris' book is found in *New York Times* reviewer Michiko Kakutani's characterization of it (October 2, 1999) not so much as a biography, but rather a "...loony hodgepodge of fact and fiction..." and a "...cloying, egocentric novel...." Following that same line of thinking, astrologers tend to mistrust what is supposedly a recorded time, but a map based on it shows Reagan's rising Mars and setting Pluto lines 125 miles west and 116 miles east of Moscow, respectively.

CHAPTER 2: Lines and Crossings

1. The cross-indexed archives of these personal testimonies collected by Jim are for the present stored with a small library of his personal papers available for researchers to use, by appointment. Their current location at the time of publication was at Astro Numeric Service (www.astronumerics.com) in Ashland, Oregon, though this may change in the future.

2. Orbs in Astro*Carto*Graphy are no different than orbs in any other area of astrology—they are a range of values determined mainly by experience. In the original edition, the orbs were specified in part as inches on a standard Astro*Carto*Graphy map (still available from Astro Numeric Service in Ashland, Oregon at astronumerics.com), but these have been replaced here by units more applicable to modern mapping software. On a printed map, the relationship between miles and inches depends on the size of the map, and the projection used. Mapping software such as Esoteric Technologies' Solar Maps (used to check both this and the first edition) compensates automatically for these factors.

CHAPTER 3: Shadowed Planets: Stages of Psychological Growth

1. See note 5 in Chapter 1.

2. The four stages shown in Table 1 combined with the occurrence of "unaspected planet" in Table 2 brings out an interesting relationship between Jim's "shadowed planet" and Robert Couteau's "transcendental," or least-aspected planet. An unaspected planet is of course the extreme case of a planet that has the fewest aspects in a given chart. Jim's concept emphasizes the two more negative early stages of a planet's emergence, as traveling unprepared to a shadowed planet's angular lines can cause grief, while Couteau's concept seems to relate to the more positive third and fourth stages. Couteau found in studying the relationship between location and success that "...the planet corresponding to the key location was the least aspected planet in that person's birth chart: the planet with the smallest number of significant angular relationships (or special positions in stellar degree traditionally deemed meaningful) with the other planets." My observation here is greatly simplified, as both theories are much more complex, but the seeming relationship between the two deserves further study. For Couteau's work, see "The Role of the Least Aspected Planet in Astrocartography" at www.dominantstar.com/as_intro.htm.

3. "Singleton" is a term apparently originated by Marc Edmund Jones, and probably first defined in his book *The Guide to Horoscope Interpretation.* It is used to denote a planet isolated in one hemisphere of a chart (east-west or north-south), with the rest of the planets in the opposite hemisphere. As Jones says: "The singleton is a focal determinator, indicating a special capacity or a gift for some particularly effective kind of activity." Assumed in Jones' definition is the use of a house system that was probably Placidus. Whether a planet is a singleton or not under Jones' definition obviously depends on which planets (major or minor) one uses, as well as which house system. Modern usage has extended singleton to mean a planet isolated from others in a variety of ways, including zodiacal hemisphere, element, or quality. Jim's usage would likely have been closest to Jones' definition, though I haven't found any exact confirmation of this.

4. Some of the most interesting (and most notorious) examples in subsequent chapters involve a shadowed Mars in a man's chart that is angular at a location associated with decidedly "unmeek" events. One can of course find many perfectly gentle and well-balanced people living at a place where a shadowed Mars is on an angle, again bringing us back to the difference in emphasis on the four stages between Lewis and Couteau.

CHAPTER 4: Grace's Saturnian Journey

1. Grace's story was included in the book at her suggestion and with Jim's enthusiastic concurrence not only because it so clearly illustrates the basic points made in the earlier chapters, but also because it shows the part locality plays in the context of the whole chart, along with transits, progressions, and relationships.

CHAPTER 5: Winds of Neptune, Fires of Mars

1. Jim Jones was born May 13, 1931, 10:00 p.m. CST in Lynn, Indiana. This data was originally from "news sources," but according to Astrodatabank.com, it has since been confirmed over the phone for writer and astrologer Frank Clifford by the registrar. In this chapter, the section on Jim Jones is based on an article by Jim in *Dell Horoscope*, while the section on Harvey Milk and Dan White was largely written by me based on research inspired by a very brief rendering of the basic scenario given either personally by Jim to myself or in lectures. Jim may have given a fuller rendering of the case, though I was unable to find it while working on the book originally, nor have I come across it since then. When writing this chapter, at first I thought the observations on Dan White and Harvey Milk would be no more than a footnote referencing Jim's basic observations. However, with the two events so close in time, so obviously connected to the Mars-Neptune conjunction and to San Francisco, the chapter wouldn't be complete without something more substantial. As it turned out, the Milk-White tragedy is one of those cases that becomes more fascinating the longer one looks at it, which is why the intended footnote expanded to what you see here.

2. Quite close in time to the release of the first edition of this book, a horrible string of murders (some involving the most gruesome kind of torture) left by spree killer Andrew Cunanan along his Mars Descendant line from April 27 to July 23, 1997 drove home this point about the problematic nature of Mars and Neptune. At the time of Cunanan's birth on August 31, 1969, at 9:41 p.m. PDT in National City, California (source: his birth certificate obtained by Lois Rodden,

according to astrodatabank.com), Mars was precisely setting along a line that sliced within less than a degree to the east of Minneapolis, where his spree began, within less than a degree to the west of Chicago, his next stop, and to within about three degrees east of Miami Beach, where his string of murders ended with the mob-style gunning down of designer Gianni Versace, after which Cunanan killed himself. His only deviation from the Mars line occurred when he killed a man in New Jersey in order to steal his truck. Interestingly, Cunanan shows a Mars-Neptune pattern similar to Jones, with Mars in the 8th and Neptune in the 7th in Placidus. Mars' only aspect is to the nodes, and Neptune's only aspect is to Pluto.

It would be easy to list many more very similar cases, but perhaps it would be wise at this point to adapt a phrase from the legal profession to point out that "good cases make bad astrology." Astrology's malefics can produce very distinct events that often are highly publicized, so it becomes very easy to pile up examples of bad people doing bad things, thus losing sight of what good people with similar configurations do.

3. In regard to Neptune, consider another case that took place when the first edition was in press, a mass suicide instigated by someone who was almost an astrological twin of Jim Jones. This was the March 1997 mass suicide of the "Heaven's Gate" cult headed by Marshall Herff Applewhite. Applewhite himself was born May 17, 1931, 3:20 a.m. CST in Spur, Texas according to his birth certificate, and his cult was dedicated to the idea that earth was doomed and that the believing elect would be called away to a spaceship where they would live a new life, free of their earthly origins. His birth data puts Neptune on the Descendant 3°49' West of San Diego, where the mass suicide took place. In Applewhite's case, angular Mars was not the linchpin, but rather Neptune, indicating that Neptune is not simply a catalyst to such incidents, but possibly an equal player with Mars. In fact, though there is an old astrological saw that makes Neptune a so-called higher octave of Venus, there is at least an equal argument to be made that it is more closely related to Mars.

4. Jim (Lewis) once unknowingly visited one of these Sun-Mars intersections in his own map, and one evening was chased through the streets by a lunatic waving a knife. While this did not make international headlines, he never made any effort to return to that location!

5. Quoted in Randy Shilts, *The Mayor of Castro Street, The Life and Times of Harvey Milk* (New York: St. Martin's Press, 1982). Other direct quotations relating to Milk and White are also from this book. Protagonist Milk was born May 22, 1930 at 1:30 a.m. EDT in Woodmere, New York (data directly from Milk to astrologer Jack Fertig, quoted by astrodatabank.com)); according to his birth certificate, antagonist White was born September 2, 1946 at 8:13 a.m. PST in Bellflower, California.

6. Mayor Moscone was born November 24, 1929, 4:00 a.m. PST, San Francisco. Birth certificate, according to Blackwell.

7. See note 9 below.

8. Jeff Mayo, *Astrology: A Key to Personality*, Penguin Arkana, 1995, pp. 110 and 119.

9. Since the first edition, I've found more detailed accounts of White and his defense which make it clear that the point about his consumption of junk food, introduced by expert witness psychiatrist Martin Binder, was actually a minor part of a "diminished capacity" defense. Binder contended that since White stuffing himself with junk food before the murders was a drastic departure from his

normal behavior it was an indication that he was suffering from depression—a symptom rather than a cause, in other words. Possibly under questioning from the prosecutor, Binder apparently allowed that the junk food itself could have in turn further eroded White's already fragile psychological state, but this is about as close as he came to the popularized version of the "Twinkie Defense."

Also, despite the noisy (and often misinformed) journalistic derision for this aspect of the defense, prosecutorial mistakes may have played at least as much of a role in White's light sentence as anything the defense did. For one thing, the prosecution played a tape of White's sobbing confession in order to make it clear that he had done the deed, but as many jurors found White's apparently remorseful confession heart-rending, the tactic backfired.

The prosecution's failure was all the more tragic in light of a confession White may have made to a former colleague, San Francisco homicide inspector Frank Falzon, after being paroled. In an article by Mike Weis in the *San Jose Mercury*, of September 17, 1998, Falzon quotes White as saying, "I was on a mission. I wanted four of them. Carol Ruth Silver, she was the biggest snake . . . and Willie Brown, he was masterminding the whole thing."

So though the story of White's act and his ensuing defense may be a little more complicated than the simplified version of the Twinkie defense given in this chapter, the judgment of assassin Dan White as a moral coward and a hypocrite certainly stands. Having discussed this incident with Jim occasionally from the time of the assassination through Dan White's suicide, I think it safe to say that his judgment of White (not to mention those involved in the prosecution) was far less generous than mine.

10. At sundown for Jonestown, Mars was at 17°24' Sagittarius and Neptune at 17°29' Sagittarius, while on the date of the assassination in San Francisco they were at 18°48' and 17°33' Sagittarius, respectively.

CHAPTER 6: War Lines across the World

1. July 4, 1872, 9 a.m. LMT, Plymouth, Vermont. Data from father, according to *Modern Astrology*, cited by Blackwell.

2. January 30, 1882, 8:45 a.m. LMT, Hyde Park, New York. From his father's diary, cited in biography *Gracious Lady: The Life of Sara Delano Roosevelt* as saying "at a quarter to nine my Sallie had a splendid large baby boy."

3. August 11, 1874 at 12:00 a.m. LMT, West Branch, Iowa, from Blackwell from David Burner's *Herbert Hoover, A Public Life*, based on records in Friends Church, West Branch. Date contradicts August 10th, which is cited in many other sources.

4. October 1, 1924, 7:00 a.m. CST, Plains, Georgia. Birth certificate referenced by various sources, according to Blackwell, and confirmed by astrodatbank.com.

5. May 8, 1884, 4 p.m. CST, Lamar, Missouri, from family sources. Blackwell. Confirmed by biographer Richard Lawrence Miller in *Truman: The Rise to Power*, page 3, quoted on astrodatabank.com: "He greeted the world from his mother's bedroom at 4:00 p.m."

6. See note 8 to Chapter 1.

7. August 27, 1908, at about 5:45 a.m. CST, near Stonewall, Texas. Time based on "daybreak" in his mother's diary and as "sunrise" in the family Bible according to Blackwell. Astrodatbank.com says Hye, Texas is recorded on his birth certificate, with no time. The difference in location is not material as the two towns and the ranch where he was actually born are within a few miles and

a few minutes of arc of each other.

8. January 9, 1913, 9:35 p.m. PST, Fullerton Township, California. Recorded by attending nurse. Photo of birth record shown in Henry D. Spalding, *The Nixon Nobody Knows*, cited by Blackwell. Modern references cite Nixon's birthplace as Yorba Linda, but this city, which does include the home where Nixon was born, was incorporated after the family had left.

9. July 14, 1913, 12:43 a.m. CST, Omaha, Nebraska. From Ford's "baby book," according to *Fowler's Compendium*, as well as communication from First Lady's press office to Stephen Erlewine, according to Blackwell.

10. Jim used Carter's Mars lines to time the troubles of his administration, first in "Astrology Predicts the Next Likely War Zones" in the July 1978 issue of *Dell Horoscope* and then in "America at War in 1980?" in the April 1980 issue of *American Astrology*. In the first article he singled out Iran as a likely trouble spot and in the second said: "Mars, which turned retrograde in January, in close square to Carter's Jupiter (Mars Jupiter again), April 7th, makes its direct station in exact opposition to Carter's Mars (1' of arc orb). Considering the previous stress on the President's Mars—a solar eclipse, the station of Uranus, as well as its involvement with the US and the other relevant charts—this looks ominously militant in nature. It is probably the final stage of the crisis (though these aspects repeat, in lesser force, in July and November of this year), one marked by considerable tension, and perhaps military involvement." On April 7th, the United States cut diplomatic ties and imposed economic sanctions on Iran; on April 17th, Carter announced that military action was the only option if the hostages were not released; and on April 24th, he announced the abortive rescue attempt.

11. Times from his mother and other sources are given as between 11:00 a.m. and noon, according to Blackwell.

CHAPTER 7: Prisoners of the Horoscope No More

1. Helen Boyd, *The True Horoscope of the United States* (New York: ASI Publications Inc., 1973).

2. It was, in fact, this symbolism that made Jim an early adherent of the Boyd chart. Ken Irving sent the chart to Lewis for rendering as an ACG map, saying only that it was a proposed US birth chart. Lewis returned the map with a comment to the effect, "I'm converted...tell me more!" A record of both Jim's and Ken's observations on Boyd's chart at that time can be found online (as of the time of publication), at planetlines.com/wordpress. This is a transcript of a tandem lecture at the 1978 National Astrological Society conference in Tucson, Arizona.

More than 30 years after Boyd's research, the availability of original documents on the Internet at the Library of Congress site, along with notes by modern scholars and cross-referenced material that includes correspondence of the delegates to the Continental Congress, has made it possible to check her reading of events. Since Boyd could find no actual time for the passage of the resolution, she provided Brigadier Firebrace with a possible time span of two hours from which he derived a more specific time by comparing sidereal returns and progressed charts against historical events.

Recent research by Gary Noel, using the online resources mentioned above, indicates that Boyd's original time span of 10:00 a.m. to 12:00 p.m. is too early, as the official journal entry for July 6, 1775 indicates the document was "debated by paragraphs" before approval. Also, a letter from John Adams to William Tudor on that date says "We have spent this whole day debating Paragraph by Paragraph, a Manifesto as some call it, or a Declaration of the Causes and Necessities of our taking up Arms." On this basis, Noel has suggested an alternative time of 5:25 p.m. LMT. Anyone wanting to pursue the question further should begin at memory. loc.gov/ammem/amlaw/lwjc.html.

Several years prior to his rectification of Boyd's time, Firebrace had conducted a test of several possible U.S. charts by scoring each using a standard set of sidereal ingresses and progressions for a standard set of historical events. He then redid this test by pitting the Boyd chart against the previous "winner"—July 4, 1776, 12:20 p.m. LMT, Philadelphia, and the Boyd chart won, which Firebrace felt confirmed its usefulness. The 12:20p.m. time has an uncertain pedigree, as though it is mentioned occasionally in articles on the U.S. chart, no one (including Boyd and Firebrace) seems to know the source for it.

Coincidentally, when the July 6, 1775 chart is progressed (using the method called the Progressed Sidereal Solar Return, or PSSR) to July 4, 1776, the angles are close to those of the "Sibly" chart for 5:00 p.m. (the center point of two contending versions of this chart, for which see Nicholas Campion's *The Book of World Horoscopes* (Bournemouth: The Wessex Astrologer, 1999, pages 363-366).

3. Assuming of course that the time of Firebrace's chart has some reasonable basis. Problems with this are discussed in the previous note.

Appendix: Historical and Technical Notes on Astro*Carto*Graphy

1. Moments of precise angularity as defined in Astro*Carto*Graphy and in most astrological usage such as the traditional speculum (a list of rising, setting, and culmination times for a specific location) are purely geocentric, and have nothing to do with apparent rising times that may take into account parallax, atmospheric conditions, and geographical considerations. For example, the rising or setting line for a planet on an Astro*Carto*Graphy map identifies those locations at which the planet's geocentric zenith distance will be exactly 90 degrees.

2. *Solar and Lunar Returns*. Donald Bradley, (Saint Paul: Llewellyn Publications,1973), page 13.

3. *The Earth in the Heavens: Ruling Degrees of Cities*. L. Edward Johndro (New York: Samuel Weiser, Inc., 1970), Chapter VI, page 110. Johndro relocated the birth chart according to a "geodetic" scheme based on an arbitrary relationship between celestial and terrestrial coordinates, rather than the method used in locality mapping in which that relationship is derived directly from the birth chart. Despite this, the underlying philosophy that the birth chart is primary remains the same.

4. Brigadier R.C. Firebrace, "The Cancer Ingress." *Spica* 1(4): 37-39.

Resources for Using and Learning About Astro*Carto*Graphy

Licensed Distributors of Astro*Carto*Graphy Products

Astro Numeric Service (astronumerics.com): P.O. Box 336, Ashland, OR 97520, 1-800-Mapping (800-627-7464). Gregg Howe worked with Jim Lewis to provide the original computerized version of Jim's maps, sold in North America and other venues, along with a booklet explaining the basics of Astro*Carto*Graphy.

Astrodata (astrodata.com): Astrodata AG, Albisriederstrasse 232, CH-8047 Zurich, +41 (0) 43 343 33 33. Claude Weiss sells full-color maps along with an explanatory booklet in German, and also sells the German-language version of the first edition of *The Psychology of Astro*Carto*Graphy*.

Equinox (equinoxastrology.com or astrocartography.co.uk): Proprietor Robert Currey is a Jim-Lewis certified Astro*Carto*Graphy practitioner, and does personal map readings as well as selling map kits in the United Kingdom, Ireland, Australia, and other venues.

Matrix Software (astrologysoftware.com): 407 N. State Street, Big Rapids, MI 49307. Offers the report software "Astro*Carto*Graphy Explained," based on Jim Lewis's own interpretations.

Educational Resources

Astrocartography.net: "...a community site for sharing information about our understanding of ourselves and the world through Astro*Carto*Graphy." Includes articles by Jim Lewis published in various magazines over the years, as well as newly written pieces by Madalyn-Hillis-Dineen, Erin Sullivan, and others.

Continuum (continuumacg.net): Provides a continuing certification program based on Jim's original training seminars.

Jim Lewis Library: Jim's files relating to Astro*Carto*Graphy have been preserved in the Jim Lewis Library, and are available to researchers by appointment. Currently it is located at Astro Numeric Service in Ashland, Oregon. To reach them, call 1-800-Mapping (or 541-627-7464) or send email to reply@astronumerics.com.

Certified Astro*Carto*Graphy Practitioners

Maps and books are a good way to begin understanding Astro*Carto*Graphy, but an in-person consultation with a certified Astro*Carto*Graphy practitioner is better. The current list of certified practitioners can be found in the Continuum website at continuumacg.net/practs.html. See pages 273-275 for more about Continuum.

Suggested Reading

Baigent, Michael, Nick Campion and Charles Harvey. *Mundane Astrology.* Wellingborough: Aquarian Press, 1984.

Cochrane, David. *Astrolocality Magic.* Gainesville: Cosmic Patterns Software, Inc., 2002.

Couteau, Robert. *The Least-aspected Planet in Astro*Carto*Graphy: A Metaphor for the Soul*, an e-book, ©1994; posted online April 15, 1998.

Cozzi, Steve. *Planets in Locality*, St. Paul: Llewellyn Publications, 1988.

Davis, Martin. *From Here to There: An Astrologer's Guide to Astromapping*, UK: The Wessex Astrologer, 2008.; and *Astrolocality Astrology: A Guide to What it Is and How to Use It*, The Wessex Astrologer, 1998.

Harding, Michael and Charles Harvey. *Working with Astrology: The Psychology of Harmonics, Midpoints and Astro*Carto*Graphy*. London, UK: Arkana, 1990.

Hathaway, Edith. *Navigating by the Stars*. St. Paul: Llewellyn Books, 1991

Lewis, Jim. *Peter Pan in Midlife and the Midlife of America: A Personal and Collective Memoir*. Edited and with a foreword by Erin Sullivan, 2002. Available through Erin at erinsullivan.com.

Lewis, Jim & Kenneth Irving. *The Psychology of Astro*Carto*Graphy*. New York: Words and Things, 2012.

Meadows, David. *Where in the World With Astro*Carto*Graphy*, Tempe: American Federation of Astrologers, 1998.

Sullivan, Erin. *Where in the World?, Astro*Carto*Graphy and Relocation Charts*, Volume 12. London: Centre for Psychological Astrology Press, 1999. Available through Erin at erinsullivan.com.

Tanzer, Elliot Jay. *Evaluating Astro*Carto*Graphy Maps: Finding the Best Places to Live & Travel—Your Step by Step Guide*. Temecula, California: Self-published, 2010.

Some Useful Definitions

Angularity: In a standard horoscope, the proximity of a planet to any of the four "angles": Ascendant, Midheaven, Descendant and Imum Coeli, which are the cusps of the 1st, 10th, 7th, and 4th houses, respectively. The orb to allow is a longtime subject of dispute among astrologers, though most would generally agree that an area approximately five degrees on either side of an angle is the strongest. In a standard horoscope, only longitude is considered. When latitude is included, certain bodies (especially the Moon and Pluto) can actually rise and set long before or after their zodiacal degree has risen or set. Astro*Carto*Graphy lines are calculated using both longitude and latitude.

Ascendant (ASC): The point of the ecliptic on the eastern horizon at the time of birth.

Aspects: An astrological aspect is a special angular relationship between two planets, measured along the ecliptic. The most common aspects (usually called "Ptolemaic") are multiples of 30 degrees. No aspects are used in an Astro*Carto*Graphy map, since conjunctions, trines, sextiles, etc., are defined only in terms of longitude, and thus cannot take latitude into account. Maps are offered in software that appear to have aspects on them, but it is not clear what these lines actually represent or how they are calculated.

Astro*Carto*Graphy®: A registered trademark that identifies the specific locational mapping techniques and interpretive system developed by Jim Lewis.

Declination: A planet's distance north or south of the celestial equator. A planet's declination can be seen on an ACG map by finding the zenith point, represented as a circle on the MH (Midheaven) line. Planets whose zenith points are the same distance north or south of the equator are either parallel (both on the same side of the equator) or contraparallel (each on a different side of the equator), depending on the orb allowed.

Descendant (DSC): The point of the ecliptic on the western horizon at the time of birth.

Hour Angle: A planet's distance from a given location as measured along the equator. The hour angle of a planet at a given moment for a given place is defined as the right ascension of the planet minus the sidereal time at that location.

Imum Coeli (IC): The point at which the ecliptic intersects the lower meridian. The 4th-house cusp in "quadrant" house systems such as Placidus and Koch.

Line Crossing: The crossing of one planet's Midheaven or IC line with another planet's rising or setting line. The latitude at which this happens is considered to be influenced by both planets. This is the same as a "paranatellonta," or paran, as defined by Cyril Fagan (see "Historical and Technical Notes" on page 283).

Locational Astrology: General term for any method of studying the difference between astrological effects at the birth place and another location. While use of the term sometimes includes comparison of the birth chart with local charts, such as, for example, the chart for a city to which the native is relocating, it usually only involves analysis of the birth chart as it would look if the native had been born at the new location. Locality mapping such as Astro*Carto*Graphy is a two-dimensional and global form of locational astrology.

Midheaven (MH): The point on the ecliptic which intersects the upper meridian. The 10th-house cusp in "quadrant" house systems such as Placidus and Koch.

Nadir: The point directly opposite the zenith at any location. Not to be confused with the IC.

Right Ascension: A planet's distance from the vernal point, measured eastwards along the celestial equator.

Rise: The location of a planet on the eastern horizon. Astrologically, a body's rising is considered to take place when its mathematical center is on the horizon (rather than the upper limb, as in astronomy), and it is not corrected for local observational conditions such as refraction, temperature, and dip of the horizon.

Set: The location of a planet on the western horizon, with astrological setting differentiated from astronomical setting in the same way astrological rise is distinguished from astronomical rise.

Shadowed Planet: In Jim Lewis' Astro*Carto*Graphy interpretations, a planet which may be difficult for the native to integrate into his or her whole personality. Any planet which is debilitated by sign, house position, or aspect in a standard chart has the potential for being a shadowed planet. Furthermore, masculine planets in the charts of women, particularly Sun and Mars, or feminine planets in the charts of men, particularly Moon and Venus, have shadow potential.

Zenith: The point directly overhead at any location. Not to be confused with the Midheaven.

Index

American Astrology, 277-281
American Astrology Digest, 278
angles of the chart, 4, 33, 60
  house structure and, 21, 26-28
  progressed, 67-68, 71
Applewhite, Marshall, 291n
Aquarius, Sun line and, 82
archetypes, self vs. not-self 8-11, 13
aspects in Astro*Carto*Graphy, 284
assimilation, see planetary archetypes, emergence of
Astro*Carto*Graphy
  astronomical principle underlying, 6
  definition 3
  differences from standard horoscope, 16
  transits and progressions, 6
Astrology: A Key to Personality, 54, 291n

Block, Neil, see Duncan, Gary
Bly, Robert, 9, 288 n
Boyd chart for U.S.A., 71
Boyd, Helen, 70-71
Bradley, Donald, 277-279, 281
Britt, Harry, 54
Bush, George H. W., 16
  Gulf War transits and progressions, 204
  planetary links to Jimmy Carter, 65
  transits and progressions to war lines, 66-67

Cancer, Sun line and, 85
Carter, Jimmy, 16, 61, 63, 65-66
  Mars, Jupiter, and Iran, 34
Caruso, Enrico, Sun line of, 47
circumstantial problems defined, 26

Cunanan, Andrew, 290-291n

Dean, Geoffrey, 276
denial – see planetary archetypes, emergence of
Duncan, Gary, 281

Eisenhower, Dwight D., 62
exemplification – see planetary archetypes, emergence of
  Jimmy Swaggart as example of, 30

Fagan, Cyril, 277, 279-281
  quoted on Sun-Mars contacts, 47
fated occurrences, relation of to projection, 10, 11, 13, 29, 30, 34
Firebrace, Roy, 71
Ford, Gerald, 16, 293n
  war lines for Vietnam, 63

Gacy, John Wayne, 49-50
Gauquelin power zones, 286-287
Gauquelin, Michel, 288n
Gauquelin, Michel and Françoise, 4
  research findings on Mars, 60
Gemini, Mercury line and, 115
George III, 71
Grace, 36-45
  shadowed planets in chart of, 31-35
Greene, Liz, 164

Hiroshima, 62, 68-69
  Boyd chart Pluto line and, 74
  Mars-Pluto conjunction and, 75
hostile planets, defined, 8
Hotspur in Wales problem, 9
Howe, Gregg, 281
Hussein, Saddam, 17, 65-66

INDEX

Imum Coeli, 4, 21, 24, 44
  defined, 302
  meaning of planets on, 15
Johnson, Andrew, 73
Johnson, Lyndon B., 16
  war lines for Vietnam, 62-63
Jones, Marc Edmund, 290n
Jones, Jim, 16, 46-51, 58-60, 290n
Jung, C. G, 288n
  concepts relating to astrology, 7-9
  Pluto line and Zurich, 15-16
  self vs. not-self, 8
  "shadow" and progressed Sun to Saturn, 208
  stages of life, 8-9
  suppressed modes of consciousness, 8-10
Jupiter line
  differing reactions to, 34
  fame, 18
Jupiter MH line, 16
  Jimmy Carter, Iran, 63
  similarity to George Bush at Beijing, 65

Karamanli, Pasha Yusuf, 73
Kennedy, John F., 16
  Saturn zenith point and Cuba, 24
  Pluto line and Dallas, 15
  war lines for Vietnam, 62
Krishnamurti, Jiddu, 179
  Sun line of, 47
Kuwait, invasion of, 17, 65-66

latitude crossing
  definition and orbs, 25
  Mars-Jupiter, 63, 65
  Moon MH-Saturn ASC, 42
  relation to paranatellonta, 283, 298-299
  Sun IC-Mars DSC, 47
  Sun-Mars and "intense assertion", 50
Leary, Timothy, Sun ASC line of, 47

Lewis, Jim, 282, 269-275
  library, 289n
Libra, Sun line and, 85
line crossing, see latitude crossing
locality as activator of shadowed planet, 33
locality astrology, 3

Manson, Charles, 50
Mars ASC line, 16
  Boyd chart, Richmond and Washington, 73
  Dan White, birthplace, 55
  Franklin Roosevelt, Pearl Harbor, 62
  George Bush, Beijing, 65
  Jimmy Carter, Iran, , 63
Mars DSC line
  Boyd chart, Saigon, 74
  Charles Manson, southern California, 50
  George H. W. Bush, Panama, 65
  Gerald Ford, Saigon, 63
  Jim Jones and, 47
  John Wayne Gacy, Chicago, 49-50
  projection as source of violence, 47, 49
Mars IC line
  George H. W. Bush, Europe and Africa, 65
  Harry Truman, Korea, 62
  Harvey Milk, San Francisco, 55
Mars line
  assertion and courage, 60
  debilitated Mars and, 55
  differing reactions of men and women to, 34
  war and, 16, 61
  well-placed Mars and, 55
Mars MH line, 16
  Boyd chart, Berlin and Tripoli, 73
  Boyd chart progressed, Hiroshima, 75
Mars-Jupiter crossing, Jimmy Carter,

INDEX

Iran, 63
Mars-Neptune conjunction as trigger for Mars-Neptune lines, 58
Mars-Saturn-Neptune line, 21
Mather, Arthur, 276
Mayo, Jeff, 54, 291n
The Mayor of Castro Street, The Life and Times of Harvey Milk, 291n
Mays, Willie, Sun line of, 47
Milk, Harvey, 46, 51-59
    as "The Mayor of Castro Street," 52
    murdered by Dan White, 53
Moon line and emotions, 18
Moon ASC Line, 13
Moon IC line, 18
Moon MH line
    U.S.A., Moscow, and the McCarthy era, 75-77
Moscone, George, 46, 53, 59, 68, 291n
    murdered by Dan White, 53

nadir point, 24
    defined, 299
Neptune ASC line, Dan White, San Francisco, 55
Neptune DSC line, Harvey Milk, birthplace, 55
Neptune IC line, Richard Nixon, Cambodia, 63
Neptune MH line
    Boyd chart, Europe, 75-77
    Richard Nixon, Washington D.C., 63
Nixon, Richard M.
    Neptune for Washington and Cambodia, 63
not-self, 8, 10, 13, 57, 186
    planets of, 31

Olive Branch Petition, 71
orbs for planetary lines and latitude crossings, 25

paranatellonta (paran) defined, 299

also see latitude crossing
People's Temple, 46, 51
Pisces, Sun line and, 82, 85
planetary archetypes,
    assimilation phase, 11, 26-29
    denial phase (projection and repression), 11, 13, 28, 29, 39, 41
    emergence of, 7-13
    exemplification phase, 11, 28-30
    inner situations as "fate", 7, 11
    projection, 11, 28-29
    repression and denial phase for Grace, 39
planetary lines
    orbs for, 25, 284
    "travel transits" vs. residence, 18
planetary polarization
    Mercury-Jupiter, 10
    Uranus-Jupiter, 8-10
Pluto ASC line
    Harry Truman, Hiroshima and Nagasaki, 67-69, 75
    Herbert Hoover, Nicaragua, 61
Pluto IC line
    Gerald Ford, San Francisco, 63
    psychological transformation, 15-16
Pluto line
    U.S. Presidents and Nicaragua, 61-62
    war and, 61
Pluto MH line
    awareness of mortality, 19, 70
    Boyd Chart, Hiroshima, 74-76
    Calvin Coolidge, Nicaragua, 61
    Franklin Roosevelt, Nicaragua, 61
    George Moscone, San Francisco, 59
    Jimmy Carter, Central America, 61
    John F. Kennedy, Dallas, 62
    political assassination, 15
    sexual awakening, 19
    polarity reversal of Carter and Truman Mars-Jupiter lines, 63
polarization of consciousness, male-

INDEX

female, 10
Price, Leontyne, Sun line of, 47
progressed sidereal solar return, 71
projection – see planetary archetypes, emergence of

al-Qaddafi, Muammar, 73

Reagan, Ronald, 16, 66, 288-289n
Recent Advances in Natal Astrology, 276
relationships
  as activator of shadowed planet, 32-33
  assimilation and, 11
repetitive problems,
  as an indicator of an emerging archetype, 33
  defined and contrasted with circumstantial problems, 26
  shadowed planets as root of, 27
repression, see planetary archetypes, emergence of
rise-set formula, 282
Roosevelt, Franklin D., 16, 61-62, 292n
  planetary lines for war zones, 61-62
Ryan, Leo, 48

Sagittarius, Sun line and, 85
Saturn ASC line
  Harry Truman, Hiroshima and Nagasaki, 74-75
  Harry Truman, Korea and Japan, 62
  Jimmy Carter, Nicaragua and Panama, 61
Saturn DSC line
  Boyd chart, Saigon, 74
  Grace, 40, 42-44
Saturn IC line
  Saturn return challenges and, 20
Saturn lines, travel to under Saturn return, 7, 20, 39
Saturn MH line, Boyd chart, Europe, 73-74
Saturn return, 10

Saturn, A New Look at an Old Devil, 164
self, planets of, 31
shadowed planet, defined, 27
  stages of emergence, 27-29
  effect of on local angle, 30
  rules for identifying, 31
  not-self and, 31
  three modes of activation, 32-33, 42
Sibly Chart, relation of to Boyd chart, 71
Shilts, Randy, 291n
Solar and Lunar Returns, 294n
Sun ASC line, 15
Sun DSC line, 15-16,
Sun line
  fame and leadership, 18,
  Willie Mays, New York, 47
  Enrico Caruso, New York, 47
  Leontyne Price, New York, 47
  Krishnamurti, Los Angeles, 47
  Timothy Leary, San Francisco, 47
Sun-Jupiter line, 17
synastry and Astro*Carto*Graphy, 284-286

Taylor, Elizabeth, 16
Thatcher, Margaret as "relationship trigger" for George Bush, 66
The True Horoscope of the United States, 70-71, 293-294n
time as activator of shadowed planet, 32
transits and progressions, 203
Tripolitania, Boyd chart Mars line and, 73
Truman, Harry S, 16
  war lines for Japan and Korea, 62
  transits and progressions to war lines, 69
  Hiroshima /Nagasaki transits, progressions, 204
"Twinkie Defense", 53, 57-58, 291-292n

U.S.A. Birth chart
  Boyd, 71
  Gemini rising, 71
  Sibly, 71, 294n
Uranus IC line, 15
  transcendence of family, 21
Uranus MH line, 15
Uranus, Neptune and Saturn
  conjunction, 3-4

Venus DSC line, happy childhood,
  effect of on marital problems, 20
Venus lines,
  relationships, 6
  romance, 18
Virgo
  Sun line and, 82
  Mercury lines and, 115

White, Dan, 46, 50-59
  murders Milk and Moscone, 53

Yogananda, Paramahansa, 13-15

zenith distance, 294n
zenith point, 24, 303
  declination, 298n

About the Authors

Born in Yonkers, New York in 1941, Jim Lewis took up the study of astrology in the 1960s, first working as a professional astrologer for the Personal Service Department of *American Astrology* magazine. From the time he introduced Astro*Carto*Graphy to the public in 1976, Jim was an active and vital member of the astrological community. He lectured internationally, and wrote for a variety of publications, including *American Astrology*, *Dell Horoscope*, and *Astrology Now*. One of his proudest achievements was to co-found the Association for Astrological Networking (AFAN), a non-hierarchical organization meant to bring astrologers together to promote their interests through public relations, media watch activities, and legal challenges to local anti-astrology laws. He was coauthor, with Ariel Guttman, of *The Astro*Carto*Graphy Book of Maps*, and author of the annual publication *Astro*Carto*Graphy Sourcebook of Mundane Maps*. Jim received the Marc Edmund Jones Award in 1978, and the Regulus Award for Research and Innovation in 1992, both in recognition of his work on Astro*Carto*Graphy. Jim's death in 1995 left a void not only among his friends, but also within the community of astrologers and in the lives of the many people he had helped so generously over the years.

Kenneth Irving began his study of astrology in 1971, and started his astrological career at *American Astrology* magazine in 1974. He served as a staff editor from 1974 to 1977, research editor from 1977 to 1984, and was then co-editor, with Lee Chapman, from 1984 until the magazine ceased publication in 2003. Currently he is editor of *Horoscope Guide*. Kenneth has authored or coauthored articles, columns, reviews and other contributions for *American Astrology, Horoscope Guide, Correlation, The Journal of Scientific Exploration*, and other publications. He is coauthor, with Suitbert Ertel, of *The Tenacious Mars Effect*. Kenneth's particular contribution recounted the decades-long struggle between Michel Gauquelin and professional skeptics over Gauquelin's "Mars effect for sports champions," while Ertel provided a detailed defense of Gauquelin's work and an exhaustive refutation of the skeptics' efforts.

www.ingramcontent.com/pod-product-compliance
Lightning Source LLC
Chambersburg PA
CBHW071655160426
43195CB00012B/1474